W9-AFE-241

SHELTON STATE COMMUNITY
COLLEGE
JUNIOR COLLEGE DIVISION
LIBRARY

Desai, Neera.
HQ
1742 Women and society
.D475 in India
1987

DATE DUE

NOV 26 1997

WOMEN AND SOCIETY IN INDIA

Women and Society in India

NEERA DESAI
&
MAITHREYI KRISHNARAJ

1990

AJANTA PUBLICATIONS (India)

Co-Contributors:

Surinder Jetley	: Chapter on Family
Malavika Karlekar	: Chapter on Education
Usha Thakkar	: Sections on Political Participation and Law.

(The views expressed in this work are the author's own and UNESCO is not responsible for them)

ISBN 81-202-0188-4

© All rights reserved. No part of this book may be reproduced, transmitted in any form or by any means, electronic or mechanical, including photocopying, recording, or by any information storage and retrieval system, except for references or reviews, without permission in writting from the publisher.

First Published : 1987

Second Revised Edition: 1990

Published by

Ajanta Publications (India)
Jawahar Nagar,
Delhi-110007

Distributors:

Ajanta Books International
I-U.B., Jawahar Nagar, Bungalow Road,
Delhi-110007

Printed at

Kay-Kay Printer

PREFACE

The present work owes its initiative to the meeting on Women's Studies and Social Sciences held in October, 1982 at New Delhi under the auspices of UNESCO.

Those involved in the movement for introducing women's studies in the institutions of higher learning have constantly stressed the need for a text book with an interdisciplinary feminist perspective which could be useful for undergraduate studies. The University Grants Commission had also expressed its expectation that SNDT Centre would take up this work. The Research Centre for Women's Studies of the SNDT University therefore took up this responsibility as it had been involved for a long time in a programme of women's studies at the University level.

Though research-based material on women is growing in India particularly during the last decade, this material lies scattered in various reports,which exist in mimeographed form. For the undergraduate students and their teacher, unless this material is collated in a form suitable for the classroom there is the danger that the introduction of women's studies courses will prove counter productive.Further we have also been greatly concerned that curricular for women's studies should present the women's perspective.We have attempted through this work, to present as far as possible an interdisciplinary focus with a thrust that would be meaningful both for undergraduate students and general women's studies courses.

Incorporating a diversity of expertise in preparing a text-book with a common running thread has distinct advantages and we opted for inviting contributions in certain areas from researchers and teachers who have adequate experience of teaching within the Indian University set-up. The major responsibility however was inevitably ours. Since all of us were full time workers, we were always short of time and we could not meet as frequently as we would have liked to; however we did manage to have a meeting with our contributors and Ms. Koto Kano of UNESCO, in October, 1985 to discuss the first draft.

We are indeed very grateful to the three collaborators: Dr.Surinder Jetley for preparing the chapter on family, Dr. Malavika Karlekar for her chapter on education and Dr.Usha Thakkar for contributing sections on political participation and law. We realise how pressurized all of them were with various commitments.

We are thankful for the assistance given by Ms. Subhadra Patwa, Ms. Mini Rao and Ms. Suneela in collection of material. We owe a special word of thanks to Ms. Veena Poonacha for her invaluable assistance in bibliographical and other assistance in checking innumerable details during the preparation of this work.

We are happy to acknowledge the financial assistance provided by the UNESCO for preparing the text book. We would like to specially mention our gratitude to Dr.Yogesh Atal, Regional Adviser for Social and Human Sciences in Asia and Pacific and Ms. Koto Kano, Associate Expert at the UNESCO Regional Unit for all their co.operation. Dr. Vina Mazumdar's moral support and inspiration stood us in good stead.

Preparing a manuscript for publication is a laborious and responsible task. Ms. S. Vegas readily agreed to do this work. We are extremely thankful to her.

We took this assignment both as a challenge and responsibility. We would feel rewarded if we have helped in a modest way in meeting a felt need.We also hope that this work will encourage many more to serve the cause of women's studies by undertaking better and improved texts or by preparing specific teaching units on specific themes.We need such a process of continuous synthesising of existing knowledge and data to promote a more vigorous inquiry and to provide better answers to questions that have nagged all those interested in the liberation of women as much as the liberation of all oppressed people of this world.

NEERA DESAI
MAITHREYI KRISHNARAJ

CONTENTS

CONTRIBUTORS

Dr. Neera Desai has been a Professor of Sociology in SNDT Women's University for many years. A well-known pioneer in Women's Studies in India she has many contributions to her credit and holds many important academic positions. She was the Honorary Director (1974-1986) of the first Women's Studies Unit in the country set up in 1974 which has since become a Research Centre. She has done much to promote women's studies in India through her own work, as well as assistance to other centres and scholars.

Dr.Maithreyi Krishnaraj is the Director of the Research Centre for Women Studies, SNDT Women's University and has been a colleague and collaborator with Dr. Neera Desai since 1975; she has been deeply involved in research, curriculum planning and in developing feminist analyses.Her specialisation is in the disciplines of Economics and Education.

Dr. Surinder Jetley is a Reader in Sociology at the Banaras Hindu University. She has extensive teaching and research experience spanning two decades and since 1978 has done several research studies on Women's issues and has engaged herself in action programmes.

Dr.Malavika Karlekar is at present a Reader in Education at the Jamia Millia Islamia, New Delhi. She has earlier taught Sociology at the University of Delhi and done a major research study of the sweeper women in Delhi.Her current interest includes teaching and curriculum preparation for women's studies, in addition to other research.

Introduction

Women's Studies in the West

The need to incorporate women's issues in higher education system has been felt the world over for nearly two decades. Women's studies were pioneered in the United States where today, they are most-developed and well-established. Starting with about sixteen courses in 1969, in U.S.A. today there are more than thirty thousand courses offered at different levels and through a variety of models.[1]

In other Western countries, women's studies have emerged only during the last decade or so and initially operated at a low key.[2] Of course, currently many of the major institutions of higher learning offer women's studies courses in different forms. One of the primary limiting factors inhibiting rapid growth in some of the European countries is the nature of the education system which is considered to be fairly rigid, necessitating the going through of a number of bureaucratic processes. However, what is striking in some of the European countries and the United States particularly, is the fact that the initiative to introduce women's studies in the University system, largely came through a wider movement. Soon Young Yoon, while examining the relevance of women's studies in the Asian context, observes the contrast in the U.S.A. where the Civil Rights movement led to the formation of Black Studies and Ethnic Studies, and the students' movement of the 1960's demanding fundamental changes in academic institutions had played a significant role in creating a foothold for women's studies. In the West, women's studies is a 'Movement-born' programme.[3]

An important consequence of the growth of women's studies in the West has been the production of voluminous material. The new feminist scholarship during the last two decades has published anthologies, reprints, biographies, abstracts, new journals, newsletters and books. Florence Howe, one of the ardent pioneers in women's studies in the U.S.A. comments : "To gain an understanding of the new scholarship on women, whatever one's discipline, is comparable to beginning to earn a doctorate."[4]

In short, women's studies in the West have survived and have been legitimized in the educational system. They further get reinforced by the women's movement from outside.

Women's Studies in the Asian Region

In the Asian region, the concern for incorporating women's studies in the University system has been the feature of the last decade. Further, the development as well as nature and thrust of women's studies in the region are strikingly different from the way women's studies emerged and grew in the West.[5]

The pursuit of research on women's issues had been an ongoing activity in the region. However, what have been new features during the last decade, are a new focus, a new perspective and new methods. The experts of the Committee on the Studies on Women in Asia while reviewing the situation there remarked : "Moving from historical prescriptive and ideal-typical accounts based largely on scriptural analysis, the studies on aspects of women found place in social science research carried out in different soical structures and on various socio-cultural problems. But it is only recently that studies with a specific focus on women have been undertaken."[6] Though the record of research work on women is impressive, the activity of inclusion of women's studies in the teaching programmes of the institutions of higher learning is still in its infancy. The reviews bemoan this situation. It is observed in one of the reports :

"Barring the Republic of Korea, there is no evidence of the institution of a separate degree for women's studies. However, women-related topics are taught in courses in history, law, sociology, anthropology, psychology and education."[7] Only very recently are efforts being made to introduce teaching on women's studies in the institutions of higher learning.

Unlike in the West, in many of the countries in the region, the emergence of women's studies has not been invariably the product of the movement outside the academia.[8] As a result many women's studies programmes have been introduced at the initiative from above. A major push to the programmes was undoubtedly given by the Women's Decade. Besides there has been a growing concern at the lack of conceptual discussion on women's issues and dearth of published material. Though researchers on women's studies have taken woman as an analytical category, there is very limited material on some of the theoretical issues such as gender subordination, value of women's work, empowerment, feminist ideology, identity of women and others. Consequently, considerable dependence is noticeable on western ideas, models, methodologies, scholarships—which is in the long run counter-productive. There is now a growing feeling that there is a need to develop a Third World focus, even an Asian focus, to understand the gender problem. The Asian women scholars have to be involved to evolve locally relevant concepts and theories taking into consideration the specificities of different regions, like caste in India, predominance of export-oriented industries in South-East Asia, significance of multinationals in Singapore, Malaysia and South Korea, sex tourism in Thailand and migration patterns in the Philippines.[9] It is gratifying to note a beginning in this direction. For instance, for the recent NGO'85 conference at Nairobi in July 1985, about 22 activists, researchers and policy-makers prepared a document enunciating a Third World women's perspective on development, described as DAWN i.e. Development Alternatives with Women for a New Era.[10] Similarly, Asian Women's Research and Action Network (AWRAN) initiated a debate on the relevance of Feminism in Asia and special features of Asian Feminism.[11]

In sum, in the Asian region during the last decade considerable progress has been made in systematic studies focusing on women's issues, introducing women's studies in the teaching programme and undertaking micro studies with an analytical thrust in contrast to earlier descriptive studies.[12]

Women's Studies in India

In the Asian region, India seems to be occupying a significant position in terms of quantity and diversity of material in women's studies. Though the concern for studying women and organising action for improving the conditions of women is not new, what is strikingly different is the new perspective based on theoretical knowledge and ideological underpinning both in research and in action.

However, the education system has been rather lukewarm in promoting the values of equality and gender justice. In many ways the educational system on the other hand actively reinforces gender differences through curriculum and teacher bias. Only recently has some attention been drawn in to focus on women in the educational system.

The indifference of the system in incorporating women's dimensions in the syllabi was clearly made evident at the First National Conference on Women's Studies (NCWS) held in Bombay in 1981. A review of curricula in different disciplines undertaken by the NCWS, highlighted the virtual absence of women in curricula. In response to an appeal sent by the Conference organisers to one hundred universities and nearly fifty institutions of higher learning, technical or otherwise for a status report on research on women and women's presence in curricula only fifty-seven institutions responded and out of them only twenty-three institutions sent their syllabi. Even a cursory look at the syllabi of various social sciences and literature left no one in doubt about the near total absence of women in the curriculum.[13] More concerted effort was made by the Research Centre on Women's Studies, SNDT in 1984, by listing the Universities from a prior knowledge regarding places where women's studies was likely to be taught. When forty-three Universities were approached only thirty responded from among them. Of these, twenty-six Universities reported having some kind of women's studies programmes but of these again, barely twelve had teaching programmes at various levels.[14] This is a marked improvement within the course of three years—an encouraging development indeed ! While this is the history of the introduction of women's studies in India, let us see what has been the rationale for women studies.

Why Women's Studies ?

As the reviewers of the status report on women's studies in India mention, "the investigations of the Committee on the Status of Women in India (1971-1974) (CSWI) represent the watershed in the field of women's studies in the country. Starting with a new perspective, these investigations collated, for the first time, a large body of data on different aspects of women's lives, and identified unexpected trends in women's situation such as declining sex ratio, declining economic participation rate and growing gaps in life expectancy and mortality rates between men and women."[15] Three decades after Independence, and after three deacdes of planned development the picture of women's position that emerged was startling in its grimness. Women's position has worsened considerably in every sphere with the exception of some gains for middle-class women in terms of education and employment. They being the more visible sections of the society, their advance generated a myth that unlike some of the Asian societies, women's status in India is very high; that women are able to perform their dual roles adequately and they get considerable support from their men. The Constitution also provided equality to women. Thus the myth not only was entrenched but it developed a complacency and acquiescence among women.

Veena Mazumdar poignantly recalls this complacency even among the members of the CSWI. She says : "On the women's issue itself few members had seriously questioned their own attitudes to the implication of sex equality before 1975, and had seen the women's question as obsolete in Independent India. The CSWI's enquiry was a revelation, and an intense personal experience which shattered their complacency transformed their consciousness and made them question their own lives, values and their arrogance of knowledge."[16]

Thus, whereas some of the women leaders were quite satisfied with the role they had played, the actual growing number of dowry deaths, sexual violence, prostitution etc. revealed a different picture.

Women's position was worsening in practically every sphere, with the exception of some gains in education and employment for middle-class women. Women were found in the least paid jobs, working long hours, and bearing full responsibility for the home by fetching fuel and water; by doing work in family production units, without being paid for the labour; by bringing up children and caring for the sick and the aged. There was growing violence against women—rape, wife battering, family violence, dowry deaths and prostitution. This was the stark reality for millions of women.[17] The declining value of women was surfacing in almost every aspect of life.

Another significant feature to be noted was that since the 19th century social reform movement days, women have been looked upon either as victims of social practices or targets for development as in the post-independence period, but never as participants in development. This attitude is prevailing inspite of the fact that women did take part in the nationalist movement, trade union movements, the Kisan movement, etc. In fact as it has been observed by various scholars on the women's movement, neverthless political parties also very reluctantly recognised the role of women in the moulding of a new society. They were perceived in the limited role of an auxiliary force to be mobilised in times of mass action. Similarly the indifference of the planners and policy-makers was exposed when the document of the framework for the Sixth Five-Year Plan was released and it contained exactly six references to women and did not reflect any of the ideas which had emanated from the various expert groups, official and non-official, during 1975-1980.[18] After a good deal of lobbying, the final document incorporated a substantial part of the analysis on women's situation. There was a growing acceptance of the notion that women have to be considered as equal participants in shaping the new society rather than as victims to be saved or objects of welfare.

The above circumstances give rise to a pertinent question : How did the academicians look at the women's question ? A number of reviews on researches in India on women have brought out a few features of research activity in this field.[19] The researches of the indologists, sociologists, social historians, and anthropologists, particularly of the pre-independence period, highlighted and criticised inhuman social practices or provided descriptions of the position of elite women in the family, marriage and kinship network. By and large the studies glamourised the position of women in the earlier periods. A trend survey of research on women revealed that up to the seventies the focus of research was primarily on women's role in the family, kinship and other institutions. Studies on working women during the sixties were essentially studies of urban educated working women. Further the role conflict of the middle-class working woman acquired prominence in Ph.D. studies in Sociology. While the legal studies focussed on scriptural and statutory family laws, which affectd mainly the urban, educated upper class women, the customary laws which governed the lives of the majority of women were out of the purview of the researchers. The studies on employment of women were largely concerned with women entering the modern sphere, and women's labour force participation. There were hardly any studies on women in agrarian situation or of the lower strata. The middle-class bias of the study not only limited the coverage but restricted the perspective in the analysis of the situation.

Since 1970, the research interest in women has not only gained momentum but also has given rise to new questions in the field of employment, such as supply characteristics of women workers, impact of technology on women, female headed households, conditions of work, female-poverty, authority and power in the family, nature of political participation, women's grassroot organisations and analysis of the women's movement. New dimensions are suggested in understanding women's position in the past. The conventional methods of studying women are being replaced by using case studies, oral histories, folk material and non-Brahminical sources. One of the striking limitations of the researches in India is the dearth of conceptual, theoretical and methodological work. The detailed micro level studies have to be woven within the conceptual frameworks which could enhance our theoretical understanding of the problems. Further, such theoretical exercises can enrich discipline also. Agarwal's remarks in this context are relevant : "Women's studies can play a significant role in expanding the scope of theoretical research in the Social Sciences. For instance, the attempt among the western feminist scholars to understand the basis of women's oppression and subordination and the form it has taken historically has helped to highlight many of the limitations of existing theoretical frameworks offered in the Social Sciences."[20] Western experience would be of limited relevance. Hence it is necessary to develop a greater Third World focus to evolve locally relevant concepts and theories taking account of the specificity of social structures.

A major concern amongst those involved and committed to women's studies movement is that though all these developments are gratifying, yet they need to be incorporated in the mainstream teaching. There is an urgent need to stress again that women's studies are not just a new area of study but are intended to practically break all conventional definitions of discipline. For achieving this objective a formidable effort to combine teaching, research and action is necessary. Remedying the phenomenal dearth of systematic teaching material for various courses and for a variety of audiences is a stupendous task but absolutely essential.

Objectives of Women's Studies in India

The first National Conference on women's studies held in 1981 started a serious debate on the objectives of women's studies in India. In the wake of growing activity for introducing women's studies in the curricula, this question acquires more importance. On the one hand, women who have been non-participants in the courses have to be made participants as a sort of compensation for ignoring women as actors or subjects in the transformation processes. On the other hand care has to be taken that sins of omission are not compounded by sins of commission. Women are not to be misrepresented nor mystified while introducing them in the courses. Women are neither to be deified nor denigrated. Disciplines like Sociology, History and Political Science teach topics such as women's position or their participation as part of the general study of institutions of family, marriage, education and elections without providing the women's perspective. In history, for example, women's life appears only as description of upper class or of royal families and symbolising more often a mystified image or a self-denying or suffering type. Disciplines like economics, psychology, education have yet to be made sensitive to women in their disciplines.

However, the purpose of women's studies is not just inclusion of material on women. The purpose is to stimulate desirable changes in women's status rather than reinforcing reactionary values. The purpose is to examine and redefine the conceptual frameworks of disciplines so as to evolve new formulations which could accommodate women's experiences. Women's studies should not be one more discipline added which would perpetuate the elitist bias of our academic institutions. The organic knowledge on women has to be enriched through interaction of theory and field experience. Women's studies have to be a bridge between the academic and the grassroot workers.

It is in this setting that women's studies in India should be considered both as an instrument for women's development and as a necessary step to develop the knowledge base of various disciplines.

Since 1981 a series of seminars and workshops have been held to evolve perspective, structure and training for women's studies programmes. The U.G.C., the apex body for policy and support for higher education in India, has accepted the need for introducing women in the curriculum of the University system by providing financial support to various activities like organising seminars, workshops and summer institutes, conducting researches on women and encouraging establishment of centres of women's studies at departments of universities. Quite a few committed individual faculty members have taken the initiative of starting cells or units of women's studies in their universities, colleges or departments. In the face of this supportive climate and keeping in view the multiple functions which women's studies in India ought to perform, at a recent seminar held in New Delhi, in April 1985, on perspective, and organisation of women's studies units in Indian Universities, organised by the Research Group on Women's Studies, Department of Political Science, University of Delhi, a list of objectives was agreed upon. They provide the approach and the thrust of women's studies in higher education.

The objectives for incorporating women's studies within the University system are both academic and social. These are :

1. To change the present attitude values in society regarding women's roles, and rights, to one of equal participation in

all social, economic and political processes and national and international development.

2. To promote awareness among women and men, of the need to develop and utilise women's full potential as resources for national development in its economic, political and socio-cultural aspects ; to question existing values ; and to promote awareness of their social responsibilities so as to participate equally.

3. To counter the reactionary forces emanating from certain sections of the media, economic, social and political institutions, that encourage the demotion of women from productive to mere reproductive roles.

4. To revitalise university education, bringing it closer to burning social issues, to work towards their solution, and to produce sensitive persons able to play more committed and meaningful roles in developmental activities for women in all sectors.

5. To fulfil a special responsibility to produce for all levels of the educational system, teachers who are aware of the need for non-sexist education, and who would actively pick up the challenge to promote values of social equality, including gender equality, secularism, socialism and democracy.

6. To update university curricula by incorporating the results of new scholarship and the issues raised by the latter as they challenge some of the established theories, analytical concepts and methodologies of various disciplines.

7. To promote increased collaboration between different disciplines in teaching, curriculum designing, research and extension activities since women's studies are interdisciplinary by nature.

8. To generate new and organic knowledge through intensive field work. This would help in the generation of data essential for evaluation and correction of development policies and programmes and in extending the areas for academic analysis, into hitherto neglected sectors. For a better understanding and investigation of the problems experienced by women at the grassroot level, a closer contact between institutions of higher education and groups directly involved in action, would be very valuable. This could ultimately assist women to enjoy their rights within the family, the community and at

work. Such contacts would also help universities and colleges to design their extension activities in a more meaningful manner.

9. To contribute to global debate on the women's question through rediscovery of the debate in India from ancient to contemporary periods by means of research and translation from Indian literature including folk literature.

Need for Teaching Material

Acceptance of integrating women's issues in the curriculum is undoubtedly a vital step in educational reconstruction. Equally important is the providing of teaching and reading material for women's studies courses in achieving the above mentioned objectives.

A major handicap, as mentioned at the UNESCO Expert's meeting, is the paucity or non-availability of reading material as well as the need to brief university teaching staff on the approaches and latest developments in this new area of research and teaching.

In the present university structures, along with the restructuring of the courses, provision of reading material is essential for two or three reasons. There is the fact of rigidity in the educational system where the introduction of new courses has to traverse through various labyrinths of educational bureaucracy and face the apathy and indifference (if not overt opposition) from the authorities and faculty members to introduce women's studies. The absence of reading material could in this milieu provide a very convenient excuse for delaying the introduction of women's studies. Secondly as mentioned earlier, women's issues have to be discussed differently and not in the stereotyped rote style of examinations. For developing sensitiveness to women's problems, and to understand their sources, provision of relevant material is a pre-requisite for introducing women's studies in the curricula. The problem with regard to material is not merely one of paucity. In fact during the last ten to fifteen years, substantial material based on hard data has been generated. The main problem is that it lies scattered in various studies and reports. It needs to be organised, collated and reformulated with a special perspective in order to provide an understanding of the devaluation of women and to evolve programmes for positive actions necessary for redeeming the situation..

This has to be the context of women's studies in India and ours is a modest effort in this direction.

II

One of the important concerns, amongst the western feminists, as observed earlier, has been to understand the cause of women's subordination. The women's studies activists and academics world over, agree that women at present have a lower status than men; that socially, economically and politically women are discriminated against and this state of affairs is unfair and must be changed. However, there is a difference in the analysis of the origin of subordinate status of women; why the lower status has still persisted; what strategies are to be devised to end this subordination and such other queries. Within the women's movement there have been three major ideological positions described as Liberal Feminism (LF), Radical Feminism (RF) and Socialist Feminism (SF). They differ in their analysis of the causes of the subordinate position of women and consequently in their action programmes. The review of the position and perspectives of these three types of feminism have relevance to our present exercise, in terms of providing a context for examining women's situation.

Another important issue which needs reference is how is it that the debate on women's issues surfaces only at certain periods of time and why there is a phase of sudden descending curve in the interest on women's issues leading to silencing of women's voices for decades ? In the U.S.A. for instance, the 19th century marked the raising of women's demands for access to education, equal rights in entering professions, equal right to vote, more legal rights.[21] etc. After the achievement of franchise in 1920, for nearly four decades thereafter the women's movement subsided to such an extent that one wondered whether there was really any such movement at all. Similarly in the 1960's a second wave of feminism spread in almost all parts of the western hemisphere and there is a feeling that in the U.S.A. there is a backlash after the late seventy's as Betty Freidan describes in her book, *The Second Stage*.[22] In India too, as will be seen in the subsequent discussions, the women's movement emerged in the 1920s and lasted for twenty years. With independence a sort of apathy and quietness prevailed for nearly three decades, and in the seventies there was a revival of the debate on women's issues.

Let us first discuss in brief the three perspectives.

Liberal Feminism

The historical origins of contemporary liberal feminism goes back to 18th century—the Enlightenment period of Western Europe. It was the Age of Reason. The triumph of reason was the key conviction. Institutions and ideas which could not stand the critical test of reason have to be repudiated and discarded even though they may have been existing for ages. It was natural that one of the many subjects the thinkers of this era touched was the nature and role of women. Another important tenet of liberal philosophy was individualism, by which it was meant that the individual possesses the freedom to do what he wishes without interference from others. Besides other theorists, Mary Wollstonecraft as a liberal thinker is well-known for her ardent support for woman's cause. Her work, *A Vindication of the Rights of Women* published in 1792, is perhaps the first, serious, systematic work. The basic idea is that women are first and foremost human beings and not sexual beings. Women are rational creatures. They are capable of governing themselves by reason. Hence if women are to be denied natural rights, it must be proved that they have no rational capacity.[23] John Stuart Mill, an ardent Liberal, argued, in his famous work, *The Subjection of Women*, "the existing relations between the sexes, the legal subordination of one sex to the other, is wrong in itself, and now one of the chief hindrances to human improvement, and that it ought to be replaced by the perfect equality admitting no power or privilege on the one side nor disability on the other".[24] One of the important corollaries of the positions of the liberals was that they accepted the common arrangement by which the man earns the family income and the wife superintends the domestic expenditure. The wife if she goes out to work will not be able to perform the tasks of child rearing and house management well and, therefore, a wife should contribute by her labour. Thus the sex role differences are accepted but with a proviso that both are considered equal. Hence women should have civil rights, they must have the right to vote and they must be given education. Indian social reformers of the 19th century talked practically in the same vein as giving the right of education to women so that they become better wives and mothers, removal of social customs like `sati', child marriage, ban on widow remarriage etc.[25]

The liberal feminism which flourished in the 1960's, did not provide more insights into the roots of women's inferior status. However, the feminists began to extend the concept of equality beyond the earlier emphasis on formal equality in the civil and political sphere. They thus demanded child care facilities, talked about the rights of poor women and control over one's reproductive life. Liberal feminism argued for equal rights for women but accepted the existing social order as valid and advocated for improvement of social customs, institutions, laws, attitudes, without altering the social structure, particularly the family. They also subscribed to the hope that an accumulation of reforms will transform society, but radical restructuring is not necessary.

Radical Feminism

A very significant perspective but one perhaps much distorted by the media, is the radical feminist perspective about women's subordination in society. Although the beginnings of radical feminism are considered to coincide with the beginnings of the second wave of feminism around 1969-1970, it has been contended that radical feminism has important ties with liberal feminism, the feminists who spoke of sexual politics before Kate Millett. However, liberal feminism overlooked the necessary connection between sexual oppression, sexual division of labour and the economic class struture. Hence their claims remained reformist.[26] Today, the radical feminists have replaced the struggle for vote and for the legal reform with the demand for the destruction of patriarchy.

The radical feminists' main contention is that the roots of subordination lie in the biological family, the hierarchical sexual division of society and sex roles themselves : factors which must be fundamentally recognised if true gender equality has to be established. The proponents of radical feminism contended that the biological distinction i.e. male/female is used to distinguish social functions and power. The dictum that anatomy is destiny, operates in the present society through sex role distinctions. The biological differences result in the male domination of power over women. Patriarchy is identified by the radical feminist as an autonomous historical fact more rooted in biology than in economy and they consider gender relations to be the fundamental form of oppression. Kate Millett, Shulamith Firestone, Germaine Greer, Ellen Frankfort, are some of the more well-known radical feminists who see patriarchy as male control over women's fertility. It is the male hierarchical ordering of society. A more important contention of the radical feminists is that the patriarchal system is preserved via marriage and the family through sexual division of labour in the society. As patriarchy is rooted in biology, and the battle lines are drawn between men and women. Patriarchy exhibits itself in a great variety of forms, but in all such forms, the avenues of power are in the male hands. Sexual politics is the politics of patriarchy. Patriarchy's chief institution is the family. It perpetuates the sexual division of labour through socialisation. Further the family is maintained by the principle of legitimacy, thus the stigma against out of wedlock children. The feminists aver that though there is no biological reason why reproduction and socialisation should occur in the family, however, this has been the basic pattern in the historical societies. Thus the nuclear family is considered to be an impediment to the full realisation of equality, which contention is very different from the liberal feminists' perspective on family.

Man being the enemy and subordination seen as the biopsychological supremacy of male over female, the radical feminists' main plea is not only removal of all sex distinctions, but for many, there seems to be no place for men in their life span. Sexual preference, control over one's body, free sexual experience and collective child care are some of the action programmes outlines by the radical feminists. Masculine hostility manifests itself through rape, pornography and sexual violence. The overthrow of male dominance requires a complete sexual revolution which would destroy traditional sex taboos; through consciousness raising, women should be made aware of this dominance, solidarity among the women be developed and women should be self-reliant so that they are not dependent on men in any sense.

Socialist Feminism

As theory and practice, socialist feminism is very much in a nascent process of construction. As women became involved in socialist theory and debate, certain problems began to emerge within the Marxist discourse and a distinction between socialist women and socialist feminists began to develop.[27] Feminists who were devoted to socialist goals nevertheless found inadequacies in the argument that subordination of women in a capitalist society arises because this serves the needs of capitalism, when confronted with the persistence of gender inequalities in socialist societies like the USSR, Cuba, Eastern Europe and China. The Marxist approach was found to have limitations in terms of inadequate formulations regarding both the political-processes of socialist societies and the analysis of women's oppression entirely through the concept of class. Feminists within the socalist fold have been struggling during the last decade to come to grips with the reality of gender oppression in society by formulating patriarchy as a process in dialectic interaction with class society. No unified theory is as yet visible nor are the answers definitive but the questions they have asked are extremely relevant.

According to socialist view, women's inferior status is rooted in private property, and class-divided society. Sexist ideology and structures such as the family maintain women's inferior status in society. Oppression is inclusive of exploitation but reflects a complex reality. Power is derived from sex and class and this is manifested materially and ideologically in patriarchy and class relations. The major task is to discover the interdependence of class and patriarchy. For the socialist feminists it is imperative to understand the operation of hierarchical sexual ordering of the society within the class structure. They also feel that overthrow of the capitalist system by itself will not mean transformation of patriarchal ideology. It would be necessary to organise struggles simultaneously against capitalism and patriarchy.

According to socialist feminists, the powerlessness of women in society is rooted in four basic structures : those of production, reproduction, sexuality and socialisation of children. Family as the radical feminists believed, was an institution which reinforced women's oppressive condition. Family and economy should not be looked upon as separate systems but as vitally interacting systems. The unequal and hierarchical sex roles operate in both the domains of family and economy.

The socialist feminists have raised the whole debate of domestic work. The orthodox Marxist analysts considers housework as producing only use value but not exchange value. A group of socialist feminists argue that women's oppression is based on unpaid housework. Child-bearing, child-care and housework are material activities resulting in products. The debate further focussed attention on the issues of women's position as housewives and of domestic labour's contribution to the reproduction of social relations. Of course the discussion is carried on in a broad Marxist framework.

Other questions raised by the socialists refer to the role of the family in strengthening sexism as contended by the radical feminists. Different approaches emerged in understanding the problem of relationship between patriarchy and the working of a particular mode of production. A very important issue related to the strategy is whether there is a place for women's movement. What is the relation of the women's movement and the wider struggles? Like the radical feminists, the socialist-feminists are not anti-man; they believe in collaborating with men if the latter support their cause and do not exhibit an instrumental approach towards women. But they do believe that women's issues are specific, they need focussed analysis and focussed attention. Hence women's groups have to be independently organised but they cannot ignore the other struggles of oppression.

Conclusion

In this section we have briefly referred to the three main approaches which have been used for understanding women's subordinate status and also for evolving strategies to establish women's equality. In the Indian context as we will notice, the dominant approach has been liberal feminist, when action has been organised taking the existing structures for granted. Some of the concepts and ideas used by the radical feminists/socialist feminists have to be critically used in India where conditions of poverty, unemployment, insufficient development prevail. For example, in a situation where other support structures are not available, the family may not be viewed as an obstruction but as a security. Similarly, issues of sexual freedom, sexual preference etc. may not be as widespread as in other developed western countries. Perhaps non-development of aggressive individualism might prove functional in the overall conditions of deprivation. In short the persepctives developed in the West are not absolutely relevant to Indian conditions. The necessity to find out which concepts are applicable, and when and how newer perspectives have to be developed, provides a good justification for developing more researches in the theoretical areas.

The Scheme of the Book

The underlying theme of the work is broadly the way major social changes in society have affected women's position, especially the development process, interacting with the pre-existing social structure. Often in development literature, the emphasis on the negative impact gives the impression that 'development' is the culprit and all the ills are attributed to it. What we have tried to show is that the obvious marginalising and devaluing of women in many ways is rather the result of interaction between a traditional patriarchal structure with capitalistic development in ways that are both complemenatry and contradictory—loosening in some ways and tightening in other ways, so that development is not a uniformly benign force improving the status of women. Much of the material presented is empirical and focusses on women in general, and not exclusively the upper and middle sections of society, so as to highlight not only the differential impact on women of social change but also the differential impact on different classes, so that what appear as paradoxes become understandable. The process is well illustrated in each chapter.

Chapter 2, on economy depicts the interaction between patriarchal structure and the emergence and growth of industrial capitalism within a given international economic order. The consequence appears to be a deterioration in women's work status for the majority of women but new opportunities for the middle-class; loss of areas of autonomy for the family producers but some Ieeway for others such as the middle class. But all classes of women experience oppression, though their forms vary. The salaried, educated women are not fully liberated and are subject to various forms of control; the poor working women face discrimination, exploitation at work and lack of support and above all male dominance at home. The interaction between patriarchal structures and the development process operates through sexual division of labour, occupational segregation and basic contradiction between women's production and reproduction roles. By reproduction, we do not mean only 'child bearing' but all functions that assist in maintaining life—the work involved in family maintenance. The pre-industrial woman worker was not a liberated woman because she too was the victim of class society and male dominance. But when other resources were directly obtained, such as food, her control over her life was somewhat better than when cash payment in a competitive set-up reduces means of subsistence. On the other hand, technological advances open up possibilities of reduction in drudgery—the average middle-class urban woman certainly does less ardous physical toil compared with her ancestors two to three generations ago.

In Chapter 3, in analysing the growth of education, we trace how liberal forces worked to improve women's education, for instance, by raising the age of marriage and emphasising education as an important means of emancipation. The right to education granted under democracy and the liberal view of education as a liberating forces is, however, undermined by limits to access to education posed by women's reproductive roles. Family responsibilities limit opportunities. In addition, for all classes of women, the content and goals of education betray a deep ambivalence between women's family roles and individual growth. The positive aspect of the growth of education is the emergence of a feminist consciousness that has exposed the contradiction between the guarantee of equality and its limits in practice.

In Chapter 4, on family, the structure of the family (or rather different structures of family life as there is no such thing as the family) is briefly described and how women are placed within it. A family is at the same time the source of retention of values and absorption of new values. Familial ties are mediated through systems of marriage, kinship and familial ideology. Socialisation is usually conceived of as 'transmission' of culture but this transmission of culture is not of fixed content. Both the content and context change. The family is the locus of the conflict between reproduction and production manifested by control over women's sexuality and fertility. Stresses and strains are felt most acutely within the family.

In Chapter 5, we see how health is not a neutral issue where access is merely one of resources. The need to develop individual rights and individual welfare under a democracy and a 'healthy' working people for development are controverted by patriarchal structures that subordinate women—the importance of a male child, the lack of reproductive freedom within marriage ; the hierarchy is claims to the resources of the family reduce women's access to family planning and general health care ; on the other hand State policies for population control target women. What could be liberating for women become new forms of oppression. In considering the health needs of women, their dual roles as producers and reproducers are not taken into account. Health programmes talk of mothers but forget their needs as individuals and workers; work policies take women as workers but ignore their needs and rights as mothers.

Chapter 6, highlights the forms of violence emerging in a society that has always had violence as a form of oppression. Earlier such violence was ideologically supported (*female infanticide, sati, harassment of widows* etc.) by a value system that extolled self-sacrifice as a necessary virtue for women. Education, freer movement, lessening of social controls are liberating forces for women but these have been accompanied by increased violence in the absence of transformation of value and ideological structures that do not view women as individuals. Added to all this is media distortion and the import of new images of women as sex objects. Deepening inequalities and struggles by oppressed sections to assert their rights (granted under a democracy) have unleashed retaliations by the more privileged, and women situated as they are in the social matrix as non-free, dependent beings become special victims.

Chapter 7, briefly depicts the various action strategies for change whose impact has been both positive and negative.

Democratic rights granted in principle are nullified by women's subordinate status. The process of development has increasingly separated the public from private and has enlarged the 'public' sphere with more formal institutions as against the earlier less formal community, caste, neighbourhood institutions. Public institutions often provide scope for women (law, for example) to escape from traditional constraints. However, access to formal institutions is limited for women and the ideolgies of many public institutions themselves reinforce traditional subordination. Actions for change have been on many fronts and their limits and possibilities are briefly examined. The deepening contradictions in society have a positive benefit in the rising consciousness of women and the growing women's movement in the country.

Though the matter is arranged under chapters and topics, there are links between them which the reader can recognise—the relationship between family, economy, education and health and how action-strategies encompass all these in the scope of their impact if not in their policy directions.

Notes and References

1. Florence Howe, *Seven Years Later, Women's Studies Programmes in 1976, National Advisory Council on Women's Educational Programmes*; also ref. *Women's Studies Monograph Series*, The National Institute of Education, U.S.A., 1980.
2. *Women's Studies International Form*, Special Issue on Strategies for Women's Studies in the 80s, Pergamon Press, Vol. 7, No. 3. 1984.
3. Soon Young Yoon, "*Women's Studies* : Is it Relevant ?", in *Samya Shakti*, Vol. 1, No. 1, July 1983, p. 5.
4. Florence Howe, (Ed.), *Every Woman's Guide to Colleges and Universities*, xiii-xiv.
5. There have been two or three major efforts to review the situation of women's studies in Asia. Leela Dube in 1980, under the auspices of UNESCO, Bangkok carried out a *Review of Studies on Women in Southeast Asia*. An expert meeting was organised, again by the UNESCO, Bangkok in Oct. 1982 to review the *Status of Women's Studies and Social Sciences in Asia* and suggest *Recommendations for Development of Research and Teaching on Women's Studies* in the region. Bina Agarwal in Nov. 1983, prepared a report of the *Current Status and needed Priorities of Women Studies in Asia and Pacific*, a project supported by Asian and Pacific Development Centre (APDC), Kuala Lumpur. All these works provide information and analysis of development and features of women's studies in Asia.

6. UNESCO, *Women's Studies and Social Sciences in Asia*, Report of a meeting of experts, 1983, p. 19.
7. Ibid., p. 21.
8. Soon Young Yoon while describing emergence of women's studies in Korea mentions that though there were various women's organisations—clubs—in Korea where women's problems were discussed, further there was a powerful students' movement in 1960s. However, their attention was focussed on restoration of democracy or unification while women's liberations was considered outdated, missionary goal or married women's problems and irrelevant to the younger generations' interests. Ref. *Samya Shakti*, op. cit., p. 6.
9. Bina Agarwal, po. cit., p. 61, 62, 63 ; also ref. *UNESCO Report*, op. cit., p. 20-21.
10. *DAWN*, Institute of Social Studies Trust, New Delhi, 1985.
11. Newsletter, *AWRAN*.
12. UNESCO, op. cit., p. 46-47, Agarwal, op. cit., p. 8-9, Desai, Neera, *Review of Studies on Middle Class Women in India, MSS Research Centre on Women's Studies*, Bombay, 1983. Krishna Raj Maitreyi, *Where Do We Go From Here*, Mimeographed, Research Centre on Women's Studies, Bombay.
13. *Report of the First National Conference on Women's Studies*, April 1981, SNDT University, Bombay, p. 41-45.
14. Subhadra Patwa, *Women's Studies' Centres in India*, Research Centre on Women's Studies, Bombay, mimeographed, 1985.
15. *UNESCO Report*, 1983, p. 47.
16. *Samya Shakti*, Vol. 1, No. 1, July 1983, p. 27-28.
17. *Samya Shakti*, Ibid., p. 34, Krishna Raj, *Why Study Women*, mimeographed, Department of Correspondence Courses, SNDT University, p. 6.
18. *Samya Shakti*, op. cit., p. 32.
19. *UNESCO Report of a Meeting of Experts*, op. cit., 1983, p. 46-47 ; also refer Agarwal Bina, op. cit., p. 10-20 ; Krishna Raj, *Research on Women and Work in the Seventies, Where Do We Go From Here* ? Research Centre on Women's Studies, 1984. Desai, Neera and Anantram, *Review of Studies on Middle Class Women's Entry on Women's Studies*, Bombay, 1984.
20. Agarwal, op. cit., p. 66.
21. Judith Hole and Ellen Levine, *Rebirth of Feminism*, The New York Times Book Company, USA., 1971, p. 1 ; also ref. Barbara Deckard, *The Women's Movement*, Political, Socio-economic and Psychological Issues. Harper and Row Publishers, New York, 1983, p. 449 ; Lise Vogel, *Marxism and the Oppression of Women, Towards a Unitary Theory*, Pluto Press, U.S.A., 1983, p. 1-3.
22. Friedan Betty, *The Second Stoge*, Summit Books, New York, 1981.
23. John Charvet, Feminism, Debt and Sons Ltd., London, 1982, p. 15 ; also ref. Susheela Kaushik (ed.), *Women's Oppression, Patterns and Perspectives*, Shakti Books, New Delhi, 1985.
24. Quoted in John Charvet, op. cit., p. 34.
25. Ibid., p. 36-37 ; Neera Desai, op. cit., p. 51, p. 66-75.
26. Zillah Eisenstein, *Capitalist Patriarchy and the Case for Socialist Feminism*, Monthly Review Press, New York, 1979, p. 16 ; also Deckard, op. cit., p. 454-460 ; Michele Barrett, *Women's Oppression Today, Problems in Marxist Feminist Analysis*, Vergo Publication, London, 1980, p. 43-47.
27. Eisenstein, op. cit., p. 5.
28. Michele Barrett, op. cit., p. 249.

1

An Overview of the Status of Women in India

Introduction

The present chapter attempts to provide a historical context to the study of the position of women in contemporary society. In order to have a better understanding of the present social structure and position of women therein, it is imperative to know the operation of various historical, political, cultural and economic factors moulding the society. And such an historical perspective is all the more necessary in the case of a society with a continuous history of more than three thousand years. It is also crucial to have a brief look at the past society, because some of the norms and values affecting women today have their roots in the past. Of course, the attempt here is only to provide a general overview and not to go into the details of periodisation and its controversy.

Though the necessity of reviewing women's status across historical phases is non-controversial, the task is fraught with innumerable difficulties. The hazards experienced while examining the position of women in contemporary society as described by Professor Srinivas, acquire much more validity in terms of delineation of women's position in early society. Professor Srinivas remarks: "It (the changing position of Indian women) has many facets and generalisation is well nigh impossible because of the existence of considerable variation among regions, between rural and urban areas, among classes, and finally among different religious, ethnic and caste groups. While in certain contexts the Indian subcontinent is a single cultural region, in many others it is heuristically more rewarding to look upon it as a congeries of micro-regions, the differences between which are crucial."[1] Historian Romila Thapar also refers to the same predicament when she remarks: "Within the Indian sub-continent there have been infinite variations on the status of women, diverging according to cultural milieu, family structure, class, caste, property rights and morals."[2] Besides, the difficulty of providing a monolithic picture of women's position at various phases of development, there is a serious difficulty of locating authentic sources which can help construct a profile of Indian women. This problem has acquired significance when history is being looked at through subaltern sources and with a feminist perspective. Thus, while on the one hand, historical documents that have been discovered and used by the mainstream scholars, tend to be elitist,[3] on the other hand, the historians who have attempted to build up history from the very beginning have not paid enough attention to the women's question.[4] Recently, some women historians and Sanskrit scholars have attempted different interpretations of the original Brahminical texts; also, some of them are trying to discover new data sources. Sukumari Bhattacharya, a Sanskrit scholar, while unravelling the picture of women in the Mahabharata mentions, "The Mahabharata presents two different pictures of women, one of which emerges from its prescriptive section and the other from the core section and there is a clear dichotomy between the two."[5] Further, she feels that women in the core epic behave with much greater freedom while those in other sections are presented as mere chattels. Similarly Uma Chakravarti, a feminist historian, while examining various sources of Ramayana story, remarks: "An analysis of the development of the Sita legend in a historical context however reveals that the emphasis on chastity and the assumption that ideal marriage is based on female devotion are aspects which were grafted on to an originally simple story. Over the centuries important details added to the story have had a crucial influence on the shaping of the feminine identity."[6] Thus only the beginnings have been made to reconstruct history from the women's perspective. India's past being a very lengthy one much concerted and collaborative efforts are to be made to attain the goal.

In order to study the development of women's position, the present chapter has been divided into three very broad periods. The first period, from 800 B.C. to 1800 A.D., described as the precolonial period is the longest one which studies the condition of women. The second one covers the period from 1800 to 1947, ie. the pre-independence period and the third the post-independence period. Periodisation has been arbitrary, but since the main purpose is to get an overview of the position of women, this scheme seems to be adequate. Further, it is also necessary to point out that in this overview, we have been able to give a generalised picture basically of Hindu upper caste women. The matrilineal society of Kerala in the South, and the matrilineal tribal societies prevailing among the Garos and the Khasis in the North-eastern part of the country provide a qualitatively different social setting for the women in those areas. Similarly, Muslim women or the women of the scheduled castes have different norms and problems. However, in this exploratory work it has not been possible to go into these diversities.

Before we describe the position of women in pre-colonial India, it would be useful to look at the normative structure and class/caste base of the Indian society, which provide a fundamental structural context for understanding women's status.

Normative Structure of Traditional Indian Society

The Vedic texts and the Dharmashastras (the codes of sacred and social duties) are said to constitute the norms for Brahminism and the religious practices for the upper castes. Prabhati Mukherjee while looking for evidence for examining the women's question in ancient India, considers that the Arthashastra of Kautilya and Manusmriti, broadly covering the period from 400 B.C. to 500 A.D., are sources for getting insights into the normative structure determining the behaviour of women.[7] Brahminism after the first millenium A.D.

moved away from the centrality of sacrificial ritual emphasised in the Vedic texts and instead emphasised worship through devotion to the deity and selfless action projected as the need to act in accordance with one's *Dharma*, i.e. duty. Dharma referred to the duties regarded as sacred which had to be performed in accordance with one's *varna*, *jati*, and sect and which differed according to each of these. The constituents of Dharma were in conformity to ritual duties, social obligations and the norms of the family and caste behaviour as stipulated in the Dharmashastras. The major concern was with ritual purity. The performance of sacred duty heavily enmeshed in social obligations was so important that absolute individual freedom only lay in renunciation.[8]

Hindu philosophy further accepts pursuit of wealth and satisfaction of sexual desires as legitimate activities though lower in the hierarchy of objectives to be attained in this life, as enshrined in four '*Purusharthas*'. Thus the householder's life is as important a stage in the life-cycle as that of a recluse. The necessity of giving oblations to the departed by the male descendants, sanctions marriage and rationalises the necessity of a male child. In this context the concepts of purity and pollution and various rituals acquire significance.

The Indian society like a number of 'classical' societies was patriarchal. Patriarchal values regulating sexuality, reproduction and social production (meaning total conditions of production) prevailed and were expressed through specific cultural metaphors. Overt rules prohibiting women from specific activities and denying certain rights did exist. But more subtle expression of patriarchy was through symbolism giving messages of inferiority of women through legends highlighting the self-sacrificing, self-effacing pure image of women and through the ritual practices which day in and day out emphasised the dominant role of a woman as a faithful wife and devout mother. We will briefly refer to some of these values and practices.

The basic rules for women's behaviour as expressed in the Laws of Manu insist that a woman must constantly worship her husband as a god, even though he is destitute of virtue or a womaniser. Women should be kept in dependency by her husband because by nature they are passionate and disloyal. The ideal women are those who do not strive to break these bonds of control. The salvation and happiness of women revolve around their virtue and chastity as daughters, wives and widows.[9] This theme has been reiterated by the recurrent symbolism of seed and the earth. Man provides the seed, the essence for the creation of the offspring; the seed determines the kind; the child's identity is derived from the father for the group placement. The role of the mother is just to receive the seed and through her own blood provide warmth and nourishment and help it to grow. Renowned anthropologist Leela Dube while referring to this symbolism comments: "One of the most significant aspects of the symbolism is how the two partners are situated in the process of reproduction. In his body man has the seed; the woman, on the other hand is herself the field.... The two partners are not on par with one another in so far as the process of reproduction is concerned. The offspring belongs to the one to whom the seed belongs. In fact he also owns the field."[10] A very sinister implication of this symbolism is that the man is the lord, master owner, or provider. A daughter or a wife is a commodity or a possession.

Besides such symbolism relegating woman to a lower position, there are rituals and practices for a woman which re-enforce her role as a devout wife and doting mother. Women perform a large number of the yearly calendrical rites.[11] These rites seek the protection and well-being of crucial kinsmen (especially husband, brother and son), the general prosperity and health of family members. Men's rites are not concerned with having *good* wives or one who will have a long life. Further, the ideal women of Indian mythology who have been extolled as paragons of virtue like Sita, Savitri, Draupadi, Damyanti etc., are women who have been dutiful, truthful, chaste, self-sacrificing women of unswerving wifely devotion whatever the temptation. The legends associated with them consistently refer to their purity and selfless attachment to their consorts. At one place wives have been mentioned as restraining all their sense and keeping their hearts under complete control; they regard their husbands as veritable gods. For women neither sacrifice nor sraddhas (penances) are of any efficacy. By serving their husbands only, can they win heaven.[12] This ideal gets re-enforced through numerous myths and legends.

One important point in understanding the value structure in Indian society is the dual concept of the female in Hindu philosophy: On the one hand woman is fertile, benevolent bestower of prosperity; on the other hand she is considered aggressive, malevolent and destructive. This dual character manifests self in the goddesses also, as there are dangerous, aggressive, malevolent goddesses like *Kali* and *Durga*; there are equally important goddesses like *Laxmi*, *Saraswati*, *Mariamman* who are benevolent.[13] Veena Das, while analysing the anthropological meaning of prevalence of the worship of goddesses, draws attention to the fact that in *shakti* form the goddess usually stands alone and is not encompassed with a higher male principle. She adds: "The principle of power finds expression in the goddesses who represent `shakti', who come to the aid of man and the gods in periods of cosmic darkness, by killing the demon who threaten the entire cosmic order. The principle of renunciation, on the other hand, finds expression in the ideals of *sati*."[14]

This duality is confusing and attempts are made to explain it. Susan Wadley, for instance, considers that there is a cultural logic in this concept. She says, "The female is first of all *shakti* (energy/power), the energising principle of the universe. The female is also *prakriti* (Nature), the undifferentiated Matter of the Universe." She further adds, "Uniting these two facets of femaleness, women are both energy/power and nature, and nature is uncultured... uncultured power is dangerous."[15] Romila Thapar in this quality sees both contempt and fear. The latter doubtless us derived from fear of pollution since women were regarded as impure on many occasions.[16] Sudhir Kakkar, while studying the inner world of an Indian child, harps upon the intimate relationship between the mother and the son, wherein for the son, the mother's original perfection remains untarnished by reality, a part of the iconography of Hindu inner world. He remarks, "In the case of a Hindu woman, at least in the imagery of the culture, maternal feelings of tenderness and nurturance occur in combination with a profound gratitude and the readiness for a poignantly high emotional investment in the child."[17]

In short, the value structure by presenting the dual character of woman, seems to have been successful in creating a myth that Indian woman possesses power, which is far from the position in readily. This whole concept is still unclear, and needs more exploration. However, it is a very valuable concept in understanding the seemingly high and really inferior position of women in India.

Caste System in India

In order to properly estimate the position of women in ancient society, a brief reference to the stratificatory system as expressed through *varna* and caste system is necessary. The *varna* principle of categorisation of society into four groups, viz. Brahmans, Kshatriyas, Vaishyas and Shudras existed in Vedic society. The four *varnas* are mentioned in order of hierarchy wherein the first three are called *dwija*, i.e. twice-born while the shudras occupy the lowest position in the society, and they are expected to serve the other three *varnas*. *Brahmans* occupy ritually and ideologically the top position of power and authority. The principle of stratification acquired normative significance, thus legitimising the over-lordship of the *Brahmans*. The *varna* scheme were empirically expressed through various caste groups, indicating the adjustment of the system to the development needs of the society.

A good deal of controversy about the caste system centres around its origin. Scholars are divided in their opinions with regard to the emergence of a stratificatory system which has such a powerful hold on both religious and secular activities of the Indians even today. The most popular and widely prevalent theory traces the origin to the Aryan invasion of India and links it to the process by which the invaders could sub-ordinate the indigenous inhabitants and integrate them as peasants and slaves in a stratified society. Thus the 'twice-born' castes are descendants from the non-Aryans. An alternate hypothesis is also put forward in which castes are looked upon as the means by which tribal societies consisting of originally equalitarian clans adjusted to inequality generated by the economic surplus. Thus theory dates back from caste system to the beginnings of class society and settled agriculture.[18] Whatever the controversies, it is clear that caste in India has existed for a very long period and that is has survived through major socio-historical changes. Gail Omvedt argues that caste has co-existed with different modes of production, right from the tributary modes to the present capitalist ones. However, she feels that caste certainly requires for its existence surplus production and economic inequality.[19]

For the present chapter we will not dwell further on the controversies, but will take up some of the features of the caste system which have direct relevance to women. Srinivas defines caste in the following words. "Caste is a hereditary, endogamous, usually localised group having traditional associations with an occupation and a particular position in the local hierarchy of castes. Relations between castes are governed among other things by the concepts of pollution and purity and generally maximum commensuality occurs within the caste."[20] Features like caste endogamy as a mechanism of recruiting and retaining control over the labour and sexuality of women, concepts of purity and pollution segregating groups and also regulating mobility of women are very crucial.

The concept of *anulom* and *pratilom* marriages by definition denigrate women. A marriage where a boy of upper caste marries a girl of lower caste is approved and called *anuloma*, while marriages of women of ritually pure groups with men of lower ritual status were considered *pratiloma*. Most serious punishments like excommunication and even death could be evoked for transgressing the norms. Woman as a guardian of 'purity' has not to lower herself but she could be raised high. Another manifestation of caste inequality is the differential status of bride-giver and bride-taker where the latter is always superior. Even within the caste there are groups which are considered superior and for climbing high in the status ladder, the bride-givers have to give compensation in terms of dowry.[21]

The other very important feature of the caste system is its control over women's labour. Caste not only determines social division of labour but also sexual division of labour. Certain tasks have to be performed by women while certain other tasks are meant for men. In agriculture for instance, women can engage themselves in water-regulation, transplanting, weeding, but not in ploughing. With upward mobility of the group, women are immediately withdrawn from the outside work. Physical mobility is also restricted through caste norms. The significant symbol of the low status of women in society is that the women of lower castes are accessible to men of higher status, while there is a very severe punishment for men of lower castes who dare to approach any women of higher groups. Evidence has been documented in various studies and folk literature.[22]

The linking of women and shudras together is one more evidence of the low position of women. Prescriptions and prohibitions for shudras and woman were the same on many occasions. The prohibition of the sacred thread ceremony for both women and shudras, similar punishment for killing a shudra or a woman, denial of religious privileges etc. are some of the illustrations which indicate how caste and gender get entrenched.[23] In fact medieval saints through their plea for direct access to god and elimination of intermediaries provided a space both for women and shudras in the religious sphere.

In short, the caste system not only provided a legitimisation to feudal relation of production but ideologically also provided justification for the subordination of women.

Position of Women during Pre-colonial Period

Many scholars aver that the position of women in a given epoch has to be studied in the context of the material culture of the society concerned. In studying Indian women, some historians have attempted to link the economic development of the society with the position of women. Suvira Jayaswal contends that society in the Rig-vedic period was still predominantly pastrol and nomadic, it did not produce enough surplus to allow any section of society to be completely subordinated or withdrawn from the process of production.[24] This perhaps explains comparatively better the situation of women in the vedic period in terms of access to education, religious rights, freedom of movement etc.[25] As observed earlier, though historical data is not enough to build up a detailed linkage, it has been noticed that the growth of a class society, which manifested itself in the form of varnas and the decline in position of women have occurred simultaneously.[26] This decline dates back from the period of Manusmriti i.e. 500 B.C. to 1800 A.D.

Manav Code provided a legal and ideological legitimisation for a pattern of social structure which lasted for more than a thousand years. The code laid down the basic framework for a hierarchical caste structure, patriarchal joint family with the oldest male as the supreme head of the patrilineal kin group, and the subordinate status for the shudras and women. Even the Bhagavad-Gita, one of the most sacred books of the Hindus, places women, *vaisyas* and *shudras* in the same category, and describes them all as being of sinful birth. According to Parasarsmriti, punishment for killing either a woman or a shudra is identical.[27] We will briefly provide a picture of women during this period.

The birth of a daughter which was not source of anxiety during the vedic period, became a source of disaster for the father during the post-vedic phase. Thus it was said that the birth of a son is bliss incarnate, while that of a daughter is the root of family misery. Education of women which was an accepted norm during the vedic period, slowly began to be neglected and later on girls were totally denied any access to education. Upanayana or the sacred thread ceremony which was performed to initiate a person into the vedic studies, was prohibited in the case of women and shudras by the Manav codes, thus closing the doors for any formal education to women. By circa 8th century A.D. the marriageable age for girls was lowered to 9 or 10 years which not only gave a final blow to any effort at educating women but began the sinister practice of prepuberty marriages. Girls in the ruling class families did receive some training in military, administration and fine arts. There were a few outstanding scholarly women like Gargi, Maitreyi and Atreyi who provided an alternative style of female existence. Similarly, Amrapalli, the famous courtesan of Buddhist literature declined to give up her invitation to a meal for the Buddha in favour of the Lichchhavi princes who wished to edge her out and host the Buddha themselves. Meera, a renowed poetess of the medieval period preferred to live her life as a devotee of Krishna rather than enjoy the luxuries befitting a royal queen. However, these are exceptions. Mainstream life for the upper caste women was confined to the four walls and restricted to serving kin members. The subservience of woman is precisely summed up in the famous injunction of the Manav code, where it is stated that a woman should never be independent. As a daughter she is under the surveillance of her father, as a wife, of her husband and as widow of her son.

In a patrilineal society where considerable concern for ritual purity is emphasised, women play a vital role in the protection of the purity of the group. Veena Das remarks, "Women were literally seen as points of entrance, as 'gateways' to the caste system. If men of ritually low status were to get sexual access to women of higher status, then not only the purity of the women but that of the entire group would be endangered. Since the main threat to the purity of the group came from female sexuality, it becomes vital to guard it. Most groups solved this problem by the custom of prepuberty marriage."[28] Marriage at an early date, marriage within the caste and even in the subcaste, prohibition of *pratilom*, marriage where a woman of higher caste marries a man of lower caste, marriage as a sacrament whereby a woman is bound in wedlock till she dies, were all practices which suggest the control of sexuality. Nothing can be compared with the most tragic and subservient condition of a high caste widow. She was not only forbidden to remarry, but she was considered an inauspicious, harbinger of ill-luck for the family. She had to forgo all the good things of life so that she may not be attractive enough to lure any man. In the medieval period she was even expected to die either on the same pyre with her husband or follow him and become *sati* (truly, devoted wife). Treatment of the widow thus at times bordered on the inhumane and callous levels.

Despite the overall social and cultural sub-ordination of women, it is surprising to find that law givers recognised the right to property, particularly that which was known as *streedhan*, women's property. Manu defines *streedhan* as "that which was given to her before the nuptial fire, in bridal procession, in token of love and which she has received from brother, mother, father or husband".[29] Later, the law givers particularly from 7th century A.D. liberally interpreted the term *adya* i.e. etc. to enlarge the scope of *streedhan* and included even such property as acquired through inheritance, purchase, partition, chance and adverse possession.[30] How far in reality this liberal interpretation was accepted is a debatable point. Some historians feel that this liberal interpretation was linked up with the growth of individual right on land in an agrarian feudal society which developed during the early medieval period.[31]

Along with this liberal tradition in the society, we come across two major religions, Buddhism and Jainism described as shramanic religions providing options to women from living such a servile life. Buddhism particularly, which flourished from 5th century B.C. to 1st century A.D. kept open three alternative roles for women. The first included the roles of wife and mother which were the most common roles for women envisaged in the texts. The image of a devout wife is not different from that which was prescribed by Brahminical texts. The second role within which a woman appears is that of a courtesan. In Buddhist literature she does not seem to be suffering from social condemnation. However, she was still under male control and dominance. Finally for women, the role of a bhikkhuni was thrown open after initial resistance from Buddha himself. As a bhikkhuni, a women had greater freedom and more mobility ; but inside the *Sangha*, women experienced severe discrimination which in a way perpetuated their subordination.[32]

Chakravarti considers that the dictum that adultery and theft are the two major offences against which the king must be rigorous, suggest the development of an agricultural economy and an urban culture.[33] In spite of the discriminatory treatment meted out to *bhikkhunis* in the order, many of them saw themselves as being liberated from the drudgery of the paestle and the mortar.[34]

Another liberal current which to some extent widened the horizon for women was the *Bhakti* movement—the medieval saints' movement. The saints emphasised salvation through devotion to a deity wherein no intermediary such as a *pandit* or a *purohit* was required. The *Bhaktas* vehemently attacked ritualism and overlordship of the Brahmans, used the vernacular as a language of communication and opened the gates of religion for women. Not surprisingly it is the *Bhakti* movement which produced women saints like Meerabai and Lalla in the North, Andal and Akka Mahadevi in the South and Bahanabai in the West. As the movement did not basically challenge the unequal social structure and limited it only to individual salvation, it could not fundamentally affect gender subordination.

In concluding this vast phase of history in the context of women's position, it may be mentioned that particularly after the establishment of class society and the rise of private property in the post-vedic period, women's position in the society declines. Patriarchal values relating to sexuality and regulation of her movement, thus controlling her purity, get entrenched during this phase. K.P. Jayaswal, an indologist commenting on the nadir reached in women's position in the puranic period, wrote : "It was not the wife of the time of Kautilya who would bring an action for defamation or assault and become defendant in the court for beating her husband; it was not the wife of the Manav who regarded 'mutual fidelity to be the higher duty. It was the wife of *Yajnavalkya's* age permeated to the core like pickle....with the dharma of abject obedience and unnatural tolerance."[35]

The overwhelming concern for purity and maintenance of honour through a woman resulting in underpinning of her role as wife and mother, exercised through both overt and covert regulations, seem to have been necessitated by the material development needs of the society. Perhaps with the efforts of the feminist historians we might in future be able to see linkages between the material culture and value system which will surely deepen our understanding. Generally the deterioration in the position of women is explained by the established historians as being a consequence of the conquest of Aryan over non-Aryan women in the Aryan household or with reference to the victory of the patriarchal tribes over indigenous matriarchal people or imposition of Brahminical austerities on society or foreign invasions in India leading to more constraints on women's life especially as a consequence of Muslim invasion.[36]

As mentioned earlier, we have ignored regional, caste, religious, class and such other differences and have provided a very generalised picture of the position of women in pre-British society. The effort basically is to highlight the formulation and influence of normative structures which are persisting till today. A woman during this vast span not only occupied an inferior position but was made to feel that her position is subordinate to men in the society. Subsequent sections will depict whether this situation has changed or not.

Position of Woman During Pre-independence Period

Though the first cultural contact of Indian society with the western world began in 1498 A.D. when Vasco De Gama anchored his ships on Indian shores, a more lasting impact came with the British rule, particularly after 1820. The advent of British rule did not merely mean a new political rule, but it also had deep-rooted implications on the economy and the ideology of Indian people. Particularly after industrial revolution in England, the rulers turned India into a colony which produced raw material for Britain. The country passed through complex economic and political developments due to the working of merchant, industrial and financial capital. The imperial system initiated the capitalist mode of production but retained many pre-capitalist institutions like the caste system and inhuman socio-religious practices. Besides initiating a limited capitalist mode of production, the introduction of cash transactions, commercialisation, and cheap machine made goods had a far-reaching impact not only on the economy but also on the entire social structure.

The use of English language as the medium of instruction significantly affected the education system. Further, for the newly emerging middle-class, English language provided a gateway to the ideology of liberalism which enshrined the values of liberty, equality, respect for the individual, secularism etc., though in colonial India, the application of these values was limited to the extent that it did not harm the interest of the rulers.

During the period there were two major movements which affected the position of women. These were the Social Reform Movement of the nineteenth century and the Nationalist Movement of the twentieth century. Both these movements raised the question of equal status of women. The Social Reform Movement has been regarded as a key to the intellectual processes that went into the making of modern India. The issues which attracted the attention of the nineteenth century social reformers were *sati, the ill-treatment of widows, the ban on widow marriage, polygamy, child marriage, denial of property rights* and *education to women.* Social reformers felt that these social evils should be eradicated by raising consciousness and making people sensitive to the injustice perpetrated on women. They thought that by giving women the access to education and by enacting progressive legislation, social change could be initiated. Raja Ram Mohan Roy, Ishwarchandra Vidyasagar, M.G. Ranade, Mahatma Phuley, Lohitwadi, Durgaram and others from all parts of the country raised their voice against some of the unjust practices, while revivalists like Dayanand Saraswati, Swami Vivekananda and Annie Besant believed in reviving the old vedic society presumed to be the ideal society for women. One of the important offshoots of the Social Reforms Movement was the establishment of the National Social Conference in 1887 which provided a forum to the reformers from all parts of the country to discuss various practices and institutions which needed to be reformed. In their annual meetings women's problems were always raised.

Another very powerful force which helped change the position and attitude towards women was the Nationalist Movement particularly during the Gandhian phase. Though in the liberal and militant phase of the freedom movement, Indian women were slowly entering the political field, a more significant mobilisation, however, took place after 1920.[37] In the Non-Cooperation Movement of 1921 and the Civil Disobedience Movement of 1930 new techniques of struggle like picketing and boycotting of foreign goods and liquor shops and non-cooperation in various governmental activites were used which provided avenues for mass participation. Gandhiji, apart from being a political leader was also a critic of some of the outmoded social institutions. He vehemently criticised the custom of child marriage, prohibition of widow remarriage, temple prostitution and the custom of purdah. Of course, his own concept of woman was a peculiar blend of religious and rational elements. He, therefore, had immense faith in the woman's inner strength and her moral appeal. In the various Satyagrahas which were launched, not only the upper class urban women participated but at many places simple unsophisticated rural women also assumed leadership. Aparna Basu summarises the contribution of women in the Nationalist Movement : "Women organised themselves into groups and were willing to join processions, face police firing and go to prison. They broke the salt law, picketed shops selling liquor and foreign manufactured cloth. There were women who joined terrorist groups and helped in editing and distributing banned newspapers and in manufacturing bombs."[38] While evaluating the Gujarati women's response to Gandhi during 1920-1942, Aparna Basu comments that it was an impressive record. She remarks : "Women indulged in various kinds of activities ranging from mass scale popular agitations, constructive work among Harijans and Adivasis, to formal institutionalized electoral politics."[39]

In short it is useful to note that the movement for emancipation of women in India began in the 19th century, when the social reformers initially were critiques of outmoded social practices and they attempted to change some of these practices by applying the rational and humanitarian criteria to the problems. They further laid great stress on the education of women as a liberalising activity. The nationalist movement not only drew a large number of women to political activity but it also generated strength and confidence among women which helped them to organise and to fight for their own cause, rather than depend upon the 'benevolent' men in society to promote their cause. The formation of the All India Women's Conference in 1927 was a crucial event in women's march towards equality.

The pre-independence period thus marked the beginning of awareness of the sufferings of women due to oppressive social customs. During this phase a favourable climate was created to improve the status of women through legal reforms. Many laws were enacted which tried to eradicate certain social evils. Though the act legalising remarriage of widows was passed as early as 1856, there were many other laws which were passed during 1920-1940. To mention a few, the Child Marriage Restraint Act, popularly known as Sarda Act prohibited marriages below the age of 14 for a girl ; The Hindu Women's Right To Property Act recognised women's right to property in joint family property. Besides the social legislation, there were other laws which affected women's work status, such as limiting hours of work in organised industries, prohibiting night work, restricting work in the mines establishment of creches etc.

With regard to the economic position it may be averred that though women of the lower strata have been working for wages, the middle-class women's entry into the world of work appears more significantly after the Second World War. A few women did take up some professions like law, medicine, teaching, etc. but their number was very limited. Hence, during this period we do not find many voices raised regarding women's dual role or the burden of working women.

In short, during the phase prior to independence, an awareness of the need to remove social disabilities of women was created ; the doors of education were opened for them ; women's

organisations emerged to represent the needs and cause of middle-class urban women; political participation of women increased · women's mobility. Finally through several legal enactments, women's unequal position was being rectified.

Contemporary Position of Indian Women*

Earlier in the chapter, we mentioned the difficulties of giving a representative picture of the position of women in India in pre-British society. The task of attempting to do the same exercise for the contemporary period is more hazardous as there has been a differential impact of factors of change on different sections of women. This has further resulted in creating contradictory images of women. Middle-class educated women, particularly in large urban agglomerations, who are working and moving freely, generate an impression that Indian women's status has substantially improved. Moreover, there is evidence of capable, efficient, powerful women at times with political clout, which reinforces this impression.

But in small towns or rural areas or in city slums, women still suffer social and economic oppression. In small towns and villages, upper caste women even today are confined to home bound activities and involved in responsibilites and interests limited only to their kith and kin. The growing instances of suffering socially and economically by women of scheduled castes and scheduled tribes generate despair, frustration and expose the inter-twining of caste, class and gender forces. The back-breaking drudgery of housework by women as well as the long hours spent in activities like fetching water and bringing firewood in the rural areas are known to all. Professor Srinivas's observations in this respect are worth noting. He says : "While at the bottom level of the rural hierarchy women do both intramural and extra-mural work, the latter being paid for while the former is not, immurement of women characterises the top level."[40]

Does this mean that there has been no change during the last thirty years ? The achivement of Independence in 1947 generated a feeling of optimism and buoyancy among the people.

*Since all the subsequent chapters are dealing with more detailed discussions on different aspects of women's position, in this section only notable changes which have ocurred in Indian society affecting women, have been briefly highlighted.

Under the leadership of Jawaharlal Nehru it was decided to take a path of directed social change based on three axes, viz., the creation of a democratic secular Constitution, planned development based on a mixed economy and state support to social welfare activities. We will briefly discuss each measure and its relevance to women.

(a) *The Constitution Guaranteed Formal Equality*

The Preamble to the Constitution of India resolved to secure to all its citizens justice—social, economic and political ; liberty of though, expression, belief, faith and worship ; equality of status and opportunity ; and to promote among them fraternity, assuring the dignity of individual and the unity of the Nation. To attain these objectives, the Constitution guarantees certain fundamental rights and freedoms, such as freedom of speech, and protection of life and personal liberty. Indian women are beneficiaries of these rights in the same manner as Indian men. Article 14 ensures equality before the law and Article 15 'prohibits any discrimination'. Article 16 (1) guarantees equality of opportunity for all citizens in matters relating to employment or appointment to any office under the State.

Besides the Preamble, the Directive Principles of the State Policy embody the major policy goals of the Welfare State. Though these principles are non-justiciable, these are nevertheless pointers to the fundamental vision of a socio-political order. The State is expected to take notice of these principles while formulating laws. Free and compulsory education for all children upto the age of fourteen, right to an adequate means of livelihood for men and women equally, equal pay for equal work, and maternity relief are some of the specific directive principles. In short, Fundamental Rights as well as Directive Principles not only provide the framework of the ideals of the State, but they are the instruments to attain the national objectives of justice, liberty and equality. By adopting the principle of adult franchise the government sought to establish a democratic republic.

Besides providing a formal structure of equality, the government, as it is found in many of the Third World countries, used law as a major plank to change society. The enactment of Hindu Law guaranteeing the right to divorce and remarriage to Hindu women, the Inheritance Act providing equal share to women in the property, and the establishment of the principle of monog-

amy are some of the important innovations introduced in the Indian social structure affecting women's status and role. The Termination of Pregnancy Act, The Maternity Benefit Act, The Dowry Prohibition Act etc. are some of the measures of relief for all women irrespective of caste, creed or religion. Significant legal measures have been introduced during the last decade. The Criminal Law (Second Amendment) Act 1983, provides crucial amendments concerning women in the Indian Penal Code. A nationwide anti-rape movement during 1980 forced the government to review the rape law. In the amended law, custodial rape has to be punished, severely putting the burden of proof onto the rapist. In 1984, the Government conceded the demand of women, to establish family courts for the speedy conduct of matrimonial disputes, through the provision of an informal procedure of conciliation. It also authorised the courts to seek the help of social workers, specialists, psychologists, recognised organisations and insitutions for resolving disputes. Thus law is seen not only as an instrument to remove social disabilities but also as a tool for empowering women.

The establishment of women's cells and the creation of a Ministry for Women's Affairs are positive steps in the direction of improving the position of women.

(b) *Economic Policy*

The enormous problem of poverty leading to various imbalances and discriminations for vast numbers of people posed a formidable problem to Indian rulers. Planned development was considered to be the most efficient way of meeting the problem. This policy measure has serious implications for Indian women. Free India adopted a path of development based on mixed economy with a very great emphasis on industrialisation. It accepted the pattern of dual sectors, viz. public and private. In the sector where social and economic overhead capital was large, i.e., coal, iron and steel, ship-building etc. and where capital was not likely to be attracted, the State took the responsibilities, while over the other development areas the State has only power to regulate and control. There have been considerable shifts in the different plan periods, i.e. from 1951 to 1985, with regard to major thrusts, in economic development.

During the late sixties and early seventies it was realised the world over that a single dimensional measure of economic development in terms of GNP is inadequate both as a goal and as a catalytic agent generating development in other sphheres. The contention that prosperity in one sector or one class would gradually spread to other sectors or other classes, proved to be an illusion. Various studies have shown that poverty and unemployment have the worst effect on women leading to the phenomenon of feminisation of poverty.[41] It is now recognised that the policy of economic development which relies heavily on high technology, multinational collaborations, export promotion and encouragement to private sector, paves the way for a higher degree of concentration of capital and extremely exploitative relations of production having very serious implications for women.

(c) *Social Welfare State*

India's emphais on being a Welfare State had significant impact on Women's Status and Role. The Government of India, in 1953 established a Central Social Welfare Board with a nationwide programme of grant-in-aids, for promoting welfare and development services for women, children and underprivileged groups. The Board has its state counterparts, and it aims at providing assistance to voluntary agencies, improving and developing welfare programmes and sponsoring them in areas where they did not exist. This programme of the Government, on the one hand, encouraged the growth of a large number of women's organisations and on the other hand, provided status and position to many of the erstwhile active women social or political workers. Proliferation of Mahila Mandals is a striking phenomenon of this period.

Conclusion

The three major policy measures which we have described, have affected women's position significantly. The constitutional recognition of equal status for women and progressive legal enactments have undoubtedly empowered Indian women with juridical equality. Inducting of women in some of the decision-making bodies creates hopes of action on the part of the rulers. One of the striking achievements during the last forty years has been the acceptance of the need and spread of women's education. Many urban girls are getting opportunities of entering the portals of higher education. There have been more opportunities for middle class and upper class women to go in for remunerative work. More women are seen working in non-traditional jobs and are also holding decision-making posts.

On the other hand, the colonial heritage of poverty, unemployent, deprivation of basic needs such as adequate nutrition, health service, sanitation etc. have not been eradicated; nay, some of them have been accentuated. In international relations there is a growing hold of the multinational corporations. The national government's effective control over production and allocation of resources get attenuated and policies pursued are often inimical to national interests. Commercialisation, modernisation, export-oriented development, growing reliance on private sector and profit motive as the main objectives of economic activities have all affected women adversely. Not only has women's employment in the organised sector been reduced, but expansion of the informal sector has put women in the category of a reserve army. The increasing feminisation of poverty is a matter of grave concern.

Patriarchal values and normative structure established some two thousand years ago still persist though in a different garb. Motherhood and the ideal of a faithful loyal, self-sacrificing wife are projected through the media and the education system. The reality of the subordinate position of woman is indicated through adverse sex ratio of girls, the growing domestic violence, increasing number of dowry deaths and rape cases.

The relative ease with which Indian women secured juridical equality, entered professions and occupied positions of power has led to the myth that Indian women enjoy a very high status in society; they are able to balance their two roles very efficiently and that they wield power naturally. This myth has been eroded during the last ten to fifteen years. There is a growing awareness that men and women suffer from discrimination and deprivation. The problems of educated urban women become more serious since the discrimination and disabilities operate in more subtle and covert ways. Thus the dual existence of women holding high positions and yet undergoing various types of suffering continues.

One very hopeful development which has occurred during the last ten years is the emergence of a women's movement wherein women have started raising their voice against inequality, patriarchal values and the inegalitarian social structure. The new leadership, we hope, will not only expose the myth of the high position of Indian women but will adopt more positive steps to raise the stauts of women.

Notes and References

1. M.N. Srinivas. *The Changing Position of Indian Women*, Oxford University Press, Bombay, 1978, p. 7.
2. Romila Thapar, "Looking Back in History", in Devaki Jain, *Indian Women*, Publication Division, Ministry of Information and Broadcasting, Government of India, New Delhi, 1975, p. 6.
3. A.S. Altekar, *The Position of Women in Hindu Civilization*, Motilal Banarsidas, Delhi, 1962 ; P.V. Kane, *History of the Dharmashastra Literature*, Poona, 1930; Upadhyaya, *Women in Rigveda*, Lucknow, 1933.
4. Ranjit Guha defines "'Subaltern' as a name for the general attribute of subordination in South Asian Society, whether this is expressed in terms of class, caste, age, gender and office or any other way." However, a search for a picture of women's position drawn through non-traditional sources to counteract elitist male bias of historians in subaltern studies proved fruitless, Ranjit Guha, *Subaltern Studies*, I, II, III, Oxford University Press, New Delhi, 1982-1984.
5. Sukumari Bhattacharya, "Women in Mahabharata", a paper presented in a Seminar on women and culture, organised by Indraprastha College, New Delhi, 1981, p. 1.
6. Uma Chakravarti, "The Sita Myth," in *Samya Shakti*, Vol. I, No. 1, July 1983, p. 70. Chakravarti also advocates looking into Therigathas stories by the nuns for getting subjective recollections of the theris concerning specific nature of women's oppression in relation to Hindu Brahminic ritual.
7. Prabhati Mukherjee, *Hindu Women : Normative Models*, Orient Longman Limited, New Delhi, 1978, p. 7.
8. Romila Thapar, "Syndicated Moksha, in the Hindus and their Ismas, *Seminar* 313, Sept. 1985, p. 17.
9. Buhler, *The Laws of Manu*, V, p. 195-197 and p. 327-330.
10. Leela Dube, "The Seed and the Earth," Paper presented at the Tenth International Congress of Anthropological and Ethnological Sciences, New Delhi, 1978, Mss. p. 8.
11. *Vratas* such as *Karva Chauth, Kevda Trij, Vat Savitri, Gauri Puna*, are all undertaken either by an unmarried girl to get a good husband or by a married woman to retain the husband or by a mother for the welfare of the son.
12. Sudhir Kakkar, *The Inner World*, Oxford University Press, 1981, p. 67.
13. Susan Wadley, "Women and the Hindu Tradition," *in Women in India*, two persepctives, by Jacobson and Wadley, Manohar, 1977, p. 114; also refer to Veena Das, *The Mythological Film and its Framework of Meaning in Indian International Centre*, Quarterly, Vol. 8, No. 1, 1981.
14. Veena Das, op. cit., p. 48.
15. Wadley, op. cit., p. 116, 117.

16. Thapar, op. cit., p. 10.
17. Sudhir Kakkar, op. cit., p. 79, also ref. p. 104.
18. Gali Omvedt (ed.), "Land, Caste and Politics inIndian States," *Teaching Politics*, University of Delhi, Delhi, 1982, p. 11-12; also refer to Uma Chakravarti, Towards a historical sociological of stratification in Ancient India, *Economic and Political Weekly*, Vol. XX, No. 9, March 2, 1985 for a different interpretation of the relation of caste system and production processes. Uma Chakravarti contends that linkage of a caste with production system seems to be a misrepresentation of reality particularly for the post-vedic and pre-Christian period of India history. According to her at that time the caste categories were more in nature of theoretical constructs. Using the non-Brahminical sources, Chakravarti shows that early Pali texts categorise people into *Kshatriyas, Brahmans* and *Gahapatis* who are considered high while *Chandala, Vena, Nishada* etc. are considered low. The Gahapatis were high status group closely associated with agriculture. They were the major employers of labour *dasas*. Thus she avers that the empirical reality of the stratificatory system was based on those who controlled means of production and not on ritualistic stauts.
19. Ibid., p. 12.
20. M.N. Srinivas, *"Caste in Modern India and other essays"*, Media Promoters and Publishers Pvt. Ltd., Bombay, 1978, p. 3.
21. Neera Desai, "Caste, Class and Gender", paper presented at the Sociology Conference, Surat, Dec. 1984. p. 15-16; also refer to Veena Das, in Nanda (ed.), op. cit., p. 132-133.
22. Veena Das, op. cit., p. 143-144 ; also ref. Desai Neera. op. cit., p. 18-20.
23. Altekar, op. cit., p. 204, 317, 326.
24. Suvira Jayaswal, 'Position of Women in Early India", A Historiographical reappraisal, Paper presented at the First Conference on Women's Studies, 1981, p. 2-3 ; also refer to R.S. Sharma, *Indian Feudalism*, Macmillan & Co., Delhi, 1980, p. 112, 113, 277.
25. A.S. Altekar, op. cit., p. 10-13, 196-197.
26. Jayaswal, op. cit., p. 5.
27. Thapar, op. cit., p. 9.
28. Veena Das, "Indian Women : Work, Power and Status," in *Indian Women* ed. by B.R. Nanda, Vikas Publishing House, 1976, p. 135 ; see also Neera Desai, *Women in Modern India*, Vora & Co., 1957, p. 20-24.
29. Altekar, op. cit., p. 220.
30. Ibid., p. 223.
31. Jayaswal, op. cit., p. 6, also ref. Thapar, 1975, p. 11, ref. Sharma, op. cit., p. 112, 119.
32. Uma Chakravarti, "The Rise of Buddhism as Experienced by Women", a paper presented in the Seminar on Women's Life Cycle and Identity, 1981, p. 4.
33. Ibid., p. 1-2.
34. Ibid., p. 7.
35. K.P. Jayaswal, *Manu and Yajnavalkya*, 1930, p. 232.
36. S. Jayaswal, 1981, p. 5 ; Mukherjee, op. cit., p. 5; Omvedt Gail, *Land, Caste and Politics in Indian States*, p. 19-20.
37. Neera Desai, 1957, op. cit., p. 136-137.
38. Aparna Basu, in Nanda (ed.), op. cit., p. 39.
39. Aparna Basu, in *Samya Shakti*, Vol. 1, No. 2, 1984, p. 6.
40. Srinivas, 1978, op. cit., p. 12.
41. For detailed discussion refer to Chapter 2 of this book.

2

The Economy

The relationship of women to the economy is a special problem area in women's studies. Why do we need to study women's role in the economy separately ?

First, because a good deal of women's work remains invisible. Its exact nature, scope and intensity are either not measured at all or partially and erratically measured. Secondly, the valuation of women's work is subject to influences and forces which are different from those of men. Simple laws of supply and demand are not uniformly applicable. Women workers form a special category. The kind of work they do, where, how, under what terms—all these are determined by women's position in society. They have speical responsibilities, not shared by others; they face various kinds of cultural taboos ; their child-bearing functions place them in a different position. Thirdly, one needs an explanation as to why women's position is a subordinate one. Lastly, changes in society affect men and women differently. As a category of workers, they, therefore, need special focus, attention and analysis because the problems and issues that face them are different.

In this chapter, we see how the goals of development and the policies followed influence the outcome. In colonial India, imperial interests dictated economic policy and their impact in a gender-asymmetric society descended with extra severity on women. In post-independent India, development models adopted and the interests they served within a profit-oriented framework influenced policy options in many directions. The impact of these on the masses, particularly women, have not been for their benefit. In what precise ways these various forces affected women is described in the following pages.

SECTION I

WOMEN'S ECONOMIC ROLE IN HISTORY

To gain knowledge of the present, one has to look at the past; but as data or references are practically non-existent, we can only begin with a recent past for which some records are available. These records of the colonial period are subject to many biases and inaccuracies but when even our present day sophisticated information systems are not free from such shortcomings, there is no harm in using them to get a broad picture. The colonial period is particularly relevant because it was during this time that cataclysmic changes rocked our social, economic and political structure. The exercise at reconstructing women's economic history must be of the nature of informed (and bold) guesses. Later, we use contemporary data to get a profile of the female work force.

Firstly, the most disastrous and ridiculous distortion is the use of the words *working women* and *non-working women* in current usage. It is as inappropriate as the terms *vegetarians* to distinguish between meat eaters and non-meat eaters, because every one eats vegetarian products with or without meat. Men and women both work. The difference lies in the kinds of work they do; where it is done, how it is done, for what kinds of rewards and so on. If by 'work' we imply broadly 'economic activity', then women *have always worked*. It cannot but be otherwise. The material requirements for survival demand everyone's cooperation. According to anthropologists, women were the major producers of food, clothing, crafts, many different tools through most of the human history.[1] In fact, this continues to be so in all those societies of the world where production is mainly for subsistence and not for sale. In India too, growing food, processing it, spining and weaving, basket making, clay modelling, extraction of 'soma' juice, preparing perfumes and many other materials for consumption were women's contribution.[2] References to women's economic activities are extremely sparse in Indian history and even for the middle age where much historical research by eminent historians like Irfan Habib or Bipin Chandra have helped to build a composite picture of the economic structure of India. Before British inroads into India, women's roles find no mention and whatever information can be gathered has to be by inference. Our first records begin with the British. These were travellers' accounts, various administrative documents and finally the Census. In the Census records we get for the first time some rough quantitative estimates that tell us something of the range and degree of the economic involvement of women. These documents are not accurate but they happen to be our only source. The patterns and trends in women's economic activities that became noticeable from the late nineteenth century till the beginning of the twenteith century excited the attention of scholars like D.R. Gadgil and subsequently other.[3] This interest is, therefore, recent. Throughout the last hundred years, two very prominent features stand out with regard to women's economic activities : (i) a continuous and impressive decline in the number of women reported in the work force ; (ii) major shifts in their occupational distribution. These two changes can be attributed to major convulsions induced by colonialism and the development of capitalism but what is significant is the differential impact it has had on men and women. This emphasised the different connection that women have with the economy. We need to study the forces that determine the degree of involvement that women have in different economic activities and under what conditions these are altered or become alterable. Research has hardly begun in this area, and hence we have no definitive answers to the many riddles that have surfaced. Nonetheless, we cannot abandon our concern with these issues arising out of a value commitment that women's subordinate position in the economy needs rectifying to enable them to get an equal and fair opportunity for human development. We, therefore, attempt to examine women's position and connection to the economy from this normative stand-point and not step short at merely describing where they are.

Economic Structure of India in Pre-British India and the Place of Women in it

Industrial capitalism, transplanted on Indian soil by colonial rule created major discontinuity for the Indian economy. The social organisation of production in precolonial Indian was not comparable to the feudal society of Europe before the industrial revolution. In India land did not belong to any private landlord. Even the king did not 'own' the land. He merely appointed revenue collectors (Zamindars or Jagirdars) who enjoyed only the right of revenue collection. The king had the right to transfer this entitlement to any person so that this was not a hereditary property right. Land belonged communally to the village as a usufruct, i.e. right of use. This land could not be sold, bought or transferred. Cultivators jointly cultivated the village lands and divided the produce. The village as a whole was collectively responsible for paying revenue to the state which was fixed as a share of the crop and could be paid in cash or kind. Along with agriculture, every household carried on the work of spinning and weaving. Artisans living in the village produced the non-agricultural goods needed by the tillers of soil and had a fixed share of the agricultural produce as payment. Craft production was never a full-time occupation but subsidiary to agriculture except in the towns. Village artisan families pursued their crafts on hereditary basis and had a caste monopoly of their particular craft. Unlike the insecure craftsmen of feudal Europe, the Indian craftsmen (and women) enjoyed economic security though not necessarily prosperity, because they supplied the needs of the village on a customary basis. In the cities that were either pilgrim centres, trade routes of administrative quarters of the ruling classes, artisans gathered to supply the luxury needs of the nobility. The mass of peasantry had no direct market related connections with these urban artisans. Whenever the court moved, the industrial towns moved along. In this predominantly household form of production, women were family-labour. In addition, many women were engaged in different independent occupations, food processing crafts, trade, and were paid in cash or kind. (More details of their economic activities are available from mid-nineteenth century, after the British had already established their rule.)

British intervention took two phases : the first phase when the East India Company monopolised trade from India, and the second phase when India came under direct British political control and the industrial development of England initiated a process of disintegration of Indian economy.[4] The first phase led to a growth of India's trade and vast expansion of merchant capital ; a process which, had it continued, might have led to economic development of India. This was the phase when Indian manufacturers received a tremendous boost. In the second phase, Britain curbed Indian industries by clamping heavy duties and flooding the country with British manufactures. This phase is usually referred to as 'deindustrialisation' of India, when Indian industries suffered massive and irrevocable destruction. In this process vast numbers of urban and rural population became reduced to poverty. Women as *major* partners in the economic activities of the household lost out more than men as the occupations in which they were engaged declined drastically.

This tragic story of conversion of a prosperous economy into a nation of mass poverty begins in the seventeenth century. From the beginning of the sixteenth century, Indian goods had entered Europe directly through sea routes. This gave a big boost to urban crafts. During 1618-1619, India exported 13,000 pieces of calico but by 1720 the quantity had reached 1,502,498 pieces. The value of Indian piece goods exported to England was £ 2.8 million in 1796-1797 but had risen by £ 26 million by 1809-1810.[5]

After 1757 (Battle of Plassey), the East India Company having acquired a monopoly over Indian trade through usurpation of political power, began a reign of organised plunder. Indian merchants were prohibited from buying from local producers but were forced to buy them from the company and were allowed to function only as agents.

"Where did the capital for the Industrial Revolution in England come from ? Spectacularly large sums flowed into England from overseas—from the slave trade and from 1760 the organised looting of India."[6] India which had been the world's textile giant was forced to import British yarn and British cloth and various other products. Great market towns like Murshidabad, Surat, Malda became desolate. The Governor General's report of 1835 stated, "The misery hardly finds a parallel in the history of commerce. The bones of cotton weavers are bleaching the plains of India."[7]

A big catastrophe for India was the introduction in the mid-eighteenth century of a new system of land tenures—the Zamindari and the Ryotwari. By this, the peasantry lost control over land; the power of merchants and money-lenders increased. The tax collectors who had earlier only rights of revenue collection over the land, now enjoyed ownership rights. The tillers of the soil had to acquire the right of use which previously they had enjoyed as a matter of course. Tenancy had to be bought. They could do this only by agreeing to share the produce at terms grossly unfair to themselves. Land ownership rapidly passed into the hands of money-lenders and merchants with a resulting multiplication of tenancies and sub-stenancies. Even the *ryotwari settlement*, by which the 'ryot' became the owner, contained merely nominal rights, the power of the monied classes being overwhelmingly oppressive. Even Brahmins acquired land. While the economic functional basis of caste broke-down, its ideological hold continued. Extortion of high rents drove many peasants to abandon cultivation. All this added to the growing demographic pressure and created land hunger and speculation. All this coupled with technological backwardness led to parcelling of land.

A study done on Kerala traces the impact on women due to historical changes in land rights in the colonial period and land reform legislation after independence.[8] Kerala State had a matrilinial system where women had rights of ownership in land and house and this right was transferred from mother to daughter. This was associated with a joint family (the *tarawad*) where the mother, her daughters, all her brothers and sister's descendants on sisters side, all lived together. The eldest daughter was the most important person and the son recognised the priority of the mother. This system was followed by 26 castes. Prior to British rule, there were three classes who had rights in land : the landlord (called *janmi*), the protector (called the *kanak-karan*) and the peasant who was the actual tiller. Nobody *owned* land. British legislation converted the janmis into land owners. Land became a saleable commodity for the first time as was happening elsewhere in India. This led to severe rack renting and eviction of tenants. Along side, the western educated classes were influenced by the British views on matriliny as a *primitive* custom. During the nineteenth century these major changes in land relations led to the break up of the *tarawad*. Women's place that had been rooted in the land and caste hierarchy was severely disturbed. Many women were cultivators and tenants (especially among the Nayars) but only labouring women had direct involvement in the production. These agricultural labourers were agrestic slaves and women agricultural labourers exceeded men workers in all castes, according to early census records.

All over India, the artisan classes thrown out of work by deindustrialisation also flooded into agriculture as their last resort. During 1921-1931 agricultural labour had increased from 21.5 million to 31.5 million.[9] There was a break-up of the village community, but all communal institutions did not vanish, reciprocal exchange of (*Jajmani*) services has persisted right upto the present day.

This pauperisation of India is indicated in the fall in food production.[10] During 1893-1894 to 1895-1896 output of food crops per capita was 587 lbs. but by 1936-1937 this had declined to a mere 399 tbs.

There were no urban slums till mid-eighteenth century. Artisans though often paid just enough to cover their subsistence, lived comfortably, consumed ghee, wore good clothes and hoarded gold and silver. Though income and wealth was unequal, the condition of the people was not uniformly miserable.[11] All this general devastation necessarily affected women to a greater degree. Before we see the displacement of women in this process, it will be useful to have some idea of the range and diversification of women's activities in this period. For this we have to turn to some British observers and Indian historians of the arts and crafts in India. It is only recently that women scholars are probing this area.

There was not only enough cloth to clothe every women in Assam but a sizeable surplus for export! In North India, Muslim women manufactured silk strings for trousers, necklaces and bracelets. They also did fine embroidery. "Every house in India is like a nursery of the beautiful", remarked Birdwood, paying a glowing tribute to the unrivalled excellence of handicrafts of

Indian women. In the North, women themselves bought wool, washed it, dried it and then wove them into blankets. There were other regional specialisation in craft : *chikan* work in U.P., *quilting* in Bengal, *tie and dye* in Rajasthan, *rug* making in Sindh and Baluchistan.[12]

Besides spinning and weaving, there were many occupations in which women were engaged, not only for their own consumption but also for sale. All over India several lakhs of women did rice dehusking for which they received payment in cash and kind, enough to ensure a decent living. Milking of cattle, cleaning them, cleaning cattlesheds, selling milk, butter, ghee—all these were always women's jobs. Women carried on marketing of vegetables and fish.[13]

There were many other crafts like the making of lac, gold and silver ornaments, mats of superior quality, etc. Besides all these occupations, there were many others, like tattooing, hair-dressing, mid-wifery, and laundry. Making cowdung cakes for sale continues even to this day. Then as now, women fetched fuel, fodder and water for themselves as well as for others and were paid for it. There were many women even in Bombay in the eighteenth and nineteenth centuries called *water-carriers*. There were no urban slums till mid-eighteenth century.[14] Artisans, though often paid just enought for their subsistence, lived comfortably, consumed ghee, wore good clothes and hoarded gold and silver. Though income and wealth were unequal, the condition of the people was not uniformly miserable ! All this general devastation necessarily affected women to a greater degree. Before we see the displacement of women in this process, it will be useful to have some idea of the range and diversification of women's activities in this period. For this we have to turn to some British observers and Indian historians of the arts and crafts of India. It is only recently that women scholars are probing this area. The economic activities of women in the nineteenth century were varied ; these continue till today but in a severely attenuated form !

From the accounts of Buchanan, Birdwood, Allen[15] and Hall[16] we can give a profile of the economic activities of women. Spinning and weaving was the biggest national industry of India, next in importance only to agriculture. Women from all castes and classes, except the highest. spun cotton yarn for sale to weavers. In Bihar and Bengal almost every family had jute looms and women worked on them.[17] In the Brahmaputra valley, from the rearing of silk worms to spinning and weaving of silk, women were responsible for all the tasks.

Displacement of Women—Some Illustrations

Apart from the writings of travellers and craft historians, a few women scholars have recently done some work on women's role in specific occupations. Atchi Reddy has given a vivid description of female agricultural supervisors and their high status a century ago.[18] Reddy points to the large number of free female farm servants who out-numbered men. There was in Nellore, a special practice of female supervisors. Even women of higher castes were agricultural labourers. Female supervisors were used in this region because (a) there were many women from Brahmin households, who had land but could not supervise cultivation and (b) male supervisors could not attend to female servants. In 1883 cultivators with farm size of 400 acres employed 45 female supervisors, but as farm size decreased, the number of female supervisors also declined.

Reddy describes the typical working day of a female supervisor. "She began work at 6 a.m. in the busy season and 8 a.m. in the slack season. Her day ended at 8 or 9 p.m. during crop cutting season. Sometimes harvesting continued at night. She also worked in the landlord's house, did minor work in the fields, supervised preparatory work before the labourers started their work, discharged the duties of an adult female member of the landlord's family in the case of the latter's absence from the fields, carried food to the fields, distributed it to the workers and carried the vessels and sometimes collected food from the farm servants' houses in case the workers had to provide their own food."

These supervisors were full time, had no unemployment and their wage equalled that of other farm servants. Female wages often exceeded that of males. From 1893-1895 to 1916-1920, the average female wage was 92 per cent to 94 per cent of male wages.[19] Thus the position of female agricultural labourer a century ago was not at all bad. Today the female landless agricultural labourer is among the poorest.

TABLE 2.1

Women Workers in Bengal in Selected Occupations

(1881-1931 — Figures in '00)*

	1881	1901	1911	1921	1931
1. Producing and selling ordinary fuel	201	208	276	119	39
2. Making and selling dairy products	—	215	223	166	182
3. Silk worm rearing	—	301	141	23	5
4. Cotton textiles	1703	462	450	519	357
5. Silk textiles	—	34	94	36	10
6. Jute textiles	435	262	508	542	388
7. Basket making and allied handicrafts	617	454	429	297	198
8. Medicine	121	126	152	105	113
9. Instruction	3	12	18	26	50
10. Domestic service	1337	801	1107	1158	4198
11. Rice husking	—	2131	2703	1696	1390

*Mukul Mukherji, ibid

Work Participation—Males and Females

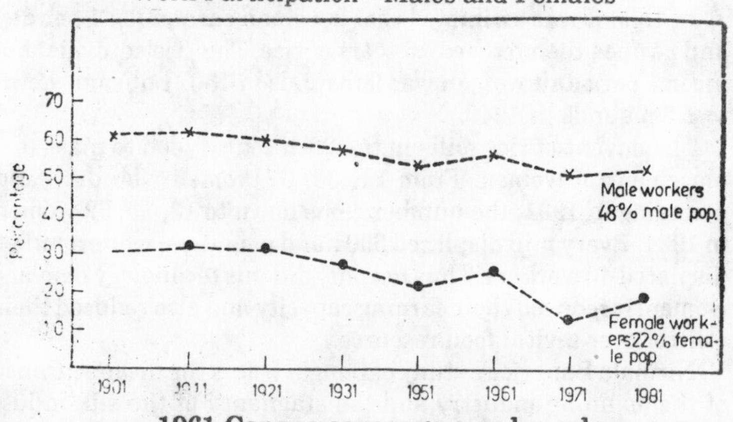

1961 Census coverage was broader
1971 Narrower definition

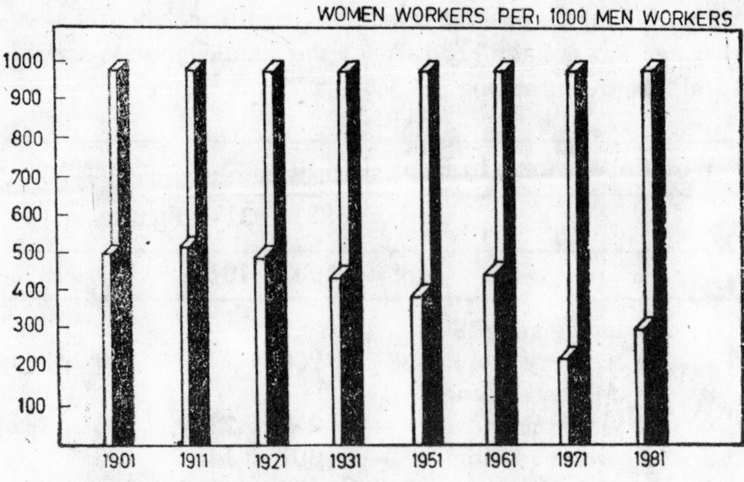

Another sad story of decline in women's livelihood is traced by Mukul Mukherji[20]. who records the devastation brought by the introduction of rice mills and hullers on women who had rice dehusking as their major source of livelihood. Until the advent of mechanised processing in the early twentieth century, dehusking was the exclusive preserve of female labour. It was done by a *dhenki* (a rough wooden beam with food peddals, pressed by two women). In 1901, around 25.2 lakh women were still occupied in rice pounding (about 22 per cent of women of 15-59 years of age).

In 1833 it was estimated that a woman earned Re. 1 per day and a rupee then fetched 16 seers of rice. The rice equivalent of income per adult woman was 9 maunds in 1807 but came down to 1.5 maunds in 1949.

The advent of rice mills in the 20th century led to mass displacement of women. From 21, 30, 67 women who did hand pounding in 1901, the number came down to 13, 10, 62 women in 1931. Every mill displaced 500 hand pounders, while a huller displaced 40 workers. Thus not only did this technology displace women; it reduced their earning capacity and also reduced their control over a vital food resource.

Nirmala Banerjee's study of Bengal traces the disappearance of the spinning industry and the stagnancy of the silk industry.[21] By 1824 with Bengal importing British yarn, millions of workers were thrown out of jobs, half of them being women.

Early Beginnings of Factory Production

By the mid-nineteenth century most of the great crafts of India had declined. Handloom-weaving suffered the most serious setback. In Western India, records are available that document this decline. Traditional brocade and *Khinkhab* cloth in Broach had declined to one thousandth of their traditional volume. In Navsari district in Gujarat every Khati and Tais caste household used to have two or three looms which women worked, but these had vanished by the mid-nineteenth century. Parsi women who had woven sacred threads and tapes for cots, rough dhotis and khadi abandoned their occupations. Machine-made *zari* replaced the once famous handwoven *zari* of Surat. In Dhulia, Malegaon and Sholapur in Maharashtra many weavers switched over to bidimaking. Similarly, the new steam-driven gins displaced the hand-gins operated by women. Use of kerosene reduced oilseed pressing by women and the new aniline dyes replaced Indian dyes. The reduction in hand-weaving also affected bamboo-workers who used to supply the bamboo shuttles.[22]

Women Get into Factories, But at What Cost ?

In the mid-nineteenth century the first factories were set up. Textile mills came first to Bombay and Bengal Presidencies. The first mill was opened in Bombay in 1854 and by 1877 forty-one mills had been set up. Jute and cotton spinning mills grew around Calcutta drawing in migrant workers from Bihar, U.P. and Orissa. Mines and plantations employed predominantly family labour. With the system of indentured labour, men and women (usually married couples) migrated to Sri Lanka, West Indies, Malaysia, and Burma to become industrial workers. Generally, however, women usually with one or two able-bodied men, stayed in the villages while other menfolk migrated. However, in the Bombay region women were employed in the ginning factories under deplorable conditions.

The factory commission of 1885 state, "The ginning season lasts about eight months and in five of which the hands work from 5.00 a.m. to 10 p.m. and in the remaining three, they work day and night. The hands are mostly women ; gins and presses never stop for meals ; as a rule, the hands take their meals at the gins...., three parts asleep and a child at the breast....the women would have worked 23 out of 24 hours." Plantations and mines employed large numbers of women and children. Despite these instances, Indian factory labour was predominantly male unlike the Lancashire model which exploited the labour of women and children in a big way.

Beginning of the Twentieth Century

The introduction of female labour in the industrial sector was a false start. After 1901 begins the story of a steep secular decline in women's labour force participation. Technological changes, foreign competition, changes in demand, legislative actions designed to protect women were all acting in combination. The relative weight of these factors is still under dispute. While such changes affect any labour, the severity of their negative impact on women calls for adequate explanation.

Between 1911 to 1961, the worker rate had fallen for both sexes, but while the decline for males was only 8.0 per cent, the decline for females was 18 per cent. More severe was the progressive deindustrialisation for women to a greater extent than for males.[23]

Sinha and Ambannavar have tried to map the changes in different sectors of female employment. Ambannavar disaggregates each sector and compares the new industries and old industries.[24] The new industries are paper and printing, rubber, coal, petroleum, transport equipment and technical goods which were highly organised, capital intensive and urbanbased. In these new industries, in the first sixty years of this century, total employment grew to a level of 1500 thousands but the share of female workers was only 86 thousands, which gives a ratio of male to female as 70 : 4.

In the older and more traditional industries, the changes were not uniform. There were some that declined over a period, such as processing of foodgrains, manufacture of various food and vegetable products, nets, ropes, cordage, footwear and earthware where female labour dwindled with the mechanisation of these because these were industries with high female concentration. The appearance of rice mills, it was seen, was inimical particularly to female employment. In the second group of industries, such as cotton textiles, an initial decline was offset by later expansion. Between the mid-nineteenth century and early twentieth century, cotton textiles (handloom and handspinning) were affected badly by competition from British manufactures and their exports through heavy duties. But with the establishment of mills in India, employment picked up. In 1919 women formed 20.3 per cent of the mill employment which rose to a peak of 22.9 per cent in 1930 but thereafter declined progressively from 18.9 per cent in 1934 to 14 per cent in 1939 with automation of reeling and winding.[25] A third group, such as dairy products, textile garments, made up textile goods, structural clay products attracted female labour to a considerable extent.

Though there were these sectoral variations, the fact remains that during the first half of this century, while male industrial employment reached 2632 thousands, female employment was just 510 thousands. For every one job for women, 12 were created for men.

In the service sector the female work force decreased by 189 thousands while that of males increased by 3237 thousands and opportunities for males were greater in the better paid administrative, defence and professional jobs.

In trade and commerce, the disappearance of village weekly fairs, the growth of towns, transport and large scale commercialised operations eliminated women. In construction too, males displaced females.

The disappearance of older household industries posed a special dilemma for women because they faced more immobilities in seeking work than men. 'On the demand side, the secondary sector rejected women, the service sector did not expand sufficiently and the primary sector overcrowded itself."[26] The slow growth of economy and technological change created conflicts between the people's need for employment and the actual pattern of growth of output. Lack of gainful employment resulted in growing poverty. The impact of fall in labour demand fell most harshly on women because of the impossibility of their gaining new skills or altering their social role in the institutional system. As a result unremunerative, unrecognised occupations increasingly stayed with them in the midst of growing poverty. The intensification of this process in town caused high female mortality and subsequent decline in sex ratio.

The biggest declines occurred in those sectors which had traditionally relied on reciprocity of support, where wages were a mixture of cash, kind or goods and services from those households in the community which purchased mainly by barter, a variety of goods and services from those producers in the community who were trained in it as a caste monopoly. These producers had a fixed clientele, whose volume increased with the growth of population. This was the traditional *jajmani* system, remnants of which still survive in parts of the country (e.g. in Maharashtra we have the bara balutedars or 12 major such contract-castes). The system covered not only the needs of the cultivators, like agricultural implements but other goods like footwear, clothing, housing material, utensils, cutlery, pottery etc. plus personal services. This method guaranteed a secure source of livelihood to women and their disappearance caused untold hardship to women, who could not readily move out of the village or find alternate employment.

What has never been investigated fully is the effect all this had on women's health. Famines, epidemics and disease took a heavy toll of women throughout the 18th, 19th and 20th centuries.[27] Before this, large scale famine and pauperisation were unknown. The chief consumers of goods produced within the village in cottage and household industries were the poorer sections of the rural population. Famines and drought decimated the poor and the artisan classes to poverty. Thus both demand and supply for the cottage industries which had engaged women not only declined, but created conditions for the rapid decline in the female population.

The Trend Continues

Acharya's[28] study on the impact of technology in seven groups of industries (food, tobacco, electrical goods, chemicals, nonmetallic products, textile and minerals) demonstrates the deepening capital intensity in these sectors and their effect on female labour absorption.

TABLE 2.2

Average Capital Intensity and Employment in Six Major Industries

	Total Employment	*Women Employment*	*Output*	*Energy*	*Capital Accumulation*
1950-1958	+ 25%	+ 22%	+ 60%	+ 90%	160 %
1959-1970	+ 33%	+ 15%	+ 170%	+ 90%	550 %

Technical change in the economy had a definite anti-employment bias. If we see the trends of female employment in the factory sector, we can see the slow, tardy absorption of females:

	1927	1937	1947	1950	1956	1967
Women as % Total Workers	7.0	14.2	11.6	11.3	11.9	10.6

To conclude, the factors responsible for the decline in female employment were the following : (i) structural changes in the economy which eliminated what were female occupations ; (ii) the new industries that sprang up were inhospitable to women, because of a new ideology about men's and women's spheres ; (iii) many of these new industries were urban-based which made it difficult for women to combine child care and domestic work along with paid work outside the home, firstly because urban activities required some level of education, long distance travel and long hours of absence from home and secondly because unlike in the rural area they had not much kin or

TABLE 2.3

Securlar Decline in Female Labour Participation

Year	*Female Workers as % Female Pop.*	*Male Workers as % Male Pop.*	*Pop.-Sex Ratio (No. of females per 1000 males)*	*Female Workers as per 1000 male workers*
1901	31.70	61.11	972	504
1911	33.73	61.90	964	525
1921	32.67	60.52	955	516
1931	27.63	58.27	950	450
1951	23.31	54.04	946	408
1961	27.93	57.12	941	460
1971	14.22	52.75	930	215
1981	20.85	53.19	936	367

(Based on Census Figures for 1971 and 1981 including marginal and secondary workers.)

Deindustrialisation of Female Labour 1881-1951

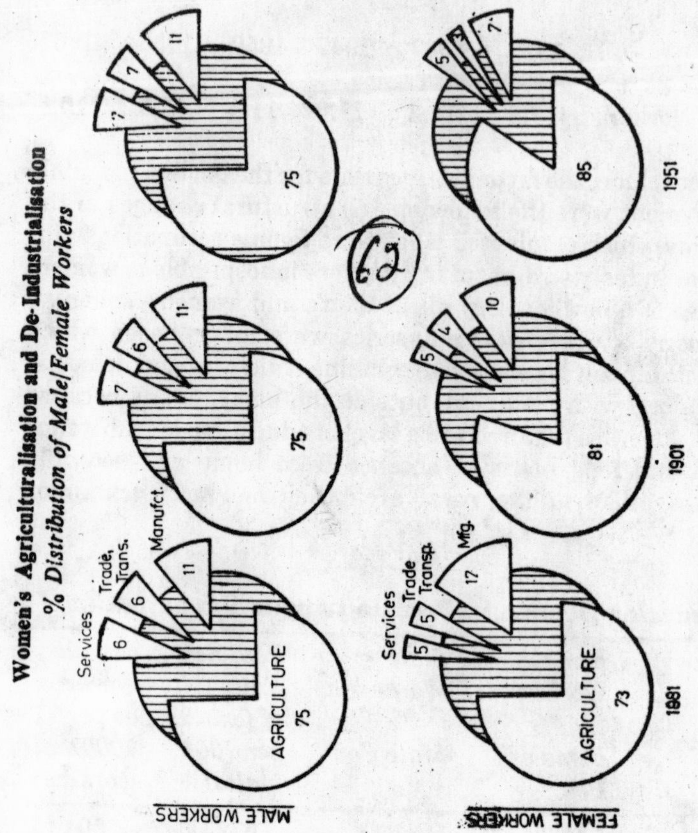

Data Compiled from figure's provided by Thorner

Source : Alice Thorner, *Economic Weekly*, Sp. No. July 1972.

neighbours' support; (iv) while work organisation changed in form and content, women's roles did not change, for they still carried the sole responsibility for child care and domestic work. If this is the picture of the last two hundred years, what of the present ?

SECTION 2

THE STRUCTURE OF FEMALE EMPLOYMENT IN CONTEMPORARY INDIA

Displacement Continues

We have seen in the preceding section, the tragic story of the negative impact of economic development on women. This historical trend has not been reversed in any significant way in the last three decades. If anything, portends are even more grim. A useful indicator is labour force participation rate, measured as number of workers as a percentage of the total population of the relevant group. In 1971 there was a drastic dip in the female labour participation rate, which in 1981 improved slightly; various doubts as to whether this was because of definitional changes have been set aside by more recent analyses that clearly point not only to a real decline for women but also to their displacement by male labour. Analysing Census data for twenty populous cities of India, Mitra asserts that neither definitional changes nor demographic variables can account for the decline in female labour participation in 1971 to the lowest level ever recorded.[29]

During 1961-1981 the participation of males in the workforce had been falling, and this decline is closely associated with the growth of male population being faster than their absorption in the labour force, but for women, the reduction was mainly due to their substitution by male labour. The reasons are (i) technological change altering the occupational structure in ways that favour males and the absence of expansion in those sectors of the economy where female labour is largely employed; (ii) growing unemployment and sluggish growth of income per capita resulting in insufficient opportunities for potential female workers.

Mukhopadhyay and Ghosh have analysed the Census data for 1961, 1971 and 1981 by making adjustments for definitional changes and dividing the three decades into three blocks : 1961-1971, 1971-1981 and 1961-1981.[30] They have tried to isolate the relative impact of three kinds of changes on female work participation : (i) effect of change in the ratio of female workers to total workers; (ii) effect of change in the aggregate level of employment ; (iii) effect of change in the sex ratio of the population. The three factors were found to be remarkably similar irrespective of the direction in which female work participation moved. Because of these three factors they were able to show conclusively that the *displacement of the female worker by the male worker was the most dominant over time and space*. This was most pronounced in Haryana and Punjab where the decline was 90 per cent. In Maharashtra, Tamil Nadu and West Bengal the decline was 58 per cent, 61 per cent and 68 per cent respectively. In more than half the districts, the substitution of female by male workers accounted for more than 60 per cent of the total shrinkage in the female labour force. The sex ratio in the population did not exert any influence. When total employment increased, female share improved but whenever total employment declined, female share dropped more rapidly (*first to fire, last to hire* is a well-known characteristic of female labour all over the world).

Conclusion

In the last 70 years very little structural change has taken place in female employment. Not only has no transfer occurred from agriculture to non-agriculture sector but also a renewed concentration has actually occurred in agriculture. Within the last twenty years also there has been no reversal; in fact there has been a further accentuation of the basic tendency of over-crowding in agriculture. The proportion of female agricultural labour was less than one-third of the total female work force in 1951; by 1971 this had risen to more than 50 per cent. They gained little in manufacturing and their employment in services plateaued in 1951. Industrialisation of India has not drawn women in even after independence and planned economic development for more than three decades.

Rural Urban Differences in Work Participation by sex 1961-1981

	RURAL	URBAN	
1961	58%	52%	Male
	30%	11 %	Female
1971	54 %	49 %	Male
	13 %	7%	Female
1981	52%	48 %	Male
	16 %	8%	Female

Female Child Labour

Children below 14 years, both boys and girls participate in productive activities despite the expectation that they will be attending school and despite laws against child labour. For the female child, induction into adult activities, both household work and other production related work begins early. As the accompanying table indicates, while male child labour is declining, female child labour has not declined—in fact it has increased slightly. Even this is an underestimate because it includes only main workers. What it implies is that millions of female children do not get the opportunity of even acquiring a modicum of basic education. (Literacy rates for females at all age groups is abysmally low.) If we separate the age group of 5-14, 31 per cent of females in that age group participate in work.

Even though the females enter the work force early, their work span is shorter than for males. Opportunities for acquiring experiece, skill and training are thus lost early.

Income Group and Women's Employment

Many micro studies have demonstrated the inverse relationship between income level of the household and women's participation.[31] The lower the income level, the greater is the pressure on women to seek work to sustain themselves and their families. The relationship between earning income or being employed by

Work-Participation Rate by Age, Sex, Rural-Urban areas 1981

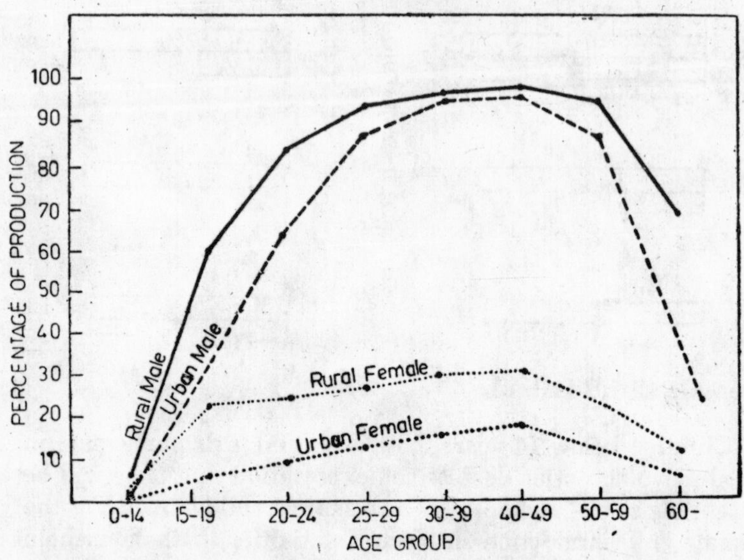

itself is not an indicator of status. The kind of work done, the terms under which it is done, the reasons for which it is done are really what matter. To the majority of female workers, who are also poor, work is not a matter of choice, nor is it ennobling because most of it is unskilled, back-breaking and tedious with inadequate rewards. They are generally engaged in those activities that society dubs as *low status*.

Household per capita expenditure in low income families and female work participation rate brings this out clearly.[32]

TABLE 2.4

Female Work Participation Rate by Monthly Expenditure Status in Low Income Families

Monthly per Capita Expenditure (Rs.)	Female Work Participation Rate	
	Rural	Urban
Below 50	36	24
Below 100	28	16
Below 200	24	15

The poorer the family, the greater is the work burden on women. It is often assumed that a decline in female work participation rate indicates voluntary withdrawal by woman. If this were true, there ought to be high dependency rates for women (i.e. women economically supported by men) but the actual ratios of dependency and the high turnout of women job-seekers refute this suggestion.

Regional Differences

One of the striking structural characteristics of female labour in India is the regional difference. In general, South-West and Central parts are the regions where women's work participation is high; North-East and North (excluding tribal areas) by contrast have low participation (see map).

The reasons are both cultural and historical as well as economic. Secondly, one must remember that in all these figures of work participation etc., definition of what is *work* excludes many economic activities that may be done in the home. (We later on discuss this point at greater length.) Relative poverty, absence of purdah, less severe patriarchal traditions, closer ties with maternal kin even after marriage may be conditions that do not inhibit women from working outside the home. The South and West are rice growing areas where female labour is traditionally employed in transplanting, weeding and harvesting. West Bengal, also a rice growing area, however, behaves differently. Various attempts to isolate *the determining variable* have been fruitless[33] and the phenomenon appears to be a complex interaction of cultural and economic factors.

Occupational Distribution in Industry : Limits to Choice

The picture in 1971 and 1981 shows continued concentration in agriculture. In industry also women are only in some sectors. In plantations, they constitute 72 per cent of the work force, in the tea estates they constitute 90 per cent of the work force, in other industries their representation is scanty.

We notice how selectively they are employed. The highest concentration of women outside agriculture is in food products, tobacco, beverages and textiles. Women are employed in sanitary and domestic services, in education and in health services.

Women's Work Participation—Regional Difference

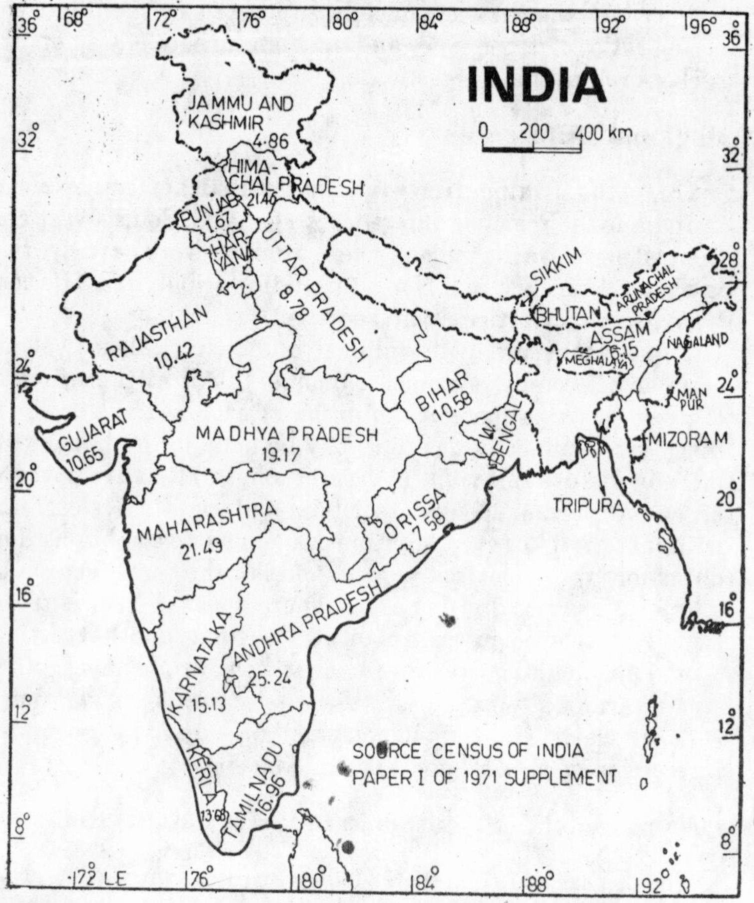

The first two are low status, ill-paid jobs, the last two are *female jobs* such as teaching and nursing. Of the one hundred and fifty occupations mentioned in the occupation survey of the country, women appear only in thirty occupations.

Household and Non-Household Sectors

India even today harbours a large segment of household production units that are precapitalist in mode of production though increasingly subject to market forces. These household industries by and large have a low technological base and are labour intensive. The majority of those relying on these stag-

Ratio of Women to Men Workers in Different Industries

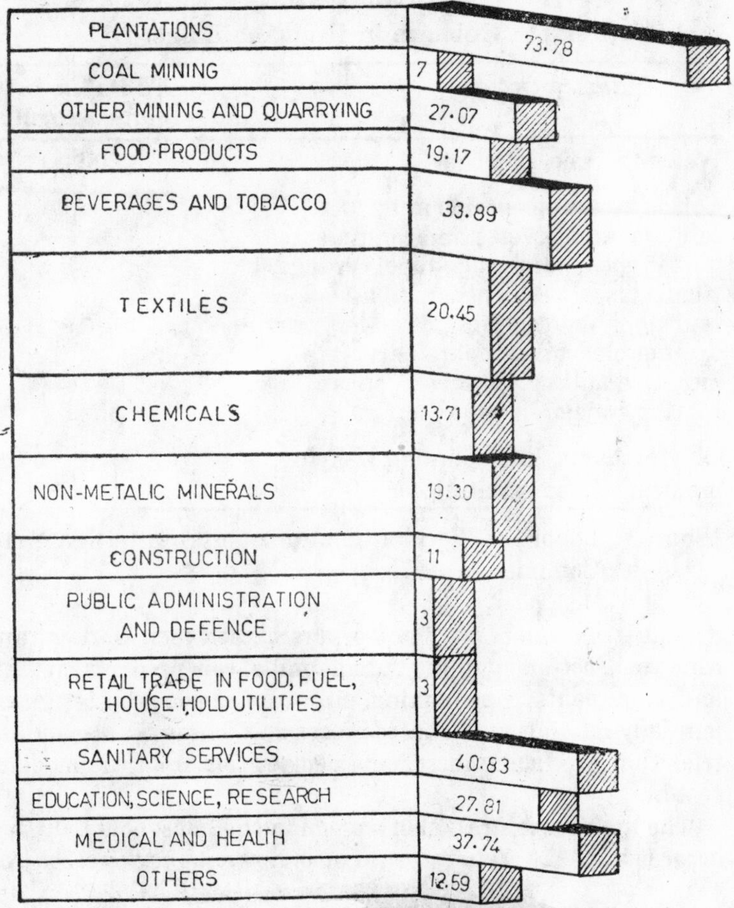

(RATIO: WOMEN WORKERS PER 100 MEN)

nant industries face dwindling demand, raw material shortage and returns hardly sufficient to ensure more than mere survival. These are also occupations with various historically determined reciprocal ties with landlords and upper castes in the rural areas, that reduce chances of free market prices for their products. The household industry has only 25 occupational groups whereas the non-household industries number more than 10,000. The most important structural feature of female non-agricultural work force is its heavy concentration in household production relative to men and their inferior position in the modern non-household sectors. Within groups of household industry where women are employed, there is once again a striking concentration.

TABLE 2.5

Female Workers in Household Sector*

Industry Group	*% Total in Manufacturing*
Weaving, cane, bamboo	80-90
Cotton spinning outside mills, pottery, coir products, sweets and condiments, butter ghee, edible oils, rope, cordage, sugar-gur, shoes, leather, silk work rearing, khadi, tanning, jewellery, cotton dyeing, bleaching, embroidery, lace, bidi, rice milling, garments, sheep rearing, wools, livestock	60-80
Clay products, jute spinning weaving, medicines, iron-smelting	10-30

*Source : Report of Working Group set up by the Planning Commission, 1978.

Industries where women workers exceed men workers are canework, cotton spinning outside mills, coir products, sweets and condiments, rope making, silkworm rearing, butter-ghee-jam-jelly-making, and tobacco processing. These are also industries that are facing increasing competition from the modern sector.

The high concentration of women in the household industry accords them the status of *family-workers with no direct control over earnings*, where patriarchal control is most closely exercised.[34]

TABLE 2.6

Work Status of Males and Females in Household Units*

	Urban		Rural	
	Male	*Female*	*Male*	*Female*
As % of total workers				
Agriculture working on own farm :				
(a) in own rights	63.20	20	61	29
(b) as helper	26.04	75.7	35	64
(c) as farm labour working for wages	10.76	4.3	4	7
As % of Non-Agricultural Workers				
In own household enterprise/profession :				
(a) As helper	10.33	38.7	7.1	25.0
(b) In own right	56.27	44.6	33.6	32.2
(c) Salary/Wage	33.40	7	39.3	43.8
As % of total workers in all categories				
Casual Wage labour	22.04	31.0	10.0	59.0

*Source : Seal, ILO/ARTEP, op. cit.

Even in the non-household sector, such as in trade, business or professions, they rarely have the status of employers. Women working as *family workers* are twice as many as among men.

TABLE 2.7

Employment Status of Males and Females in Non-Household Sector*

	% of Workers	
	Male	*Female*
Employers	5.0	1.32
Employees	62.21	65.50
Single workers	27.48	23.73
Family workers	5.31	9.45

*Source : Seal, ILO/ARTEP, op. cit.

Taking all these characteristics together, what it all amounts to is that 73 per cent of women workers are in the *unorganised sector* because women's share in factory employment even in 1981 was only 12.4 per cent of total work force. This implies that for a given demand of labour in these sectors, increase in women's participation would require more sharing by men both in economic activity as well as housework performed at present by women. Secondly the *unorganised sector* also implies insecure unprotected employment; labour intensive output with poor value added production, i.e. long hours of work with little reward.

Taking a few major industrial groups we find that even within the industry which employs women, women are selectively employed only in a few narrow range of tasks.

This absence of diversification makes women workers vulnerable to retrenchment when automation occurs in specific tasks/operaions. The question of occupation segregation of women is a major problem area. The actual situation is rationalised as *women being good at certain tasks*. This is *never* the real reason. One needs to know, why women are employed in these tasks. The reasons could be partly historical, in that women initially entering some occupations, stayed there. At other times female preference may be dictated by the distinct advantages of female labour to employers.

In another study done by Sinha,[35] it is reported that 72 per cent of women in mines and plantations are in the unskilled category. The technical-professional female workers account for less than 10 per cent and they are largely health-personnel attending creches, etc. The number of women in any supervisory capacity is zero. In mines other than coal, 89 per cent of the women workers were unskilled workers. In studies done on white collar jobs, the absence of women in higher posts and in supervisory-decision making posts has been repeatedly noticed.[36] A study on public enterprises noted that the representation of women at the executive level was 25 per cent, at the technical level 15.8 per cent, at the assistant level 19.5 per cent. But at the receptionists level 100 per cent, stenotypist 60 per cent. But at the receptionists level 100 per cent, attendants 19 per cent, sweepers 12 per cent, daily wage earners 97 per cent. A study done by the Ministry of Labour on the public sector showed that women employees in Class III category (clerical) constituted 83 per cent of the total women employees. In R and D establishments where women are 60 per cent of total employees, more than 50 per cent of the total women are reported to be doing non-scientific work.

TABLE 2.8

Job Categories with 50% of more Female Workers*

Industry	*Total No. of jobs in indy.*	*No. of jobs where Ware in large nos.*	*Name of jobs where F is largely or exclusively employed*
Cotton textile	28	1	Reeling
Jute textile	37	1	Hand sewing
Silk textile	33	5	Picker, Examiner, Receiver etc.
Wollen	26	1	Darning
Bidi	11	1	Rolling
Cigarettes	20	2	Case packing Head packing
Paper	27	1	Rag sorting
Match	26	4	Hand rolling, box filling, frame filling, etc.
Cashewnut	20	7	Sweeps shelling, grading, etc.
Tobacco proc.	23	8	Checking, sweeping, drying, grading, etc.
Tea, Coffee pl.	7	1	Plucking
Rubber pl.	6	1	Field work
Coal mines	26	1	Shale picking labourer carrying
Manganese	28	5	Sweeping, sorting, cleaning, dressing, etc.
Mica	20	2	Surface labour

*Source : Report on Second Occupational Wage Survey, 1963-1965, Vol, I.

In the higher administrative cadres, the representation of women is woefully low :[37]

	Females per 100 males
Supreme Court Judges	0
High Court Judges	2
IAS	9
IPS	0.09
Indian Education Service	5
Higher posts in S & T organisation	Less than 1

Women applicants who had registered with employment exchanges in cities had sought the following jobs to a greater extent than men : labourers, school teachers, sweepers, typists, stenos, clerks, telephone operators, midwives, ayahs, cooks and key-punch operators.[38]

Public and Private Sector

In the Public Sector the total number of women employees was around 1.7 million and in the private sector 1.2 million. In the various ministries of the Union Government, in 1984 except for the Home Affairs where women employees was 5.80 per cent of the total and Communicaions which had 7.2 per cent women, representation in other departments was insignificant. The Finance Ministry had only 0.8 per cent women. Overall, in all the Ministries women employees were barely 2.5 per cent of the total labour force in 1984.

Educational Composition of the Labour force*

	Female	*Male*
Illiterate	52.59	48.43
Literate upto middle school	28.56	41.63
Secondary school	13.79	7.39
Graduate and above	5.06	2.55
	100.00	100.00

*Source : NSS 32nd Round.

An interesting phenomenon is the higher proportion of graduate women. There has been a rapid increase of higher education for women in the last three or four decades and their entry into white collar jobs has been extremely significant. There is thus a clear class difference in the employment experience of females. New opportunities in the growing tertiary sector are education-related and therefore, women with higher education have found greater opportunities. The typical curve for aggregate female labour takes a U-shaped form with respect to education, at the bottom level of very little or no education, most women work because they are poor. In the middle, with modest education, women's participation tapers off because the kind of jobs that will be available are *low status*. At higher levels of education, more prestige giving jobs are available; also work becomes more a fulfilment and a way of improving social mobility for the family by getting better joint incomes.

We have seen the way sexual division of labour operates in the labour force, whereby women get slotted into specific sectors and within each sector, specific occupation and within each occupation, further concentration into a narrow range of specific operations. Agriculture, the oldest and most extensive employer of women, exhibits a similarly detailed sexual allocation of tasks and operations. The reasons for these vary from region to region and appear to be mostly culturally determined. Some of it could be due to certain tasks being more easily combined with household responsibility. One of the greatest myths that is sustained is that women do *light* work. The arduousness of most women's tasks is never acknowledged because of a patriarchal shroud that covers up the actual labour input, the energy expended on different tasks, etc. One of the best ways of demolishing the myth would be to have men do female tasks to discover how hard they are. Some of the cultural taboos pertain to (a) whether a particular work is done outside the home, (b) whether it is done in male company, (c) whether some tasks will be *polluted* by women. Age also makes a difference. Young unmarried women and pubescent girls have greater taboos about mixing with strange men or men outside the kin group. Some of these taboos are safeguards by the family against the all too common sexual exploitation of young females. For the poor women, for example, tribals or untouchables and lower caste women, the sheer necessity to earn exposes them to sexual exploitation by employers.

TABLE 2.9

Sex-wise Allocation of Tasks

Task	*Rajasthan*	*West Bengal*
Ploughing/Digging	Mainly male	Totally male
Sowing	M & F; usually more M.	Totally male
Irrigating	Totally male	Totally male
Harvesting	M & F (More F)	Predom. F.
Cutting grass	Predom. F	Predom. F.
Weeding	Predom. F	Predom F.
Husking, winnowing, parboiling	M & F (More F)	Totally F
Cattle/Goat grazing	Male (occ. F)	Totally M
Milking/feeding cattle	M & F (More F)	M & F
Minding poultry	F	F
Groundnut picking	F	—
Vegetable plucking	F	—
Making straw mats	F	F
Ropes, quilts etc.	F	F
Selling (grain, veg., fish) locally	F (Sometimes M)	M
Selling (-do-) long distance	M	M
Manual labour	Mostly M	M
Household work :		
Cooking, grinding, cutting chopping, cleaning, sweeping, washing clothes, utensils	Almost entirely F (M do 5%)	Almost entirely F

Note : The authors give time spent by men, women, children on task.

We reproduce a detailed task allocation by sex—the allocation done by a woman researcher[39] in the appendix.

In case one thinks this is true only of one region, we can find such sex specific allocation of tasks in all regions; there may be minor variations but there is a broad pattern in agriculture and allied occupations, wherein crucial productive resources are not handled by women (plough, seeds, canals, important commercial outlets etc.)

Data from Rajasthan and West Bengal indicates the sexwise allocation of tasks.[40]

SECTION 3

CONDITIONS OF WORK IN THE UNORGANISED SECTOR

Agriculture

Though women are major partners in agriculture, their contribution is unrecognised and undervalued. Besides, many productive activities of women in agricultural households are hidden under the label *domestic work* and hence become totally invisible.

TABLE 2.10

Percentage of Women Reported as Doing Household Duties who Participated in Specified Activities for Family Benefits*

	% W. in activity out of those engaged in house work	
	Rural	*Urban*
1. Free collection of fish, game	6.24	0.80
2. Free collection of firewood, dung etc.	14.34	3.11
3. Maintenance of kitchen garden	4.70	1.35
4. Work in household poultry	11.06	3.11
5. Sewing, tailoring, weaving	3.77	6.65
6. Tutoring children	0.48	2.19
7. Bringing water from other villages.	1.35	—
8. Any one of these specified activities.	21.78	12.33

*Source : NSS 32nd Round.

In addition to those women formally included as workers in the Census or national surveys, more than a quarter of the rural women and more than half of all women are engaged in these *unrecorded* activities.

Women's contribution in wages in proportion to that of men in landless households is estimated to be 1.2 or 1.6 to 1.0. Only a mere 4 per cent of women cultivators and less than 20 per cent women agricultural workers are literate. This makes it difficult for these women to move out to other jobs. In 1981 in the age group of 5-9 only 25 per cent of girls were attending schools against 40 per cent of boys and in the age group of 10-14 only 29 per cent girls against 58 per cent boys attending schools.

Many women in agriculture are self-supporting. Nearly 17 per cent of cultivating women and 16 per cent of agricultural workers have no male support because of widowhood or separation.

There is a close connection between rural poverty and high incidence of female agricultural wage labourers. Indices of poverty are also closely associated with days of employment available, level of agricultural productivity, type of cereals grown etc. Sen[41] has demonstrated the correlations between high proportion of agricultural wage labourers in regions characterised by inferior grains, low agricultural productivity and high unemployment, in her study of 91 districts for the country as a whole. While those getting work for less than four hours a week were only 5 per cent among the males and 20 per cent among the females. The female agricultural labourers were worse off than the women in cultivating households in terms of employment. While only 10 per cent of women in cultivating households wanted employment to add to family resources, more than 50 per cent among female agricultural workers were seeking work.

Agarwal[42] has reviewed all available data and studies to show the inter linkage between gender, poverty and agricultural growth. The question that has been posed in recent years is : does the burden of poverty fall more heavily on women than on men ? In studying the dimensions of poverty, the focus has hitherto been the *household*. The poor household is identified and the estimates of persons who are below the poverty line are arrived at by multiplying the number of *poor households* by the average size of household. The basic assumption in this exercise is that all members of the household are poor and second, that all are equally poor.

Evidence for inequality in income and consumption levels between women and men within the household comes mainly from studies on intra household food distribution, health care and energy expenditure on work. All the studies done so far in different regions of the country point to a shortfall of calories per day per woman.[43] Among the poorer households with gross deficiency and malnutrition, the deficiency among women was 25 per cent more than for men. In times of distress, more women went hungry than men. Whichever way it is calculated (relative to energy expenditure or other indices of malnourishment), the data points to the inferior status of rural poor women vis-a-vis men of their class. It is also well established now that children's nutritional status depended on whether or not the women were employed and on the wages of the mother rather than the employment of the father or his wages. Wherever women are earning anything, almost the entire amount goes to feeding the family whereas even among the poorest household a man retains a sizeable portion of his wages for personal needs like tobacco, bidi, liquor etc.

Feminisation of Poverty

The nature of women's responsibilities give them very little leisure for rest, recuperation or improvement of skills etc. Under conditions of extensive deforestation their work in collecting fuel has increased enormously. Whereas earlier they walked 1 km—2 kms., today they sometimes walk 10 kms. a day. Fuel scarcity not only increases work burden, it also reduces nutritional levels by difficulty of freshly cooked food which is essential for most food used in the tropics.

Women also have unequal control and access to cash.[44] Wages for agricultural work even when paid to women are taken over by men. In some regions where husband-wife teams or family labour is employed, the cash is handed over to the male. Seasonal fluctuations in employment affect women much more because their work is more task specific. In some places, this subordination leads to sexual exploitation also, as in some districts of Uttar Pradesh (as for e.g. reported from Jaunsar). Women from bonded labour households are sold to brothels by the husbands to repay debts; the women have to stay in prostitution till the debts are cleared.

India has witnessed a phenomenal agricultural growth which has wiped out earlier foodgrain deficits and has led to accumulation of food stocks. Yet this has had no significant impact on reducing the incidence of absolute poverty in rural India because rising output has been accompanied by rising prices due to price support policies and extensive unemployment that leaves people with reduced purchasing power..In the regions of the highest agricultural growth (Northwest) there is least incidence of poverty but discrimination against females persists. Dowry has replaced bride price in almost all places. In the eastern states where there is relative agricultural stagnation, the women and children bear a disproportionate burden of poverty. In these regions there has been an increasing female responsibility for the economic maintenance of families due to male migration, desertion etc. The southern states come somewhere in-between. According to Visaria's analysis, 9.6 per cent of all households in the country are female-headed. The majority are widows and what is very significant is that 40 per cent of the females in female-headed households live alone whereas only 8 per cent of males live alone. This implies that the women have to fend for themselves. That poverty and female-headed households go together is established by both Visaria[45] and Parthasarathy.[46] In Visaria's analysis, the household expenditure of female-headed households was half that of male-headed households. According to Parthasarathy, among the poor households of every agricultural class, the proportion below the poverty line for females was consistently higher.

Detailed studies on women in agricultural households are only beginning to surface. Joshi[47] in a broad survey based on demographic and secondary data, village economic surveys, anthropological studies and farm management studies confirms what we have already detailed above. The agricultural labourers who are the bulk of the women workers in agricultural, come from social classes that traditionally have a low social status. Poor literacy, irregular employment, heavy work burden and sexual exploitation are all mentioned. Saradomoni and Mencher[48] also draw attention to heatlh hazards posed by long hours in muddy water with the risk of parasitic infections in villages ;

different types of work arrangements ; impact of pregnancy that interrupts wage earning capacity when it is most crucially needed. Women work at lower rates than males even when their total average hours of work exceed that of men. In times of unemployment, women take up bidi making. The crucial role of women's earnings to family survival means that any episode of unemployment pushes the family into poverty.

Sethi[49] in her field survey found that not only do all occupations in which females are engaged carry a lower wage rate but even in similar occupations like harvesting, reaping, weeding etc. the male wage rate is always higher than the female rate for similar number of hours of work. Farm owners say they prefer females because they are 'cheap' and 'hard working'.

The occupational structure of families in Punjab is different from other regions. First, overall female participation in Punjab is the lowest in the country. There are more females in secondary and tertiary sectors in the state. The proportion of female agricultural workers is lower than in other States. They are employed on seasonal and casual basis and are engaged in picking cotton, harvesting of wheat, fodder cutting, weeding, sowing and construction work from four to six months a year. The average working hours are rarely less than 12 hours per day on wages that range from Rs. 5.20 on different tasks depending on the sex allocation of tasks. Picking, transplanting and winnowing, because these are tasks for the females, are paid lower even though they are ardous, demanding longer hours without any kind of facilities. The sheer need for income has pushed many Punjabi women into agricultural wage labour despite strong cultural taboos. Sethi also found that household work and child care continued to be totally the women's responsibilty even though they were also doing wage work. These women did not have any decision-making powers within the household and the worst trend of all is that the practice of dowry has reared its ugly head even in the poor, agricultural labour households.

The most vivid description of the life of toil, deprivation, insecurity and low social status of female agricultural worker is brought out by Gulati.[50]

Mazumdar[51] states categorically in the book *Role of Rural Women in Development* : "Rural women who constitute the largest group have been not only bypassed by the development process but their traditional roles and status in society have been altered adversely by the nature of development process itself." Some of the major conclusions made in the book are :

(a) In substistence farming with high female participation women work on a complementary basis with men but their control over resources is not necessarily assured.
(b) In labour intensive cash crop economy, women work harder but they have no control over earnings.
(c) In regions where there have been land reform and new technology, women's roles have been affected often in contradictory ways.
(d) In small farm households landlessness has emerged where women are hardest hit.
(e) Individual male migration has posed social hardship to women.
(f) The existing system of marriage and kinship place women in a subordinate position.
(g) There is total absence of social services for women in agricultural work.

The status of the women in agriculture depends on their class. The most hit are the landless.

Industry

The Indian economy has even today only *pockets* of factory type establishments that use modern technology, have hired workers covered by labour laws and where workers are organised in unions. The terms *organised* and *unorganised* are loosely used to mean many different things which in practice occur together. By and large two important features distinguish the organised from unorganised—scale of operation and organised labour. Technology often goes with scale of operation but not necessarily. The most telling feature of the Indian economy is the extremely decentralised character of production units.

The Economic Census 1980 conducted by the Central Statistical Organisation has revealed that at the all India level (excluding Assam) there were 18.41 million enterprises engaged in different economic activities other than crop production and plantation with 53.58 million persons working in them.

TABLE 2.11

Employment Status of Female Workers in Non-Agricultural Household Units*

Economic Activity	*Employment in own account*			*Employment in establishments using wage labour*		
	Total No. (00)	*Female*	*F%*	*Total No. (00)*	*Female*	*F%*
1. Mining, Quarrying	2353	49	(2.0)	807	101	(12.5)
2. Manufacturing, Repair	22909	5512	(24.0)	73926	7249	(9.8)
3. Electricity, Gas, Water	21	1	(4.7)	2193	59	(2.6)
4. Construction	655	24	(3.6)	1588	268	(16.8)
5. Wholesale and Retail Trade.	27618	2010	(7.2)	26421	1503	(5.6)
6. Restaurants and Hotels	2657	327	(12.3)	8874	372	(4.2)
7. Transport	1759	33	(1.8)	7285	194	(2.6)
8. Storage, Warehousing	468	6	(1.2)	1816	115	(6.3)
9. Communications	5	—	—	2955	202	(6.8)

10. Financing, Insurance, Real Estate and Business Services.	1157	23	(2.0)	10664	876	(8.2)
11. Community, Social and personal Services.	6173	803	(13.0)	63175	10221	(16.1)
12. Others	193	18	(9.3)	3898	270	(6.9)
	63664	8769	(13.7)	203602	21430	(10.5)

*Source : *Ec. Census 1980* : *Statement 6* (Published in 1985).

Of these 92 per cent were non-agricultural and 73 per cent of them did not use hired labour. They were in other words family enterprises or *self-employed* units. Of the total units 62 per cent were in the rural areas≤≤though the non-agricultural units were fewer. From the point of view of number of enterprises and number of persons working in them, manufacturing and repair, wholesale and retail trade, community and personal services were the three most important activities.

Among the non-agricultural establishments that use hired workers, more than 2/3rd of them were in urban areas. The female share in the total employment was more in own account enterprises than in establishments that hire labour. In the former, their share was 1/5th while in the latter it was only 1/8th.

Women's employment in the unorganised sector consists of self-employment in petty trade, food processing, or in family units of traditional occupations or manufacturing establishments that are small workshops scattered geographically or in various forms of putting out systems.

In recent years, considerable attention has been paid to the development of the informal sector, as the unorganised sector is also called, and women's concentration in it. Because of rapid industrialisation and mechanisation that have destroyed traditional crafts, poor women in the world face extensive and acute unemployment. Their retention in traditional 'unorganised' units as well as their entry into new types of unorganised units appear to be because of special difficulties women face in gaining entry into the more structured units such as illiteracy, low technical skill and lack of opportunity for acquiring either literacy or new skills. Over and above, women's mobility is restricted due to family obligations as well as attitudes regarding what is permissible work for them. The major problem for women is not being pushed out, which is true in some sectors, as staying where they are. While men move up through education to higher jobs, women continue to hold traditional occupations that ensure basic survival for the family. Women's employment in petty ventures provides men and society in general, an insurance against unemployment and sickness, against inflation and wage cuts. Thus, though *overall* female employment has declined without question, there are essential sectors in rural and urban areas that employ women in large numbers. A woman's capacity to earn in the Indian context, far from giving economic independence is only a means by which she maintains herself, her children and family. Her obligation to her family extends to supporting it in need by earning.

Under a programme of women's studies especially focussing on women of the poorer classes, a good many studies were done on women by the Indian Council of Social Science Research (ICSSR) in a wide range of occupations in the unorganised economy.

Karlekar's[52] study on women of the sweeper caste vividly illustrates the growing inequality in status between the men and women. Whereas the men are moving into white collar services that require some education, the women continue to do scavenging. The study depicts the struggle of these women in combining their roles as wife, mother, unpaid domestic help and economic provider.

The woes of the bidi and tobacco workers of Nipani[53] are a classic case of dire exploitation. As many as 16,000-17,000 women work in dingy tobacco godowns at a pitiable wage of Rs. 4.80 per day. Walking 5 to 6 miles from their villages, they leave their homes before dawn and reach back late after dusk. Working long hours, often 18 hours with barely half an hour for nursing a baby (so much for consideration of motherhood) amidst tobacco dust and insecticide, the women often face sexual harassment. Checkers can reject their product for non-compliance. This industry *prefers* women—because they are cheaper, docile and easily cheated.

The women firewood pickers[54] climb the foothills of Girnar to collect firewood and their daily feet gives the lie to notions of *women's work*. Here is a description of their daily routine :

Rising very early, many hours before dawn, they tie loaf made the previous night in a piece of cloth, pick up an empty tin of water, arm themselves with small axes, a length of rope, walk to the toll station before day break, buy their entry pass, and walk hurriedly to the forest in groups. They fill their tin with water when they pass a pond. After 3 to 4 hours of walking, they hang their food bundles on a tree. They take off their saris, tie up their petticoats, and armed with the axe and rope, go deep into the forest. There they cut wood, pick up dry twigs, keep calling each other to keep track of each other. They break for lunch and stack their collected wood. Lunch is just dry-roti and chilli, onion or garlic. By evening, they tie their bundles with rope and come down the hill with the load on their heads. They sell the wood and when they reach home, it is 10 p.m. They carry on an average 2 mds. and earn less than Rs. 1.20 per month. Accidents take place often. Harassment by traders and forest guards are common, but merchants get away with truck loads of timber by bribes to forest officials. The firewood picker families are constantly in debt.

The scene may be different ; the occupation different but the essentials of the story remain—be they cashew workers, coir workers, fish-graders, bidi workers or lace workers, cartpullers, or coolies, domestic servant—name any occupation, it is the same unvarying story of long hours of work, poorly remunerated with little prospect of upgrading. Women in the unorganised sector have insecure jobs, are kept on temporary or casual basis, with not even the barest of welfare facilities, under conditions that pose health hazards. Where social taboos against working outside the home prevail, women produce at home, on piece-rate basis and become victims of traders' malpractices. This is so in Bhatty's[55] study that examines 264 households where women contribute more than 45 per cent of the household income. When household income increases, the proportion contributed by women declines but not the absolute amount. In fact the absolute amount increases because the average number of women bidi workers per household increases with a rise in household income. There is no slackening of effort and they continue to work 11 hours. The association of rising household income with rising household size arises because of labour intensive activity. Per capita income does not increase. Women continue to work to stay where they are. Whenever alternate job opportunities become available, men are quick to step out.

In another study of a growing urban centre,[56] it was found that 90 per cent of women were in unskilled jobs. The distribution of female workers per 100 male workers was as follows : 240 (bidi), 171 (domestic work), 79 (garbage disposal), 27 (head load), 10-20 (trade/construction), 65 (teaching), 60 (Nursing, health personnel). The porter women (those who carry load) in this city contributed 50 per cent of the household income, their daily wage being between Rs. 1.50 to Rs. 3.00 "Entry into the urban social productive process or rather into the fringes of this process has disrupted the pattern of women's former existence in the village without giving rise to any new kind of integration."[57]

There are some studies on domestic servants.[58] Work herein is in individual households, with paternalistic employer-employee relationships, but the tediousness of the work, lack of security and low wages are compensated by easy availability of the job—one sector that has proliferated in the absence of household technology. Domestic service by women raises many tricky questions about women's liberation. Domestic work done for others fetches a wage—in that sense it is a way of valuing work otherwise not valued. On the other hand, class differences are maintained between women and the relationship of maids to mistresses is an uneasy and antagonistic one. Improving the lot of domestic servants, organising them etc., can be some useful measures. One may also view it as making some contribution to women's economic status. On the other hand, maintenance of a non-contractual relationship is problematic—making the tedious job more pleasant but it also makes for a type of patron-client relationship that postpones the emergence of *free labour*.

Cashew processing employs 90 per cent female work force. Here there is a clear gender division of labour, where loading, unloading and roasting are done by men, and women do shelling, peeling, grading and packing. Despite the fact that women cashew workers contribute more than 44 per cent family income, their status at home remains the same and they receive no help in housework. Though paid by piece-rate and paid low, they have a sense of loyalty to their employer and do not change their employment, and unions exist only in the factory sector.[59]

Coir is another female dominated industry which employs over five lakh persons. A sample study of 400 women found they are paid 75p.-88p. for 100 husks. Export orientation and mechanisation have led to the emergence of monopolistic forms. At the same time, there is a process of decentralisation which has led to closure of organised factories and expansion of unorganised units. The combined effect of this is the displacement of women from the organised sector and their concentration in the unorganised sector. The status of women within the household was low; alcoholism and wife beating among the men and total responsibility of the women for housework represented the typical features of lower class women's lives.[60]

Many studies corroborate the fundamentally subordinate position of women in the unorganised sector and their easy exploitability. In a major, comprehensive study by Banerjee, some basic issues such as the following are addressed[61] :

(a) the character of female labour supply and the social vulnerabilities of female labour ;
(b) its advantage to the employer and society ;
(c) new methods of production organisation that combines organised and unorganised forms in ways that segment the labour force.
(d) their rationale (or rather absence of rationale) for sexual division of tasks.

The characteristic of female labour supply according to Banerjee is its lack of response to wage rates and its determination by level of family income. Because women aim to make up a deficit in family level of income which is already very low, they are prepared to take up any work and at any rate. Employers are able to take advantage of the short term considerations of women workers and the absence of alternatives they face by hiring them at wages far below their productivity. Sexual division of tasks has no rationale and has little connection with the special biological role of women because child bearing and child rearing in reality are given no recognition. Women work at hard tasks during pregnancy and when motherhood creates special needs, they are deprived of even their ordinary needs. The shift of workers between occupations has little effect on relative wages so *overcrowding* by women is not the real cause of low wages. Women accept any clear family taboos about work even if it means foregoing opportunities. But where there are new occupations and no established taboos, women are able to enter. However, even prejudices of employers can create inequalities. The upshot of it all is that women in paid employment are treated as deviant, and discrimination in the labour market stems from this. At the same time, ironically, women's family obligations are so strongly laid that the ultimate responsibility for family survival, which implies also economic responsibility, rests on their shoulders. As the main purpose of work is to keep the family intact, argues Banerjee, work cannot improve women's status but only maintain male dominance within the household. However, that work by itself cannot achieve an enhancement of status would be true of work under any exploitative situation, whether for men or women.

In a situation where organised industrial growth has slowed down, the needs of the economy are not by people's self-help efforts. However, the resources for operating viable units or improving productivity are so meagre that the majority of *self-employed* are caught in a trap of low productivity. *Own-account* description assumes that producers have a measure of control but for the thousands of self-employed workers, the lack of resources makes them an easy prey to middlemen and traders. The retention and expansion of the *unorganised sector* in a planned economy was based on the rationale that consumer goods would have to be produced by these units to offset the emphasis on heavy industries that public investment will mainly concentrate on. A dual economic structure resulted in creating two classes of workers. The advantages to the employers of the small scale sector for escaping union activity, of various taxes, of labour laws etc. have resulted in a conscious exploitation of precapitalist forms of production. Women's fate is inextricably linked up with this development model. Given their social disabilities and discrimation, they are unable to enter the *organised sector*. Their need for earning income or obtaining bare necessities drive them into the only sector that recruits them.

Section 4

EARNINGS DIFFERENTIAL

The most glaring discrimination against women is in wage inequality ; not only unequal pay for equal work but unequal pay for work of comparable worth. One of the clear cases of bias lies in the definition of many women's jobs as being of *lower skill*. It is on the basis of value judgements and not on any objective standards of skill component, or actual output that these categorisations are based.

In rural areas, especially in agriculture, women's back-breaking work is conveniently treated as deserving less than the rewards paid to the males even for identical operations.

The irrationality of wage differences emerges when actual studies on productivity are carried out. In farm management studies female labour time is taken as being equal to 3/4 or of male labour time, measured as a standard 8-9 hours per day on an a *priori* assumption. In an actual field study done to test the introduction of new farm machinery,[62] much to the surprise of investigators, female labour was found *three times* more efficient.

Wage-Difference in Agriculture

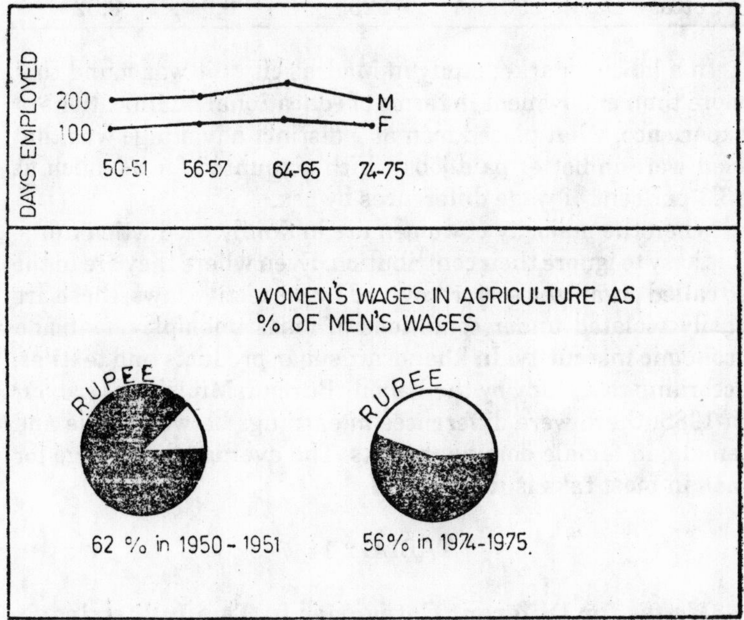

Type of Equipment	*Picking Rate per labourer in mtrs. per minute*		*Hours taken for the same job*		*Potato yield in kg. per 20 mtrs.*	
	M	*W*	*M*	*W*	*M*	*W*
1. Spring time cultivator	1.6	5.2	192	53	17.1	23.6
2. Potato digger elevator	1.4	4.0	185	69	18.2	23.9

In another study on the silk reeling industry[63] which covered 9,000 reeling establishments, the wage rates had no relation to productivity.

TABLE 2.13

Productivity per Labour Day in gms. per Raw Silk

	Units exclusively	*Units exclusively*	*Average/wage/day Rs.*	
	M	F	M	F
Charkha	357	443	6.82	5.55
Cottage Basin	293	325	8.94	6.52

In a labour market study in Madras city[64] it was found that more than endowment in terms of educational qualifications or experience, what placed men at a distinct advantage was that men were in better paid jobs which accounted for as much as 86.3 per cent of wage differences by sex.

When the majority of women are in family production units, it is easy to ignore their contribution. Even where they are in the so called organised sector, covered by protective laws, these are easily violated under conditions of mass unemployment and economic insecurity. In khandsari/sugar products and textiles, according to a study by the Labour Bureau, Ministry of Labour in 1985, there were differences in earnings between male and female, in female dominant tasks. The average daily wage for men in most taks is Rs. 9.

TABLE 2.14

Wages for Different Categories in Two Industries

	Daily Wages in rupees	
	M	*F*
Khandsari/Sugar		
General labourer	6.88	5.86
Packing and wrapping	—	5.53
Wrapping (piece rate)	—	2.74
Cotton Textile		
Cotton : Picking	7.70	5.57
Sweeper	7.66	6.61
Lint Carrier	9.26	8.53

In the organised sector inequalities persist. Precise data on this is not available but micro studies give plenty of evidence. Sinha's study on women in mines and plantations has illustrated the earnings gap.

1. **Average Weekly Cash Earnings** (*in Rs.*)
   (*work above ground*)

	AP	*Assam*	*Bihar*	*MP*	*Maharashtra*
Men	120.69	124.08	108.38	116.84	113.08
Women	110.01	116.66	97.45	103.90	109.50

	Orissa	*W.Bengal*	*All India*
Men	106.98	108.15	111.67
Women	121.90	99.92	102.45

In coal mines, female earnings are 80 per cent of that of males. In non-coal mines, female earnings are less than men's by as much as 50 per cent. In plantations too, there are differences but not always unfavourable.

		Assam	*West Bengal*
Tea	M	3.08—3.66	3.47—3.85
	W	3.32—3.82	3.36—3.68

Despite the passing of the Equal Remuneration Act in 1976, these blatant discrepancies continue.

Even among the educated workers, women earn far less than men. Among highly qualified Science and Technology personnel, while women's wages are 90 per cent of men at entry point, stagnation in career produces a wage gap of 60 per cent by the time the women are in their 40's.

The report appearing in the Indian Express, Nov. 1, 1985 is not an uncommon phenomenon. (See next page)

Section 5

MIDDLE CLASS EMPLOYED WOMEN

One of the striking features in post-independence India is the phenomenal increase in the number of employed women from the middle class. The spread of higher education has been rapid

60 mills violate labour laws

By Nachiketa Desai
Express News Service

AHMEDABAD, Oct. 31.

An estimated 10,000 workers, more than half of them women, have been employed as contract labourers in the 60-odd textile mills of the city in utter violation of the labour laws.

The labourers, engaged by contractors to do various kinds of work in the textile mills, are paid less than Rs. 8 for 10 to 12 hours of hard work per day, according to a study sponsored by the Union Labour Ministry.

The study, conducted by Dr. Sujata Patel, revealed that the contract labour system was a recent phenomenon dating back to 1967-69 when the textile industry was facing a crisis. The system, which was first introduced in the bobbin cleaning department, had spread to other departments of the industry where normally permanent workers are employed.

Dr. Patel argues that the contract labour system could not have spread so rapidly without support from the Textile Labour Association, the only recognised union of textile workers.

Obviously the system of contract labour was beneficial to the mill management as it cut down the expenditure on the management's share towards provident fund, gratuity, medical allowance, bonus and various other incentives being given to permanent employees.

That the contract labour system is being encouraged by some representatives of the Textile Labour Association has been brought to light by another study conducted by Ms Renana Jhabvala.

In her study on the decline of women work force in the textile mills of Ahmedabad, Ms Jhabvala has cited several instances where representatives of the union were running contracts of the mills.

Ms Jhabvala found that the contractors used to pay kick backs not only to union representatives but also to Labour Department officials.

Following a public interest litigation filed recently, the Gujarat High Court has appointed a 10-member fact-finding team comprising five lawyers and five officials of the Labour Department to investigate into the prevalence of contract labour system in the textile mills.

The team visited about a dozen mills during the last 25 days and found that the contract labour system existed in all the mills. According to a member of the team, in one of the mills the contractor was himself the representative of the union.

The team is expected to submit its report to the High Court some time next month.

A startling fact brought out by both Dr. Patel and Ms Jhabvala was the employment of child labour by the contractors in the mills.

Both Dr. Patel and Ms Jhabvala have stressed the need for organising contract labourers in the textile industry to ensure a fair deal to them.

Ms Jhabvala, who has traced the history of textile industry in her study entitled "closing doors", has described how the mill management and the TLA have been favouring retrenchment of women workers. She pointed out that the strength of women workers, who constituted 20 per cent of the total work force engaged in textile mills of Ahmedabad in 1925, had come down to 2.5 per cent in 1975.

Ms Jhabvala says "neither the union nor the employer nor the relatives are interested in helping the woman retain her job"

She says the organised sector, particularly the textile industry, tended to discriminate against women.

"A good mother cannot be a worker, and as being a woman almost inevitably means being a mother, women should be excluded from the labour force, is the prevalent ideology in the organised sector", Ms Jhabvala says.

It is because of this attitude towards women that the mill management as well as the union have been displacing women workers, first compelling them to work as contract labourers and then rendering them jobless altogehter, Ms Jhabvala adds.

after independence. The rate of growth of higher education for women has been faster than that of men, though either in absolute numbers or as a proportion of total enrolment, women continue to lag behind. This has created a vast pool of educated woman-power. Simultaneously, there has been an expansion in the tertiary sector of the economy, more rapid in its increase than that of the secondary sector. The proliferation of the administrative-bureaucratic jobs stimulated a demand for educated personnel. Developmental efforts and growth in welfare services also meant a sizeable expansion of various professions such as scientific, technical, medical and para-medical. While thus opportunities for employment were opening up some changes in attitudes to women's employment among the middle class were visible. From the once widely held view that only widows or single women without male support should seek a job to the idea that an employed woman adds prestige to the family, marks a transition in the value system of the society—an area worth a deeper sociological inquiry. "My husband permits me to work," "my in-laws do not object to my working" are statements that we come across frequently. This acceptance is on the other hand hemmed in by many conditional clauses that reduce the potential of this opportunity for a genuine liberation of women. There are considerations such as : whether the job has social prestige ; whether it is above or below that of the husband ; whether it means mixing with men ; whether it permits women to continue to perform their domestic responsibilities and so on. The words used are "allowed", "not objected to" etc. which imply that is not a right of every woman but granted to her as a matter of munificence. The control over the income earned is not necessarily in the woman's hands. Nor does it always improve the woman's position with respect to authority and decision making, within the family.

As the reasons for earning are more for improving or maintaining the standard of living of the family or to cushion it against inflationary pressures, women's own interests are not fully served. Girls earning to collect their own dowry or remaining unmarried to support parents are fairly common. Whatever research has been done on this class of women, shows clearly that middle class employed women spend almost entirely what they earn for the improvement of family welfare, barring some exceptions. The notion that such women hold jobs to earn 'pin-money' is an utter falsehood. Women's earnings in middle class families go towards better nutrition for all, better schooling for children, more extra curicular activities for children, more amenities for the family, acquisition of durable consumer goods etc. The most immediate beneficiaries are family members. Nevertheless, there have been some gains for women themselves, such as acquiring some measure of social and psychological space, greater social interaction outside their immediate kin group and higher self-esteem. But these gains have been also offset by a heavy price, in terms of greater physical, mental and emotional strain, induced by the necessity to manage two roles. Employment outside the home on terms and conditions identical to that of men does not absolve them from their socially imposed domestic responsibility. The dual burden exists for women of all classes, but the nature and degree varies as between classes. The middle class woman's job is cleaner, better paid, less arduous physically, but she has anxieties and responsibilities that are of different intensity especially with regard to children, which call for intellectual and emotional care besides mere physical feeding. As an educated woman, she shoulders extra responsibilities. Going to the ration office,bank, doctor's clinic for children, attending school meetings, meeting family's social organisations such as rituals, festivals are all the woman's jobs and the man in the family is taken to be "too busy" to do these. For housework, a servant's help may be available and for chid care, they can fall back on either kin support or hired help but none of these fully absolve the employed woman's responsibilities, for men are still unwilling to share them, by and large. Whatever support services are available are individual, private provisions and their availability is not guaranteed but depends on luck and circumstances or family's willingness. The strain of attending to two roles provoked a spate of research and in fact for the first three decades after independence, this was almost the exclusive concern of research on women.[65] A consequence of the dual role was the loss of promotional opportunities in their careers. It became clear that professed equality in education and employment even for those who gained a foothold remained unfulfilled given unequal opportunities and unequal responsibilities.

It is only recently that attention has begun to dawn on some fundamental issues that go beyond documenting the role-conflict : Why are women penalised in their careers for performing an important social role ? Why are sex roles so rigid that men do not share in family maintenance though women are doing men's work ? Does not the family belong to men as much? Do they not derive much gain from the income of the employed woman ? There appear to be differences in the attitudes as between different cultural groups within the middleclass—the business class, the upwardly mobile nouveau riche, the traditional learned class, the more patriarchal and feudal north etc. Barring, a small minority, women's employment is not seen as important to themselves and hence there is not much sympathy for a woman who is ambitious. She is seen as aggressive, masculine and neglectful towards her family. Faced with these social strictures, it is not surprising that most women play down their career ambitions. Where there are exceptions and women have achieved distinction, many of them would say, "we have to work twice as hard to gain recognition" or they could do it only because their husbands were supportive.

That employment by itself does not guarantee independence or improved status for women is proved also by the middle class experience where they are better off than their poorer sisters in other ways : health, education, material resources etc. Fundamental changes are needed in the structure of family, work-arrangements and value systems. Faced with these uncomfortable questions, many women become defensive and proclaim : 'we do not want to compete with men' ; 'we do not want to neglect our children' etc. This comes from a misinterpretation of feminist critiques of society that examine the bases of inequality. These are : (a) unequal responsibility and work burden (b) non-recognition of the value of women's family maintenance work which results in an employment structure that ignores this, and the workplace is so structured as though nobody performs this (c) the application of standards of performance that disregards the unequal conditions under which this work is performed, namely that women have to do their jobs with one hand tied behind their backs.

The dilemma of the middle class woman is a genuine one for in a situation where the family is the only economic and emotional support and non kin solidarity groups are absent, she is unwilling to lose this. There is a misunderstanding on the part of researchers too in blaming women for their lack of career commitment. Employers are unanimous in their appreciation of women workers as more sincere, dependable, hard working—in other words, committed. The contradiction comes from a wrong word like 'commitment'—it should be 'ambition'. All the same there is some truth in the observation that girls are not trained for taking their careers seriously ; instead, marriage is regarded as their main destiny. All adults need family life, work and personal growth and there must be a balance in the combination, but for women, there is a major loss in shutting off the last two.

The consciousness of middle class women has risen noticeably in the last decade ; witness the growing women's movement in the country. The questions that had been earlier avoided are now being asked. This is a sign that things must change.

SECTION 6

UNEMPLOYMENT : FEWER DOORS OPEN FOR WOMEN

Data on unemployment (including all persons seeking or available for work) was for the first time canvassed in 1981. Other sources of data are on the number of job seekers currently registered with Employment Exchanges. During the period 1970-1980 the number of females in the 'Live Register' multiplied three times. Female job seekers on the employment exchange registers from 1/8th of total job seekers—a proportion far in excess to their representation in the work force. The rate of increase in unemployment of females was 2.3 per cent per year, against only 1.6 per cent for males during the decade. Significant changes noticeable in the employment exchanges are : (a) proportion of educated applicants both among males and females has been rising and is nearly 60 per cent now and (b) placement of job seekers has slowed down due to the sluggish growth of the economy creating little new employment opportunities for new entrants. The increase in educated job seekers was as follows :

TABLE 2.15

Job Seekers	*Male*	*Female*
Matriculates	+ 9.4%	+ 11.7%
Undergraduates	+ 16.8%	+ 19.2%
Graduates and Postgraduates	+ 12.3%	+ 15.1%

Source : DGET, 1985, *Employment Review*.

Even educated women have more difficulty in getting jobs. Among the women applicants, in professional, technical and related works, and in administrative and managerial works women accounted for barely 0.2 per cent job applicants ; clerical category covered 5.30 per cent but semiskilled and unskilled job seekers were 94.5 per cent.

For women :

(i) Open chronic unemployment is twice as high as for males.

(ii) Open *current* unemployment is equally severe and twice as high as for males.

(iii) Even for the usually employed females spells of unemployment creating acute under-employment exist for one in four female workers as against 3 in 10 for male workers.

(iv) Unemployment rate rises with the level of education.

The NSS has compared in its three rounds chronic unemployment, but the figures are still not accurate because of inadequacy of coverage.[66]

SECTION 7

IMPACT OF TECHNOLOGY

Is technology gender neutral ? Who takes decision on introduction of new techniques and whose interests are served ? Are technological changes in different spheres of productive activity also accompanied by changes in the ownership of the means of production, division of labour, generation of surplus and its accumulation and labour absorption ? Can questions of technology be studied without considering production relations ? Can these be analysed without considering the nature of power relationships within the household ?

The relationship between technology and socio-economic structure is a complex one. New technologies in certain spheres while throwing women of some classes out of employment have also increased household incomes in some others. Even where more employment or more household income has accrued to women, it has not necessarily altered the status of women, as pointed out by innumerable micro studies, where woman being an earner or the family's income level being better does not alter fundamental inequalities between men and women in control over crucial resources and authority in decision-making.

When technological changes take place in the context of an increasing integration of the Indian economy into the world market systems, technological policy has to balance the needs of productivity gains, egalitarian distribution of income, provision of basic needs for all and the safeguarding of our biosphere from deterioration. As the economy moves from subsistence to a modernised, monetized sector, often women are the worst losers. Their real incomes shrink with uncertainties of cash income and much of the self-provisioning they were able to do no longer becomes possible. The work rhythm of new types of work can also disturb the time and energy balance of woman's work.

The skill component of women's training is at present grossly inferior to that of men. At higher levels, not only should one worry about women's inferior access to prevailing skills but also their participation in the generation of new technology.

The relation between technology and women have to be examined for the following :

(a) Impact on employment
(b) Impact on nature of work.
(c) Impact on heath and nutrition.
(d) Impact on general social status.
(e) Availability of technology for increasing productivity, and lessening of drudgery.

Scattered evidence throughout this chapter have shown that by and large, the impact of technology for women has been negative.[67] Even where a class of women *are* getting technical education, the choice of courses tend to be sex-stereotyped. For example, nearly 50 per cent of women trained in dress-making remained unemployed.[68] Secondly, even where the women have received proper training in new skills, the rate of unemployment among them is higher than among males.[69]

As many of the skills given are intended to promote self-employment, in the absence of enterpreneurial skills, credit and marketing facilities, women are unable to set up their own production units. In addition, various kinds of family restrictions confine and narrow their choice of occupations.[70] Even at higher levels of scientific and technical education, the rate of unemployment is high. National studies also indicate considerable wastage of woman's scientific talent by their preponderance in non-research posts.[71]

Technology in Industry

In rural and other small industries, technology has displaced women. In the fishing industry, even though women play a dominant role in the production process and in marketing, the socio-cultural values of fisherfolk assign inferior status to women. The introduction of nylon nets fabricated by machines no doubt improve the catch but has reduced women's job opportunities in net-making. The introduction of the auction system in marketing forces women to compete with large traders, and women have lost much of the control they had earlier through income from fish vending. The new assets created by technology are invariably owned by men.[72]

Gulati[73] in her study of the impact of new technology on women in Kerala points to a less severe impact wherever women have enjoyed some degree of power and authority and wherever they gained access to new technology. However, the introduction of trawlers on the whole has been very problematic in two ways :

(a) Creating wide class disparities within the fishing community;

(b) Destroying the coastal fish availability due to intensive deep sea fishing and thereby endangering future yields. The effect of this on different families have to be examined.

A Bombay study[74] records higher income levels to trawler owners but impoverishment of others and the lack of control of women over household income and resources, their loss of marketing opportunities due to long distance truck operated marketing outlets displacing house to house retailing or local market sales etc.

What is true of fishing is true of traditional dairying. The setting up of new large scale, highly commercialised cooperative dairy units and daily processing has left women out of cash income.

In all these instances, we notice that technology alters simultaneously forms of production. In the export industries the changes in nature of the market, forms of production and technology combine to create pressures and generate a special set of vulnerabilities for women.

In cotton handlooms, woollen cottage industry and hand block printing there has been mass displacement of women.[75] Between 1974-1981 there was an addition of 2.31 lakh cotton powerlooms which started as unauthorised looms but have been regularised since by the Government. (Recent estimates of powerlooms put it at a total of eight lakhs). They have put out of action an estimated 13.86 lakh handlooms in the country. One handloom provides work for four persons. Converted into person year basis one handloom employs 2.4 persons of whom 0.9 are women labour. On this basis, the disruption of the handloom industry has extinguised 28.64 lakh jobs, half of which were held by women involved in pre-weaving tasks. The new jobs created by powerlooms were only 5.58 lakhs. In five states (Tamil Nadu, Andhra, Gujarat, Maharashtra and U.P.) 2.55 lakh handloom women workers were displaced between 1961 and 1971.[76]

In the woollen cottage industry (Jammu and Kashmir, U.P., Rajasthan, Punjab, Haryana, Maharashtra, Andhra and Karnataka), 200,000 women are employed as part of family production units well integrated with sheep rearing. It is an industry which not only meets the demand for warm clothes, from locally produced raw materials with inexpensive tools, without using power and employing hereditary skills but provides seasonal employment in non agricultural months. Woollen spinning and weaving has now been taken over by mills, leading to massive unemployment for men and women. In addition export of sheep and lamb meat has reduced raw material for this cottage industry.

In the hand-printing industry the benefits of an expanding demand for printed textiles have gone to machines instead of to unemployed men and women. An estimated 250,000 jobs have been lost, a major section of the losers being women because the comparative employment per unit of output between hand-printing and mill printing is 15 : 1. In the name of export promotion technological change is introduced but the aggregate increase in export earnings conceal employment distress at the micro level and the creation of greater inequality, for the sections that gain and the sections that lose are different.

Coir industry has been facing the threat of mechanisation. The tobacco-units that employ over 90 per cent female labour are responding to the collective struggle of women in the Karnataka border by threat of mechanisation.

There are no precise quantitative estimates of the extent of labour displacement by industry, nor do we know much about the nature of the victims and what policy options exist.

Technology and Agriculture

Agricultural growth has taken place mainly in the areas where new agricultural technology in the form of HYV has been adopted. Their impact on women vary as between classes and regions. Agarwal[77] has attempted a class/gender analysis on the differential impact of different components of the new technology. (a) The new irrigation based HYV cultivation (b) mechanisation of different operations like threshing (c) mechanisation through tractorisation. Her conclusions, supported by field data from Andhra and Tamil Nadu are as follows :

(i) Employment opportunities in certain agricultural operations linked to the HYV irrigation package increased, and

(ii) employment in those operations generally for female and male labour that were mechanised, led to a reduction in labour demand.

There were differences in impact for different classes in agriculture. There were some who benefited from increase in real wage rates and larger number of days of employment due to double-cropping while others were worse off. But whatever increase in employment did take place was nowhere commensurate to the total agricultural labour available for work. Women in small cultivator households faced increased work burdens by having more farm work in addition to their normal household duties. Among marginal land holders, many lost land due to tractorisation leading to eviction of tenants to facilitate large areas for agricultural operation. Only those cultivators gained who were in a position to invest in the new technology. Only women from large farmer's households benefited, but even among them the household work increased, like cooking for hired workers. Whenever farm size increased, hired labour replaced family labour. Thus while new agricultural technology led to some increase in employment and real wages for some, for others it led to increase in unpaid work.

Sen[78] also examines the HYV regions (Pujab-Haryana and Tamil Nadu) and while agreeing with the above findings makes some pertinent observations regarding changes in land relations. In both regions as a result of land reform legislation while there was a decline in absentee landowners this was offset by consolidation of land by rich farmers, growing insecurity of small tennants due to tenant switching, and evictions. Many of the pre-existing reciprocal relations and ties between owners and tenants that guaranteed minimum year round subsistence broke down. Nevertheless tenants used to farm and pay share cropping and bonded labour were replaced by wage labour. In addition the new technology needed more cash for inputs like fertiliser, pesticides and water. As a result, risks of cultivation increased and land was lost by many small farmers. There was also tenant eviction. Thus, despite some increase in demand for labour, there was further increase in landless agricultural labour in Tamil Nadu, where there had already been a large number of small tenants and agricultural labour. In the North, where there were a large numbers of medium farmers and not many absentee landlords and very few landless labourers, the new technology led to subdivision of land. Hence demand for agricultural labour improved wage rates. Women of small farm households began working as casual workers to sustain household income. In Tamil Nadu on the other hand eviction of small tenants led to non-brahmin women working as casual labour to keep the level of household income from falling. Thus the effect of new technology in the two areas differed. In the North, while the range of tasks performed by women changed, women's employment overall did not decline but in the South, due to a pre-existing large surplus of labour, when new technology eliminated some traditional women's tasks, there was a decline in employment. Thus the crucial difference is created by the kind of contribution women's wage employment makes to small farming households and the extent to which a reserve army of unemployed labour acts to push women out of employment. There are many questions that need looking into, such as, do relations of subordination get strengthened or weakened by women's wage labour ? Does women's wage labour alter the sexual division of labour at home ? What impact do peasants' organisations have on women ? These questions await investigation.

So far we have mainly talked of displacemnt. A related issue is access to new technology.[79] Throughout the regions of agricultural modernisation, until recently women were never invited for training, for extension service programmes even though they are the major partners in agricultural production. The operation and maintenance of machines requires trained labour and when the use of machines on the farm increases, men are the first to get permanent employment. Women, therefore, get relegated to the status of casual workers. Women are given only those jobs which cannot be done by machines or are unpleasant. New technology is labour saving for men but for women it has increased drudgery.

In view of this dysfunctional effect of technology it would be desirable for policy purposes to first obtain adequate information on the specific needs and requirements of women. Before any new technology is used its likely effects on women should be assessed.

After devoting attention to the energy consuming and frequently under-productive work of women in producing and processing staple foods, hoeing and weeding, in providing fuel and water, some new technological solutions have been offered. There are distinct advantages in selecting and maintaining simpler devices and equipment for rural women, such as, thin walled tanks, simple hand pumps and mud brick stoves, better containers for food, use of solar energy, biogas energy etc. By concentrating on *basic technology* rural women who have so far been bypassed by modern technology could increases their productivity. Wherever experiments in involving women have been carried out, their response has been enthusiastic. Technological policy is inevitably entangled with the problem of poverty. Technology indicates power. Access to it and control of it are questions of the balance between political and social objectives.

Technological change can spell absolute deprivation of women at work by simply eliminating their designated tasks in the labour processes (we saw examples of this in the textile industry and coal mining) or by promoting male substitution (as for instance in rice milling, fish processing). Technical change can also alter the nature of women's work (assembly line production instead of craft work), severely increasing the strain as well as hazards of work.

Technology cannot be turned back. It can serve humanity by lightening physical toil. Human society has two halves : men and women, and women do not wield equal power and choice in the use of technology. A great deal of women's work is arduous and very little has been done to lighten the drudgery of tasks like fetching fuel, water, cooking, washing etc., which take away a good deal of women's time. The problem is not simply one of availability of technologies. Division of labour within the household, modes of production and land tenure systems are all a complex package of social and economic factors that create resistance to appropriate choice. Secondly, the conflict between transfer of technology from abroad and its immediate short term gains in growth and developing indigenous technological capabilities that have a long term effect of reducing mass poverty has never been resolved in the Indian context. The import of technology and the neglect of basic needs technology have more serious repercussions for women. The impact of technology should not be viewed solely in terms of *employment* without regard to what kind of products are produced and for whom. Hence the question of choice of technology is not just a matter of technical rationality but one of social goals.

SECTION 8

EXPORT INDUSTRIES

A new phenomenon that has emerged since the late sixties is the growth of export industries. A shift in policy towards promoting the growth of the economy through incentives for the growth of exports took place at a time (a) when world trade in certain products was expanding rapidly, providing opportunities for many third world countries (b) when import substitution by an accent on *self*-reliance began to wane as a result of various bottlenecks in public investment including foreign exchange crises. One of the outstanding advantages Third World countries enjoyed was low labour costs. New export products like garments, food products, electronics offered opportunities for expansion. Though these were *modern* industries and involved new skills as in electronics, the uncertain and fluctuating international market (i) makes employers prefer a temporary, easily dismissed labour force, (ii) makes labour unrest or organised labour struggles costly. Added to this is the advantage of decentralised units that offer a lower capital base. Women have been selectively drawn into this sector but on terms that continue to exploit their vulnerabilities in the labour market.

A series of studies done on export industries reveal that the new opportunities women have received in a *modern* sector have only entrenched them in their inferior status as workers. Studies on the Garment Industry[80] show that the industry resorts to widespread subcontracting; the industry is highly centralised because certain innovations like bandcutting make their decentralising easy though a few big firms do exist. The women are employed in selective tasks only such as in thread cutting, button stitching, tailoring etc. and their chances of holding supervisory, managerial or the more skilled jobs, such as that of cutters are absent. There are no wage norms at all, and there are wide variations in methods of operation and payment. Production organisation also varied where different levels of technology coexit simultaneously.

Women workers recruited are of younger age groups, with some education (primary and above) and characteristics that enable employers to retrench labour whenever not needed because the majority of women are casual workers. Though proportionate to the total labour force, female workers form only 20 per cent in the big garment assembly units, females are employed in large numbers of avoid the hazards of *unionisation* which a predominantly male labour force is likely to engender. Males are employed in the decentralised scattered units which makes unionisation difficult. Secondly, females are used on *put out* basis (pieces are give to be done at home) which makes wage norms and unionisation unlikely. As a whole the wages in this industry are low compared to the profit margins enjoyed by the exporters.

In the food processing industry[81] women are hired as cheap casual workers in dispersed units often on a piece rate system, wherein wages are determined more by the industrial strucutre and export value. There are also a large number of home workers. For the majority of the women workers (fish processing, papad, masala, canning etc.) the survival of families would be difficult without women's earnings. Women are involved in this industry mainly in manual processes such as cutting, peeling, packing etc. Thus the emergence of 'modern' mechanised units has resulted in down grading of women's traditional skills and food processing.

The most serious form of exploitation occurs in the so called Free Trade and Export Promotion Zones.[82] Two such zones have been established—one mainly an electronic unit and the other a multiproduct one.

In the electronic zone in Bombay, there are 92 units that employ 5465 males and 1524 females, but what is disturbing is the concentration of females in semi-skilled and unskilled categories. In a sample survey of 48 units the distribution was as follows :

	M	*F*
Unskilled	27.08	23.05
Semi-skilled	39.35	69.26
Skilled	33.57	7.69
	100.00	100.00

Women were more in assembly jobs while men were in the preparation of software :

Type of concern	*Male*	*Female* (*% distribution*)	*Total*
Components	2.92	97.08	100
Software	65.00	35.00	100
Consumers' products	30.00	70.00	100
Others	18.58	81.42	100

The female workers earned less than Rs. 500 per month, an average level of 1/4th to 1/5th of the wage available at similar skill level in established firms that make other non-export products outside the zone. Facilities available were minimal increment was very low so that years of experience conferred little advantage. The bulk of the workforce was unmarried, aged between 17-25. Most of the women had joined in order to see a younger brother thorugh college, collect their own dowry or help the family during the unemployment of the main breadwinner. Unionisation was discouraged and only a small proportion were members of unions. The threat of dismissal discouraged labour struggles. The well-meaning argument of generating employment becomes oppressive for women when their *cheapness* and *docility* are what they are used for. The charm of cheap labour may not continue long abroad if further automation takes place, reducing cost differences in which case Export Promotion Zones may become agents to sell these products.

Kandla Free Trade Zone has an equally dismal story.[83] Of the total workforce males constitute 4783 and females 3401. The educational level of the female worker is primary level and the age level is below 20. The majority are unmarried. The FT Zone at Kandla has readymade-garment units, knitting units, electronics, pharmaceutical, brush and bristle making units. The bulk of labour is recruited through unlicensed contractors. Average wages ranged between 300-600 depending on the industry.

These women workers in addition to hours of work at the factory do household chores. Their total work day began at 4 a.m. and ended at 10 p.m. Any attemp to organise was severly dealt with by the influence of the panchayat and Mahila Kalyan Samiti (an Upper class women's Organisation). A successful strike in 1982 was broken by police firing which since has terrorised the workers into passivity.

KFTS & SEEPZ are categorised as *essential services* thereby outlawing strikes. They are also free from various Labour laws.

The policy of Free Trade Zone is riddled with many contradictions, not the least being the propagation of female labour as *cheap labour*.

SECTION 9

CONCEPTUAL BIASES IN MEASURING WOMEN'S WORK

Women's work has been particularly sensitive to biases in methods of enumerating workers. Coverage will vary according to what is counted as *work*, whether it is an activity that results in sale and brings income, i.e. *gainful activity* or whether it is an activity that adds to the resources of the household/society, regardless of it resulting in sale or not, i.e. *productive activity*. In India, the major data sources on work-participation are the National Sample Survey, the Decennial Census and the Statistics of the Directorate General of Employment and Training. The National Sample Survey (NSS) is undertaken periodically and is a detaile, indepth coverage of selected villages and districts and is a good source for rural employment, levels of living etc. The NSS has been changing its scope and has changed its definitions from time to time so there are great variations in coverage, especially that of female labour. The Decennial Census is the most comprehensive data source in the Indian context. While advanced countries have many forms of registration (birth, death, marriage, school, tax, unemployment, social security etc.) in poor countries, where the population is predominantly rural and formal organisations and institutions are fewer, the Census is almost the only source for much of the information we need on a particular population. Biases and distortions in the Census regarding women's work then have far reaching implications for women. The Directorate General of Employment and Training collects data only for the urban *organised* sector. As women are mostly in the unorganised sector, even in urban areas women's work participation is grossly under estimated.

Let us look at the Censuses in India. Between 1901-1951 the approach was that of gainful workers[84]. Only in 1891, the population was classified according to sources of livelihood which meant that all members of a household besides the workers in the household who were supported by that source of livelihood were included. No separate estimate of workers then was possible. Between 1901-1921, the Census classified people into workers and dependents but the term *worker* included any one deriving an income who might not be working (such as retired persons and those deriving rent income). As most property is in the name of men, there will be over-counting of men and undercounting of women. The 1911 Census stated : "A woman who looks after her house, cooks the food is not a worker but a dependent. But a woman who collects and sells firewood or cowdung is thereby adding to family income and should be shown as a worker. So also a woman who regularly assists her husband in his work but not one who merely renders a little occasional help." This broadened the coverage to include women doing work in family units but a lot depended on who the question was put to, who answered and interpreted. From 1931 to 1957 there were three classifications : earners, dependents and earning dependents. The self-supporting were those who earned enough to support themselves; earning dependents were those who earned an income but not enough to support themselves. Household members who jointly cultivated land and jointly earned an income were to be counted as workers, but as Sinha states, "The instruction that non-earning dependents do not include women and children who take part in the cultivation of land as unpaid family helpers was ignored in many States."[85]

The undercounting of workers in the Censuses between 1911 and 1951 was as follows :

TABLE 2.16

Degree of Undercounting in the Census*

	Female (%)	*Male (%)*
1911	6.1	2.1
1921	6.1	2.0
1931	19.15	5.0
1951	24.5	11.2

*Source : J.N. Sinha, *Monograph on 1961 Census*, pub. in 1972.

From 1961 onwards, the approach shifted not to income earning but to productive work, but the classification of *main workers* and *marginal workers* led to undercounting of marginal workers, wherein by definition women tended to be consigned.

Women's work encompasses several different categories and what is included or excluded is arbitrary and subject to biases caused by : (a) the gender of the respondent as well as the enumerator ; (b) cultural perceptions regarding women's role ; (c) words and terms used in the questionnaire that tend to exclude what women are actually doing.

Women do household work which includes cooking, washing, cleaning, child care. In the rural areas of the Third World, there is no woman who is just a housewife. Most of the time and energy of rural women is spent in providing types of goods and services usually bought for money in the advanced economies. Women in these economies undertake expenditure substituting work that augments the family's resources, fetching fuel, fodder, fetching water for cattle and household, managing kitchen gardens, poultry, small animals cattlecare, food processing such as threshing grain, dehusking, storing, grinding or milling grain. For instance, anthoropologist Health who has examined 398 subsistence economies finds that while in most societies women were responsible for 50 per cent to 80 per cent of food production, only in 6 per cent of societies did women not participate at all.

In addition to various types of subsistence work, women also participate in all kinds of family enterprises, be they farms, family household industry, fishing,shops and other commercial enterprises. They are unpaid family workers but they often get excluded or undercounted by definition or conceptual biases.

The estimates of unpaid family workers given by the Committee of Experts on Unemployment,[86] show the extent of undercounting.

TABLE 2.17

Extent of Undercounting of Unpaid Family Workers

(In Millions)

Age	*Males*		*Females*	
	Excluding unpaid family labour	*Including unpaid family labour*	*Excluding unpaid family labour*	*Including unpaid family labour*
10-14	6.97	13.06	4.15	9.30
15-19	18.54	27.77	7.55	14.87
20-24	23.88	31.15	7.73	13.91
25-29	22.85	26.95	6.96	11.86
30-34	21.49	23.16	6.35	10.40
35-39	18.83	19.93	5.86	9.31
40-44	16.73	17.29	5.35	8.28
45-49	14.86	15.20	4.67	7.09
50-54	12.69	12.96	3.70	5.52
55-59	10.00	10.23	2.58	3.82
60-64	7.20	7.40	1.54	2.25
65-69	4.80	4.96	0.91	1.33
Total	182.99	214.42	57.96	98.83

While for males the undercount was 31.43 million, for females the undercount was 40.87 million and the undercount for females predominated in the 15-34 age groups.

We can see that both in 1951 and 1961, there was a strong possibility of under enumeration due to definitions and also how the definitions were interpreted by enumerators. In 1961, workers did include those who were seasonally employed but who had done some regular work of more than one hour a day throughout the greater part of the season with or without remuneration or in regular employment for fifteen days preceding employment. The term productive work was interpreted as production for sale because of the clarification given in the Census that an adult woman can be counted as a worker who "in addition to household work is engaged in work such as rice pounding, for sale or wages, in domestic work for wages or for minding cattle or selling firewood, making and selling dung cakes for sale etc".

The 1971 Census was definitely biased against women, because it included as workers only those who reported themselves as participating in economically productive work as their main activity. This meant that women whose main activity was domestic work or due to cultural perception reported themselves so, were counted as non-workers even though these women spent a significant portion of their time in the fields. A supplementary question on secondary work was added but this did not provide any accurate estimate. The major difficulty was that unpaid family workers were counted as workers only if they satisfied a time criterion regardless of the extent of the contribution. A major difficulty that arises in the case of women is the overall fuzziness between what is productive work and what is "domestic" work. The latest Census in 1981 adopted a more liberal definition of work in so far as a person is enumerated as a worker even if he or she works for a few days during the year, preceding the day of enumeration but once again the definition of "productive work" creates problems for women in family enterprises.[87]

Apart from exclusion, the frequent changes in definition and coverage preclude any valid estimaion of trends over time. This difficulty is accentuated in the case of women workers because of the erratic way in which interpretations of their participation tends to be carried out. This non-comparability is not the only consequence. Actual changes cannot be separated from spurious changes.

The data on unemployment is inadequate and imprecise. We do not have correct answers to questions such as (i) What proportion of rural women are workers, (ii) what proportion of rural women so counted are available for work, (iii) for what period are women workers (unemployed) who are willing to work, (iv) what are the characteristics of the involuntarily unemployed by economic position, age, education, number of dependents etc. ?[88]

The National Sample Survey is not free from bias either. The sample selection itself predetermines the scope. There is a prior question that separates persons in the labour force from those outside. The reference period has been changing—daily status, weekly status and current status. Those persons who fall outside the labour force in the process of enumeration cannot have their day to day activities recorded. Female participation rates are highly sensitive to not only schedule chosen, the particular set of concept, procedures etc. but the actual surveying itself. During the 27th and 32nd round of the NSS, the usual status and subsidiary activities differences do not fit inter-state differences. In Nagaland where matriliny[89] prevails, participation of females is significant and the reports are also closer to reality but in Andhra and Madhya Pradesh, reported participation is less than actual participation.

There is, therefore, a serious problem of *perception*. Male investigators interview a male respondent regarding the work of the women in the household. Rigid sexual division of labour results in male ignorance of what women do, how long they work etc. Even if the respondent is female, the answers tend to reflect cultural perceptions.

The measurement of the labour force depends not only on definitions but actual questions. Are you a worker ? Are you seeking work ? Are you available for work ? These are the questions employed but in a socio-economic condition when a person is not working but also not seeking work and is not available because of bondage, household resources, lack of knowledge of work available etc., the answers will not be accurate and will reflect these conditions rather than the exact state of unemployment.[90] Categorisation of workers into agriculture, non-agriculture, self-employment and so on conceals the nature of employment, the form of contract, the relative security of employment and thus predetermine the analysis.

Household surveys also record merely certain formal characteristics but not who uses them under what terms. All kinds of stratification are used such as income, assets, regional and cultural features, religion, ethnicity, but sex and age distinctions do not emerge across the board. The family household becomes the final unit of sampling and while a few specific questions may be addressed to women, traditional classifications are treated as homogenous around sex. Perception is restricted to the role of women as mothers and occasionally as supplementary bread winners. The definition of who is the head of the household is faulty. *Whoever is regarded so* is inaccurate when in many households women are responsible for the economic maintenance of the household to a greater or lesser degree and often solely responsible.

This brings us to the point : What is the nature of female economic activity that evades capture ? It cannot be that it is because they do home based work because men also do home based work and they are counted as productive workers. Primarily it is because of the use of domestic activity as a code. Women perceive themselves, are perceived by others mainly as engaged in domestic activity even when they are engaged in income earning either in a formally visible way or in indirect and invisible way as unpaid family labour or are engaged in free collection of goods and services.

The priority criteria used in questionaires, "What is your *main* activity ?" even when time criterion is used evokes responses from women as domestic workers. The efficiency with which their other activity which is productive work is netted depends on the degree of visible marketability. The fact that women are uniquely responsible for a zone of work, (domestic) gives them this distinction of being difficult to net. Given that this is the most regular commitment women have, the respordent, even if a woman, would not say anything different if slotted as a domestic worker. Even when the question asked is about how much time they spend on productive work, domestic work would be a high priority activity for all women. Devaki Jain suggests that the respondent should not be given the option of discussing her usual status so that the attention can be deflected from the prior classification of worker non-worker to capturing actual activity. She asks[91] :

"Unless we count women not only be giving them their rightful place but also have a perception of the quantum of labour time they put in, in support activities, how do we even see what is happening to the trend, how do we assess investment in relief from the household burdens, how do we interpret technological choices, how do we plan employment promotion ultimately for poverty alleviation ?"

Some time allocation studies of women's work in two states, (using the productive criterion) done by ISST, New Delhi on districts previously surveyed by NSS, found considerable undercounting of female work.[92] Women spend 150 days a year doing weeding, more than 200 days cutting grass, 60-120 days in harvesting, 30 days a season in dehusking, collected groundnuts daily, fed and milched cattle for 240 days and cut fodder for 240 days. Had women better access to water, fuel fodder, this would release them for visible, gainful activity.

Implications of Biases and Inadequacy in Evaluating, Enumerating Women's Work and Why a Special Focus on Women in needed :

(i) The interests of men and women within the household are not the same. This may relate to how income is spent, earned etc. Studies have shown that men go for consumer luxuries but women spend their earnings on family needs. Women's work has a high welfare component. (ii) Women's income and consumption get reduced in absolute terms because of less time and energy. (iii) Women's gain from increase in household income depends on their control over that income. (iv) Women are deeply involved in cultivation but in normal practice, when addressing the head of the household, the head is always presumed to be a male. The conferring of the headship on males, irrespective of who actually bears the responsibilty entitles him to privileges such as credit; he acts as the owner of not only the assets but also of the human resources in the household. The head of the household is not always a principal earner. The household sector contributes as much as 73 per cent to the national savings in the private sector and 889 women per 1000 men are in this sector, but definitions like *head of household*, *productive worker*, *main activity* etc. reduce these women conceptually to a dependency state. (v) Ignoring variations in patterns male-female work leads to policies that benefit only men. The peak/lean seasons of activity in agriculture do not coincide for men and women. (vi) In the absence of data on women's work, technological choices eliminate women's jobs and reduce them to poverty. In Rajasthan, a significant number of women worked receiving wages for four hours for 150 days in weeding. But when weedicides were introduced, they lost jobs. In an UNDP project to upgrade the woollen industry, work was shifted to worksheds and Muslim women who used to spin yarn at home last their jobs. (vii) In farm management studies, women's labour time is taken to be 3/4 to 1/2 of male labour time on the assumption that women are less efficient. (viii) Unless data is provided on the asset position of women, sensible policies cannot emerge. In Kaira district where milk cooperatives were set up, when data on women's work was obtained by classifying landless houses into those who did agricultural labour and others in the dairying houses, it was found that in dairying houses women did both agricultural labour and dairying work and had four hours of extra work than in other houses. (ix) When formulating basic needs service deliveries, we need clear understanding of the work pattern of women in different occupations. (x) A priori assumptions made regarding productivity of women distort the data.

"There is one major distorting device operating at all data collection concerning women, above and beyond interpretation difference or collection facilities. This is a set of cultural assumptions about the secondary importance of anything women do; it produces under registration of women from birth to death; an underenumeration of women in employment, independently of other forces that also create undercounting of populations in general."[93]

To sum up, the undercounting and undervaluation of women's work emerges because of :

- (i) definition of productive work/gainful work;
- (ii) questions that slot on a priority basis on who is a worker;
- (iii) respondent bias—when male, due to notions of women's work; when female, due to self-perceptions one one's major responsibilities;
- (iv) seasonal, intermittent nature of women's work that makes it difficult to fit it in with notions of *regular* work.
- (v) their provision of subsistence goods being non-monetary get excluded;
- (vi) difficulty of separating housework, collection of free goods, unpaid famly labour and wage labour in the case of women;
- (vii) unpaid female family labour do not get counted as the respondent is usually a male head;
- (viii) definition of who is head of household is biased against women, who despite shouldering all the economic responsibility are not defined as *heads*.
- (ix) ignoring of intra-household differences that lead to ignoring women as producers, consumers, decision makers in policy planning.

We need to improve the accuracy of data, modify definitions to eliminate cultural bias, evolve a sounder empirical base for assessing time/energy/output contribution of women, the differential impact of technical and other changes on different classes of women and differential seasonal variation of men's and women's work.

Even after doing all this, a crucial problem would remain. Why is it that the important work of women in "domestic work"—cooking, cleaning, washing, care of the young, sick, elderly—finds no place anywhere as *work* ? How do we get recognition for this work ? The contribution to the national income of these services that women render free ranges between 1/4th to 1/2nd of national income. Yet a woman is regarded as *dependent*; the moment marriage breaks down, she is without support from the very home that she helped build. (Legal maintenance is a pittance.) Her involvement in the provision of services to the nation, gives her less time and energy for *gainful* activity and yet she is declared as *voluntarily* unemployed and not seeking work. Her unequal status in the labour market is a punishment meted out for performing these valuable services to society.

Issues and Theoretical Implications

The history of women's work points to the following essential characteristics :

1. The women bear an inordinately heavy work load whose returns are not commensurate with their work. They have the responsibility for housework and child care; in a country where the majority are poor, they also have the responsibility to earn and provide the wherewithal for survival; they also engage in collection of free goods (fuel, fodder, minor forest produce etc.) that take up considerable time.
2. The decline of craft production has led to deskilling for both men and women but men have moved partly into the modern sector and learnt modern technical skills. For women, loss of their past skills has meant being pushed into unskilled manual labour, agricultural work, construction and domestic services.
3. Wage disparities between men and women workers operate all along the line. They partly reflect differences in

skill, experience which in itself is the consequence of prior discrimination in access to education and training. Some of this lack of access is due to cultural inhibitions and injunctions but a lot of it is due to sexual division of labour that confers responsibility for family work uniquely to women and creates immobilities of various kinds. The labour market makes no allowance for this burden by providing services that would lighten it. The family expects the woman to do both the work. Hence her choice of work is often dictated by what is available easily, what is feasible, and can be combined with her other responsibilities.

4. Occupational segregation is the further branching out of the sexual division of labour. What are men's jobs and women's jobs get culturally defined. These have little relation to biological differences but what is interesting is the fact that the differences are not neutral; they are hierarchical and confine women to a subordinate position. Once occupational or task segregation takes place, they tend to be retained against all other rational criteria. Only in new forms of production there is greater neutrality.
5. Labour market discrimination takes place by exploiting the vulnerabilities of women. They are paid lower wages, confined to lower skill jobs, have less access to promotion or on the job training, or have no access to secure, better paid jobs.
6. Most technology has had an adverse impact on women by eliminating women's jobs in many cases.
7. There are clear differences in the work done; the arduousness of it; the degree of choice that is available; the extent of the *double-burden* (family work and other work); the degree of access to employment opportunities and employment—equipment in terms of human resource development as well as auxiliary resources such as land, credit, marketing, etc.

Any consideration of women's role in the economy provokes two basic questions : (1) Why is women's role not recognised ? (2) Why do women have such an inferior position in the economy ?

While the exact pattern that has resulted in India is due to a certain type of interaction between industrial capitalism and patriarchy, there are general theoretical questions that emerge in the examination of women's differential experience as economic participants. Women's studies theory and research have identified two or three major processes that are embodied in the position of women in the social strucutre. First there is a pervasive sexual division of labour that is extremely resistant to change, either in practice or in ideology. One corollary of this is occupational segregation of women—which permits differnetial treatment. The connection between the sexual division of labour and all other influences that affect the position and power of women are complex but highly integrated. It affects the socialisation process, it influences the notions of masculinity and femininity and it results in demarcation of spheres of influence with the male having more power. It leads to waste of female potential and ignores individual differences in capacities and abilities within each sex. It restricts autonomy for women and by restricting their experiences of the outside world, limits their capacities in performing even their limited roles.

Another corollary of defining women as solely responsible for family care means that their incursion into the labour market made inevitable by inadequate incomes of males or absence of male earners is seen as deviant behaviour and hence the pervasive notion of the woman worker as *supplementary earner* without any objective criteria regarding the total resources contributed to the household, or time and energy spent. A woman who earns as much as 50 per cent or sometimes 100 per cent of the income of the household is still a supplementary earner, who is so regarded by every one. A man who is unemployed, or who is in seasonal employment or earns little is still a primary-earner. A woman who spends almost 10-12 hours a day rag-picking may earn very little ; her husband may earn as much in one hour. She remains a *marginal worker* by definition. The treatment of women's contribution to family based production units reveals this bias. A man who merely sits at the loom is the primary producer. The woman who does all the preceding operations and has to put in 3 to 4 times as much labour in-but is only a *helper*. Because they are not defined as bread-winners, the utility of women's income is placed lower ; were they to be freed from the task of bread-winning they ought to value leisure highly. Yet we find that women seek alternative avenues of work, even if it is at a low level. It is their desperate need for "bread-winning" that places their labour supply at a lower level. This is the paradoxical situation. Their need to make up a gap in income is the primary requisite and hence their labour supply curve assumes a different form.

These factors affect the wages paid to them and the conditions of work offered. Women are "preferred" in certain lines of work, certain operations in industry and agriculture which involve long hours, tedium with lesser returns because men will not be availble for such work.

The status of a woman worker defined as a supplementary eaner, following upon the sexual division of labour becomes acute in a monetised economy. The demand and the wage for female labour is conditioned by the supply characteristics of female labour such as low skills, need for intermittent participation due to reproduction, child care etc. We know that these supply characteristics are themselves induced by both cultural forces and the impact of previous economic sanctions against them.

These supply characteristics are also determined by the structure of the household—whether it is a joint family, nuclear family etc. The process and rate of household formation influence women's economic position. These processes are affected by fertility rates, mortality rates, migration, asset position, social-legal sanctions on property transfers, urbanisation etc. Fertility in turn is modified by age at marriage, customs, legal reforms etc. Women's work patterns are conditioned by these structural changes. Women's lives are in fact more radically transformed by demographic and development changes than are men's lives. Modernisation involves expansion of the masculine domain and shrinkage of the feminine. Women staying in the traditional sphere as allotted by sexual division of labour, become increasingly handicapped. Development then proceeds on one masculine leg. The interface between women's reproductive role and productive role which women alone combine is subject to influences that affect reproduction—pre-natal care, post-natal care, feeding patterns, family planning, male control over female sexuality and fertility. What happens in the interface has immediate bearing on women's production roles. These influences are again different accordingly to the class status of the household. Among the poor no matter what else happends, the ultimate economic responsibility devolves on the woman.

The intermittent nature of women's work, their partial and selective absorption in industry and other sectors has led to the theory that women are a "reserve army of labour". The model does not quite fit developing economies with mass unemployment. There is also the fact that there are occupations which men refuse to do even if unemployed because they are lowly or perceived as *women's job*. There is also the fact that women are preferred when the taking of a permanent labour force is risky for the employer, when his product faces uncertain market fluctuations in demand.

Women's loyalty to their household and their inferior political status prevents their unionisation and this is used for offering them inferior working conditions.

The connection between women's housework or generally reproductive work and the economy is as yet little understood. It provides several functions to the economy. It is not merely their unpaid characteristic that gives women lower status but that it is an obligatory work. Women's status it was felt would improve by drawing them into the labour force. Even in socialist countries, while they have drawn women into production and wage work, housework and child care continues to demand a sizeable part of women's time and energy. The sexual division of labour persists, preventing women's fuller participation in all social political activities and even within the economic sphere. This denies them equality in position and power.

We do not have an integrated theory of women and the economy but what we have seen in the way their cultural definitions and patriarchal ideology induce a different set of parameters for them and prevent equality. Development processes appear to accentuate this inequality by drawing more men in, by eliminating previously available opportunities for women and by not giving equal opportunity to women to enter the modern sector. Class differences mute this process for whatever opportunities are available become available to better classes.

There is a theory that women's labour force participation is a U-shaped curve. In the initial stage of subsistence production, women participate to a great extent in production ; as development gets initiated, craft and other traditional lines of occupation decline leading to a big fall in women's participation. As development reaches a higher stage, women's participaion picks up because of the expansion of the tertiary sector. This model fits the developed countries but may not fit the newly developing countries that are embarking on models of development that are not employment generative. Secondly, even within the advanced economies, while women's overall employment may be high, they face all the problems that are specific to them : lower wages, occupational segregation, part time work, insecure employment etc.

These issues need greater attention, study and research to yield a satisfactory theoretical model. It is to the credit of feminist research that these have come to the fore.

SECTION 10

EMPLOYMENT POLICIES AND PROGRAMMES

Legal Safeguards

The legal provisions that specifically apply to women workers are : (a) the abolition of night work except in some occupations such as nursing, telephone operators etc. ; (b) provisions that prohibit work involving lifting of heavy weighs ; (c) prohibiting underground work for women in the mines ; (d) Maternity Benefit Act; (e) provisions for creches and (f) Equal Remuneration Act. These are discussed in the section, *Women and the Law.*

Legal safeguards for women workers have not been a uniform blessing. They have been used by employers as an argument against the employment of women despite statistics that show that the costs to the employers of maternity benefit is less than 1 per cent of total expenses. Hardly 1.5 per cent of women employees claim the benefit. This study by the labour bureau of the claims made under the Act and claims fulfilled show the low use of the Act, but nevertheless, women workers are seen as a *burden*. Secondly, enforcement of legal provisions has been very ineffective. These provision do not apply to the unorganised sector and so most of the women workers are not covered by any legislative safeguards.

Other Employment Policies and Programmes

Several committees have made recommendations regarding the employment of women. The Committee on the Status of Women had made far reaching recommendations.[94] It had suggested : (1) reduction in the period of service for qualifying for maternity benefits ; (2) reduction in the limit of women workers in establishments from 50 to 20 for provision of creches ; (3) extension of time beyond 7 p.m. for women ; (4) development of training and employment programmes ; (5) creation of part-time employment ; (6) employment information ; (7) provision for re-entry ; (8) better enforcement of law and (9) unionisation of agricultural workers and other sectors presently not covered.

An interministerial committee went into these provisions and accepted some of these, while rejecting the first two. A National Plan of Action[95] was formulated by the Government of India which identified the problem areas as :

(i) limited overall opportunities for wage employment ;
(ii) attitudinal barriers to women's employment ;
(iii) employer prejudices ;
(iv) inadequate training ;
(v) lack of information and guidance ;
(vi) inability to combine housework and child care responsibilities with wage work in the absence of support services.

Action plans were proposed to take care of these and also the promotion of self-employment for women as well as greater opportunites in other areas. Special training programmes were also considered. Very little concrete action has been taken and support services are nowhere available.[96]

A working group set up on Employment of Women for the Sixth Plan basically advocated : (a) diversification and expansion of education and training opportunities for women ; (b) human-power budgetting of the female labour force in all comprehensive area development plans and designing appropriate programmes to offer a variety of training and work opportunites to women ; (c) promotion of self-employment and small industry employment among women by ensuring a reasonable share of credit and other inputs for them and (d) a higher rate of investment in *women-concentrated* industries and occupations.

The Working Group categorically stated : "Without a deliberate policy and a specialised agency to identify, promote and assist individual women and women's groups to develop necessary information and skills to undertake income-generating activities and to actively promote their support by the major supporting agencies; mere directives to the existing promotional agencies will not help." The Plan also realised that unless there is a speical plan for women with specific earmarked funds in sectoral plans, women will not benefit. The Working Group also recommended a compact Directorate for Women's Development in each State.

Another Working Group on Personnel Policies for bringing in greater involvement of women in science and technology, set up by the government also recommended a series of measures along similar lines.

These recommendations are laudable. The impact of these programmes is at present not visible. The economy in general is facing a crisis of inadequate growth and recent policies to stimulate growth do not promise greater employment. In the event of such growing mass unemployment, it is not clear how these well intentioned programmes are going to work. A net gain, however, due to research and lobbying by women is that women's economic roles are at least moving to centre stage for the attention of society.

APPENDIX

Sex-wise Distribution of Work

	Male/Female Participation in percentage	
Nature of Work	*When hired*	*When self-employed*
1	2	3
1. Ploughing	100 M	100 M
2. Hoeing	100 M	100 M
3. Sweeping up dry leaves etc. carrying and burning it in the fields as pre-monsoon soil treatment	SN	SN
4. Filling baskets with kitchen ash or cowdung for manuring	60—70M, 30F	SN
5. Carrying the manure basket-loads to the fields	100 F	SN
6. Carrying baskets of seeds to fields	100M—80F	SN
7. Sowing the paddy seed by broadcasting	100 M	100 M
8. Cutting out green leaf for manure :		
(a) If from house compounds and easily accessible bushed	30M—70F	SN
(b) If cut from slopes and ridges less easily accessible or from trees	100 M	100 M
(c) Collecting leaves cut down, bundling and carrying head-loads to the field	30M—70F	SN

(*Contd.*)

APPENDIX—*Contd.*

1	2	3
9. Spreading the green leaf by broadcasting it in the fields (swinging and throwing twigs of it far out)	90M—10F	90M—10F
10. Submerging the leaf manure by tramping over in muddy rice-transplanting bed of the field	90M—10F	90M—10F
11. Covering the narrow boundary ridges (about 2-4 feet broad) with sticky soil to stand the monsoon flooding	100 M	100 M
12. Levelling the ploughed slushy field with draft animals	100 M	100 M
13. Transplanting :		
(a) Picking the paddy seedings and banding them	10M—90F	20M—80F
(b) Carry bundled seedling to the transplant	20M—80F	30M—70F
(c) Planting the seedlings	10M—90F	30M—70F
14. Weeding	100 F	100 F
15. Harvesting :		
(a) Building the harvested stalk	30M—70F	SN
(b) Carrying it to threshing yard	SN	SN
(c) Threshing	20M—80F	40M—60F
16. Cowdung washing and preparing Threshing yard	100 M	100 F
17 Winnowing :		
(a) Standing over four feet high level and dropping grain	90M—10F	70M—30F

(Contd.)

APPENDIX—*Contd.*

1	2	3
(b) Fanning against the dropping grains to waft out chaff	10M—90F	30M—70F
18. Preparing huge haystacks shaped conically to resist wind and rain :		
(a) Building it up to a height of 20 to 30 feet	100 M	100 M
(b) Lifting up bunches of hay using a supply-lead pole	30M—70F	30M—70F
19. Beating the hay to get remains of paddy sticking to it	10M—90F	SN
20. Measuring out paddy :		
(a) Filling the volumetric measure with paddy	20 M—80 F	SN
(b) Lifting it an dropping out counting loudly	100 M	100 M
(c) Carrying measured paddy and stocking it in cabins	SN	SN
21. Lift irrigation :		
(a) Lifting water in large wooden buckets	100 M	30 M—70 F
(b) Helping in it by pulling a rope to the lever device	10 M—90 F&C	SN&C
22. Boiling the paddy and drying it in the sun for parboiled rice	10 M—90 F&C	SN&C
23. Husking paddy and making rice (split size, granule size)	100 F	100 F

(Contd.)

APPENDIX—*Contd.*

1	2	3
24. Night watching or ripe fields of cron or harvested stalks in the field at night, care taking of water courses	100 F	100 M
Horticultural and allied work :		
25. Fencing :		
(a) Cutting bamboo thorns by climbing up bamboos	100 M	100 M
(b) Collecting thorns, bundling and carrying	20 M—80 F	SN
26. Preparing firewood :		
(a) Cutting huge logs and splitting	100 M	100 M
(b) Hewing pieces into handy sizes for storage	70M—30F	SN
27. Tree climbing, plucking, fruits such as coconut, arecanut, jack fruit, or climbing tree for any purpose	100 M	100 M
28. Husking of coconuts for sale except when in small number of less than 20-30	100 M	100 M
29. Cleaning homestead yards and coating cowdung lotion for drying and processing of any cropyield (grains, straw)	100 F	100 F & C
30. Watering the vegetation with shoulder loaded earthen containers	100M—90F	SN & C
31. Cutting grass for fodder from the hill slope areas	10M—90 F & C	10M—90 F & C

(Contd.)

APPENDIX—*Contd.*

1	2	3
32. General caretaking of draft animals	100 M	100 M
33. Cattle grazing and guarding crops against stray cattle menace	100 F & C	100 F & C
34. Cleaning cattle sheds daily and dumping the dung in storage pits	100 F	100 F & C

Note : M : Males; F : females; C : children male or female of 8 to 15 years; SN denotes sex-neutrality which means that a male or a female can be employed.

Notes and References

1. Evelyn Reed, *Women's Evolution,* Pathfinder Press, New York, 1976.
2. Padmini Sengupta, *Women in India*, Ministry of Information, Government of India, New Delhi, 1964.
3. D.R. Gadgil, *The Industrial Evolution of India in Recent Times*, Oxford University Press, Bombay, 1954.
4. Various economic historians such as Bipin Chandra, R.C. Dutt, A.K. Bagchi, have amply demonstrated this.
5. Quoted in Anupam Sen, *The State, Industrialisation and Class Formation in India*, Routledge and Kegan Paul, London, 1982.
6. Quoted in S.N. Sen, *History of Modern India*, 1765—1950, Wiley Eastern Ltd., New Delhi, 1979.
7. S.N. Sen, Ibid.
8. K. Saradamoni, "Changing Land Relations and Women : A Case Study of Palghat District in Kerala", in *Women and Rural Transformation*, ed. Vina Mazumdar, Concept Pub., New Delhi, 1983.
9. Anupam Sen, op. cit.
10. Anupan Sen, op. cit.
11. George Birdwood, The Industrial Arts of India, *Idarah I Adabiyat*, Delhi, 1974.
12. H.J.R. Twiff, *A Monograph on the Art and practice of Carpet Making in the Bombay Presidency*, Government Central Press, 1907.
13. Francis Buchanan, *A Journey From Madras Through The Countries of Mysore, Canara and Malabar*, London, 1807; *An Account of the District of Bihar and Patna, 1811-1812*, Patna, 1922.
14. Tapan Raychaudri, "Historical Roots of Mass Poverty in India," *Economic and Political Weekly*, Vol. 20, No. 18, May 1985.

15. B.C. Allen, *Monograph on the Silk Cloth of Assam*, Assam Secretariat, 1899, Navrang, New Delhi, 1974.
16. Basil Hall, *Travels in India, Ceylon, Borneo*, George Routledge and Sons, London, 1931.
17. T.N. Mukherji, *Art Manufacturers of India*, Navrang, Delhi, 1974.
18. Atchi Reddy, "Female Agricultural Labourers of Nellore, 1881-1981. *The Indian Economic and Social History Review*, Vol. 20, No. 1, 1983.
19. Reddy, ibid.
20. Mukul Mukherji, "Impact of Modernisation in Women's Occupation—A Case Study of the Rice Husking Industry of Bengal," *The Indian Economic and Social History Review*, Vol. 20, No. 1, 1983.
21. Nirmala Bannerjee, "The Bengal Experience", Seminar Paper, Technical Seminar On Women's Work and Employment, ISST, New Delhi, April 1982.
22. M.M. Joshi, *Urban Handicrafts of Bombay, Deccan*, Gokhale Institute of Politics and Economics, Pune, 1936.
23. Alice Thorner, "The Secular Trend in the Indian Economy, 1881-1951," *The Economic Weekly*, Special Number, Vol. 11, Nos. 28, 29, 30, July 1962.
24. J. Ambannavar, "Changes in Economic Activity of Males and Females in India," *Demography India*, No. 42, 1975.
25. M.D. Morris, "The Emergence of the Industrial Labour Force in India—A Study of the Cotton Mills", Oxford University Press, Bombay, 1965.
26. J.N. Sinha, "The Indian Working Force—Its Growth, Change and Composition," *Census of India*, 1961, Vol. 1, *Monograph* II, Government of India, New Delhi, 1972.
27. Ashok Mitra, *The Status of Women, Literacy and Employment*, ICSSR, Allied Pub., Delhi, 1979.
28. Sarathy Acharya, *Transfer of Technology and Women Employment in India*, ICSSR (unpub. mimeo.), 1979.
29. Ashok Mitra, op. cit. (see footnote 27).
30. Sudhin Mukhopadhyay and Bhanushika Ghosh, "Sources of Variation in Female Labour Force Participation—A Decomposition," Technical Seminar on Women's Work and Employment, ISSI, Delhi, 1982.
31. Devaki Jain and Nirmala Bannerjee (ed.), *Women and Poverty—The Tyranny of the Household*, Vikas, New Delhi, 1985.
32. *Women's Activities in Rural India*, A Study Based on NSS 32nd Round, Department of Statistics, Government of India, June 1981.
33. Leela Gulati, "Interstate Differences in Female Labour Force Participation", *Economic and Political Weekly*, Vol. 10, Nos. 1-2, 11 Jan., 1975.
34. K.C. Seal, "Women in the Labour Force—A Statistical Profile", in *Women in the Labour Force*, Asian Regional Employment and Training Programmes, ILO Geneva, 1981.
35. J.N. Sinha, *Employment of Women in Mines and Plantations*, Labour Bureau, Ministry of Labour, Government of India, Simla, 1978.
36. Vanmala, "Employment of Women in Andhra Pradesh, Public Enterprises" in K. Murli Manohar ed., *Women's Status and Development in India*, Society for Women's Studies and Development, Warangal, 1984.
37. *Women in India—A Statistical Profile*, Ministry of Social Welfare, Government of India, New Delhi, 1978.

38. Directorate General of Employment and Training, *Employment Review*, 1985.
39. C.V. Kala, "Female Participation in Farm Work in Central Kerala", *Sociological Bulletin*, Vol. 25, No. 2, Sept. 1976.
40. Devaki Jain and Malini Chand, "Report on Time Allocation Study, Its Methodological Implications", *ISST*, New Delhi, 1982.
41. Gita Sen, "Inter Regional Aspects of the Incidence of Women Agricultural Labourers", in Devaki Jain, Nirmala Bannerjee ed., *Women and Poverty*, op. cit.
42. Bina Agarwal, "Women, Poverty and Agricultural Growth," *Journal of Peasant Studies*, Vol. 13, No. 4, July 1985.
43. Srilata Batliwala, "The Energy, Health and Nutrition Syndrome", in *Women and Poverty*, ed. Devaki Jain, Nirmal Bannerjee, op. cit.
44. A.K. Chakravarty et al., *Health Status of Rural Population, Singur* as quoted by Bina Agarwal, op. cit. (see 46).
45. Pravin Visaria and Leela Visaria, "Indian Households with Female Heads, Their Incidence, Characteristics and Levels of Living", in *Women and Poverty*, op. cit.
46. G. Parthasarathy, Rural Poverty and Female Heads of Households, Need for Quantitative Analysis, Paper, Technical Seminar on "Women, Work and Employment", ISST, New Delhi, 1982.
47. Rama Joshi, *Status of Women Agricultural Workers*, ICSSR, 1973 (unpub., mimeo).
48. K. Saradamoni and Joan Mencher, "Muddy Feet, Dirty Hands—Rice Production and Female Agricultural Labour", *Economic and Political Weekly*, Review of Agriculture, Vol. 17, No. 52, Dec. 25, 1982.
49. Raj Mohini Sethi, *A Study of Agricultural Labour in Punjab*, Dept. of Sociology, Chandigarh, unpub. 1981.
50. Leela Gualti, *Profiles in Female Poverty*, Hindustan Publ., New Delhi, 1982.
51. Vina Majumdar, *Role of Rural Women in Development*, Allied Pub., New Delhi, 1978.
52. Malavika Karlekar, *Poverty and Women's Work*, A Study of Sweeper Women in Delhi, Vikas, New Delhi, 1982.
53. Bidi Workers of Nipani (author not mentioned), *Economic and Political Weekly*, July 22, 1978.
54. A.N. Buch and Ela R. Bhatt, *Firewood Pickers of Girnar*, S.E.W.A., Ahmedabad, 1978, also see N. Nagbrahman and Srikant Sambrani, "Women's Drudgery in Firewood Collection", *Economic and Political Weekly*, Volume 18, Nos. 1-2, Jan, 1-8, 1983.
55. Zarina Bhatty, *Economic Role and Status of Women*—A Case Study of Women in the Beedi Industry in Allahabad, World Employment Programme, ILO, Working Paper, 1980.
56. Sulabha Brahme, *Economic Plight of Hamal Women in Pune*, ICSSR, 1978 (unpub. mimeo).
57. Ibid.
58. Amarja Pawar, *The Pune Domestic Servant's Revolt*, ISRE, Bombay, 1982 (mimeo).
59. K. Aravindakahan Nail, *Women Workers in Cashew Industry*, ICSSR, 1978 (mimeo).

60. Molly Mathew, *Women in the Unorganised Sector, Coir Industry*, ICSSR (undated) mimeo. Also "Lace Makers of Narasapur" by Maria Mier, ILO, Zed Press, London, 1982.
61. Nirmala Bannerjee, *Women in the Unorganised Sector*—The Calcutta Experience, Hyderabad, Orient Longman, 1982.
62. R.N. Kaul, H.S. Kalhat and M. Shyam, "Potato Digger Elevators—Performance Studies", Punjab Agricultural University, as quoted in Bina Agarwal, op. cit. (see footnote 50).
63. M. Johnson Samuel and S. Erappa, *Women Workers in Silk Reeling Industry*, Seminar Paper, Indian Historical Association, Madurai, 1983.
64. S. Usha, *Male, Female Wage Differentials in an Urban Labour Market* : A Case Study of Madras Metropolitan Area, Unpub. Ph. D. thesis, Univ. of Madras, 1981.
65. Neera Desai, *Review of Research on Middle Class Employed Women*, Paper, ISI, Seminar, "Women, Work and Society", Delhi, 1982.
66. National Sample Survey, 38th Round, 1983, Report 315, Key Results, Dept. of Statistics, New Delhi, July 1985.
67. This is illustrated both historically and the continuing displacement in recent times. For eg. B.B. Patel, "Technology, Employment and Occupation of Women Workers in Gujarat", MIDS, Seminar on Women, Technology and Forms of Production, Madras, Oct. 1984.
68. A Study of Utilisation and Wastage of Training Programme of National and Regional Vocational Training Institutes for Women, ISST, Delhi, 1985.
69. Census of India, 1971, Technical Personnel and Degree Holders, Vol. 7, G. Series.
70. Indira Hirway, *Women and Technology*—A Study of KVIC Gujarat, Seminar Paper MIDS, Oct. 1984 (op. cit. footnote 71).
71. Maithreyi Krishna Raj and Madhavi Mehta, Unemployed Postgraduate Degree Holders in Science in Bombay, Research Centre for Women's Studies and Council of Scientific and Industrial Research, 1982.
72. Karuna Ambarasan, Factors Influencing the Role and Status of Fisherwomen—A Study of Three Villages in Chengleput District, Tamil Nadu, MIDS Seminar, op. cit., 1984.
73. Leela Gulati, *Fisherwomen on the Kerala Coast*, ILO, Geneva, 1984. Also Kalpana Ram, "Coastal Fisherwomen of Kanyakumari, Tamil Nadu", Paper, Second National Conference of Women's Studies, Trivandrum, 1984.
74. Sudha Mokashi, *Maharashtra Rajyatil Sagarl Masevari Vyavasache Swarup va Jadan-Dachan*, SNDT University, unpub. Ph D. thesis, 1982 (in Marathi language).
75. Devaki Jain, *Displacement of Women Workers in Traditional Industries*, ISST, 1984.
76. L.C. Jain, "End of Handloom Industry", *Economic and Political Weekly*, Vol. 20, No. 27, July 6, 1985.
77. Bina Agarwal, *Agricultural Modernisation and Third World Women* : Pointers from Literature and Empirical Analysis, WEP/ILO, Geneva, 1981. Also : Ruchira Chatterji, *Marginalisation and the Induction of Women in Wage Labour*, The Case of Indian Agriculture, World Employment Programme, ILO Geneva, 1984.

78. Gita Sen, *Women and Agrarian Change in India*, pre-publication, mineo, 1985.
79. Elizabeth Keily, "Appropriate Technology for Women", *Development Forum*, June 1976, A series of studies were gone on export industries.
80. U. Kalpagam, *Women Workers in the Readymade Garment Industry*, MIDS, Madras, 1981 (mimeo). M. Krishna Raj, *Socio Economic Condition of Women Workers in the Garment Industry in Greater Bombay*, ICSSR, 1983 (mimeo). Rukmini Rao and Shaniba Hussain : *Invisible Hands—Women Working in the Garment Industry*, ICSSR, New Delhi, 1983 (mimeo). Nirmala Bannerjee, *The Role of Women Workers in Export Industries*, ICSSR—Indo-Dutch Project, 1983 (mimeo).
81. Neera Desai and Prema Gopalan, *Changes in the Food Processing Industry From Traditional to Modern Forms and its Impact on Women's Role and Status*, ICSSR, Indo-Dutch Project, 1983 (mimeo). (A similar study was done by Surinder Jetley under the same programme for Haryana).
82. R.N. Sharma and Chandan Sengupta, *Women's Employment at SEEPZ*, Unit for Urban Studies, Tata Institute of Social Sciences, 1984 (mimeo).
83. Sushila K. Trikla, *Women Workers in Kandla Free Trade Zone*—Report for Indian Council for Research in International Economic Relations, New Delhi, 1985.
84. J.N. Sinha, *The Indian Working Force*—Its Growth and Changing Composition, op. cit., Chpater I, Conceptual Clarifications.
85. Ibid.
86. Report of the Committee of Experts on Unemployment, New Delhi, 1981.
87. J.N. Sinha, 1981, "Economic Census Data—A Note", *Economic and Political Weekly*, Vol. 17, Feb. 6, 1985.
88. Bina Agarwal, "Work Participation of Rural Women in Third World : Some Data and Conceptual Bases", *Economic and Political Weekly*, Vol. XX, Nos. 51 and 52, 1985.
89. Ibid.
90. Devaki Jain and Malini Chand, *Importance of Age and Sex≤*—Specific Data Collection in Household Surveys, ESCAP, Bangkok, Sept. 1980 (mimeo).
91. Devaki Jain and Malini Chand, *Domestic Work, Its Implications for Enumeration of Workers*, ISST, New Delhi, 1982 (mimeo).
92. Devaki Jain and Malini Chand, A Report on Time Allocation Studies, op. cit.
93. Elise Boulding et al., *Hand book on International Data on Women*, Sage Halstead, New York, 1976.
94. Report of the Committtee on the Status of Women, "Towards Equality", Ministry of Education, Government of India, 1974.
95. National Plan of Action, Government of India, 1975, Sixth Five Year Plan, 1978-83 First Draft.
96. There have been a few studies evaluating Women's projects. Two of these are :

    Kumini Dandekar, *Employment Guarantee Scheme—An Employment Opportunity for Women*, Gokhale Institute of Politics and Economics, Orient Longman Ltd., New Delhi, 1983, and Devaki Jain, *Women's Quest for Power*, Vikas Pub., New Delhi, 1980.

3

Education

The development of women's education is integrally linked with the perception of roles within the Indian society. As we shall see, views have changed little and an exogenous factor such as education has had minimal impact on the liberation of women from age-old prejudices and beliefs. The formal system of schooling based on evaluation, agewise distribution into classes, and certification, often at a location spatially removed from the homes of pupils, came with colonial rule. Prior to the establishment of such institutions, children learnt basic literacy skills, familiarity with the scriptures and so on at *tols*, *pathshalas* and *madarsas*. Even after the introduction of formal schools, indigenous modes of transmitting knowledge as well as zenana or home education for girls continued.[1]

Taking into account what were deemed to be the particular needs of women, the British supported *zenana* system: the colonial rulers were primarily interested in formal education of men and not of women in India. While in part, this approach was in keeping with the overall attitude that women, whether of Indian or British middle classes, should be trained not for careers, but to be good wives and competent mothers, it also reflected a general indifference to prevailing social relationships and role expectations of the subjected people. The education of girls and of women was regarded as the legitimate responsibility of Indians : it neither suited nor interested the rulers to take much initiative in this area. However, as will be clear from the next section, various reports on education noted, in often meticulous detail, the state of female education in India.

Socio Historical Perspective

In 1891-1892, over three lakh girls were enrolled in primary and secondary schools; yet only two per cent of them were being educated at the secondary level[2] : as girls reached puberty, they were rapidly withdrawn from the formal educational sphere, which meant among other things, exposure to the external world. The privacy of the *zenana* system was mooted to be eminently suited for those whose primary aim in life was to be that of home-maker. The *Review of Education* of 1886 pointed out that Indians "at large encourage or tolerate the education of their girls only up to an age and in standards at which it can do little good or according to the point of view, little harm".[3] The notion that education can be harmful for girls is widely relevant even today. While recent figures show that 75 per cent of girls in the relevant age group are enrolled in the country's 5 lakh primary schools,[4] and school enrolment of girls over the last hundred years has indeed increased substantially, such figures only tell a part of the story.

Clearly then, the education of girls was, and continues to be, influenced by a range of factors which are considerably different from those affect boys' education. When, by the middle of the nineteenth century, the newly emergent middle class got interested in the education of girls, they did so for a variety of reasons. With the establishment of the Bethune School in Calcutta in 1849, Indian initiative in the sphere of women's education was formalised. In the years following not only were a number of schools started, particularly in the three Presidencies, but also the *zenana* system of education flourished. While educated men often taught women in their family, *zenana* education or group teaching within a suitable home was soon recognised as a feasible alternative to education in a school. By the end of the century, the Government of India started funding tutors for these rapidly expanding home-oriented schemes of education. In 1882, the Education

Commission stressed the importance of *zenana* education in a culture where women's seclusion was still prevalent. In the Bengal Presidency, by 1907 the number of girls being instructed through this system had gone up to 1431 recorded cases, as against 1200 at the end of the earlier quinquennium.[5] Apart from the advantages of limiting women's exposure to external influences, this method allowed for learning over a number of years which could often be continued—or even started—after marriage.

The historical roots of prejudice against women's education, and later, against its expansion in non-traditional areas, lay in a basic conviction that there was something special about women's nature which would be destroyed by excessive education. Access to various scientific theories from the West served to reinforce the belief in women's uniqueness, if not their inferiority.[6] The rudiments of reading, writing and a little arithmetic, hygiene, needlework, embroidery and the vernacular language as well as English were regarded as being more than adequate for girls. There were not only debates on the kind of syllabi and textbooks to which girls should have access, but also little unanimity about the amount of education to be given to them. While a number of the more radical social reformers argued for granting of education of girls, because they as much as boys needed to develop their total personalities, there was another forum which demanded educated daughters. Western education had created a new breed of young men who expected something more from their prospective brides.[7] As an article in a popular Bengali women's journal pointed out, "Soon it will be difficult to get bridegrooms for girls of upper and middle class Hindu families unless these girls are given some education." Not only were college-educated boys looking for girls who were more than literate, but it was also considered: "A marriage between an educated man and an illiterate girl cannot be a happy one; discord and disagreement will naturally be the result of such a marriage."[8]

In other words, there were certain tangible benefits to be had from giving girls some basic learning, skilfully interwoven with fables, stories or even moral education which taught the value of obedience, patience, chastity and of course, the joys of motherhood. By and large, the aim of education was to create not only competent wives and mothers but also intelligent companions for Indian men who had received western education. Its liberational role emphasised by the radicals was clearly to be subordinate to the wider social goal which stressed willing acquiescence and not a questioning and enquiring mind. Even when girls from a few families ventured into higher education, they were trained to be teachers, nurses and perhaps doctors: in a *purdah* society there was a growing demand for female doctors to attend to women. Science, engineering, and other male-dominated areas were regarded as being too taxing as well as time-consuming for girls whose chief goal was to be successful wives.

When the national movement gained momentum by the second decade of the present century, women supported menfolk in their endeavours and occasionally joined pickets and marches. It was Mohandas Karamchand Gandhi who legitimised the active participation of women. What is of particular interest is that he did so by stressing his belief in their innate non-violent and self-sacrificing nature; he felt that this characteristic made them suitable proponents for the philosophy of *satyagraha*. The success of Gandhi's appeal lay in the fact that he was reaffirming and not contradicting existing sexual stereotypes. In a fast-changing environment charged with the heady appeal of self-rule, families supported the participation of their womenfolk in non-violent protest; they boycotted foreign goods and surrendered jewellery for the motherland. Sacrifice at home was matched by sacrifice in the wider political arena.[9]

Whether it is the position of early reformers, views of leaders of the national movement or policy statements of the post-Independence period, there is an unmistakable commitment to the development of the nutrient, beneficient aspect of a woman's nature. She is to be the embodiment of Sita, the pure and chaste wife of the Hindu God Rama who paid dearly for her act of disobedience in crossing the Lakshman rekha or line of protection. But a woman is also *shakti*, or the female power who destroyed *mahisasura*, the powerful buffalo-demon, when all other male gods had failed. This duality of the female principle has instilled in the minds of policy markers as well as householders the importance of developing the *right* kind of education for girls.[10] Consequently, educational goals for girls are substantially different from those for boys. As we shall see, strategies to attract girls and women to learning are to be accordingly designed. For their survival and unity, families stress the benevolent and unifying apsects of feminlity. By and large, irrespective of whether the formal structure of the family is joint or nuclear, the ideological basis is that of a joint family with a strict hierarchy of authority and patterns of subjugation of women, particularly of those in the reproductive age. Among the middle-class, higher education of a certain kind as well as jobs in any technological area are often regarded as potentially disruptive—if not destructive—of family harmony, the linchpin of which is the supportive woman. Male kin fear that their control over women's lives may be marginalised with too much education or education of the wrong kind. Further, in the latter half of the twentieth century, the new educational and work ethos stressing competition and success may well come into conflict with the demands of the family network.

It is precisely over an interpretation of roles then that a conflict arises between the ideals of womanhood and the ideals of education. The purported aims of education which are the creation of a certain measure of independence of thought, a spirit of enquiry and of objectivity could well threaten the well-maintained differences between the sexes. As we have seen, a workable via media between the two sets of ideals was eatablished in British India with the idea of separate curricula and subjects for boys and for girls. A brief look at the relevant sections of post-Independence Commissions and Committees on education will show that this ideology of differentness is carefully preserved.

Shortly after Independence, the University Education Commission headed by Dr. S. Radhakrishnan was set up. In its chapter on women's education, the all-male membership appeared to have advanced little over the views of enlightened Indians of a few decades ago. They were firmly committed to the belief that *a well-ordered home helps to make well-ordered men*. The mother who is *enquiring and alert* and familiar with subjects such as history and literature will be *the best teacher in the world of both character and intelligence*. Yet it was clearly prudent to argue that as women have "demonstrated their ability to think and work alongside of men", much of education could be in common. Nonetheless, due to differences between the sexes, *the greatest profession of women is and probably will continue to be that of home-maker.*[11]

Between 1950-1951 and 1960-1961, for every hundred boys enrolled in primary school, the number of girls rose only from 39 to 44; for general education at the college and university levels, the relevant figures improved from 16 to a mere 27.12 Clearly, the policy towards women's education had to be looked at from various angles. Accordingly, the National Committee on Women's Education which was set up in 1958 under Mrs. Durgabai Deshmukh was to enquire into low enrollments, reasons for wastage, as well as examine the scope for vocationalisation. The Committee prefaced its analysis and recommendations with the two existing views on women; the dominant opinion was that a woman did not have much of a role to play outside the home and even if she did, this was *definitely secondary and subject to the demands and exigencies of her role within the home.* The other view of course was that a woman should *have open to her all avenues to life which are open to men.* Nonetheless, the Committee hastened to add that education was in no way to prove a threat to family life; equally, if women were to perform a multiplicity of roles, it was essential that *our men should also come forward to join the women in work within the home.*[13]

Quoting various agencies concerned with the implementation of education, the Committee felt to *a greater or lesser degree that some of the subjects taught to boys are not related to the aptitudes, interests and needs of girls.* There was a need therefore, for the introduction of more courses in the fine arts, nursing, home science, dietics and so on.[14] That views on the differentiation of curricula were reflected in enrolment figures is clear from the fact that in 1955-1956, while the number of girls in vocational courses in schools numbered 31 to a hundred boys, at the college level, only 7 girls to the same number of boys were studying for a professional degree.[15] In an attempt to investigate the basis of such streaming, a Committee was appointed by the National Council for Women's Education on the Differentiation of Curricula for boys and girls headed by Mrs. Hansa Mehta in 1962. In its report, the Committee stated quite unequivocally that while girls did have responsibilities at home, these could not be made the criteria for dividing subjects on the basis of *sex and to regard some of them as 'masculine' and other as 'feminine'*. It further added that such stereotypes did more harm than good, and forcefully pointed out that *the so-called psychological differences between the two sexes arise not out of sex but out of social conditioning.* Thus the blame for discrimination in access was laid squarely on the home and wider society. Recognising that social transformation could not be achieved overnight, the Committee agreed that *for some time to come* certain psychological differences as well as those in roles and responsibilities would *have to be accepted as matters of fact*. The long-term aim, however, should be to fight against such prejudices.[16]

Two years later, the Kothari Commission spoke of the need for equalisation of educational opportunities; yet there continued to be an unstated ambivalence towards the role of education in the lives of girls : while their schooling was to be expanded, it was not clear whether this was for the individual benefit of the recipients themselves, or because they were to be responsible for *full development of our human resources, the inprovement of homes* and so on. At the same time, the Commission accepted women's right to work outside the home, adding that there was no case for a differentiation of curricula. In other words, the modern Indian woman had to be equipped to carry the dual burden of rearing the right type of citizens as well as for bringing home a pay-packet. Education had no role to play in disturbing the sexual division of labour within the home, based on the convenient argument that women are better at certain tasks than men.[17]

In 1974, the Report of the all-women committee on the Status of Women in India felt that it was high time that a realistic evaluation of attitudes towards women and their education was made: reiterating the Hansa Mehta Committee's position, the CSWI felt : "Inequality of the sexes is built in the minds of men and women through a socialisation process which continues to be extremely powerful." Rather than acting as agents of equality, schools which *reflect and strengthen the traditional prejudices* through curricular differentiation and the *classification of subjects on the basis of sex and the unwritten code enforced on their pupils* are in fact agents of the existing social system based on gender and class inequalities. Not only did the Committee support the common curriculum upto the Class X stage but felt that at the senior secondary level, girls should have free access to vocational and professional courses in keeping with local needs. University education needed to be made more relevant for all, while at the primary school level both boys as well as girls should be taught music, simple craft and needlework.[18]

In its latest document on the state of education in the country, the Ministry of Education has given a fairly candid appraisal of the existing situation. However, as is the case with most government documents, it softpedals the issue of solutions and the problems inherent in making the system work. It points out that girls' enrolment is far lower than what it should be and recommends the need for *special remedial programmes for girls and children of poor and illiterate families.* There is an urgent demand for more women teachers and single sex schools as parents hesitate to send their daughters to school unless certain minimum conditions are fulfilled. The document also notes : "Though the performance of girls compares favourably with that of boys, relatively fewer girls seek admission to professional courses other than those pertaining to medicine, teacher-training and nursing." However, the document ignores some of the drawbacks in the system, and lays the blame for low enrolment rates exclusively on family bias. It states : "To a great extent this disparity is more the result of economic and occupational problems and cultural biases of society than the accessibility of educational facilities."[19] The right kind of institutional facilities which will minimise the handicaps for girls are neither available nor adequately planned for.

Whether it is the tribal girl who wants to go to school but has to help her mother with weaving and cooking, or it is the urbanite who aspires to be an Astro-Physicist but has to be content with a degree in Home Science, an overweaning concern with the correct performance of roles comes into conflict with objective educational goals. Whilst for the majority of girls the mandate of poverty makes decisions relatively easy, for those for those who are in a position to go beyond the first few years of school, social and familial notions on what a girl should be doing takeover. Equipped with arguments on a woman's essential nature, her abilities at expression rather than at abstraction, family members have little difficulty in channelising options. That such arguments are not peculiar to India alone is clear from the debate in the West on the superior verbal skills of girls and their lack of aptitude for subjects which require spatiotemporal competence. While feminists have been trying hard to prove that such scientific arguments are rarely free from biases, of relevance here is the fact that years of conditioning has led to the internalisation of stereotypes in the minds of growing girls; not only do they feel that they would be unable to cope with Science and Mathematics but also that as their primary role is excellence in the private realm of the family and not in the public sphere of employment, there is little need to participate in more challeniging subjects and courses. The following sections deal with the interaction between such value systems and the access to education at various levels.

Before going on to the next section, it is useful to take note of a basic dilemma which has confronted many involved with the expansion of education in the post-Independence period. This is the conflict between two sets of goals—that of quantative expansion of education and its selective, quantitative growth.[20] In a highly inegalitarian society based on deep cleavages founded on class, caste, religion and gender differences, the ideal of quantity or education for the masses comes into conflict with the ideal of quality or education for an elite who will put the country on the world map. This conflict relates not only to values but also to tangible decisions on the allocation of scarce resources. Irrespective of this difference in priorities, the overriding aim of most modern educational systems is to provide training for occupational betterment. In India, for the less privileged, some years in school or participation in the non-formal sector help in skill-training. Even for the upwardly mobile middle-class, the contemporary urban school in the fee paying sector, which supposedly purports to fulfil objectives such as development of the total personality, training the child for participation in higher education and providing the basic accoutrement for a better lifestyle etc., in reality fall far short of fulfilling them. For these select few, schooling with its unimaginative syllabus is really the beginning of a long process of competition, elimination and preparation for a career. But for those in the mass education sector in the poorly equipped government insitutions, there is no hope for any kind of prolonged training.

The important points to be taken into consideration here are that (a) irrespective of the level of education being considered, boys have an advantage over girls in terms of access, retention and future use of their training and (b) in the case of the small fraction of the population which can exercise the option of going in for higher education, girls are invariably concentrated in the lower status, less competitive and rapidly multiplying colleges for general education. In this, girls from the upper middle-class and middle-class share with the first generation literate son of a farmer or shopkeeper, a common destiny. There is a distinct dividing line between the high status and relatively few medical colleges, institutes of technology, management and engineering and the bulk of higher education institutions comprises the proliferating degree colleges, polytechnics and technical institutes. While by and large the former are the preserve of boys from privileged backgrounds, the latter cater to their sisters as well as to boys who are unable to succeed in highly competitive selection tests which assume a fluency and familiarity with a certain subculture as well as the English language. Thus, the dual system of higher education which separates a select, self-perpetuating elite from the majority trained in indifferent institutions is devided not only on the basis of socio-economic status but also on the basis of sex. The relevant difference here is that while boys from certain backgrounds often cannot succeed in gaining admission to elite institutions, the girls in question are not allowed to try to succeed. This point will be discussed at greater length later.

In general, the role of the educational system in the life a girl is to reinforce the values of consistency and obedience. In addition, the family creates an awareness of and preparation for her future life in her husband's home. For boys the stress is on competition and career. Theoretically, it is difficult to envisage how the same school system can have different sets of aims and consequences. This will become clearer when we look at the content of textbooks, the narrower choice of courses for girls and the low rate of women's participation in higher education. Further, where the pervasive media reaffirms existing social values on the division of labour within the family as well as in the external world, the task of changing stereotypes becomes difficult.

Access and Retention

The following graph indicates the disparities in male-female literacy rates. Further, while there were 1,055 illiterate women to a 1,000 illiterate men in 1911, the former figure went up to 1,322 women to a 1,000 illiterate men in 1981. This gender gap is due mainly to the growth in absolute numbers.

Further, there are substantial regional imbalances and differences : in Kerala, a state known for its general level of awareness, female literacy figure according to the 1981 Census is 24.8 per cent, in rural areas it is around 18 per cent, while in the towns and cities women's litracy has gone up to 47.8 per cent.[21] At this point it is necessary to understand the implications of the term literacy. In the contemporary context, it is assumed that the basic skills of reading and writing are acquired through the formal school system or throgh non-formal education. However, in order to be meaningful a minimum of four to five years of training is essential so as to ensure that recipients do not lapse back into illiteracy.

Any talk on the current national goal of universalisation of elementary education (hundred per cent enrolment upto the age of 14 years) must take into that enrolment is only a part of the picture: if, in 1990, all girls upto the age of 14 years were indeed in schools, it would no doubt be a source of great satisfaction to policy planners. However, it is of equal importance to see where these children are in 1995. Are they still in school or are they back at work in the fields or at home? For instance, in 1975-1976, 66.1 per cent of girls in the age-group of 6 to 11 years were enrolled in primary school classes, mainly in Class I. If we look at the 1980-1981 figures, namely at the time when these girls should have been going into Class VI, their enrolment figure in class VI had fallen to 29.1 per cent. In other words, before primary schooling is over, well over 50 per cent

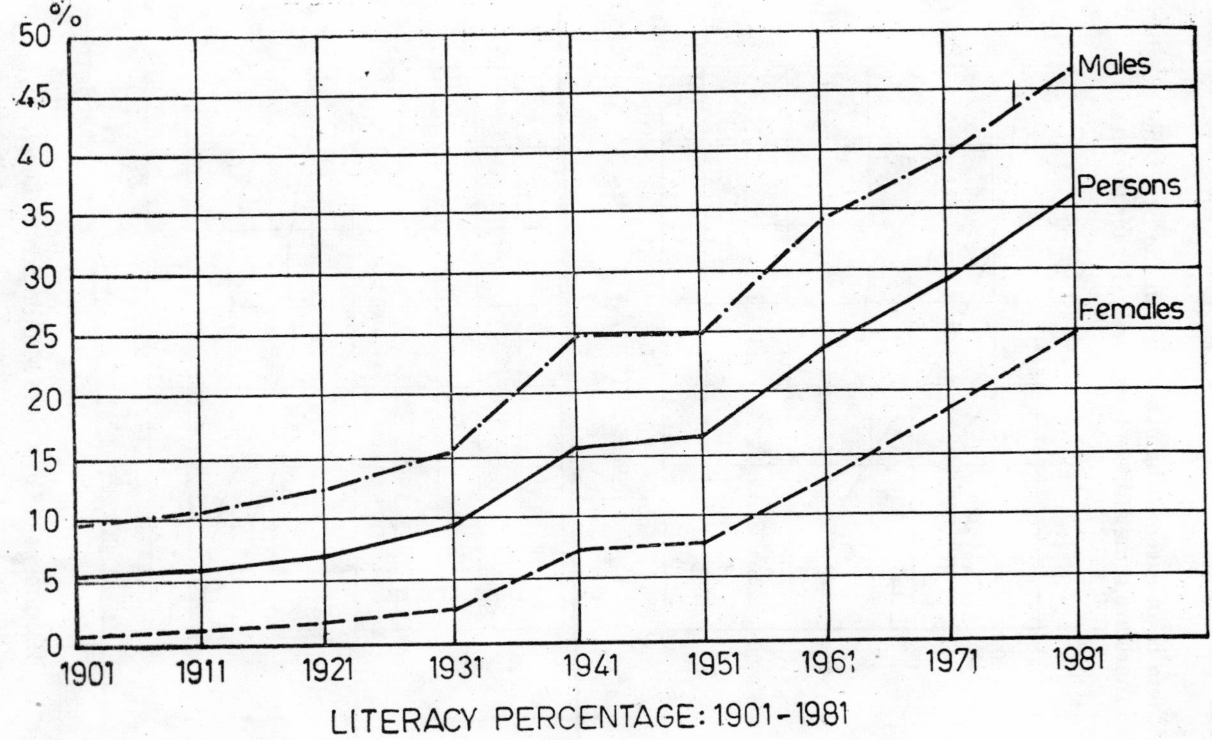

LITERACY PERCENTAGE: 1901–1981

(There is an excenrating over 100.0 in the first table because there are some students who are older for the class.)

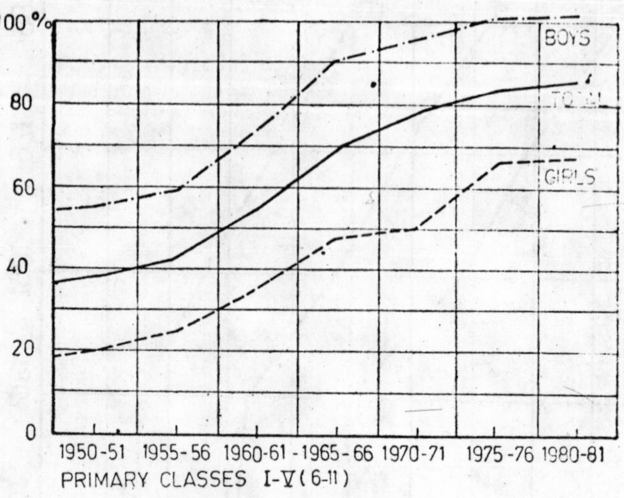

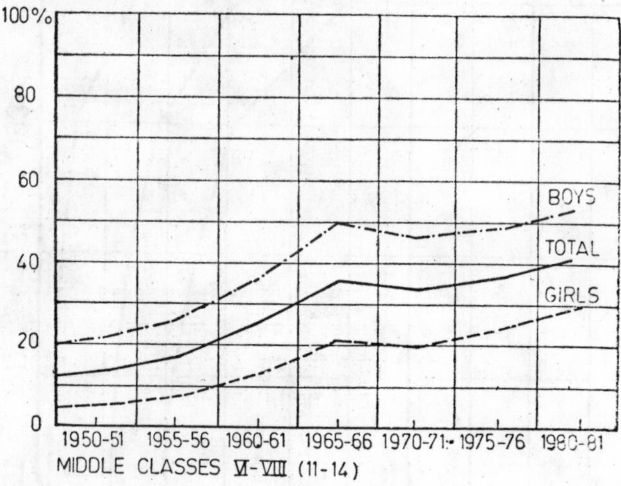

Enrolment of Girls upto Middle School Level.
Figures are a percentage of relevant age-groupwise population.

of those initially enrolled leave the system. The picture is almost as bleak for boys at this level of education. In a situation where 44 million children are a part of the labour force and every third household has a working child, it is clearly simplistic to hope for a high rate of participation in education: national strategies for development have to contend with family strategies for survival.[22]

On the whole, girls constitute only a third of total enrolments at every level of schooling and their drop-out rate is higher than that of boys. In the graph it is clear that though overall enrolments have been steadily rising with each Census recording, there remain substantial differences in male-female rates of participation.

While girls' overall school enrolment increased from 64 lakhs in 1951 to nearly 400 lakhs in 1981, this still accounted for only 12 per cent of the relevant age groups at all levels as against a figure of 20 per cent for boys. It is now more or less accepted that an obstacle impeding universalisation of elementary education is the non-participation of girls. Further, the likelihood of the rural girl being out of school is much higher than that of the urban girl. At the secondary level, while only 13 per cent of girls in the relevant age group are in school, a meagre 17 per cent of these are from the villages.[23] There are a number of reasons which keep girls away from school. Important among these are (i) the high cost of education because of earnings forgone in poor families. (ii) social factors such as early marriage and a widespread belief in female seclusion, increasing the demand for girls schools and women teachers and (iii) discriminatory processes at work within the school system itself. We shall take up each of these reasons in some detail.

I. *The High Opportunity Cost of Education*[24]

As is clear from the figures on child labour, the existence of poor families is heavily dependent on the work of children and of women. In such a situation, the returns on education—which normally means a few years of schooling—are low. Being in school means forgoing the opportunity to earn or help in the home, thereby releasing adults for productive activity. In a poverty situation, the costs in real terms are too high and schooling is seen as a poor investment which provides no definite access to better employment. Further, more girls than boys are employed at an early age and if there is a question of choices; boys are more likely to be given the option of a few years of schooling: it is hoped that it may improve employment chances.

A number of studies in urban slums have borne out that formal schooling has a marginal role in the lives of girls. A recent Delhi study among the Balmikis, a sub-caste of the North Indian Bhangis or sweepers found that as girls were expected ultimately to combine housework with marriage, schooling was of little consequence. Almost 75 per cent of mothers whose sons were being educated wanted them to complete school, while 50 per cent with daugthers admitted that their girls had not studied beyond Class III. They left school because they had got jobs, were married off, or were needed to help with the housework. As a woman commented:

> Why should I waste my time and money on sending my daughters to school where she will learn nothing of use? What does the Hindi alphabet mean to her?... Too much of schooling will only give girls big ideas and then they will be beaten up by their husbands or be abused by their in-laws.[25]

In a Bombay slum it was found that illiteracy was three times as high among the women and girls than among the men; women in migrant *bastis* in Delhi were prepared to send their daughters for a few years to primary school, but hoped that their sons would finish school. The authors noted that while "parents tended to have unrealistic educational and employment aspirations for their sons", they did not "consider education very important for their daughters". Part of the reason could be the increasingly higher minimum educational requirement for any kind of employment potential. This increases competition among boys and to that extent reduces the family's willingness to spare scarce resources for girls' education up to an extended period which alone will make it meaningful for any employment possibilities. At the same time, there was a generational improvement in enrolments, and a larger number of girls than their mothers were reported to be in school in each of the above studies. Most importantly, the ability to write letters home after a girl was married was regarded a vital function of literacy : such communication is essential in a situation of substantial female abuse.[26]

II. *Social Factors*

One important social factor affecting participation in education is early marriage. Though girls now marry at an average age of 17, pre-pubertal and child marriages are not uncommon. Increasingly, among the middle-class, an educated, if not employed daughter is an asset in a competitive marriage market; however, there are certain limitations to the nature and extent of education as well as to the kind of employment to which girls can have access. A survey sponsored by the Committee on the Status of Women in India revealed some significant attitudes to the education of girls. While a statement that girls should not be given any education at all was categorically rejected by the majority, many felt that higher education for girls was not necessary. Parents' willingness to send girls to school depended on whether certain facilities are available such as more girls' schools, more women teachers and nearness of schools to their homes, better transport and toilet facilities.[27] While the latest government document states that 95 per cent of the population is within a kilometre of a primary school and 80 per cent has the same facility as far as middle school is concerned, the same document admits the lack of vital facilities in schools such as potable water, buildings, blackboards, and so on.[28] The document also noted that though the rural sector caters to a much larger segment of the population, relative expenditure on this sector is comparatively much lower than the money spent on urban schools. Nor is it that schools in the towns and cities are all well equipped; however, the question of facilities acquires particular importance in rural India as it is linked to the urgent need to reach out to village girls.

While children in general are affected by inadequate or substandard facilities, there are certain specific disadvantages which impede the education of girls. Though in India, as in other parts of the world, teaching is a preferred occupation for women, yet today, only 27.8 per cent of all school teachers are women. While this is a marked improvement over the previous record of 14.7 per cent at the time of Independence, there is clearly a need for a far more rapid expansion in the cadres of women teachers. In order to encourage women to go in for teaching the Education Commission[29] of 1964 suggested that there should be special allowances provided as well as residential accommodation for women teachers in villages. In addition, there should be schemes introduced to encourage part-time teaching degrees through correspondence and so on. Since 1983, the Government of India has sponsored a new scheme by which it will provide financial assistance for the appointment of women teachers in the nine educationally backward states. However, it is not unusual for women to face resistance from their families as well as feel hesitant themselves when it comes to taking up jobs in unknown rural areas.

Though the financial viability of co-educational institutions is undoubtedly much higher than running several single sex institutions with low rates of enrolment, by and large, the Indian situation demands segregation as a precondition for the mass schooling of girls. Nothing this requirement, the Secondary Education Commission of 1953 and the National Committee on Women's Education recommended the stepping up of the establishment of all girls' institutions. Yet, latest figures show that the ratio of such institutions to all institutions is only about 10 to 15 per cent, whereas the overall enrolment of girls is approximatly 35 per cent.[30] However, it is not enough to set up an institution for girls; it is essential to see that it has access to the same kind of facilities enjoyed by boy's schools: studies suggest that they are often without teachers and have to make do with substandard teaching material. Further, and this leads us logically to the next point, girls' schools often do not have access to facilitites for the teaching of certain subjects such as science and mathematics. When equipment and trained pesonnel are in short supply, they tend to be assigned to boys' schools or at best, to those run on co-educational lines. The suggestion for creating more girls' schools on the face of it appear to be an immediate solution to the reluctance of parents to send girls to co-educational institutions. It is not clear what is the relative weight of this factor against other consisderations such as distance of the school, lack of women teachers, opportunity costs of girls' education and non-availability of child care services.

III. Discrimination Within Schools

The issues relating to the education of girls clearly do not end with ensuring a higher rate of enrolment in schools: there are certain processes within the school which work to reinforce stereotyped notions of what it means to be a girl. While some influences are more subtle than others, the end product is a perpetuation of inequality between the sexes. Two specific aspects of the inner life of the school are dealt with namely the content matter of text-books and the access of girls to certain kinds of courses.

(a) It is now being increasingly recognised that the text-book, whether it teaches English or Mathematics, can, through the use of characters and symbols in certain situations become a powerful medium for the perpetuation of stereotypes and role models. For instance, a NCERT-sponsored study of Hindi text-books which are widely used in the country found that the ratio of boy-centred stories to girl-centred stories was 21:0. Again when the books made biographical references, 94 out of 110 relate to prominent men. In the thirteen English language text-books published by the Central Institute of English, Hyderabad, boy-centred stories outnumbered girl-centred ones by eighty-one to nine. Further, the general tenor in books in both the languages was to portray boys as courageous, achieving and interested in science and technology; girls and women were rarely portrayed in roles associated with economic activity or independence. A study of Marathi text-books found that even when girls were seen as being employed they were invariably portrayed in menial and subordinate roles.[31]

Taking note of the fact that such gross deviations from reality could indeed affect self-perceptions, the Women's Education Unit in the NCERT recently undertook projects to devise handbooks on how text-books should be written so as to improve the status of women. The handbook for Mathematics demonstrates aptly how change in attitudes can be introduced through a supposedly value-neutral subject. Thus, where earlier, problem sums would deal with shopkeeper Joshi's purchases at the wholesale market and the monthly expenses of Mr. Sathe, the suggested problems ask students of Class III to work out how much Lakshman had in his bank account before he distributed equal sums to his daughter and to his son. At the middle school level, ratios, graphs and equations are introduced through the biographical details of women scientists and mathematicians. Of greater importance than the sums themselves are the instructions to teachers who are asked to weave in the text while teaching students how to solve a problem.[32]

The originators of these innovative handbooks are well aware of the fact that unless the teachers are convinced of the need to teach more imaginatively, children will concentrate on the solution only and not on the text. Clearly this is the crux of the problem : teachers are by and large a conservative force, who are not easily convinced of the need to teach or preach greater equality between the sexes through Mathematics, Physics or Hindi. Nor is it easy to start the process of textbook revision or ensure that the same text-books are to be taught in all the schools in the country. Further, text-book writers themselves are singularly resistant to change as they feel that radical deviations would clearly disturb the well-entrenched expectations of both the school community as well as the family. However, the need to constantly review what is going on within the school is made even clearer if we look at what girls are making of their education.

(b) One major advantage of the 10+2+3 system (where 10+2 refer to the years in school and +3 to the time spent on a first degree) is that it makes the learning of Science and Mathematics obligatory for all students upto the Class X (10) level. Yet, though this pattern of education was officially adopted in 1968, it has still to be accepted in a few states. Consequently, under the old scheme, schools, continue to offer Home Science and Art for girls rather than Science and Mathematics. However, we also find that schools under the new scheme find ways of countering the system due to the professed inadequacy of teaching staff. Thus in the Jama Masjid area of Delhi, which caters to a largely Muslim population, girls' schools are unable to offer Science and Mathematics because qualified women teachers are not available. It is also not improbable that such schools are in fact catering to the demands for education of a certain kind for girls from an essentially *purdah* society.[33]

That the notion of what is right and proper for a girl to study permeates the educational system in general, is evident from the kind of choices that girls make at the +2 level that is, for Classes XI and XII. A recent study of Delhi schools indicated that while girls constituted about 60 per cent of the Arts stream and about 30 per cent in the Science and Commerce streams, over 40 per cent flocked to the relatively new Vocational stream. Further, the subject-wise breakdown of vocational options showed that girls were concentrated in Typing, Weaving, Textiles, Health Care and Beauty Culture, while boys chose Opthalmics and Optics, Auditing and Accounting in addition to Office Management. Again, for the socially useful-productive work, options in a non-academic area which children can opt for in Classes IX and X, choices are "markedly sex-typed and girls continue to do the same tasks in school as are assigned to them at home".[34] However, a look at the performance of girls in school leaving examinations in various parts of the country indicate that not only is the pass level of girls higher than that of boys but also those who have have opted for the science stream often fare as well-if not better than their male.[35]

The scientific aptitude of girls is represented in school leaving results. However, two important questions need to be asked here: first, how many girls who fare well in Science at the Class X examinations do in fact opt for it at the +2 stage and second, how many of those who offer Science for the final school leaving examination continue with it or with related subjects at the degree level? While it is difficult to give precise answers, there are indications that in some of the best schools in the country there is only one girl to four boys in the Science section. Further, classroom observations of trainee teachers show that these girls are quiet and reserved non-participants. While they were diligent about their home-work and performed well in unit tests, they rarely took part in discussions which were dominated by the boys.[36] The fact that they were in a minority may have accounted for their low degree of participation. Nonetheless, those who taught Classes VI and VII found that girls were as assertive and definite in their point of view as boys, indicating that adolescent girls soon internalised the need to be submissive and obedient, rather than be questioning and argumentative, particularly in a male-dominated environment.

While the following section deals with enrolments in higher education, it would appear that far fewer girls do in fact go in for Science and Technology than would be reasonable to expect from their school-leaving results.[37] Clearly then, there are important non-academic factors which influence choices at the age of sixteen or seventeen. These are related to social and familial expectations of what a girl's basic role in life is to be; if, as in the majority of cases, it is assumed that she is to be a good wife and devoted mother, who may, if she has time, work as a teacher or as a clerk, there seems little point in investing time and energy on a career in Science and other related areas. Again, if it is a question of investment of scare family resources, these are invariably spent on the technical education of a boy. Even if his sister has similar aptitudes, she more often than not, redirects them to traditional feminine oriented courses. Underlying many of these decisions is of course, a deep-seated conviction that a woman's basic nature equips her to perform better in certain areas than in others. Even when school results point to the contrary, families—and indeed girls themselves—choose to believe that there can be no true fulfilment in combining too many roles, or in competing to enter the male-dominated disciplines. That such beliefs operate even more in the realm of higher education will be clear from the next section.

Higher Education

Despite regional variations, going to college is by and large an urban middle-class phenomenon, which is more marked in the case of girls. The total girls' enrolment of about 10 lakhs accounts for 1.5 per cent in the age group of 17-23 years.[38] This works out to 38 girls for every 100 boys in higher education. Interestingly, the proportion of women to men is higher at the postgraduate level than at the undergraduate level. This would suggest that once women in certain areas are able to break through the barriers of prejudice, they proceed to acquire a further degree and perhaps jobs in those areas. The following bar chart records some interesting trends in women's

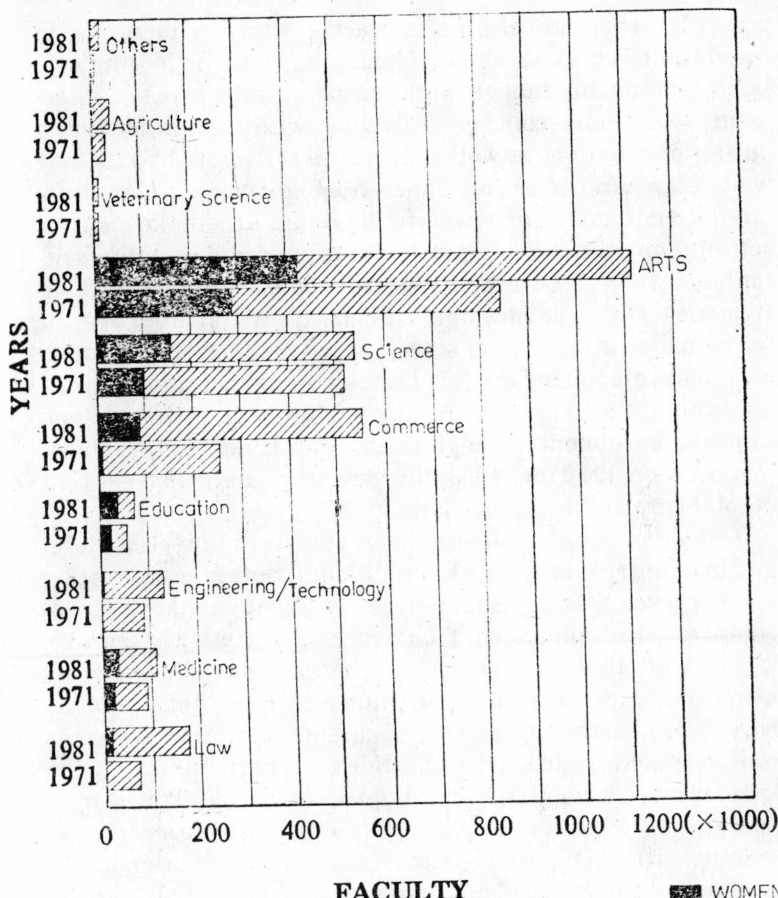

Women in Higher Education

higher education : for instance, while enrolments in the traditional areas of the Arts and Education continue to expand so are those in Science, Commerce and Medicine. Medicine acquired respectability as a profession for women by the end of the last century as women doctors were needed for the families of the emergent middle-class. The present trend of high capitation in medical colleges might act as a further deterrent. However, qualifiactions in a particular area do not always mean that women will be in a position to take up jobs of their choice. For example, women trained in medicine generally opt out of private practice which is lucrative, in favour of lower salaried, fixed hour jobs in public hospitals. It is not improbable that a work situation that involves interacting with male colleagues, dealing with men patients in a variety of situations as well as being on call for night duty may well deter parents or husbands from allowing their fully qualified daughters or wives from taking up employment or setting up practice. Apart from undermining the self-confidence of a girl who has invested many years of her life to rigorous training in a competitive area, such attitudes result in the under utilisation of scare skilled resources. The unemployment rate among qualified women in science and technology is almost fifty per cent.[39] Latest figures show that though women's enrolment in engineering has gone up seventeen-fold between 1960 and 1983, they are still barely five per cent of total enrolemnt in that discipline.[40]

The increased general enrolment of girls at university level and their entry into many non-traditional courses is interesting as it proves that at certain levels reservations against co-education are diminishing.[41*] Looking at the country as a whole, it is clear that though overall enrolments for girls is increasing each year, these continue to be much below that of boys. Secondly, the expansion is apparent in traditional areas as well as in non-traditional areas. However, participation in the latter is much lower than what could be expected if choices were made purely on the basis of academic ability. Due to a variety of reasons, girls do not compete to the extent that is commensurate with their school leaving results for coveted seats in Science, Engineering, Architecture and so on. Instead, they tend to flock to the burgeoning colleges and polytechnics, many of which are of indifferent standard, for degrees and diplomas in courses regaded as respectable and appropriate for girls. As M.N. Srinivas has perceptibly pointed out, in a highly competitive marriage market, a girl's connubial circle narrows to those who are better educated than her. Rather than being regarded as institutions for acquiring knowledge and perhaps providing training for a vocation, "colleges and universities provide respectable waiting places for girls who wish to get married".[42]

---

* A micro study of Jadavpur University by Malavika Karlekar, is a good illustration of this trend. Some data from this study is given in the Appendix.

The functions of education for a boy are clearly very different from those for a girl. As an exogenous factor, education continues to be viewed with some suspicion by those committed to the notion of the obedient, virtuous and benevolent woman. Its liberating potential is to be clearly avoided; at the same time there is today a growing awareness of the need to educate girls. Access to college education is no longer a preserve of the westernised urban elite, though certain courses continue to be dominated by them. The dilemma caused by exposure to the external world coupled with the need to keep intact the notion of female dependency is resolved by stressing the suitability of some areas of study and the need to avoid others. That the making of such choices may in fact result in the suppression of genuine interest and talent in some other field is not regarded as being of much consequence. Of primary importance is the need to preserve the unity and prestige of the family nexus. Too much education or education of the wrong kind can without much difficulty, tarnish the reputation of a kinship group which depends on among other things, the eligibility of its daughters.

Alternatives to Formal School : Non-Formal Education and Adult Literacy Programmes

The target groups for non-formal education are those children who have to work for a living. It is hoped, that when not at work, with the right type of encouragement they will find their way to functional lieracy and non-formal education classes. However, progress in this area has not been particularly satisfactory; taking note of the slow expansion in the alternatives to formal schooling. The Central Government has recently introduced a new scheme of financial assistance on a 90:10 basis to the nine educationally-backward states so as to stimulate enrolment in the age group of 6-14 years. During 1983-1984, seven states were granted aid to set up 10,000 non-formal centres. Apart from running classes on more flexible lines than what is provided within the structure of the formal school, courses are shorter and more intensive.[43] However, as with all the other sectors in education, the curriculum has to be relevant and the teacher needs to have a commitment and an approach which are in many ways different from that of a conventional school teacher. This is not always possible, and evaluations of such programmes have shown that the non-fromal teacher—often an unemployed youth—rarely understands his role fully. Nor is the material to be taught always relevant. At a non-formal late evening class in Uttar Pradesh, an observer noticed five children yawning while the educator read out to them the needs of pregnant women. The children chanted after him and later he read out from pamphlets on potato-growing, horticulture and poultry keeping. Not only was the teacher oblivious of the need of his pupils but also it was clear that there was a lack of co-ordination between him and those in charge of organising lesson plans.[44]

Though there have not been enough follow-up studies on the impact of non-formal education on girls, there are sufficient indications that this scheme, like all those affecting children who have to combine productive work with other roles, will suffer until the issue of child care facilities is solved. As experts have pointed out: "Though the provision of child care facilitites has been recognised as an essential instrument to improve women's access to education, to vocational training, to employment and even for political participation,[45] not much has been done to systematically work towards a comprehensive strategy by which women's other roles are given due cognisance while envisaging a role for them in the educational process." A consistent finding from studies among the urban poor is: "Woman and elder girls are considerably hampered in their activities by the lack of institutionalised child-care facilities." This not only affects their capacity for work and schooling but also means that babies and little children are often neglected. The recent proposal to involve *anganwadis* in the promotion of primary schooling appears to take this problem into consideration. Under this scheme, pre-primary classes will be organised at the location of the Integrated Child Development Scheme (ICDS) until the age of three years. Subsequently, primary classes would be organised at the same location and would enable girls to come to school with their younger siblings who would be taken care of by *anganwadi* workers. At the higher level it is proposed to organise learning through the Open School system and the Open University.[46]

The National Adult Education Programme (NAEP) was launched by the Janata Government in 1978 with the aim of bringing those in the age groups of 15 to 35 years within the ambit of literacy, within the next five years. Like most governmental targets, this too was clearly unrealistic and even today, only 52 per cent of the illitrates covered by this scheme are women. However, there are indications that well-run programmes may well benefit entire families. An extensive study in a backward part of Andhra Pradesh[47] shows that an integrated programme of education with basic maternal and child health nutritional services resulted in a high degree of awareness and receptiveness to modern health practices. Follow up studies on programmes built around women in various stages of pregnancy and early childhood showed that knowledge on nutrition, health and general development through the Mother Child Centres (MCCSs) and Functional Literacy Classes (FLITs) had increased considerably. Minor ailments were dealt with more competently and dietary practices of both pregnant women as well as infants appeared to have been influenced by the government-run programmes. Whether in fact women would retain their commitment to a different approach to the body needs to be seen; what is important, however, is that they were receptive to change.

Recently, organisers of income generating schemes for rural women in Punjab reported that some familiarity with numeracy helps in learning simple costing exercises. While calculating aggregates for a number of days at a time was difficult, women easily learnt how to compute their daily earnings. This helped them in dealing with exploitative middle-men as well as with family members who were interested in appropriating most of their earnings. A major criticism against the adult education programme for women, however, is that they by and large reflect a middle-class world view and rarely take into account the vital role of their client groups in production. Such programmes stress the role of home-maker and provide training in conventional areas such as health, nutrition, child care, home economics, sewing, embroidery and so on. While these are undoubtedly important, it is equally relevant to train such women-most of whom are earners—on how to increase productivity as well as provide information on alternate channels of employment and create awareness of their rights as workers.[48]

Clearly then, like elementary education, alternatives to schooling suffer because of their basic irrelevance to the lives of those whom they are supposed to benefit. In India, apart from the urban middle and upper middle-class elite and the increasing rural population which considers it worthwhile to invest in the education of daughters, the bulk of women and girls participate in education only when it does not conflict with their basic goal of earning a livlihood. The role of education has to be viewed as a part of the wider strategy for improving the general living conditions of the majority of the country's population. For girls, social expectations are different. Women are supposed to be the natural upholders of family unity, responsible for the perpetuation of the lineage as well as for the physical well-being of various generations. Therefore, their participation in education is greatly dependent on how much value society places on it.

While middle-class boys too have to face pressures of various kinds when making choices, these are of a qualitatively different nature. In a male-dominated society, the stress imposed on boys by the syndrome of achievement, examination and selection is not inconsequential; yet there is a commitment to getting into and in succeeding in a wider range of courses through open competition. Theoretically, girls are supposed to have access to the same courses as boys. In practices, if they are allowed to go to college, they tend to flock to a few, selective *feminine* areas of study. Boys are socialised to compete and succeed, and girls to accept and to participate in well-demarcated, 'safe' educational realms. This is reinforced by portrayal of women in the media, particularly films and advertising.

Entertainment through glossy magazines, television serials and the cinema celebrate the sexual division of labour. When the media is used for educational purposes, for instance in radio programmes on agriculture, the role of women is, more often than not, neglected. Though there are an increasing number of articles and reports appearing in leading newspapers on atrocities against women, high female-infant-mortality rates, discrimination in employment and so on, these have to compete with a fantasy world which transports a woman onto a yacht, a snowy hillside or a discotheque on the arm of a handsome young man wearing the latest in men's fashions. This juxtaposition of reality with escapism results more often than not in opting to dwell only on the latter. Not only is the escapist point of view presented in a much more attractive manner, but it also allows for a release from the daily routine. Statistics on how many girls leave the educational system, or analyses of why women do not want to become scientists are only unwelcome reminders of existential reality.

Thus, any thought of reforming text-books or trying to create awareness among women of their potentialities and many roles has also to contend with the invidious influence of media extravaganza; with television reaching out to more and more areas in India, the competence of the educational system in changing attitudes has to be seriously assessed. If social attitudes hold the key to educational expansion, then clearly there is a need to explore ways in which these can be modified. At one point of time, women's organisations as well as women's institutions did have an important role to play in convincing families on the need to educate daughters. This was in the heady days of the freedom struggle when the basic concern was with the liberation of the urban middle-class woman. In the late twentieth century, the issues are far more varied and complex. If we accept that governmental initiative by itself is neither equipped nor committed to a systematic expansion of women's education at every level, there is a definite case for collaboration between different agencies. Field studies indicate that voluntary agencies have been quite successful in mobilising support for various programmes; it may be worthwhile to initiate pilot projects for expansion of girls' education in limited areas. If a group of villages is chosen to test out alternate strategies for encouraging girls to come to school, it may be possible to isolate factors which families regard as important. For instance, in a remote part of Madhya Pradesh, it was found that while in a particular village, no girls attended school, at the next village, not only was school enrolment high, but also a daughter was being prepared for college. After conducting preliminary investigations, the researcher concluded that while everthing else was in common, the second village had become more innovative because of its access to urban areas.[49] More micro level studies of this kind may well help in the development of comprehensive strategies for educational expansion.

While entrenched attitudes are not easy to root out, a concerted strategy organised by governmental agencies together with others in the area may well work much better than having several conflicitng schemes supposedly working for the promotion of gilrs' education. It needs to be remembered that not only are men planners and administrators indifferent, if not hostile to the question of changing attitudes to girls, but often women themselves are not convinced of the benefits to be realised by giving girls more freedom of choice. The sexual division of labour within the family is the result of generations of socialisation. Any re-socialisation is bound to bring with it some undesirable instability. Resistance to change can only be overcome by introducing it slowly as well as by demonstrating that every new situation need not be destabilising. This could be achieved by well-though out programmes limited to a small segment of the population as a first step. For this kind of a strategy which is sensitive to disparate needs, it is essential to have a responsive governmental machinery as well as cooperation not only with other agencies in the area but also from the beneficiaries of such schemes. The best proponents of education for girls are those who have benefited from it and are committed to its expansion. Any educational strategy must aim not only at gaining new converts, but also at enlisting the support of those who have been, and continue to be pioneers in stepping out.

APPENDIX

Data from Jadavpur University

The enrolment of girls and boys in the Arts Faculty over a twenty-year span show that the concentration of girls in a few feminine subjects continue, though the percentage enrolement of girls in the traditional scientific disciplines of Physics, Chemistry and Mathematics is also going up significantly.

(See graphics on pages 165 & 166)

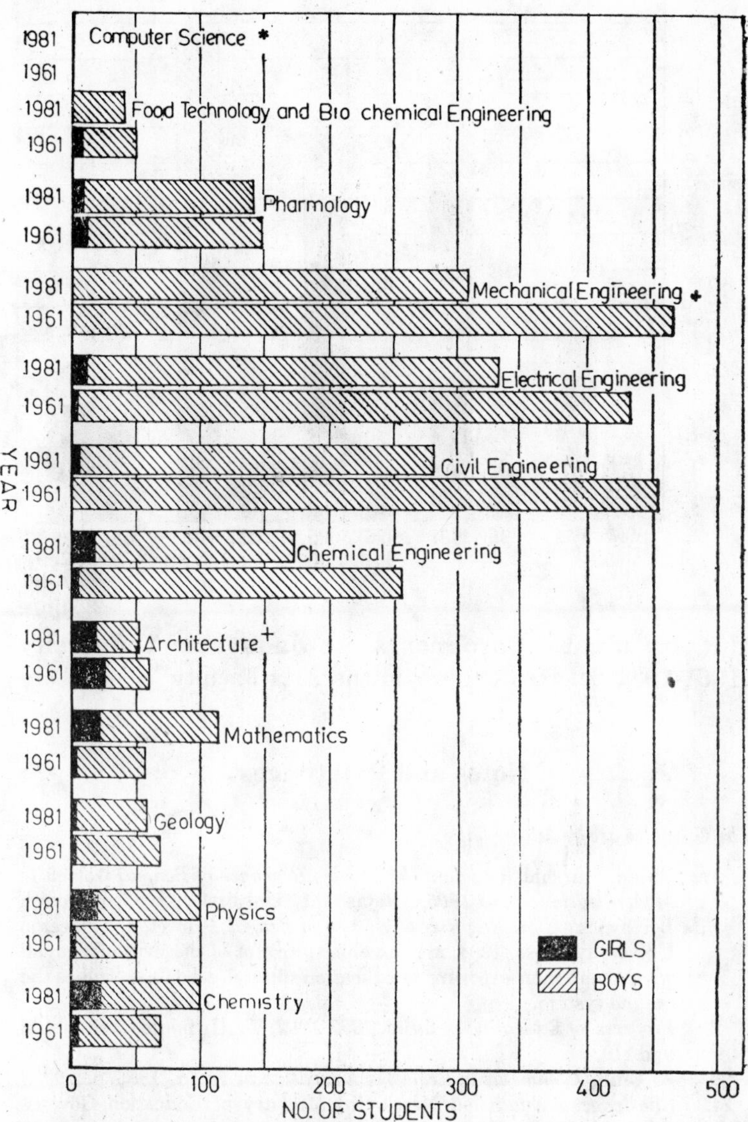

Undergraduate Enrolments at Jadavpur University
Science & Engineering Faculties
*No Enrolments +Course introduced in 1977

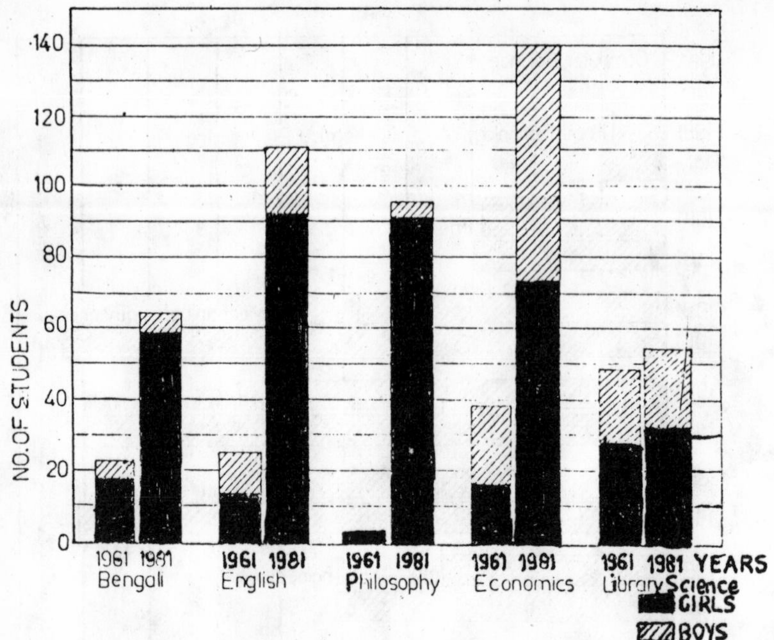

Undergraduate Enrolments at Jadavpur University (1961-1981) Selected courses in the Arts Faculty

Notes and References

The Graphics are by Aditya Pal

1. Gulam Murshid, *Reluctant Debutante* : *Response of Bengali Women to Modernisation, 1849-1905*, Rajashahi University, 1983; Meredith Borthwick's *Changing Role of Women in Bengal*, Princeton, Princeton University Press, 1984, are excellent account of the lives of Bengali women and their exposure to education through schools as well as the *zenana* system.
2. *Progress of Education in India, 1897-1902*, Vol.II, figures from p. 106 and 110.
3. A. Croft, *Comments in Review of Education in India*, 1886, p.279.
4. *Challenge of Education*, New Delhi, Ministry of Education, Government of India, figures from p. 1 and 34.
5. *Progress of Education in India, 1907-12*, Vol.I, p.213.
6. Dorothy Griffiths, Esther Saraga, *Sex Differences and Congnitive Abilities: A Sterile field of Enquiry*, chapt. in "Sex Role Stereo-typing" edited by Oonagh Hartnett, et al., London, Tavistock Publication, 1979.
7. Murshid and Borthwick, op.cit.

8. Ibid., 41.
9. M.K. Gandhi; This view of Gandhi has been put forth in "To the women of India", in *Young India*, April 10, 1938.
10. Sudhir Kakar, *the Inner World*, New Delhi, Oxford University Press, 1980. Margaret Cornmack, *The Hindu Women*, Asia Publishing House, 1961, Bombay, A detailed description of the socialisation process of Hindu girl.

    C. Dimmit and J.A.B. Van Buitenen, *Classical Hindu Mythology* (translated), Rupa, 1983 (reprint), New Delhi, is a good introduction to some of the important Hindu myths. C. Rajagopalachari, *The Ramayana*, Bharatiya Vidya Bhavan, Bombay, 1982. An eminently readable life of Rama.
11. Report of the University Education Commission, 1948-1949, Vol.I, Delhi, Manager of Publications, 1950, p. 393-395.
12. Report of the Education Commission, 1964-1966, NCERT, New Delhi, 1971. The National Council of Educational Research and Training publishes textbooks used in most Indian Schools as well as sponsors research in education.
13. Report of the National Committee on Women's Education, 1958, New Delhi, Ministry of Education, 1959, p. 7-9.
14. Ibid., p.86.
15. Education Commission, op.cit., p.240.
16. Report of the Committee on the "Differentiation of curricula," 1962, in J.C. Aggarwal, *The Progress of Education in free India*, New Delhi, Arya Book Depot, 1984, p. 395-396.
17. *Education Commission*, p.238.
18. *Report of the Committee on the Status of Women in India*, New Delhi, Ministry of Education and Social Welfare, 1975, p. 281-282.
19. *Challenge of Education*, op.cit., p.38-57.
20. J.P. Naik, *Equality, Quality and Quantity*, New Delhi, Allied Publishers, 1975.
21. Vina Mazumdar and Balaji Pandey, "Perspective on women's Education. 1971-1981", Unpublished paper, 1985, p.1. R.K. Bhandari, "Educational Development of Women in India," New Delhi, *History of Education and Culture* 1982 (statistics for the graph), p.13.
22. *Indian Express*, "Figures of 44 million children in India's labour force," 27 August, 1985.
23. R.K. Bhandari, "*Educational Development of Women in India*," New Delhi, Ministry of Education and Culture, 1982, p.36. The graphs are based on figure on p.35.
24. Jagdish Bhagwati, *Education, Class structure and Income Equality World Development*, Vol.1, No.5, May 1973. The opportunity cost argument is death with in detail.
25. Malavika Karlikar, *Poverty and Women's work*, New Delhi, Vikas Publishing House, 1982, p.121-122.
26. Ibid., p.124-125. *Data of slum studies*.
27. *Towards Equality*, Report of the Committee on the Status of Women in India.
28. *Challenge of Education*, op. cit., deals at length with 'lack of facilities in schools', p. 27, 34.

29. R.K. Bhandari, op. cit., Table 18, p.46.
30. Ibid., p.57, p.54-66 deal with various handicaps in girls' education.
31. Kamlesh Nirchol, *The Invisible Woman*, New Delhi, Amalatas, 1978. *Women and Girls as Portrayed in Hindi Text Books*, New Delhi, NCERT, 1976. In *Vasudha, Dhagamwar, women who use the Marriage Act,* India International Quarterly, Vol.12, No.1, 1985, Marathi textbooks have been analysed.

NCERT, has brought out three handbook on textbook writing, namely *Status of Women through curriculum,* elementary *Teachers Handbook*, 1982, *Status of women through curriculam*. Secondary and Senior secondary stages 1984, and *Status of women throgh Teaching of Mathematics—A Teacher's handbook, 1984*. All three are interesting and informative.

33. *Challenge of Education*, op.cit., p.43, discusses the non-implementation of the 10+2+3 system particularly in respect of the education of girls. Observation on schools in the Jama Masjid area were made by a Muslim girl student of Jamia Millia Islamia, who has studied in one such school.
34. Usha Nayar, "Education of girls at the secondary level in India," unpublished paper, 1983. It gives a detailed analysis of streaming of students in different disciplines at Delhi School.
35. *Patriot*, New Delhi, 25 May, 1985. A report which confirms "What National data in Education in India," Volumes clearly show.
36. Jamia Millia, observation of B.Ed. student.
37. Rajani Kumar, "Secondary Education for Girls, The What and How," *Education Quarterly*, October 1982, Vol. XXIV, No.4, analysis of Delhi, applies equally to the rest of the country as U.G.C.'s data on women's enrolment discipline-wise shows.
38. R.K. Bhandari, op. cit., p.36, Statistics for the bar chart are given on p.37.
39. *Census Volume on Degree for elders and Technical Personal*, Govt. of India, 1971.
40. *Challenge of Education*, op. cit., p.19.
41. See Appendix.
42. M.N. Srinivas, *The Changing Position of Indian Women*, New Delhi, Oxford University Press, 1978.
43. "*Women in India*," country paper presented by the Ministry of Social and Women's Welfare, New Delhi, 1985, p.47-48.
44. Susheela Bhan, discusses this in her, "The National Adult Education Programme," in A.M. Shah and S. Bhan's (ed.), *Non-Formal Education and the NEAP*, New Delhi, Oxford University Press, 1978.
45. Mazumdar and Pandey, op. cit., p.7.
46. *Challenge of Education* op. cit., from p.90 onwards, it discusses various alternatives 'Anganwadis', provides basic facilities such as immunisation, additional nutrition and functional literacy to infants and pregnant women.
47. Victor Jesudasan, et al., *Non Termal Education for Rural women to promote and Development of the young child*, New Delhi, Allied Publishers; it gives a full appraisal of the project in Andhra Pradesh.
48. *Opinions* Gleaned from conversations with those working with women's groups.
49. *Observations* of a researcher from the Indian Social Institute, New Delhi.

4

The Family

The current knowledge about the family describes it as the basic social unit in which all of us—men, women, and children—live in a network of mutual ties and obligations. It is expected to meet the basic needs of all its members and provide a sense of belonging and togetherness. It is in the family that we have our first experiences of joy and sorrow, love and hate and other shared experiences. In times of crises we turn to the family. It prepares us as social beings through transmission of tradition and the cultural, moral and spiritual values from one generation to another.[1]

Family organisation forms the basic core of a given society's sexual division of labour, marital norms and a system of control over resources, rights, duties and privileges of the members.

Significance of family for the women is even more vital than for men, as one can talk of the social problems of the latter without involving the family, but for the former, one cannot speak about their social problems without dealing with their family functions. Motherhood is a supreme goal which is socially celebrated, and is to be performed within the domestic domain along with her experiences of work and leisure. While a man is allowed an independent existence, woman's survival is not socially conceivable without the family. The social value placed on the familial role of women is also responsible for her subordination to man and for her lack of access to economic and political resources, even when she contributes equally or more to the family economy. Thus while the family throttles women's aspirations towards positions of power and equality, it also places significant responsibilities on them and provides almost the only means of social survival in the majority of societies today.

What women do for the family has been analysed by the social scientists in a variety of ways. Women's role and status have been described to put forth their functions towards the family. Their ritual roles and symbolism in religion are listed at length. Accounts of women's activities in different social groups have been documented. These studies emphasise the stability, durability and persistence of this form of social living and its functionality for social order.[2]

Yet there is hardly any discussion on what family means to its different members. Surely, all of us do not experience the family in the same way. For some of us it means security, resources, power, shelter and life-long insurance aginst a harsh world. For others it may be an existence with uncertainty, insecurity, assetlessness and a threat to be thrown out of its membership without notice. More women in the family are likely to be in the second group—at least in the major family systems of the world—patrilineal, patrilocal and often patriarchal, marked by unequal gender relations of power running along gender lines in which men's power and women's subordination is accepted as a social norm. It is not surprising therefore, that women have a low position in this society which is reflected in lower life expectancy, lack of access to education, health and employment opportunities, widespread practice of female neglect and abuse, such as wife beating, leading to female suicide and bride burning as the ultimate fate for the hundreds of powerless women every year.

The existence of alternate structures turns out to be variations on this dominant theme such as the nuclear family, the communes etc. Yet we would like to identify any supportive structures which are comparatively more favourable to women and explore the possibilities of perpetuating them.

In its present form the family organisation represents an oppressive institution for women, inconsistent with the ideals of equality, justice and development. It seems doubtful to achieve these ideals in the present ideological structure and values governing the dominant family structure, unless a deliberate direction is forthcoming from the oppressed group—that is the women themselves—and the other institutions in the society especially, the State.

We will present an analysis from a feminist point of view of different forms of family organisations, modes of descent and the nature of the institutions of marriage, inheritance etc.- which "provide the major contours of the socio-cultural setting in which women are born, brought up and live their lives".[3]

Using the cultural-historical context, an effort will be made to describe the roots of these institutions and the major variations in the different regions, castes and religions in the Indian society. With a continuity in its long history, *the past lives with us even today vividly, obstinately and sometimes obtrusively and must be known by everyone interested in the present.*[4] The picture that emerges may be typical of the situation in most of its general features (as inferred from the literature available) though it is possible to find exceptions. If we find a disproportionate emphasis on the Hindu family, it is due to the fact that this is the dominant form of Indian family in which the majority of women live and which has its imprint on the other family structures too.

The typical Indian family is the joint family. It has endured as long as the records exist. In the most extensive work on family and kinship in India, Irawati Karve defines the joint family as "a group of people who generally live under one roof, who eat food cooked in one kitchen, who hold property in common, participate in common family worship, and are related to one another as some particular type of kindred".[5] This pattern is found all over the country and even among other religious groups such as Muslims, Christians etc. Even when there is no ancestral and immovable property, families with two-three generations of patrilineal kinship can be found living together.

In ancient days, since agriculture was the mainstay of the economy and all services were paid for in land, every Indian had a small family holding in some village—may be just a strip of land or for an artisan, just a small house. With the diversification of the economy and people moving out in trade, armed forces, civil services, etc., member may stay away even in distant places but the connection of a family with a locality lingers long after a family has finally migrated out of the village. The general assumption that the joint family is a typically Indian institution is based more on the value placed on jointness rather than the actual number of such families. For in the development cycle of the family there is constant formation and fission of units. A point comes in this process when from the parent joint family elementary units may separate which in course of time will grow into a joint family. There are two major modes of descent in India:

(1) Patrilineal Descent
(2) Matrilineal Descent

Patrilineal Descent

Barring a limited number of matrilineal communities concentrated in the south-western and the north-eastern regions of the country, the family in India is largely patrilineal and patrilocal. The core of the family are the males who trace their descent from a common ancestor. The women are brought as brides and the young daughters are given in marriage to unrelated males of the same or higher caste, never to a lower one—at least not if it can be helped. The scope of this family includes multi-generational membership: three to four generations of males related to the male ego as grandfather and his brothers, father and his brothers, cousins, sons and nephews, and their wives, unmarried daughters and sisters.

In reality such complex or extended families may be few in number and what one finds are much smaller joint families. As the constant formation and fission continues, the essence of the concept of joint living is the desirability of mutual obligations, joint landed property and pooling of resources, labour and skills when the family lives by a family enterprise.[6]

In the joint family, there is no exclusive one-to-one relationship. The women in one's mother's classificatory category and age group are all 'mothers'; the same applies to the men also. Grandfather's brothers are addressed as 'grandfathers'. Thus, child-rearing is not the exclusive task of one woman. There are aunts, grandmothers, sisters, who look after a young child's needs, while fondling the child and bringing him up is under the care of grandfather, uncles, etc. This concept of *sharing* child-care may be welcome to the western woman who finds mothering an exclusive responsibility thrust upon her. But one has to live in a joint family to experience the lack of access and control over one's children. In fact, a parent is not expected to even fondle one's own child in the presence of elders or show attachment to own ones children in preference to children of husband's brothers.

Preference for Male Offspring : In the patrilineal family, a son is looked upon as the natural successor, supporter and heir of the family. A father relives through his son. Unlike a daughter who must change loyalties after marriage, a son is considered to be a good investment and an insurance for the future. The strong preference for a son has to be understood in terms of two institutions interlinked with the family : property and religion.

In the Brahmanical literature woman is considered the property of man, and if any rights could be conferred on her, they were through the husband. Theoretically, a wife was the co-owner of the property with her husband but this right remained only a juridical fiction.

The religious requirement of a son is an even more compelling reason for male-preference. A son alone is qualified to carry on the patrilineage, perform the rites of lighting the funeral pyre and propitiating the souls of agnatic ascendants through *shradha*. Women who could not produce sons had a miserable existence, and more often than not, a new wife would replace her.[7]

The social basis of gender hierarchy is rooted in the system of social stratification. Just as the social distance became greater between the castes, so also were the controls on women's sexuality. In maintaining social distance in the hierarchy, women's role in the ritual purity of the upper castes is crucial and they are seen as 'gateways' of the caste group. If a woman was to marry a man of a lower ritual status, their children will have a status lower than that of the mother. Thus the descendants of such an alliance will lower the prestige of the whole group. It is for this reasons that the patriarchal family with male descents considers it vital to control the sexuality of women but not of men. Practices like pre-puberty marriages with *ritually correct* men, ban on widow-remarriage and the practice of sati are means of containing the women within the caste and family fold.

Men are given a free hand in choosing their women and can marry in the lower status group without affecting the status of their progeny. They may do so for gaining political power or wealth. There is a dearth of eligible boys in the privileged upper castes such as Brahmins, Thakurs, Rajputs etc., due to this practice. The prevalence of female infanticide, and female suicide may be associated with hypergamy.*

It is difficult, however, to prove that the texts also reflected the actual social reality as it affected the masses of the people. As M.N. Srinivas puts it: "Educated Indians derive their idea of the joint family not from what they see and experience but from the epics, folktales, Hindu law etc."[8] The same is true of other institutions. Not only is there discrepancy between the social norms fixed in writing and the actually practised behaviour, but there is also a wide gap between the family as it was found in the different castes within the same region. There is a popular belief that Indians traditionally lived in joint families which began to disintegrate under the impact of individualism introduced by the British rule. Yet, the bulk of the lower castes and poorer people may have never possessed the physical resources to maintain extended kinship structures. The upper castes and wealthier people may have lived in the kinship system similar to the joint family described in Hindu law.

Thus the landed upper castes in the villages and the stable upper caste population in the cities may have provided the model for the description of family in the scriptures and to the observers. Some of the features of the model are: belief in and practice of Vedic teachings, prohibition on polluting food (beef, alcohol etc.) and people (impure castes engaged in menial services), belief in the doctrines of Karma, Dharma, Maya, Moksha etc. The type of family and kinship system and

* Marrying above one's caste.

marriage customs emerging from this patrilineal model give a generally low position to its women.

Women's role under the Brahmanical law is to facilitate, the male mode of descent by producing sons. She is the 'field' (*kshetra*), man the seed (*beej*).[9] The seed is considered to be superior to the field. By and large, the Muslims have similar notions about women's subordinate role, sex segregation and seclusion of women as well as concepts regarding patrilineal and patrilocal family. However, wherever marriage between close kin exist as prevalent among some Muslims and in the South, no sharp distinction exists between bride-givers and bride-takers. Some of the adverse features for women in the Indian system are:

(1) The woman is a social dependent.

(2) Her worth is measured in terms of her ability to produce male children through whom the patrilineality is perpetuated.

(3) She has no share in the property. This is now sought to be corrected by law, yet cultural norms still hold strong.

(4) A woman does not belong to her father's family, while membership in the husband's family is conditional to her 'proper' behaviour.

(5) Women have no direct participation in 'high' religion—though they have the principal obligation to arrange, observe and continue the local traditions and rites pertaining to welfare of sons and husband. Women have responsibilities, while men have power.

(6) Women are controlled by the family in every aspect of their life.

In spite of the limited number of communities where matrilineal descent is found, the system is of special significance from the women's perspective.

With laws ensuring equal inheritance to sons and daughters, the future family's evolution to bilateral relations alone would ensure a symmetrical and egalitarian institution.

Matriliny had a strong base among the Nayars and Tiyyars of Kerala. It is found among several temple servant castes, occupational castes, and some forest tribes. In parts of Karnataka and Tamil Nadu too Matriliny is found.

The Muslim (Moplahs) of northern Kerala and of the Union Territory of Lakshadweep (classified as scheduled tribes) are other examples of matrilineal society with a unique social organisation. While other matrilineal societies have undergone a great deal of change, the Lakshadweep islanders are found to be the least affected by processes of change. A typical matrilineal joint family in Kerala called 'tharwad' is formed by a woman, her sons and daughters and daughters' sons and daughters. The husbands of the daughters are occasional visitors who never stay in the house, and the sons go to visit their wives and children at the wives' mothers' houses. There are no relations by marriage. There was of course a limit to the size of this type of joint family; in course of time there would emerge offshoots as for example, when the house became too small, and a new nucleus formed around which another 'tharwad' would develop. The woman is not dependent on her husband nor does she derive her status from him. She has dignity and right which cannot be ignored even when a male, like her brother or mother's brother may assume a position of authority as her manager. The husband is never fully incorporated into this family unit, and does not enjoy any rights over his children or wife's property.

In fact the women's brother among the Nayars of Kerala, may yield considerable power in making decisions over property matters as well as in several other public functions. Yet these functions are performed on behalf of the sister.

The Nayar women did not engage in any productive work, yet enjoyed full property rights and inheritance, and succession is continued through women. Their lack of participation in productive work is more than compensated by their matrimonial relationship with the upper status groups—the Namboodri Brahmins—which were instrumental in enhancing the social and political status of their families.[10]

The Muslims of Kerala (Moplahs) also provide the daughters the right to share in the parental property. But this is seldom put into practice. They have the custom of marriage between close relatives, particularly children of siblings and exchange marriages. The most preferred alliances are between the children of two brothers. This way the property remains within the family. The sons-in-law are resident members of the family.

There are, however, differences in the matrilineal cultures of the north-eastern and south-western regions, both between them and among the different communities within them[11]. The north-eastern communities of Garo and Khasi and the Pnar in the States of Meghalaya and Assam live in matrilineal society, where the husband comes to live with the wife's people and tends her land. The women have always been participating in the subsistence economy and therefore manage to look after the economic functions in their families. Among the Khasis, the youngest daughter gets a larger share in ancestral property, as she is entrusted with the care of the aged parents as well as performs the family rituals, death rites etc. The Garos entrust this function to one daughter who then inherits the property. This practice is different from the Nayar system in which all girls are co-sharers.

The materilineal family seems to be, at least apparently, a system with less internal stresses and strains than are inherent in the patriarchal set up. Rivalries of brothers, co-wives, and between mothers-in-law and daughters-in-law do not form the theme of their folksongs.

The concept of family with husband is not the nucleus, it is the mother-child dyad which is central, suported by a woman's own family of mother, brothers and sisters.

Some of the typical features of the matriarchal family system are as follows:

(1) Women are not social dependents of men.

(2) They are the perpetrators of the family line and the children owe their social placement through the mother, acquire their share in movable or immovable property, and also acquire positions of authority through (as the heiress's brother) her.

(3) The women are not under social pressure to produce male children, or to prove their fertility as a pre-condition to their position in the family.

(4) A woman is a full member of her matrilineal group and continues to be so even after her marriage.

(5) She has important religious and social responsibilities which she fulfils as the heiress of the family property.

(6) She controls her own life and her children. In case of breakdown of marriage, children remain with her.

There are, however, contradictions in the system. The suppression of fatherly inclination brings much alienation between the father and children. "He is insecure because of minimum rights over his wife, hardly any rights over his children and only right to use in the ancestral property."[12] The man is never fully incorporated in the wife's group, but is needed in the mother's group and may enjoy a position of authority and decision-making there.

These features of the matrilineal society give an impression that women are all powerful matriarchs. Contrary to this notion, one finds that political power and social control is exercised by men—they may be husbands or matrilineal kin. Although the line is contrived through women, power rests with men. The division of labour between the sexes emphasises differential rights and expectations. Men's superior physical qualities are recognised; war and politics is left to them. Rulers, chiefs, elders and managers of property are men. The modern forces of change are further strengthenig the position of men. With opportunities of education, new avenues of livelihood, and geographical mobility, a man gains control over his wife and children as the breadwinner. Several legal measures now enable an individual to demand his/her share in the property. Tenancy laws discouraging absentee landlords have led to splitting of land and breaking up of joint families, like the 'tharwads'.

The British notion of the male-dominated conjugal family and the impact of English literature depicting this model of the family has affected the outlook of young men. Their mobility to other regions of the country, where patriliny prevailed, has also brought changes in the few areas where matriliny was predominant. These changes have been detrimental to women's status. As they move towards sanskritic rituals, dependency on male increase, and dowry emerges as a consideration for settlement of marriages.

Tribal Family

The third type of family is that of the so-called primitive tribes of India. With the coming of Aryans, with their cattle and plough, the jungles were burnt pushing the tribals southward and eastward where they were then cut off from active intercourse with the life in the plains.

> The Aryans and those of the original people who remained in the jungle possibly lost some features of their original culture...and exchanged ideas, words, materials and processes.

Irawati Karve notes that some primitives use a kinship terminology which is made up substantially of sanskritic words. Thus they are an organic part of the Indian life and cannot be treated separately as something fundamentally different from the rest.

The differentiating features are between agriculturists (mostly Hindus) and forest dwellers (mostly primitives). One finds a mixture of patrilineal and matrilineal modes of descent among them. The tribal family is usually set up in nuclear households with the sons moving out after getting married, within close proximity to the father's residence. Among some tribes (like the Bhils of Rajasthan), at least one son will stay with the old parents. The cultural norm among others is for the sons to continue staying with the parents and separate after the death of the father (as among the Tharu and some Gonds). By and large, the nuclear household is the most common form of domestic grouping among the tribals. Joint families are characteristic of land-owning and trading classes.

Changes in the Structure of Family

The scholars on family and social changes observe that the nature of family organisation is closely related to its economic base. Yet even in families in which livelihood is earned from work in factories, offices, labouring of various sorts, in places far away from their ancestral villages, the patriarchal ideology and joint form of family exist as a cultural norm.

In fact the nuclear family, or the modern conjugal family of husband, wife and children may not necessarily be a symmetrical family. If the wife has brought a dowry and the man thinks himself to be the master who deserved it, with the additional role of being the breadwinner, oppressive domination can be as much or even worse than in the joint family structure. In such a set up, the woman is denied even the occasional emotional support of other women that she enjoyed in the joint family. Thus what emerges is patriarchy as the dominant form of family in which the gender construction is oriented towards hierarchic relations between the sexes.

The joint family, due to constant splitting has fragmented the land base to such an extent that there are not many really large households living off the land. In the cities, among the affluent business class, there is more likelihood of large joint families living in spacious palatial houses with enough resources to go around. Thus there are less joint families than ideologically conceded to. This is due to the value placed on the upper caste Brahmanical model of family living. The variations along caste, and occupation lines have been recently studied and they reveal that the preponderance of upper castes is associated with higher jointness in family living.[13]

The same family may assume different types of stages in its developmental cycle. Pauline Kolenda has listed twelve types of families in her study ranging from single person and nuclear (with husband, wife and children) to joint families or lineal (across generations) as well as collateral (in the same generation) joint type. She has also noted that a woman finds joint living very oppressive and desires a separate house of her own. In this effort a woman, presumably, would succeed when she has in her control, important means of rewarding or punishing her husband for his compliance or non-compliance to her wishes. The wife's bargaining power is more among such groups where there is a custom of remarriage of divorced women and the practice of bride price. The other favourable factor is the ability of her natal family or lineage to provide strong economic and social support.[14]

A.M. Shah observes in his study on Gujarat that a joint family is somewhat more characteristic of higher castes and the least characteristic of the untouchable castes. There is no conclusive relationship between landownership and type of family and while the majority of the households are nuclear (husband, wife and children) the majority of the people live in join families, that is, they maintain emotional links with their kin, even when divided by distance.

Western sociologists believed that industrialisation and urbanisation are more compatible with the nuclear family. This may not be true in Asian societies where in urban and in industrialised centres, people retain their family network.

Whatever be the mode of descent or type of family, the woman's role as a mother is central to it and thus the meaning of life for her is basically determined by her biological function.

Marriage

The institution of marriage is the gateway to the family. It has been such a pervasive influence that practically every adult is married in India, particularly women whose only salvation lies in fulfilling motherhood. Just as family is more important to women than to men, so also marriage is more essential to women than for men. It is the only 'Samaskara' (rites) in which women have the opportunity of going through sanskritic rites. She enters the new world through marriage where her worth as a 'reproducer' confers some status on her. Exemption from marriage for women is rare and only for becoming a *sanyasin*.* There are not many *sanyasins* in India.

We have evidence from the Vedas that when the bride and groom used to be old enough they would select each other and the parents or guardians, at best, only helped them by arranging and financing the wedding.[15] Evidences of Gandharva marriage or *Swayamvara* are mostly from royal families; so we have no idea of the form of marriage prevalent among the masses. All the women mentioned in ancient texts were from royal houses or were under the protection of reputed sages. In a later period, marriages began to be arranged by parents.[16]

Caste purity was maintained by controlling the sexuality of women, as mentioned earlier, for the rules regarding marriage were more strictly enforced for women.

The completely segregated life of the young girl or the married woman was the fate of the upper caste groups who worried about maintaining strict structural boundaries. This picture is also repeated among the upper class Muslims and Christians. The women in the lower strata had to work along with their men outside their homes too and were thus exposed to the exploitation along with their men in a system marked with harsh inequalities.

Altekar gives evidence in support of inter-caste marriages as commonly prevalent in ancient times, while they began to be discouraged by 10th century A.D. By 14th and 15th century

*One who has renounced the world.

the practice was almost forbidden. Violation led to excommunication from caste and the condemnation of chidren to a low status. Nevertheless, the violations must have continued which gave rise to nearly 3000 jatis today. Some of the features of Hindu marriage, as emphasised by tradition are:

(1) The principle of endogamy—marriage within the caste.
(2) The rule of exogamy—marriage outside one's gotra and outside certain specified degree of blood relationships. In Northern India village exogamy, or marriage outside the village, is stricIty practised.
(3) *Anuloma* (Hypergamy) or the men of higher castes marrying women of lower castes was preferred to *Pratiloma*—the marriage of women of higher castes of men belonging to lower castes.

By 300 B.C., marriage had come to be so obligatory and powerful a norm for girls that they would be married to highly undesirable men if a proper match was not available. Fathers came to regard it as their religious duty to arrange the marriage of their girls before the onset of puberty. The women were socialised to treat a husband like God whose will was final for them.

The impact of these features led to denial of education for girls, extreme control over their sexuality and freedom of movement, but worst of all was the institution of dowry and the social seclusion of child widows. In a few communities that escaped the Aryan influence like those in the Malabar region, women enjoyed a better position and were married much later than their Aryan sisters.

By 200 A.D., pre-pubertal marriages were common all over India. The trend continued during the medieval times from 1000 A.D. onwards due to foreign invasions. The girls were married by the age of seven or eight years. Child-marriages of three and four year old girls were not uncommon. In the nineteenth century, several reformers, who themselves had been victims of child marriage practice, took up the cause of abolishing this custom. Lala Lajpat Rai married at the age of 12, the Gandhis (Kasturba and Mahatma) were both 13, while Mahadev Govind Ranade married at the age of eight.

The Civil Marriage Act of 1872 made consummation of marriage before the girl had attained the age of 10 a punishable offence leading to life imprisionment. Later the well-known Sarda Act of 1929 fixed the age of marriage for girls at 14 and for boys at 18. Since this Act was applicable to British India, people started performing child marriages in the nearby Princely Indian States. Today, the custom of early marriage continues in the rural areas, and among the illiterate and the poorer strata of society, where religious superstitions hold strong sway. One belief is that the father of the pre-puberscent girl earns special religious merit on her marriage. Another reason for the continuation of the custom is the fear and inability of the poor to protect their women. So by marrying them off at a tender age, they pass the burden to the other family. It is not known to what extent this acts as cultural immunity and results in escape from exploitation by the upper caste, rich and powerful men. But married status of a woman is expected to provide some immunity against such advances.

For their desire to marry off girls at a younger age to men of higher status, with higher qualifications the fathers had to pay a price. This marriage related price—dowry—is in fact the custom of giving away of the virgin daughter as a gift to the bridegroom (called *Kanyadan*), followed by customary subgifts of cash, jewellery etc. called *Dakshina*, as token gifts incidental to Kanyadan.[17] *Dakshina* was not demanded, it was given; it never involved such huge transfers of money as are found in the dowry giving groups today. Yet dowry is an integral part of the hypergamous ideology. What must have begun as a humble offering has attained monstrous proportions. Traditionally, the groom of higher status or for that matter any groom in the 'Kanyadan' marriage was given 'dakshina'. Today there is a hunt for highly educated, salaried men who are paid dowry by many group which earlier practised bride-price.*

The region south of the Vindhyas had the universal practice of bride-price. The isogamous marriages preferably of cross cousins, uncles, and nieces established symmetrical relationships. The girl retained her rights in the natal family where she had her first few deliveries. The flow of gifts was also bilateral. Whatever was received by a girl at her marriage from her own kin and from her husband was retained by her as

*Detailed discussion on this follows later.

her 'Streedhan'. She had the right to dispose or pass it on to her daughter.

The Brahmins looked down upon bride-price as an inferior custom to 'Kanyadan' marriage although it was near universal in the south as well as fairly widespread among the poorer sections of hypergamous castes, Himâlayan people and among other non-hypergamous castes in Central India. The patrilineal tribal groups of the Indian subcontinent customarily pay bride-price. It is a symbolic payment in cash or kind denoting transfer of authority over the bride from her kin group to the bride-groom's kin group. In these communities, a daughter is not regarded as a burden. But among the poorer sections, the custom of bride-price may place the man and his family in debt.

Today, the Brahmanical model is being emulated by these castes which desire to improve their status by marrying their daughters to educated and salaried men who are in short supply. Thus, dowry is introducing a new asymmetry in the South.

The increasing incidence of dowry today is found among communities with a high degree of monetisation, increased agricultural and general prosperity and access to the 'organised sector'. Srinivas views 'modern dowry' as a product of the forces let loose by British rule. Dowry today is a vulgar display of wealth by the new rich which becomes a stranglehold for the parents of poor girls who must offer similar price to procure grooms for them. Srinivas calls dowry as the modern *sati* to which women are being subjected in increaing numbers.[18]

Mate Selection

There are various patterns which prevail regarding the selection of boys and girls for matrimony. By and large, in the rural areas, such arrangements are made with the help of women who have access to both the natal and the in-laws family. The outgoing daughters and sisters and the incoming daughters-in-law play a significant role. They provide information about prospective brides and grooms, negotiate transactions and the arrangement of actual ceremonies. However, it is the older women who exercise this kind of influence. The boy and the girl seldom see each other before marriage. The parent's authority is final. The consideration for such marriages is the dowry the girl is going to bring, the status of the family and the looks of the girl. The girl's parents also ensure the ritual requirements of the relation, the prospects of the girl enjoying the same or superior status as compard to father's home and the physical fitness of the boy. All or some of the conditions may be met in a particular match.

In the cities, and to some extent in the villages too, the girls are subjected to a humiliating parade in which the boy and/ or his people inspect her. In some progressive families such meetings between the boy and the girl and their families may be arranged on an equal footing. But in the majority of the families in the middle-class, it is a painful experience for the girls.

During the freedom movement, at the height of nationalism, inter-caste and inter-religions marriages became common. Gandhiji visualised the struggle for freedom as the freedom from caste, racial and social prejudices too. Unfortunately that favourable environment evaporated quickly after independence.

Monogamy or one man-one woman marriage is a cultural norm in most parts of the country. However, the failure to produce a son or breakdown of marriage results in the man taking a second wife. The Islamic law permits upto four wives. But generally monogamy is the rule, among Muslims too.

Polygamy, to some extent is found among all religions. There is a higher incidence among tribals. The custom of bride-price brings more prestige to a person if he can afford to bring more than one wife. If the agricultural communities among them, an additional wife is seen as an economic asset who not only works on the land but also reproduces labour in the form of children. Artisan groups may also follow this practice for similar reasons. The social factors such as barrenness of the wife, failure to produce a son, illness—mental and physical—and the custom of *levirate** and *sorrorate*** marriages may lead to polygamy.

In some parts we find polygamy too; the variants being polygamy (more than one wife) and polyandry (more than one

*levirate : a widow marrying her dead husband's younger brother.
**sorrorate : a widower marrying wife's younger sister.

hus-band). The Todas of Nilgiri, Khass in Jaunser Bawar and the people of Kinnaur and Lahul and Spiti valley are polyandrous. Polyandry does not imply greater sexual freedom for women because the women have no control over their bodies nor over their children. The system is a variant of patriarchy, in which more than one man has sexual access to a woman in the family.

Among the Muslims, in spite of the legal sanction for polygamy, there is not as high an incidence of it as is believed to be. The law makes polygamy for Hindus a criminal offence, but not for Muslims. Among the former too, the legislation has not been effective in eradicating the evil.

The emergence of Islam, 1300 years ago, gave extra-ordinary rights to women. Muslim women, under the Islamic injunctions, are provided better status compared to other religious groups at least in theory. But in practice, the Muslim women face many handicaps such as polygamy, unilateral divorce, lack of support in the event of a dissolution of marriage etc.

Socialisation

The entire process of socialisation of females is to internalise the concept of dependency which is crippling to the development of their personality. In fact they have *only roles on personality*.

As mentioned earlier, the act of giving the daughter away in marriage lowers the position of the family. By the same principle, a village of bride-givers has an inferior status than the village of bride recievers (This relationship is found even when payment in consideration of marriage is bride-price and not dowry). A daughter is described as *Paraya Dhan* (another's property), *Chidiyan da chamba* (birds of passage) and by other similar terms, and hence any investment in their development is regarded fruitless. In contrast, a son is the support in old age, and a light illuminating the path to the heavens.

Socialisation for gender differentiation and sex inequality starts early in a girl's life. Since she has to leave her father's house where she spends a brief spell of her childhood she can hardly recall the time spent there and tends to glorify it. The north Indian folksongs are full of praise about the father's house which is invariably described as better, richer and a happier one. We came across a prosperous family in a Punjab village, where the mother would wake up a ten-year-old to make cowdung cakes at 4 a.m. on winter mornings—as a part of the training for her future role in the in-laws' house! There is a lot of pressure on young girls from an early age to learn the house-hold chores which they will have to shoulder as young brides. The burden of work is heaviest on the youngest bride. By the some token, in the father's house, a daughter could enjoy more leisure, if her brother's young wife was there. Since the brother's wife comes as a permanent member in her father's house, which a daughter has to leave, there is a quarrelling relationship among them. Panini, the great grammarian wrote that they are 'natural enemies'. In fact, the daughters of the village provided a sort of 'spy service' for watching (and reporting aberrations) about the behaviour of the brides.

The custom of early marriage ensured that the girls learned the tradition of the new family and transferred loyalities to the new home. After marriage, minimum contact with the natal family ensures further immurement in the husband's home. The custom of *Kanyadan* forbids the parents/older brothers etc. to accept anything from the daughter's house and the parents-in-law did not encourage frequent visits to the father's house. The folksongs of North India sung during the marriage ceremony of a daughter reveal the type of welcome she would get by different members of her father's house. *The mother asks her to keep coming, while father says come and spend some time with us, the brother expects her to come on occasions and the brother's wife says why would she need to come now (since she has a house of her own).* CSWI reports that many widows and deserted women they met told them that they could expect support and shelter from their family as long as their fathers were alive. The departure from the father's house, the choice of husband, the re-visits to the natal family are all decisions which do not involve the young girl. Summing up the whole world of women Irawati Karve says, a woman's life may not have been all sorrow. As a pet daughter, a beloved wife and an honoured mother, a woman experienced happiness, "but whatever it was, frustrated or successful, it was made so, mostly by agencies other than her own will. She was owned by someone and her master made her life". To take a few illustrations : "Draupadi was the proud princess of war-like *Panchalas*; whatever social position the Pandavas gained was due to their marriage with her and yet she was gambled away by her husband at dice play. Nala did the same thing; Sita was abandoned at the smallest breath of a scandal."[19]

No wonder there is discrimination in the allocation of resources between the sexes—nutrition, medicare, education and practically everything. Now in the urban educated families, the attitudes are changing, yet the majority of the families, even the well-to-do ones may practice discrimination in the opportunities they give to their sons and daughters. The most manifest is the denial of inheritance to daughters. This is done in a bloodless way—the daughters are so socialised that they internalise the norms of subordination to the will and happiness of others. They are taught to serve best foods to the males in the family—first brothers and father, later sons, husband, father-in-law, brother-in-law etc. They write off their share in parental property in their brother's favour in order to enjoy the 'affection' of the brothers and to ensure welcome to their visits in the natal home. How insecure and alien a woman must be in her husband's home to wish all her life for an occasional escape to her natal family and to be in their books, in case she has to fall back upon them if her marriage breaks down. This fear is a real one with her.

A woman is never a permanent member of her husband's family. "She may have to leave is she does not satisfy and she may leave if she is not satisfied." Patriliny in association with joint property, and joint family household along with the rules governing marriage prescribe a life of constraint on women and is responsible for a devaluation of her position. It is the anxiety of the parents to train her in the strictest manner so that she is used to pain. Then is she is lucky, she may live happily but if the conditions are different and difficult in the husband's house, she will not find it too difficult to adjust. Cruel logic but such is the justification given for girls' socialisation by the parents. In fact, the heart-rending scene at the 'Bidai' (send-off) of the daughter on her marriage is a testimony to the agony of parting with a child who was a part of the family.

Dowry

Dowry as a consequence of the ancient religious custom of pre-puberty marriages and hypergamy for maintaining caste hierarchy are not the only consideration for marriage today. A complex of factors reinforce the evil custom. The parents want to marry off the daughters above their status. In ancient times, it was higher caste of the boy (hypergramy) for which the parents paid a price. Now in addition to it are higher education and more remunerative occupation of the boy. In Bihar, Uttar Pradesh, Orissa and Punjab, there are well defined grades of dowry for different professional categories of grooms—an IAS commanding the highest dowry. There is competition among the parents of the girls to buy the best. Yet in U.P., thousands of marriages are arranged with boys having little education and without much prospect of a good job, with considerable dowry. In the rural society, the parents still consider it their duty to marry girls at a young age as it supposedly brings spiritual rewards. The amount of dowry a girl takes along with her is supposed to enhance her status. A well placed boy is expected to give her a secure future and a leisurely life. It is prestigious to be the wife of a man where a woman does not need to work (for a wage). Thus dowry encourages the belief that women's work in the home is non-productive. Very often the girls take up paid employment to earn money for their dowry.

The marriages of educated girls who are capable of economic independence are also settled with dowry, because the parents look for a match with higher qualification than the girl with a well-paid job.

If the girl has a permanent job there will be perhaps less emphasis on dowry in anticipation of control on continuous income she is going to bring to the husband's family.

In the custom of gift exchange e.g., in the South, Maharashtra or in Bengal, gifts are not of equal value. Whereas the boy's family may give only symbolic presents, the girl's family gives an enormous amount by way of dowry. The parents of boys justify taking dowry by saying that they have to do the same for their daughters. They also demand the expenses incurred on the son's education as he is going to give the benefit of his education and occupation by supporting the girl and her children. The entire attitude is to devalue the girl's contribution and her input into home-making. Some justify dowry as a sort of compensation to the daughter in lieu of her share in the parental property. In Hindu Law, claim to mainteneance in the joint property also included expenses on her marriage. Muslims, among whom Islamic law gives right of inheritance to the daughter, compensate instead by giving dowry. In many parts of India, the in-laws purchase gold from the cash received from the girl's father. The rich peasants in Andhra Pradesh and Karnataka give land in addition to other gifts. But this view about dowry as the female share in property just confuses the issue. It is neither transfer of wealth nor share in the father's property in the form of moveable property. On the one hand, the rich families deny the daughter an equal share with her brothers, and on the other, the poor families give much more by way of dowry than their resources permit, often incurring heavy debts to meet the demands. The salaried middle-class are the worst examples of the second type. They are also the ones who desire the daughter to be placed comfortably, while those who are the dowry receivers view it as an opportunity for one-time rise in their standard of living. Receiving a big dowry for one's son or giving it for one's daughter, are both considered to be measures of the status of a family. In this commercial transaction for status enancement, the girl is the only forgotten factor. The quick economic gain by a family/group are exhibited by the show of wealth at the time of marriage. This is found among every class. Gold may replace silver, synthetic sarees to cottons and steel instead of brass utensils, to give a few examples in the lower class's upward economic mobility. Among the more affluent ones, it takes the form of scooters, refrigerators, cars ostentatious expenditure on food, lighting etc.

Much of this wealth evaporates without trace, such as the money spent on decoration, entertainment and food. One thing it does achieve is status enhancement for the family. But the entire exercise is wasteful, without any lasting value to the daughter whose share in the parental wealth is squandered in such display.

The custom of bride-price is equally oppressive for the family of the groom. Many tribals find it hard to get a wife and incur debts to pay the price. At other places it may lead to servitude for generations for taking the money from a money-lender. In Uttar Kashi region, a woman may be sent for prostitution by the husband to clear off the debt he incurred on his marriage with her.

All these practices denote a low status of women in comparison to men. True, the girls in this group are not regarded as a curse by the family of birth and a woman has the right to leave the man if she so desires without loss of prestige, and can marry again. But the conception of women as someone's possession—of the father in bride-price giving communities, and of the husband in those giving dowry—is a degrading one and the law prohibits both the customs.

The concept of 'Streedhan' as traditionally understood in the south, included the wealth received by a woman from both her husband's and her father's family. In an event of divorce/separation/remarriage, the husband's parents would take away their part of it but the woman was still left with her parental gifts (mostly jewellery).

Hindu marriage rites emphasise the superiority of the male. While groom promises to protect and support the bride, she in turn should follow the husband, act according to his wishes, serve the elders in his family, be affectionate to the young and should remain steadfast in her duties, ready to suffer in silence. We do not know how many brides and grooms understand the 'mantras' at the time of wedding, for a vast majority are ignorant and illiterate, while those who can understand go through the ritual without much belief in them. Yet the usage that emphasises inequality in marriage continues.

The problem of dowry has been one of the most important issues in the women's movement in this country. Howeer, it is also related to the domestic and therefore private lives of women which is difficult to fight. The form of violence that take place within the four walls of the home would be treated as crimes if they were to happen on the street. But domestic violence is treated as a family affair, about which the police and the courts are also biased. A woman is always viewed as someone's sister, daughter, wife or mother—never as a citizen in her own right who also needs to live with dignity and self-respect. Demanding dowry as a consideration of her marriage is the ultimate insult to her dignity. It reflects the devaluation of women's roles in society and their powerlessness.

Attack on Dowry

The evil of dowry is emerging as the major curse on the women in our society. There seems to be no difference now in the prevalence of the practice, either religionwise or castewise.[20] The demands of dowry continue to grow, so does the harassment of young brides for continuous flow of gift and cash by their husbands' family and the inability to do so unleashes violence ranging from beating, resultant suicide and murder. (We discuss this form of violence in a later chapter)

Several women's organisations and other civil rights organisations campaigned together to press for a Bill amending the 1961 Act, to make it more effective. Thus around the 70s, the government appointed a Joint Select Committee of Parliament to look into this problem. During the same period, the Law Commission has also submitted a report on enquiry into dowry deaths. Finally in 1984, a Bill to amend the existing Act was passed whose provisions are taken up later in our chapter that includes law. Demanding dowry is a cognisable offence but cultural norms and social pressures restraint the parents from going to the law courts. Therefore, the new Bill empowers any recognised welfare institution or organisation to take up a woman's case in a law court.

The women's rights groups feel that the law is not sufficiently deterrent to the practice of dowry in its present form. Their suggestions are to further tighten it form maximum benefit to women. Some of their recommendations are:

1. To accept the Law Commission's definition of dowry: "Dowry should include among others, things estimable in terms of money demanded or taken from the wife or her parents or other relatives by the husband or his parents or other relatives at any time, i.e., before, during and after the marriage, where such a demand or taking is not properly referable to any legally recognised claim and a relatable to the wife's having married into the husband's family."
2. The ceiling on expenses on marriage should include expenses incurred by *both* the parties to the marriage together.
3. The number of persons in the 'Barat' should be limited to 25 as already done in Punjab and Haryana.

4. The law should be applicable to both bride's and bridegroom's families.
5. Minimum imprisonment should be increased to one year from six months.
6. The value of customary gifts should be fixed at Rs.5000. The gifts should be limited only to the bridegroom and not to the persons related to him.
7. The government should appoint Dowry Prohibition officers in each state, who would prepare annual reports which, in turn, would be placed before the State Legislature and the Parliament. Offences under the Dowry Prohibition (Amendment) Bill 1984 should be made unbailable and compoundable.

Widow Remarriage

There are some permissible conditions for widow remarriage in some communities (e.g. levirate marriages). The practice of widow remarriage was shunned by the upper caste Hindus as well as by the elites among other religious groups. They form a minority; yet in absolute numbers the widows are a large group of women subjected to a great deal of suffering, because though women are allowed to remarry in the lower castes, very few actually do. The number of widows far exceed the number of widowers in every Census.

The social indignities heaped on the widows from ancient times are recorded. The could not participate in auspicious ceremonies, nor be allowed to wear good clothes or eat normal food. They were to make themselves unattractive to the opposite sex and were largely debarred from public spaces, and were made to observe lifelong mourning for the dead husband. The self-immolation by a widow was an act of highest merit. Even today, many villages worship the site where a 'Sati' was committed. This might have been confined to the upper caste/ class families. Yet they formed the reference models for the rest of the society.

The Widow Remarriage Act XV was passed as early as 1856 but the stigma attached to widows continued. The economic plight of the widows is the product of an unsympathetic attitude by the society. Many were forced to flee to holy cities like Varanasi to survive on people's charity. There are an estimated 20,000 widows in that city alone.

The new laws, discussed earlier, provide the widows the right to share in the husband's property. This is, however, relevant only in the case of propertied classes. For the poor widows, several states (U.P. and Punjab) have adopted a scheme for providing a small pension. The government has now provided family pensions to widows of government servants. These relief measures help the widows, but the lasting solutions are:

1. helping the widows to be economically independent and the law should protect their rights.
2. Change in attitudes towards widows and a climate in which the widows' rights to make their own decisions are respected. Today not many men or their families approve of marriage with a widow. A concerted effort towards social education is needed for attitudinal change towards widows.

Education and Employment of Women and Changes in Family

The view that social changes, especially those related to the pursuit of higher education and employment of educated women will make possible for women, greater control over their lives and their income is not borne out by facts. In fact, in one study 77 per cent of the highly educated working women turned over most of their income to husbands or mothers-in-law.

The mere fact that a neo-local residence is formed is not a sign of the emergence of nuclear family and breakdown of the joint family. The obligations to the joint family continue to be fulfilled, such as remittances to the parental family, participation in family ceremonies, and assistance in a time of crisis. In fact, the joint family may provide the family support a woman needs for child care if she has to go out to work. A mother-in-law may look forward to a new daughter-in-law as relief from her burdens. Similarly to a young woman, a mother or mother-in-law would provide a perfect family support-system if she has to go out to work. Yet such arrangements benefit the women only if the other memebrs of the family share the child-care and the domestic responsibilities. But the ideology about gender division of labour permeates all kinds of family, because whatever sharing exists is only between female members.

The picture of the rural family shows a highly segregated world of men and women. But the women spend a great deal of time with other women. In the urban situation, except among the upper caste or class joint households, a woman is isolated from the world of women as well as from the male world. The older women in the traditional family set-up can also be tyrants because of the role they are given to implement the patriarchal values by controlling younger women and enforcing qualities of docility, obedience, submission etc. In some metropolitan cities, a new trend is also visible where the power balance between the mother-in-law and daughter-in-law often tilts in favour of the latter because of the latter's employment, superior education and greater sophistication.

Unfortunately, the educational institutions, the new economic and political institutions as well as employers share the family ideology of emphasising the traditional role of women at homemaking and child-care even when women have taken up full time employment outside the home or female industries develop where women are given wage work to be done in the household.

Among the middle-class educated woman many are forced to take up paid employment due to economic necessity, while others, after being educated, seek to become economically independent. It is assumed that these women have a more dynamic approach towards life.

The incompatibility between these two roles assumed by women lead to a double burden. There are two solutions to the situation.

1. A social climate (reinforced by educational institutions and media) emphasising sharing of household work by all members of the family—men, women, boys and girls.
2. Working women to be considered as a special group to be given favourable working conditions such as flexible working hours, transportation and housing facilities and child-care facilities.

Women have always been engaged in productive labour

along with their child-bearing and rearing functions but industrialisation has, by removing the workplace a way from home, created problems for women.

There are many who have no male around. They are separated, deserted and divorced of the so-called 'male breadwinner' who is irresponsible towards his family. Thus the women have to earn their livelihood and look after themselves and the children. Wives of migrant men, especially overseas migrants may not receive any remittances for years, leaving them to shoulder single-handedly the family responsibility. The report about this category of women reveals that the women most likely to assume economic roles outside the home are the youngest or only daughters, that residing in 'fatherless' families, and women who have experienced significant economic loss.

Impact of Education

There is unmistakably more opportunities for women in the environment today than ever before. Education is one of the crucial factors in improving women's position. For example, Kerala which has the highest literacy rate has also the lowest female infant mortality rate and is experiencing a steady rise in the age of marriage of girls. Yet the menace of dowry is infesting all communities, even in marriages of educated girls. It is reported that a large number of Christian girls seek escapism into religion by becoming nuns rather than undergo the humiliation of marriage with dowry and other kinds of oppressions which follow it.

A growing number of educated, working young women, especially in the larger cities, are thinking of alternatives to marriage and are demanding institutional arrangements like hostels for single working women who can live independently. Where such facilities are available along with employment opportunities, many women prefer to lead single lives. The educational opportunities are generally restricted to a girl in the privileged class. The wide disparities in education of women in the different strata is also reflected in the employment patterns among working women. On the one hand, women, however small in number, are entering into professions with men on equal terms. There are women engineers, architects, managers, administrators, diplomats; even politicians and ministers. On the other, a vast bulk of poor, illiterate women work in the unorganised sector, whose contribution is indispensable to the survival of the family. While economic participation of the labouring class women also gives them more or equal power in decision making in their families, it is not such a liberating fact considering the economic deprivation from which the whole family suffers. An improvement in a family's economic position results in the withdrawal of women from employment as the traditional Indian notion of high status is associated with women's confinement within the home. Another reason for such withdrawal is the greater input required for preparing the children for higher education and better skills.

The modern pressures of inflationary conditions, the egalitarian ideology and the consciousness about one's constitutional rights are making more and more women desire economic independence as a first step towards a dignified existence. Yet a decline in the opportunities for economic participation among the poorest women in the country has been observed. The Seventh Plan proposes to correct the position. The Ministry of Social and Women's Welfare has been set up to look after the problems of women as a needy group, among others.

The pressures from the wider economic forces are constantly affecting the women and their families. The pressure on land, the pauperisation of peasantry, the extinction of certain handicrafts etc., coupled with employment opportunities in the cities push out, at least the poor, to the cities. In India today, 69 per cent of all migration is rural migration, and 77 per cent of all migrants are females. In the cities these migrants live in slums where a new kind of family organisation is emerging. There is no community of one's roots, with its folk culture, tradition and norms or the values shared by members of a family. Each member of such families develops in relation to his or her work and social environment to which he or she is exposed in the city. Very often, in these families women shoulder the burden of looking after themselves and the children by taking up any work for less than adequate wages. The men are in this way in a position to exercise some discretion in choosing the type of work as well as the wages acceptable to them.

The decision to educate the girls is taken within the family. It may be noted here that there may be more *modernity* in people's attitudes rather than in their actual actions. If a family can afford to educate one of the two children, it is the male child who is more likely to be sent to school. The same is true for expenditure on higher education on sons and daughters in most families.

The major familial problem for the bulk of the families is not education, or even literacy, but the availability of employment.

Much of the devaluation of women results due to the non-recognition of their work within the family which includes various forms of subsistence production. This invisibility of the women's contribution is now being brought to life and measures are being sought at the international level to bring it under the category of economically productive work. Early marriage, preceded by cheerless childhood, a gruelling exercise in going through the agony of dowry raising by the family, the strange family as the husband's home, the anxiety about giving birth to male children, the curbs on freedom of eating, sleeping, talking and moving, the various intrigues for position among the women, the use of manipulation of males (sons) and pathetic old age and unprotected widowhood, are the various expressions of an unjust social structure—the family. A woman may go through some or all or none of these experiences. Yet to the extent that any of these dismal aspects affect a woman's life they are a reflection of an unhealthy society.

The oppression of women within the family has never emerged as a social issue because of the social values demanding privacy and sovereignty of the family. This subjects millions of women to private sufferings of various degrees. The facade of family *prestige*, *honour*, *izzat* act as constraints on their resort to legal help or social therapy. Only when the oppression takes extreme forms like physical injury and death, does it receive public attention.

The parental family undertakes the first conditioning for acceptance of an unequal status, where young girls are taught to be submissive and docile while boys are given importance and status. Girls are confined to indoor life and denied the opportunities for education and other life chances which are bestowed on the boys. This role is further refined towards more servility and dependence after marriage. Their economic contribution by wage work too may not alter this subordination of women because men control both productive and reproductive functions of women.

While poorer classes blame alcohol as the villain of the piece in the husband's ill-treatment of wife and children, in the middle-classes the situation is no better majority of the suicides and murders of women are due to family tensions. The attitudes of the law and order machinery is also negative towards women as they share the family ideology that women should keep their domestic affairs within the family, and not bring them out in the public. A 'good' woman is one who should not complain about her 'own' home and her husband/in-laws. Parents are heard saying that a girl should prefer to die in her husband's home rather than go back to the father. The withdrawal of support from the two families—the father's and the husband's—may drive a woman to the ultimate step of taking her own life (if the in-laws have not done so by burning her). The family is an institution which denies the fundamental rights and constitutional guarantees to women.

The consciousness about the inferior position of women is emerging slowly, but unmistakably:

(1) It is heartening to note that there is growing awareness about gender injustice among people, the policy-makers and the academic community.
(2) Women have started protesting in their different milicu in an organised manner—the peasant women, the factory workers, the college teachers, the housewives are reacting against injustice.
(3) The family is the biggest brake on the right for assembling and organising by women, because women are separated as individuals whose first loyalty is to their families, thus denying them the right for individual liberty. Yet unless women start the movement for democratic rights within the family, they cannot participate in the social, political and economic life of the nation. The women's voice is aginst hierarchy—of which male-female inequality is one of the many other manifestations. Thus both men and women have a stake in it.

Notes and References

1. The sociological literature is flooded with family studies which describe the roles without examining the inequalities within the family. See, as examples, Talcott Parsons, *Social Structure and Personality* (New York: Free Press, 1970) and Talcott Parsons and Robert F. Bales, *Family, Socialization and Interaction Process* (New York: Free Press, 1955).
2. Taking household as the focus, accounts of different activities of women of different social groups have been given, among others, by Mary Chatterjee, "Conjugal roles and social networks in an Indian urban sweeper locality," in *Journal of Marriage and the Family* [39, 1977 (i)]; J. Jacobson and Susan Wadley, *Women in India: Two Perspectives* (Columbia: South Asia Books, 1977); and Oscar Lewis, *Village Life in Northern India* (New York: Random House, 1958).

   The ritual roles of women and its symbolism in religion is the theme of some anthropological writings such as those of P. Hershman, "Virgin and Mother", in I. Lewis (ed.), *Symbols and Sentiment* (London : Academic Press, 1977); Susan Wadley, "Women and the Hindu Tradition", in D. Jacobson and S. Wadley, op.cit., U. King, "Women and Religion: the status and image of women in major religious traditions", in D.Souza (ed.), op.cit.

   Women in Contemporary India (New Delhi : Mandian, 1975). The Role of family for women is encountered in every feminist analysis. An excellent collection of papers is in A. Kuhn and Ann-Marie Wolpe (eds.) *Feminism and Materialism* (London : Routledge and Kegan Paul, 1978). Explaining women's role in the broader context of community and its production process also necessitates the description of family authority structure and the intra-household relationships. On the one hand, we have the accounts of paternalism leading to control on women (and men) in hierarchical structures, on the other, a social premium placed on women's dependent role. Ursula Sharma brings it out very clearly in her *Women, Work, and Property in North-West India* (London : Tavistock Publications, 1980). However, this ideology of the submissive wife is more true of the high status groups.

   Maria Mies, *Indian Women and Patriarchy* (New Delhi : Concept Publishing Co., 1980), it is a study of middle class educated women who, the author thinks, are the most oppressed under patriarchal values.
3. The first ever survey of the status of women in India was undertaken by a committee appointed by the Government of India which submitted its report on 1974, entitled: "Towards Equality", this committee on the Status of Women in India (*CSWI*) is undertaking a revaluation after ten years.
4. An extensive analysis of ancient and historical description of the family and kinship system in four linguistic regions of India, northern, central, eastern and southern, which enable us to understand the continuity and differences between regions as well as between different historical periods, is provided Irawati Karve, *Kinship Organisation in India* (Bombay : Asia Publishing House, 3rd ed., 1968). It is an irony that she being one of the few Indian intellectuals writing on women and coming

from the family of pioneers in social reforms like widow remarriage, dedicates the book to her husband with the words:
"I place my head on your feet and ask for your blessings."

5. Ibid., p.8.
6. A study of the family as it exists in residential unit and the relation between its size and nuclearity or jointness is provided with the analysis of Gujarati families as well as with the help of an excellent annotated bibliography of the family studies in A.M. Shah's *The Household Dimension of the Family in India* (New Delhi : Orient Longmans Ltd., 1973).
7. K.M. Kapadia, quotes Dr. P.V. Kane and others to give the approximate dates of the chronology of Sanskritic texts. See, K.M. Kapadia, *Marriage and Family in India* (Delhi : Oxford University Press, 3rd ed., 1980).
8. M.N. Srinivas in forword to A.M. Shah, footnote No. 6.
9. See Leela Dube, *Sociology of Kinship : An Analytical Survey of Literature* (Bombay : Popular Prakashan, 1974).
10. op. cit., *CSWI*.
11. *CSWI*, p.56.
12. For studies on the association between rural-urban residence, caste association, education etc. and jointness of family, see I.P. Desai, *Some Aspects of Family in Mahuva* (Bombay : Asia Publishing House, 1964); M.S. Gore, *Urbanization and Family Change* (Bombay : Popular Prakashan, 1968): William J. Goode, *World Revolution and Family Patterns* (London : Collier Macmillan Ltd., 1963); and Pauline M. Kolenda, "Region, Caste and Family Structure : A Comparative Study of the Indian `Joint Family'" in Milton Singer and Bernard S. Cohn (eds.), *Structure and Change in Indian Society* (New York : Wenner-Gren Foundation for Anthropological Research, 1968), p.339-396.
13. K.M. Kapadia, "Rural Family Patters : A Study in Urban-Rural Relations", *Sociological Bulletin*, V, III-126.
14. I.P. Desai, op.cit., also Vedic Index R.V.X., 27.12 quoted in K.K. Jha, *Rethinking in Marriage Institution* (Patna : Chintamani Prakashan, 1979). Pauline Kolenda finds more joint families in those districts where women's natal kin are not strong influence. The husband's kin and patrilineality are strongly related to high joint family districts. See "Marked Regional differences in Indian Family Structue", paper presented at the Asian Regional Conference on Women and the Household, Delhi, January 1985.
15. P.V. Kane, *History of Dharma Shastras* (Poona : Vol. II, Pt. I, 1947).
16. A.S. Altekar, *The Position of Women in Hindu Civilisation*, Banaras, 1956.
17. M.N. Srinivas, *Some Reflections on Dowry*. J.P. Naik, *Memorial Lecture*, Oxford University Press, New Delhi, 1983.
18. Srinivas, ibid.
19. Iravati Karve, op.cit.
20 "The Dowry Prohibition Act, 1961," *Samya Shakti*, Vol.I, No.2, 1984.

5

Health—A Gender Issue in India

Power relations mediate all social life and as such, they not only determine our environment but also define the way we react to it. Our definition of health and illness depend on the characteristics of the society we live in and our location in it. In our society, we find that as long as an individual is carrying out the assigned role, the individual is considered healthy. But the patterns of morbidity and mortality reveal the contradiction between real health needs of the individual and the actual level of health considered adequate and necessary. How does this affect and concern women ?

Power relations not only define *what is health* in the perceptions of women on their own health needs, but also determine access to health care (such as food, medical attention) and the degree of control women have over body-events that influence health, such as pregnancy or child-bearing and the amount of rest and recuperation available after sickness, after child-birth and after work.

There is also a close connection between employment, education and health. Discrimination against the girl child begins at birth. Three-fourths of the 50 million children who are not enrolled in any school are *girls*. It is estimated that 30 per cent of the total work of fuel gathering, fetching water, and farm work is done by girls aged between 6-11. Almost the entire burden of sibling care is on the girl child. Education influences mortality, morbidity and fertility through better knowledge and through a better social status.

As a part of the labour force, their needs as women are subordinated to the needs of the economy and hence these needs are not provided for. It is said that women are both to create, rear and socialise children and thus enable them to grow into the desired adults who are capable of effectively carrying out the roles assigned to them by the society. Thus women's traditional role is to give birth to and bring up the future workers of the economy. Hence for a woman the definition of health is determined by her ability to perform these functions, even though millions of women work on the farm and in agricultural activities, in the household industry, non-household industry and services. Herein lies a basic contradiction.

Thus all the nutrition programmes are aimed at pregnant and lactating women. But what about the *nutritional deprivation* suffered by girls from infancy to pregnancy? Infant mortality rates clearly show how due to deprivation, the female child morbidity and mortality rate is much higher than that of the male child, even though biologically the female is much tougher. Even if the undernourished child does not die, there is increasing evidence that the child will grow to adulthood, stunted physically and mentally. The undernourished woman will give birth to a premature child (in birth-weight, length and maturity). And what about the women who have fulfilled their reproductive roles but must continue to work for their families' survival, without enough food to meet their own needs? Hence the health of women is an important indicator of the health of the entire work force.

The changing patterns of economic development have put a heavy burden on women which is reflected in their health status. The marginalisation of farmers, landlessness, forced migration, temporary and permanent, have undoubtedly affected women's health and nutritional status. The growth of small and cottage industries has depended heavily on female labour. Most of these industries do not come under the purview of any kind of safety legislation. Women work in industries like tanning, tobacco, cashew, coir textiles, garment, fish processing and canning etc. In all these industries, they toil to long hours at low paid, unskilled jobs. Hence there are health problems related to the work place, hazards of pollutants on women who work during childhood, adolescence, pregnancy and lactation that can be dangerous both to women and foetus. There is very little information about the safety-levels of these harmful substances and more often the damage done includes, T.B., allergies, abortions, bronchial disorders, death of unborn child, anaemia, toxicity, disfiguration etc. Therefore, women have in the last decade become exposed to new kinds of health hazards.

In addition to these disadvantages, provision of facilities to the woman-workers during maternity is woefully inadequate. Hardly 5 per cent of women have legal safeguards that guarantee benefits and violations reduce the actual coverage to around 2.30 per cent. Women perform not only what the Census of India defines as 'work' but a lot of other activities that are energy consuming—cooking, collecting fuel, fetching water, looking after cattle and other animals, unpaid work on the family farm or in family craft and child-care. Calorie needs for women are calculated without regard to the actual work burdens of women, but even these norms are not fulfilled for women and girls as they eat consistently less than their requirements. Malnutrition aggravates diseases, increases risks of infections and reduces resistance to various diseases. Yet, ironically women do not consider themselves ill. In a study done by Amartya Sen, in Bengal, more men than women declared themselves ill.[1]

Women have been the major targets of family planning programmes. Even here they do not have the basic right to choice in this most intimate man-woman relationship. They do not even have the right to their own reproductivity. They have to have as many children especially, sons, as the husbands or their family desire. They have to choose the family planning method that is approved by the husband, mother-in-law and finally the doctor concerned. If they complain of side effects there is no attention paid to it—they have to suffer in silence.

Family planning programmes are population—control oriented and do not place any emphasis on women's health, emotional and psychological welfare. They do not raise the status of women by reducing unwanted pregnancy but make them victims of experimentation and state policy.

Despite being deprived of health care, women make the best providers of it. Women know herbs that heal, the songs that soothe a feverish child, the precautions to need be taken during pregnancy etc. Even the dais (the village mid-wives) had their own store of knowledge. No doubt, there were a lot of superstitious and unhealthy practices going on. But today's health system fail to see the sensitivities of the rural and uneducated women. These women are inhibited by hospital environment, the people they have to deal with, especially men, be they doctors or any other health worker, the distance to be covered from home to hospital, the money required for expenses etc. If only we could have a health system that goes from house to house.

There is little systematic data available to support any analysis of women's health status. And this in itself is a telling comment on how important the health of women is to society. Improving women's health is not just a matter of providing maternal and child health services. It must include educational programmes and social reforms. Unfortunately, a great impediment in the realisation of women's constitutional, legal and social rights has been the woman herself. In India women's health issues have not emerged as a major focus of activity or analyses within the women's movement. Women's groups are aware of the women's inaccessibility to health care services, the lack of reproductive freedom, sexual harassment of women and the extent of the sexist bias in medicine. But this has not led to any comprehensible theoretical understanding of women's health as a part of feminist theory. Nor has it raised any concerted action programmes. There have been individual campaigns, such as the demand for a ban on hormone-based contraception, on drugs for pregnancy testing and amniocentesis for sex determination. There is an inadequate understanding of the total health care that is required in terms of guarantee to women—adequate nutrition, in consonance with the energy expenditure requirements, maternal care at all stages, importance of reducing the heavy work burdens and ensuring adequate rest and leisure, health education toward preventive care and a family planning programme that would become woman centered and not population control biased.

TABLE 5.1

Sex Ratio by Age Group from 1901 to 1981*

(Sex ratio Females per 1000 males in the Census Year)

Age group in years	*1901* 972	*1911* 964	*1921* 955	*1931* 950	*1941* 945	*1951* 946	*1961* 941	*1971* 930	*1981* 935
0–4	1078	1030	1035	1023	1004	990	992	979	
5–9	955	999	960	912	945	965	955	943	
10–14	924	817	822	884	903	936	877	885	
15–19	929	930	916	991	928	944	929	882	
20–24	1092	1078	1075	1023	986	969	1051	998	
25–29	980	968	968	952	984	958	974	1007	
30–34	967	961	954	901	943	927	929	975	
35–39	882	853	841	973	914	897	872	909	
40–44	969	949	945	869	902	882	891	848	
45–49	882	849	823	863	898	884	855	836	
50–54	997	917	954	889	904	902	974	847	
55–59	919	884	860	945	935	936	861	866	
60 and above	1149	1092	1040	994	958	1001	1000	936	
Unspecified	1174	1267	—	—	—	—	863	1071	

*Source : Veena Shatrugna, *Women and Health*, Research Centre for Women's Studies, SNDT Women's University, Bombay, 1984.

Sex Ratio

The sex ratio of a population is likely to be a composite of biological and social factors which cannot be easily separated. In the case of sex ratio the role played by biological factors may be very small especially because its influence is only in the early part of life. So it is the social factors that have a significant impact on sex ratio. In the advanced countries, there is a higher death rate among males than females, but in India, upto the age of 34, the female death rate is much higher than that of males.

The sex ratio of a closed population is a function of the sex ratio of births and deaths. The difference in the sex ratio at birth is not the main cause of a male dominant population in India. It is the difference in mortality rates of the two sexes which cause the number of males in India to rise in comparison with the number of females. Mortality differentials sex-wise are considered a major determinant of sex ratio in India (Table 5.1).

There is considerable evidence on the low life expectancy of females at birth. Female mortality is higher for all age groups including 'infant', maternal and old age groups. Higher mortality of males is obvious in the mortality rates during the first day, first week or even the first month in all countries including India. But after the first month social factors operate effectively to bring down the relative disadvantage of the male in India. It is only in India that females die at a higher death rate than males after the first month of birth.

Demographic-cum-economic indicators of the adverse status of women in India are prominent. Considered according to relig-

TABLE 5.2

Percentage Completeness of Registration of Infant Deaths*

Age Group	*Rural*		*Urban*	
	Males	*Females*	*Male*	*Females*
Less than 1 week	18	17	40	39
1 week to 1 month	24	20	36	31
1 month to 6 months	30	26	50	45
6 months and over	46	36	59	47
Under 1 year	27	24	45	41

*Source : Registrar General, India, *Sample Registration System*, 1980

ion, age, rural or urban setting the sex ratio demonstrates the odds against women. The most interesting feature is that the sex ratio becomes increasingly adverse with rise in age. In 12 out of the 16 states and for the country as a whole, the sex ratio deteriorated considerably and the reasons for the continuing adverse sex ratio have been explored ever since the Census was started in 1871. This is perhaps the most prominent demographic feature in India not only because of its persistence but also because it is a dramatic connotation of the social and health status of women. Although an adverse sex ratio is a feature of relatively less developed countries, yet what worries us about the Indian situation is that this phenomenon has continued despite large scale, intensive efforts at improving the overall health status of the population. As population growth has been mainly due to falling death rates with marginal decreases in fertility, the adverse sex ratio in India has been by and large the product of adverse *female* health relative to that of males.

Almost every Census report starting with 1871, has emphasised the following : (1) the crucial role of mortality, (2) significant contribution of mortality in the child-bearing age group 15-34 to aggregate female mortality and (3) crucial role of neglect of female health in female mortality. It has been pointed out that underenumeration played an insignificant role. Neglect of female health is testified through these factors : female infanticide, neglect of female infant's life, premature cohabitation resulting in early child bearing, over-work and malnutrition. The Indian female is much more at a disadvantage even when compared to other developing countries. After the age of 34, the Indian female probably gets an advantage over the male but she is not as vigorous as females are in other countries. In India the higher death rate of the female compared to that of the male can be traced to her status as a second class citizen. Attitudes towards sterilisation or family planning with a given composition of male and female children prominently bring out the unpopularity of female children.

Differential Access to Health Care

Health surveys were conducted in the then Bombay among six rural communities of six districts in 1957 covering a rural population of 37,000. It was observed that among non-adults (i.e. age group below 15 years) there were 513 male children ailing, as compared to 730 females in the year of survey. Among the non-adults the percentage of males getting some medical treatment was much higher than the percentage of females. This was true of adult males and females. Moreover the male female differences were very striking in the backward villages that enjoyed less communication with the outside world. Women received more of free treatment, traditional treatment or no treatment at all. An ever widening gap in educational levels of the males and females, and the lower employment of females as compared to males, and in addition excessive child-bearing, all add to the inferior health status of women.

Urbanisation and industrialisation might cause a decline in fertility but a more relevant factor associated with health improvement is education because by and large education changes attitudes and outlook whereas urbanisation and industrialisation might improve the economic status of women. Moreover, urbanisation in India is a result of the spillover of the rural population into cities caused by push migration. Such migration not only does not lead to decline in fertility, it leaves personal health culture unchanged.

Mortality

TABLE 5.3

Death Rate by Sex in Children of Age Group 0-4 Years in Rural and Urban Areas from 1970-1978*

Year	*Rural*			*Urban*			*Total*		
	M	*F*	*T*	*M*	*F*	*T*	*M*	*F*	*T*
1970	55.1	61.0	58.1	32.3	32.3	32.3	50.5	55.3	52.9
1971	53.2	59.3	56.2	31.1	33.3	33.3	49.2	54.8	51.9
1973	53.1	60.8	56.8	29.6	33.4	31.4	48.9	56.0	52.3
1976	54.2	55.9	55.2	29.0	30.1	29.7	49.6	51.9	50.1
1978	53.9	54.9	54.2	30.1	31.0	30.5	49.9	50.4	50.1

*Source: *Survey on Infant and Child Mortality, 1979—A Preliminary Report*, Office of the Registrar General, India, New Delhi, 1980, p.34.

In 1979, the overall average infant mortality for males was 120 per 1000 and 131 for males, according to the latest figures as released by the Ministry of Health.

Education makes a distinct impact on infant mortality:

Level of Education of Women	*Rural*	*Urban*
Illiterate	132	81
Literate, below Primary	105	59
Primary and above	64	49

Occupation also influences infant mortality. For mothers who were in agriculture and allied occupations, it was 127 in rural areas and 119 in urban areas; but for industrial workers it was 194 in rural areas and 121 in urban areas.

Neo-Natal & Post-Natal Mortality : All India

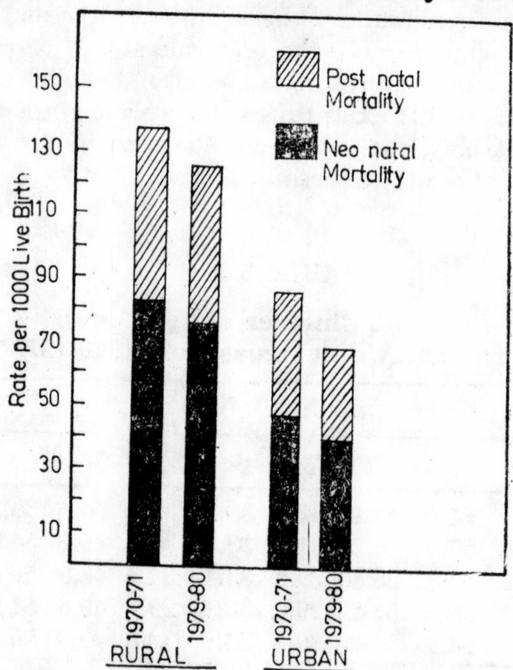

It is said that women are born to create—in India nearly 100,000 women die every year due to abortion and childbirth, a figure 100 times higher than in developed countries. Two-thirds of pregnant women in India are anaemic. Complications of pregnancy due to high fertility lead to many complications of pregnancy resulting in a high percentage of deaths. Pregnant women lose immunity to malaria and are most susceptible to viral infections. It also precipitates the development of overt leprosy and diabetes and childbirth triggers episodes of major psychiatric pathology. The difference between male and female mortality is highest in the age group of 15-35. In 1972, the infant mortality rate was 132 per 10,000 for males and 148 for females. In 1978 the same differences prevailed; male mortality being 120 but female mortality 131. Maternal mortality is 680/100,000 in rural areas. There is now a marked increase in the number of teenagers seeking abortions. Repeated abortions lead to low birth weight and obstetrical complications. Women can rarely avail of maternal leave and day-care centres or creches are few and far between; the better ones are expensive and out of reach except for the middle-class. Even in establishments that are legally required to provide creches, less than 15 per cent do so. In 1975, 1 per cent of all deaths were due to pregnancy and childbirth. In 1979 it was more, i.e. 1.1 per cent. The percentage distribution of maternal death for almost all cases was higher in 1979 than 1975.

Anaemia: This condition can make one easily tired causing blackouts and general disinterest in work with lowered resistance to infection. There can be breathlessness on walking, bone

TABLE 5.4

Prevalence of Anaemia in Different Parts of India

(Age in Years) (Figs. in %)

	1-5 Boys and Girls	*6-14 Girls*	*15-24 Women*	*24-44 Women*	*45 Men and Women*
Hydrabad	65.5	66.7	64.4	75.9	47.0
Calcutta	94.4	95.3	95.1	93.7	88.3
Madras	23.2	18.3	19.0	24.4	21.8
New Delhi	57.1	73.3	61.5	76.5	66.7

Ref : *American Journal of Chemical Nutrition*, 35, p. 1442, 1982, quoted in Veena Shatrugna, *Women and Health.*

(The lower rate in Madras needs investigation and explanation).

pains and even heart failure. During pregnancy it can be fatal if the women have any other accompanying problems like excess bleeding. The babies of anaemic mothers are smaller with very little energy reserve. Women are most vulnerable during their productive period.

Hypertension Stress plays a very large role in precipitating hypertension. In a socio-economic condition where the reality of life is hunger, semi-starved children, overwork, wife beating and insecurity, stress becomes a normal condition of existence. The incidence is rising in urban populations, especially among women.

In big cities like Delhi and Bombay prevalence of hypertension among the population is 15-30 per cent; in small towns like Rohtak: Men—5.9 per cent, women—6.9 per cent and Average : 6.4 per cent. In rural India: 3.5 per cent; urban India: 4.15 per cent. Hypertension occurs more often in women after the age of 40 years.

Diabetes

TABLE 5.5

Per cent Prevalence of Diabetes Millitus in Rural Areas

Age	*Male*	*Female*	*Total*
20-25	2.5	1.2	1.8
50	4.0	5.4	4.7
All ages	2.9	2.0	2.4

Ref : *Survey of Diabetes Millitus in rural population of India*, 21, 1192, 1972.

Women during old age have a higher incidence than men. There were more diabetic cases among the women who were undernourished.

Leprosy

The prevalence of leprosy in Madras and Greater Bombay was 15.2 per 1000 population surveyed and the age at onset for males was 31.49 years and females 29.43 years. Younger girls are more prone to leprosy than boys, spending as they do longer hours in closed ill-ventilated rooms, where contact with others who have the disease is unavoidable and there is poorer resistance due to poorer food intake (resistance to disease is related to adequacy of food intake).

Being the traditional provider of water and having to work many hours in water, women are vulnerable to water-borne diseases. Occupational hazards to which women are exposed are only just coming to light. Women have a lower capacity to sustain heavy manual and physically demanding work. They have less-tolerance to heat and vibration. In employment in certain industries like electronics, weaving and carpet-making women suffer from severe visual impairments. Hardly has any concern been directed against the effects of drugs on the people who are working in the companies producing these drugs. The workers during the work process are exposed to the same drug by way of bone, mouth, touch etc. They work for nine hours a day; day after day, year after year, producing hormones vasodilators, antibiotics etc. The major health hazards these women suffer from are deteriorating eyesight. The speedup on manually handled packing operations lead to fatigue, weakness, backaches, aching arms, feet and shoulders, as workers have no access to correct information on the hazards they face to demand safety devices.

The process of cooking itself is hazardous. Studies on rural energy patterns have shown that a woman spends a great deal of time on fuel collection. She uses stoves that are not only fuel insufficient but also expose her to heat and to serious respiratory diseases like chronic bronchitis and emphysema through inhaling animal dung-smoke. Hence respiratory disease is one of the major causes of death among women in rural India.

Nutritional Standards

Food is needed to provide energy for doing work, protein for building tissues and vitamins and minerals for the overall utilisation of energy and protein.

Energy requirements have been based on body weights, sex, climate and work done. There is a minimum amount stipulated for both men and women to survive to ensure a bare existence. Any further activity needs more energy. So the acts of working such as cooking, filling water, cleaning the house etc. needs more energy than others. More than half the women do not get the recommended dietary intake of calories, proteins, calcium, iron and vitamin A.[3] Two-thirds of all pregnant women are anaemic. According to records of the National Institute of Nutrition, 10 to 20 per cent of all maternal deaths are due to nutritional anaemia. During pregnancy a woman is required to consume at least 2500 calories per day, but an average Indian woman consumes barely 1400; for the 55 gms. of protein she needs per day, she gets 37 gms; against iron requirements of 40 mg, she gets a mere 0.2 gms. The shortfalls are even more marked during lactation. The problem of nutrition is essentially linked to poverty but for women the problem is further compounded by gender discrimination. Paradoxically, women are the chief nutritionists, being responsible for 40 to 80 per cent of all food production and in addition women; *totally support* 30 per cent of rural families. Commercialisation has reduced direct control over food supply for women; breakdown of traditional feudal ties that guaranteed minimum subsistence has been replaced by money wages that buy less and less of basic needs. Inside the family the guardians of nutrition for the family take a lower share for themselves and their daughters.

Social Conditions

There has been little or no study on the possible positive benefits of reducing energy expenditure by reducing the overwhelming drudgery of women, especially of poor women. It could be an important means of improving women's health. Energy saving may release a significant amount of women's time. In India development has adversely affected women of all classes except the well to-do. It has been observed that in villages in Punjab, where development programmes had been initiated, the health conditions of the women have actually deteriorated and the incidence of low birth weights and neonatal mortality has actually increased. Should one adopt technology to women's changing roles with the family, or adopt technology for reducing the rapid deterioration in women's social and economic situation? These questions have not been raised at all in the discussions of policy options regarding technology.

1. The improved smokeless stove, if introduced, minimises smoke damage to the eyes. This also means an economy of fuel which would result in saving of time and energy for those who have to collect and provide the fuel, but the design of the stove should adhere to the women's cooking needs.
2. Fetching water for the household is one of the most arduous and time-consuming tasks. Handpumps and tube-wells in the vicinity of the house and home filtration units of a simple design could be the answers for reduction in women's work-load.
3. The provision of sanitary latrines also merit serious attention as it would make a significant difference to the health of the community as a whole and to the convenience of the women-folk.
4. Introduction of cesspools, soak pits to improve drainage and compost pits to take care of household kitchen wastes would go far towards improving the village environment. Biogas can be used for cooking, home and street lighting, running water pumps and other agricultural implements.
5. Grain storage bins and improved techniques of food preservation would improve women's health.

Fertility

A major influence on women's fertility, female infant mortality, and female infant rejection is the pervasive son-preference. If one wants proof of the strength of patriarchy in Indian society, the obsessive desire for a male child is enough. It is a reflection of the relative value of men to women in society. All other consequences of discrimination flow from this starting point. This is a starting case of socio-cultural perversion of a natural (or biological) requirement. Biological reproduction requires in fact more women than men because one woman can bear only one child at a time normally, whereas a man can impregnate many women. For the survival of a child, it is the female of the species that plays the dominant role : carrying the baby in the womb, making the body of the baby with the tissues and nutrients from her own body, and suckling it after birth. How tragic it is that this society does not value the being who contributes most to the continuation of the species!

The influence of socio-economic factors on fertility is recognised but no systematic studies have been done. A married woman's status in her husband's household hinges crucially on her ability to produce a male child. This continued to be so despite vast changes in Indian society brought about by rapid industrialisation, urbanisation, education of women and social reform legislation attempting to reduce legal disadvantages of women. Even though there is a clear connection between fall in infant mortality and total fertility per woman and the level of education of parents, particularly the mother, many families in India continue to regard education as unimportant for girls. The Committee on the Status of Women in India (1974) had noted that nearly 20 per cent of Indian families rejected the need for education of girls while over 56 per cent disapproved of higher education for women.

Male-child preference is one major over-riding influence on fertility; the second is the universality of marriage for girls and the persistence of child marriages regardless of laws prohibiting it (Sarda Act in 1929 and the recent legislation raising the age of marriage for girls to 18). In a single district in Rajasthan in 1983, 9,000 child marriages were reported. In many cases, the future husband's name is tatooed on the waiting girl child's arms to secure her bondage. In Uttar Pradesh, Madhya Pradesh, and Bihar it is rare for a girl in her teens to remain unmarried. Early marriages for girls are sought to preserve the chastity of the girls and secondly, to ensure their sub-ordination to the bride-receiving family. Early marriages take a heavy toll of girls future physical, and mental growth; thereafter their education and employment chances diminish drastically. Early pregnancy induces high maternal mortality.

The commonest causes for divorce, separation and desertion by husbands in the villages is barrenness and suspicion of adultery. Contrary to scientific knowledge barreness is always blamed on the woman, and the man resorts to remarriage. Divorce or separation pose great hardships for women; they are suddenly forced to fend for themselves when they have in fact been denied training for it. Legislation permitting widow remarriage in 1856 has remained a dead letter. Widowed women in India cannot easily remarry even in castes that formally permit remarriage. In the 1971 Census for every 100 widows there were only 30 widowers. Society frowns on widows, who even to this day must discard coloured clothes, ornaments, the red-mark on the forehead that symbolises auspiciousness, etc. Innumerable widows spend their lifetime in destitution, seeking refuge in ashrams, often being forced into prostitution risking both their health and sanity.[4]

The institution of the joint family is a cultural feature that leads to control over a woman's fertility, and lack of autonomy for the young, married woman.

Family Planning

This is a euphemism for contraception. The family planning approach to population limitation therefore concentrates on providing new efficient contraceptives, on a national basis through mass programmes under various public health auspices.

India is the first country in the world to have a national policy and programme of population control. The population control efforts in India have been promoted in a series of Five Year Plans, the first beginning in 1951. The main appeal for family planning is based on considerations of the health and welfare of the family, more specifically of the mother and child. At the policy level, the Indian family planning programme depends for its success on the voluntary acceptance by the people, though the process of motivation and education and enlightened realisation of the good that accrues to individuals from acceptance and practice of a small family norm.

Family planning is now called family welfare and it is a mixed programme for women. The government sees *Family Welfare* as a remedy for almost every social ill. The basis of the government programme is the assumption that increasing population is responsible for the increasing poverty in India. We know that the poor have absolutely no purchasing power and hence hardly consume anything in terms of food, housing, clothes, schooling, vehicles, health etc.

In a social structure with so much inbuilt gender and class inequality, how will mere reduction in numbers, promote better distribution of available resources? The only old age security for a vast majority of the Indian people is their children. When the survival rate of children is still low, what incentive can people have for birth control? Women however do have a special stake in birth control to avoid unwanted pregnancies. Birth control knowledge, *safe* birth control devices should be available to them as a right but in ways that they can control and not in ways that are imposed on them through state policy, medical personnel and the pharmaceutical companies. Women all over the country have fought lonely battles against enforced measures by going in for sterilisation only after they have had enough children. Often many women on other hand, are forced to carry an unwanted pregnancy to term because they have been refused an abortion. Women's positive response to sterilisation after pregnancy has been quickly seized upon to promote new technologies but very little time or resources are spent on *educating* men and their families of the dangers to women by excessive child-bearing.

In promoting different methods, the family planning programme has laid heavy stress on sterilisation as an easier administrative measure than pills which require careful education, guidance and monitoring. Injectibles are now being propagated though they have been banned in other countries and evidence regarding their safety is not conclusive. If anything, possible effects on the mother and nursing mother are serious enough to sound caution, but powerful business interests, particularly multinationals, are promoting these and the government has yielded to such pressures by giving licence to manufacture them in the country and by further authorising voluntary family planning agencies to adopt them. The intra-utrinedevice (IUD) is also being promoted. All these methods are women-targeted; no attention is paid to the side effects which are extremely painful and serious, such as excessive bleeding, pelvic inflammations, severe backaches, disruption of the menstrual cycle etc. As the health care system is unsympathetic to women's discomforts, many women prefer to complete their family and get sterilised.

FAMILY PLANNING METHODS
FAMILY PLANNING ACCEPTORS BY METHODS 1968-69 TO 1983-84

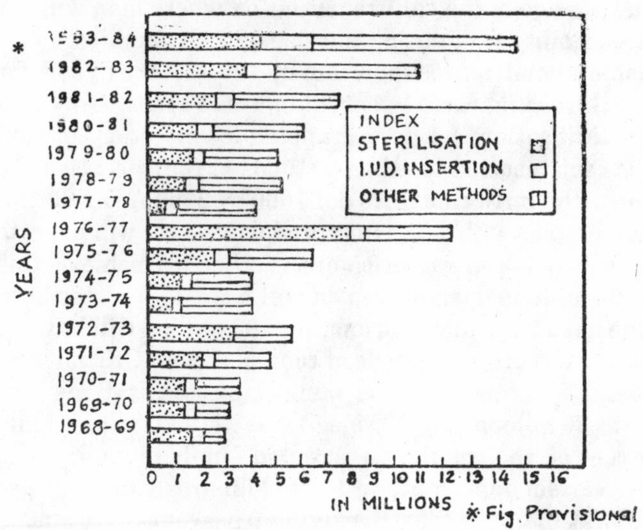

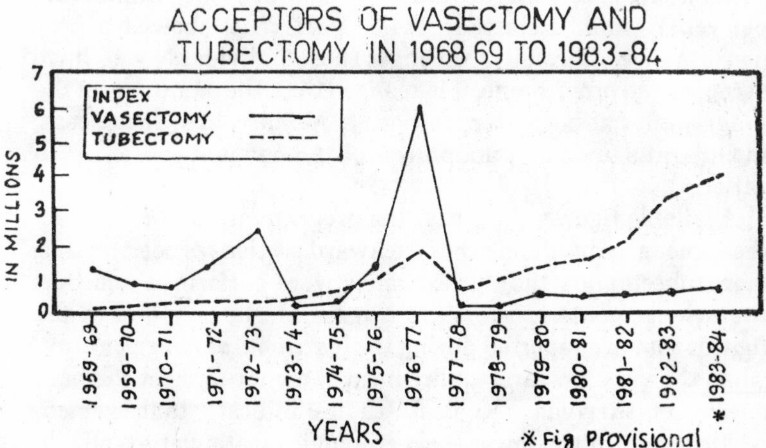

Peak in vasectomies during 1975-1976 and 1977-1978 because of the vigorous drive during the emergency period this background leading to increased resistance by men.

Birth control measures for men, condoms or vasectomies, are far simpler and safer—involving less discomfort and yet, the population control policy targets women primarily and prefers to take advantage of the cultural situation where men will not take responsibility for limiting the size of their families.

Available official figures show that by 1981-82, the figures for births of a third child was 51 per cent in urban areas. Only 23.7 accepted sterilisation, 1.1 per cent opted for insertion of IUD and 2 per cent resorted to other methods of contraception. To bring down the birth rate to 20 per 1000 by 2000 A.D., 60 per cent of the couples with wives in reproductive ages will have to accept one form of contraception or the other. To achieve this target, 102 million men or women will have to be sterilised during the next 17 to 18 years, another 102 million will have to accept IUDs and other methods of contraception. Official records show that since 1956, the number of sterilisations performed was 36 million and IUD insertions were 14 million. Only 23.7 per cent of the population accepted family planning. The numbers varied from state to state. Maharashtra (36.7 per cent), Gujarat (34.8 per cent) Kerala (32.0 per cent) were among the better achievers, whereas states with relatively large populations such as Uttar Pradesh (11.3 per cent), Bihar (12.2 per cent), and Rajasthan (14.5 per cent) showed a poor performance. Secondly, amongst those individuals who have accepted the programme, it is realised that the mainstay of the programme has been sterilisation. In Maharashtra 95 per cent, in Gujarat 91 per cent and in Kerala 96 per cent chose sterilisation.

Available figures show that the programme had better success among tribals and other backward sections of society; that more tubectomies than vasectomies were performed and that the achievements of the state targets are largely due to the figures that are reported during the lean months of agriculture, when the villagers are in dire need of money to meet the bare needs of survival. Medical studies indicate that women, particularly in the lower socio-economic strata, get extremely low nutrition and hence most of them are anaemic. Each pregnancy, delivery and post-partum period is drain on women's health.

If such women are persuaded to accept tubectomy it does not

Expectation of life at birth by sex

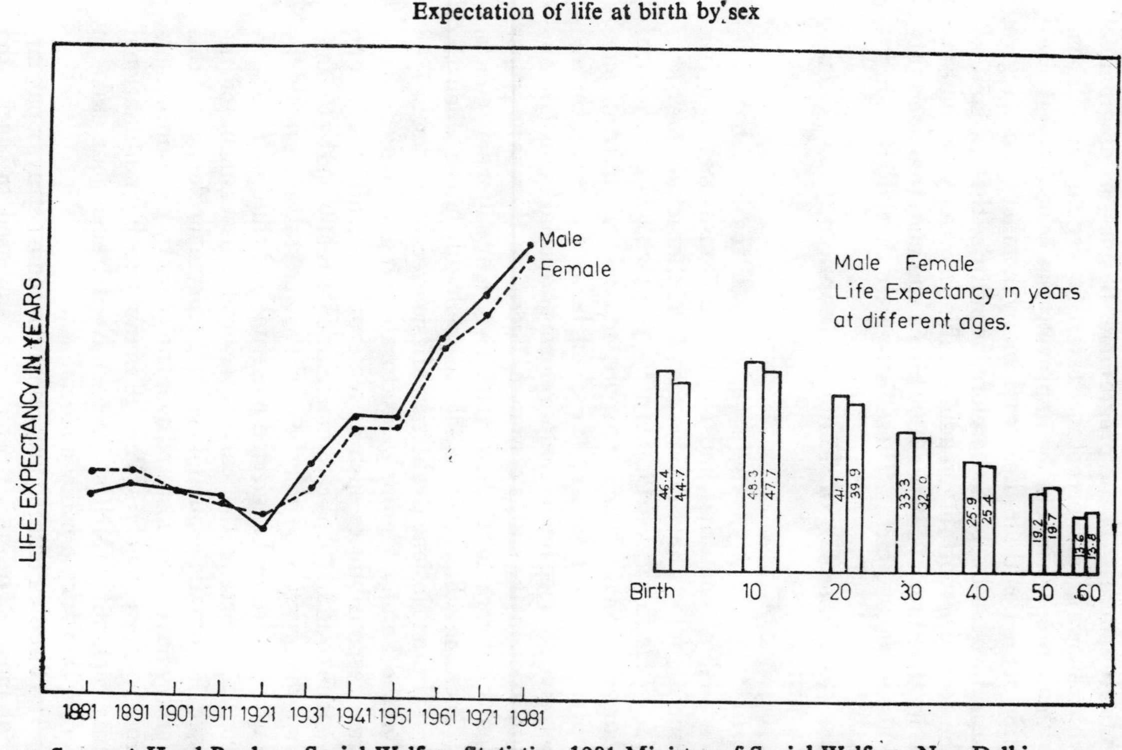

Source : Hand Book on Social Welfare Statistics, 1981 Ministry of Social Welfare, New Delhi.

indicate success of the programme. Besides, a programme which shows greater acceptance of fertility regulation methods, without proper inputs for improving the socio-cultural situation for a healthier life for all family members, cannot give desirable results. It is therefore, no surprise that in spite of the decline of mortality in adults, infant mortality continues to be in the range of 130 per 1000 births and maternal mortality 500 per 100,000 births. These figures are shockingly high.

Use (or Misuse) of Modern Technology in Family Planning

In this country, where we have yet to draft out just, reasonable maternal and child health measures, the risk benefit analysts have decided that *it is better to take the risk of side effects in the distribution of the pill through non-chemical channels than allow unwanted pregnancies and maternal mortality*. They just aim at the child bearing mechanism and perceive no need for economic reform and social changes or any alteration in the status of women. Therefore, there is no proper health network to attend to women who may suffer side-effects.

These invidious implications were already latent when the first United Nations Evaluation Mission recommended in 1966 that the Family Planning Directorate in India should be freed from responsibilities such as maternal and child health and went on to add : "This recommendation is reinforced by the fear that the programme may be used in some states to expand the much needed and neglected maternal and child welfare services." The roots of the current scientific assessment of the need for drastic population control scheme for the poor of this country have been fostered over the years by pronouncements from western scholars. The pill manufacturing multinational drug companies (MNCs) alone have a tremendous stake in seeing that such a policy materialises.

The Family Planning programme in India betrays a patriarchal bias. "Ordinary people are supposed to lack the intellectual capacity to understand what is best for themselves. People must be manipulated into striving for their own self-interest." It would not be surprising if after some time the pill is promoted as ideal for the rural and poor Indian women who lives in constant fear of rape, because the pill would protect her from its physical consequences such as unwanted pregnancy.

Clinically there is a growing feeling among doctors, planners, government and the international agencies that contraceptive should be made available in simpler ways. The potential swallower of the pill (i.e. the woman) does not even come into the picture.

In the light of the go-ahead from the Indian Council of Medical Research for liberalised distribution of the pill some dire future possibilities begin to rear their heads. Given the philosophy underlying the weighing of risks and benefits by policy makers and the objective of achieving results without radical socio-economic change, the fear that rises is if the pill is unleashed today, can injectables be far behind? The very advantages of an injectable for the illiterate, conscious women, who have access to sympathetic medical counselling, prove to be a disadvantage for the illiterate women of the Third World who do not enjoy the same relationship with the medical profession.

All these methods mentioned above are being widely publicised by the government through the use of media. But no effort at all has been made to propagate the use of natural methods of preventing pregnancy such as rhythm, safe and non-safe periods, coitus interruptus (withdrawal), abstinence and billing method (testing mucous to determine ovulation). These natural methods need widespread educative approaches, face to face guidance and most importantly tremendous willingness on the part of the health personnel. The likely long-term benefits for women as well as society at large would be much more than the short-term target oriented policies and programmes. In a social situation where the co-operation of men is not easy to win, where the construction of sexual-pleasure is almost entirely male-defined and not on mutual consideration, this may be easier said than done, but non-invasive methods of contraception that are least damaging to the health of women need to be promoted wherever possible.

It is advised that before starting on these *hormonal* contraceptive methods, a thorough medical check up should be conducted. How many can afford it, in terms of time and money? How many women could risk the slightest harm to their babies if they were aware that it would affect their breast-fed infants? Even those willing to tolerate havoc to their children are concerned. Ultimately it boils down to the paternalistic attitude of policy-makers and shapers. They feel that they know what is best for those illiterate millions who do not really understand their own needs. The risky methods of contraception are tested on females; the safe ones are reserved for males. The leadership in human reproduction research today is predominantly male.

Amniocentesis

This is a scientific technique that was supposed to be used mainly to detect genetic deformities. But today it has become very popular in India for detection of the sex of the foetus and subsequently getting rid of the female foetus. It is of special relevance to our country where the obsessive and often neurotic desire for a male offspring overrides everything else. All doctors agree that amniocentesis is a dangerous instrument of discrimination against the female foetus, conditioned as an overwhelming number of our young mothers are, by centuries of tradition to desire male children only.

One estimate that has shocked everyone, right from planners and policy-makers to the academicians and activities was that between 1978 and 1983 around 78,000 female foetuses were aborted after sex determination test in our country. (Times of India, 1982).

The government and private practitioners involved in this lucrative trade, justify sex determination tests as a measure for population control. Women have always been the worst target for family planning policies. As one author puts it, "Is it really better to be born and left to die than to be killed as a foetus?" Does the birth of millions of unwanted girls improve the status of women ? But what can be the long term implications if such a trend continues ? Will it not aggravate the already disturbed sex ratio ? Will society treat women in a more humane way if they are scarce in supply ?[6] On the contrary, there will be increased incidence of rape, abduction and forced polyandry. A random survey conducted in Bomaby with doctors and a cross-section of patients revealed that in 95 per cent of cases it was couples with two or more girls and in rare cases with one girl, who went in for amniocentesis to determine the sex of the child. Fifty per cent of these opted for an abortion if the test predicted a female foetus. But there were some rare instances of a couple with two or more sons, wanting a daughter next.[7] Isn't this a significant pointer ?

Time and again it is stated that women themselves enthusiastically go for amniocentesis out of their free will, and that it is a question of women's choice. But are these choices made in a social vacuum ? These women are socially conditioned to accept the tragic fact that unless they produce one (or more) male child they have no social worth. They can be harassed, taunted, even deserted by their husbands and in-laws if they fail to do so. Thus their choices depend on the fear of society. It is true that feminists all over the world have always demanded the right of women to control their own bodies and their fertility; to be able to choose whether or not to have child/ children and have facilities for free legal and safer abortions. While understanding these issues in the Third World context we must keep in mind the social, economic and political background of the country concerned. Lack of food, economic security, clean drinking water and adequate health care facilities have led to a situation where a woman has to have 6.2 children to have at least *one surviving male child*. There are the roots of the population problem not merely the desire to have a *male child*.

Most of the new women's organisations feel that the amniocentesis tests should be allowed under strict governmental control and only for detecting genetic abnormalities. The issue of amniocentesis once against shatters the myth of neutrality of science and technology. Hence the necessity of linking science and technology with socio-economic and cultural reality.

Health Programmes

The public health services have reflected social attitudes in considering all women primarily as mothers or potential mothers. Health services have therefore been termed as maternal and child health (MCH) services. This has resulted in a de-emphasis of general health services for them.

Health services for women and children can be improved only in association with a substantial change in their social status. This implies, first and foremost, a change in the present attitude of looking upon women and children as expendable. A vicious circle has set in. The high mortality rates of children and the social preference for sons rather than daughters leads to a demand for more children. All this leads to a deteriorating health condition of women and this is precisely what a declining sex-ratio indicates; and this is exactly the situation and attitude which society must outgrow. Basic services such as routine antenatal care (ANC), delivery, postnatal care (PNC), infant care, immunisation and treatment of ailments should be delivered to all women and children within the community. The community approach will mean the training of traditional birth attendents, dais (village level midwives), and female community health voluntreers in early diagnosis and management through simple and safe procedures and utilising them for MCH care. It has often been noted that one of the many causes of low utilisation of existing M.C.H. services is that they require attendance at distant clinics or the Primary Health Centres, for which the majority of women, particularly the poorest ones, cannot spare the time, money and energy. Hence, it should be possible to subdivide villages (and city wards) into 20 family units and train voluntary workers to look after these units. This would increase the penetration of services and intensify health awareness.

Priorities in MCH Activities

This is very crucial in the Indian context of limited resources and the need to achieve results quickly. The priorities may be as follows:

1. Care of pregnant women—including treatment of specific nutritional disorders (anaemia, etc.) beginning with the poorest sections.
2. Safe deliveries.
3. Post-natal care and care of the new born, including premature births.
4. Nutritional care of children below three years, beginning with the poorest.
5. Immunisation of mothers and children including tatanus, toxoid, B.C.G., DPT and Polio.
6. Family planning advice and services, during pregnancy

following deliveries and co-ordination with child care; medical termination of pregnancy and menstrual regulation by trained personnel.

7. Treatment of illnesses including control of infection and oral rehydration.

As described earlier, inadequate and improper nutrition are the root of most of the health problems of women and children. There is almost universal agreement that undernutrition is aggravated by repeated infections which abound in the environment of poverty and are further worsened by the lack of prompt medical attention.

What has been done by the Government of India ?

The Government's response to the deteriorating nutrition situation in the country began in the early seventies with a series of national programmes aimed at nutrition intervention, education and agricultural policy.

Mid-day Meal Programme

It was begun in 1962-1963 based on the recommendations of the National School Health Committee as a centrally sponsored scheme and was later transferred to the States with Central assistance at 40 per cent of the expenditure after the Third Plan. During the drought of the mid-sixties, it was extended to all affected areas, with most of the food supply coming from *CARE* (Cooperative of American Relief Everywhere). In 1978, it was estimated that about 12 million children in schools were covered by the programme.

While the basic aim of the above programme was to (i) increase enrolment in schools (ii) improve the nutritional status of school children; in reality the first objective has received greater priority while the nutrition component has been neglected. The programme has suffered from improper implementation and leadership, especially after it was made the States responsibility. Kerala is the only state where a consistently high percentage of children has been covered—about 73 per cent in 1970-1971.

Applied Nutrition Programme (ANP)

An expended nutrition programme to encourage village people to grow more protective foods for their own consumption was launched by the Government of India in agreement with the *UNICEF* and *FAO* in 1958 with the following objectives:

1. Production of protective foods by village community, schools and households.
2. Consumption of these items by local communities, preschool children and pregnant and nursing mothers.
3. Nutrition education of nursing mothers and mahila mandals, schools, çommunity development and health workers and other block development workers.

As the programme called for the coordination of various ministries and departments, speedy implementation was difficult. A special programme of supplementary nutrition for preschool children in urban areas was also introduced.

Food Fortification Programme

The manufacture and distribution of fortified food particularly for the vulnerable sections was mooted first by the public sector *Modern Bread* in 1968. The production of Balamul, a low-cost locally produced nutritive cereal is another major scheme in association with the Kaira District Milk Producers Union, Anand. Miltone, a proteinisolated toned milk from groundnut is produced by the government dairy at Bangalore with additional units to go into operation at Hyderabad and Ernakulam. Experiments on fortification of wheat flour, tea and salt have also been conducted.

However, where a large majority lack purchasing power, many of these products do not reach the needy; they are in fact consumed by the middle and upper classes who are adequately fed.

The Minimum Needs Programme began in the Fifth Plan. An outlay of Rs.175 crores (or 4.2 per cent of the total revised MNP) has been allotted in the Sixth Plan. The MNP Nutrition Programme will follow the traditional pattern of mid-day meals for children 6-11 and supplementary feeding of preschool children, pregnant and lactating women.

Existing Nutrition Programmes suffer from :

1. Lack of rational and specific goals.
2. Poor priority planning.
3. Inequitable resource distribution.
4. Problems in delivery systems.
5. Lack of effective evaluation, monitoring and research.

Reform in approach and policy must be brought about in these main sectors : agriculture, health services and nutrition to bring about a permanent improvement in the nutrition picture of our country.

Prejudices within the Medical System

Records of the health care system, whether public or private, show that health services are availed of much less by women than by men. The provision of facilities for women in the public health system (as measured by women doctors, beds reserved for women etc.) is also significantly less than for men. Women make the best providers of health care, but efforts to gear family, community and society towards encouraging women to pursue such professions are disappointing. By the end of 1977, the female : male doctor ratio in India was 1:4 and among postgraduates, it was 1:17. There seems to be a greater resistance to women's higher education. Men resent the fact that women take up medical college seats only to give up practising after marriage. In 1975, a study pointed out very clearly that only women doctors who temporarily and partially drop out from full-time practice are studied, but not men who drop out to do business or emigration, or take to other occupations. The maximum brain drain from India is male doctors. Despite all the constricting forces in a working life of 40 years, a woman doctor, who has an average family and who is in addition responsible for bearing and rearing her own children, nevertheless manages to carry out 7/8 of the professional work of a male doctor.[8]

Female Doctors : At the end of 1977, total male doctors registered with the Medical Council of India were 1,69,789, while female doctors were 39,544, with the male to female ratio of approximately 4:1.

From 106 medical colleges in the country, a total of 10,748 male and 2974 female medical students passed out of MBBS examination in 1977-1978 (*Pocket book of Health Statistics in 1979*) with a ratio of 3:5:1.

The 1975 Census data indicated that the proportion of women to men entering Postgraduate medical education was very low at 6:100.

Two independent studies revealed that despite a significant increase in educational opportunities for women in the field of medicine, the top and key positions in health care management are largely occupied by men.

Nurses: According to the 1971 Census there were 3979 male nurses as compared to 1,05,795 female nurses in the country. The profession so overwhelmingly occupied by females is always relegated to the secondary status. The Bhor Committee appointed by the Government recommended a nurse population ratio of 1:500 to be achieved by 1971 but it has so far been only 1:4731.

In 1970, the total number of nurses trained were 11,673. This number is almost the same as that of doctors trained. The present nurse to doctor ratio is 1:2.3 while the ideal ratio is 3:1 or more. In spite to the gross deficit in the number of nurses, the number of nursing training schools declined between 1966 and 1970. While the number of medical colleges has increased, the standard of available training facilities for nurses is extremely inferior with little administrative power to the heads of the nursing schools (who are always females) as compared to Deans of Medical Colleges (who are always males).

In spite of $3\frac{1}{2}$ years training, nurses are given only functional assignments which involve just mechanically obeying the orders of the doctors. The creative satisfaction, recognition, status and money go to the doctors, while what remains to the nurses' lot is laborious monotony. As much as 40-50 per cent of nurses and their parents feel that marriage is a problem for the nurses, as their duty hours are inconvenient to married life.

Village Level Health Workers

In the primary health centres, 96 per cent of community workers are males, despite the government guidelines to give priority to females. Taking care of the sick has been for

TABLE 5.6

Out-turn of Nurses, Mid-wives, Auxiliary Nurse-Mid-wives and Lady Health Visitors From 1950-1983

Category	*1950*	*1956*	*1961*	*1966*	*1970*	*1975*	*1976*	*1977*	*1978*	*1979*	*1980*	*1981*	*1982*	*1983*
1. Nurses (Diploma/ Certificate holders)	1282	1914	2851	5456	6257	5202	5506	5892	6788	6503	7256	8144	7351	7342
2. Midwives	1559	2605	2277	4119	5416	5578	4891	6213	6282	6164	6541	7406	6781	7299
3. Auxiliary Nurse-Midwives (Health workers female)	—	299	2083	3701	5104	5660	5506	5799	5709	6148	4264	5572	6192	5684
4. Health Supervisor (Lady Health Visitors)	53	123	315	415	479	752	720	709	650	549	483	567	653	835

Source : *Indian Nursing Council*, 1985.

centuries a woman's job, but when care of the sick has become a paid job it is captured by the male.

Health is a priority issue for women, because without mental and physical well being they cannot function effectively, nor develop their human potential. It is intimately related to social conditions, and not only to the state of medical advanced or the medical resources of the country. Education creates awareness, knowledge and the confidence to assert one's rights. Employment gives women the resources for their basic needs. The ICSSR Programme of Women's Studies in 1978 therefore identified Education, Health and Employment as the three most critical areas to improe women's status in India.

Until recently, health had not been recognised as a gender issue. Women need to develop their own organisations to spearhead the change in their own condition. Some women's groups have begun to work with women to promote awareness and knowledge of their own body functions, of the dangers they are subject to in being mere recipients of family-planning and health programmes rather than taking initiatives in demanding the right programmes, in monitoring them to see that women's interests are not overruled and in lobby/protesting against practices harmful to women. This will come about when health is seen as part of the larger issue of subordination of women in Indian society.

Our approach needs to change in order to ensure that:

(a) health and family planning becomes accessible to all women UNDER TERMS that will ensure women's welfare;

(b) full and equal participation of women not merely as recipients of the health system but as providers in that system at both the managerial and technical level, takes place;

(c) research into women's health problems, needs and occupational health hazards is promoted;

(d) new health services and appropriate technologies for meeting specific needs are initiated; and

(e) all forms of exploitation are eliminated through both social reforms and social awareness.

Notes and References

1. Amartya Sen, & Sunil Sen Gupta, 1985, "Malnutrition ofRural Children the Sex Bias," in *Women and Poverty*, (Ed.), Devaki Jain and Nirmala Banerjee, Vikas, New Delhi.
2. Veena Shatrugna, *Women and Health* ; *Research Centre for Women's Studies*, S.N.D.T. University, Bombay, 1984.
3. Suresh, N. Kulkarni, "Demographic and Nutritional Background of the Status of Women in India," Institute of Economic Growth, Delhi University (Mimeo) (undated).
4. Baidyanath, Saraswathi, "The Kashivasi Widows", *Manu's India*, Vol. 65, No.2, June 1985.
5. Veena Shatrugna, Op. Cit., p.15.
6. Dharma Kumar, "Aminocentesis Again (Discussion)," *Economic and Political Weekly*, Vol. 18, No. 24, 11 June, 1983.
7. Lakshmi, Mohan, "The Sex Determination : Controversy Continues," *Eves Weekly*, 25th September, and 1st October, 1982.
8. C. Satyamala, "Is Medicine Inherently Sexist?", *Socialist Health Review*, Vol. 1, No. 2, 1984.

Additional Readings

Padma prakash, "Editorial Perspective: Roots of Women's ill Health, " *Socialist Health Review*, Vol.1, No.2, 1984.

Meera Chatterjee, "Health for All : Whither the Child?" *Social Action*, Vol. 35, July-Sept.1985, p. 224-240.

Venkatachalam, 1962, "Maternal Nutritional Status and Its Effect on the New Born," *W.H.O. Bulletin* 26, p. 198.

C. Gopalan : "The mother and child in India," *Economic and Political Weekly*, Vol. XX, No. 4, 1985.

Malini Karkal, 1985, *Mother and Child Survial in Dynamics of Population & Family Welfare*, (Ed.), K. Srinivasan and S. Mukherjee, Himalayan Publication, Bombay.

Sujata Gotaskar, Rohini Banarji and Vijay Kancheve, "`Health ofWomen' in the `Health Industry,'" in *Socialist Health Review*, (Special issue on `Women's Health'), Vol. 1, No. 2, September 1980.

Srilatha, Batliwala, 1985, *Women in Poverty : The Energy, Health and Nutrition Syndrome, Chpater in Tyranny of the Household, Investigative Essays on Women's Work*, (Ed.), Devaki Jain, Nirmala Banerjee, Shakti Books.

Leela Gulati, "Marked Preference for Sterilization in a Semi Rural Squatter's Settlement," *Studies in Family Planning*, Vol. 10, No. 11/12, 1979, p.332—336.

Stephen Minkin, *Introduction, Contraceptive Use and Abuse*. Depe Provera, A Critical Analysis Repoint from Women and Health, 1980, Vol. 2, Summer.

Sheila Zyrbrigg, Rakku's Story, *Structure of Ill Health and the Source of Change*, Published, George Joseph, Sidma Offset Press, Madras, 1984.

Srilatha Batliwala, Daswani Mona and Leena Bakshi, "Sex Bias in Modern Medicine : Gender Discrimination in Health Training Deluxy and Personnel," *Social Action*, Vol. 35, July-Sept. 1985, p. 241-352.

Ashok Mitra, "Implications of the Declining Sex Ratio in India's Population, Allied Publishers, Bombay. *I.C.S.S.R. Programme of Women's Studies*, 1979.

Ajit Mehta and K. Jayant, *Pre-inatal Mortality Survey of India* (1977-1979), Part I. Identification of Health Intervention Needs, *Journal of Obstetrics & Gynaceology of India*, Vol. 31, No. 3, 1981. Hitesh Bhargava, S. Karma, Nirmal Pant, "Preinatal Mortality," *The Journal of Obstetrics and Gynacology of India*, Vol. 31, No. 4, 1981, p. 584-592.

P. Padmanabha, "Mortality in India : A Note on Trends and Implications," *Economic and Political Weekly*, Vol. XVII, No. 32, 1982.

Leela Visaria, "Infant Mortality in India, Levels, Trends and Developments," Economic and Political Weekly, Vol. XX, No. 32, 10 August, 1985.

Meenakshi Sharma & S. Saksena, "A Clinical Study of Pre-inatal Mortality," *Journal of Obstetrics & Gynaecology of India*, Vol. 32, No. 3, 1982.

A.K. Jain, "Determinants of Regional Variations in Infant and Child Mortality in Rural India, *Population Council*, New York, 1984.

Gandotra, M.M., Pandey, Divya, Values, "Attached to Children in Indian Society and Family Size Norms," *The Changes and Impact—Journal of Family Welfare*, Vol. 26, No. 1, 1979.

Vibhuti Patel, "Amenocentesis and Female Foeticide, Misuse of Medical Technology," *Socialist Health Review*, Vol. 1, No. 2, 1984.

Govternment of India, Ministry of Health & Family Welfare, *Report of the Working Group on Health for All, By A.D. 2000*, 1981.

6

Violence

There are crimes which are specifically directed at women : rape, sexual harassment, sexual exploitation and abuse, as in prostitution, domestic violence and pornography. In addition to these, is the murder of young married women for non-fulfilment or insufficient fulfiment of exhorbitant dowry demands. All these forms of violence have increased greatly in recent years and this social pathology requires analyis.

Violence accompanies power; it is committed to prove or feel a sense of power ; it is an instrument of coercion used to maintain power. Violence against women takes many forms and the forms vary between cultures, but what is near universal is that male violence exceeds female violence. Wars have been mainly fought by men for aggrandisement, for suzerainty, for possession. Violence may not always be direct, physical violence. We have seen how the social structure has inbuilt discrimination and oppression against women, consequences of which are mental, physical ~~and emotional~~ injury to women.

Any hierarchical system of dominance and subordination victimises the weaker sections, and this victimisation can vary from subtle pressures through the power of ideology and socialisation or open brutal oppression. The aim is always to induce the subordinate group to comply with the wishes of the stronger.

"Any individual or group facing the threat of coercion or being disciplined to act in a manner required by another individual or group is subject to violence. This is not necessarily confined to physical violence but the creation of an atmosphere of terror, a situation of threat and repraisal."[1]

Rape

The notion that a woman is to blame for rape is convenient for a male-dominated society. The allegation always is that she was provocative. She seduced. Even if she did not, she should be able to protect herself through the fire of her chastity. Mahatma Gandhi too believed that a chaste woman should be able to ward off rape and if she could not she should give up her life.[2]

In India, there are several forms of rape : (a) rape within marriage (b) rape within family (c) rape as caste/class domination (d) rape against children, minors and unprotected young women (e) gang rapes during war, political upheavals as an instrument of revenge (f) custodial rapes (g) stray, unpremeditated rapes.

Data collected from the file of the Bureau of Police Research and Statistics, New Delhi, 1985 gives the following reported cases :

States	1972	1975	1978	1979
Uttar Pradesh	577	760	820	708
Madhya Pradesh	433	565	858	790
West Bengal	285	408	477	500
Bihar	240	304	345	418
Maharashtra	238	283	360	371
Major cities				
Bombay	29	56	58	
Delhi	30	52	57	
Calcutta	15	21	23	

It is significant that rapes (as reported) are highest in the states that have a more pronounced feudal structure and which have in recent years experienced intense class and caste struggles.

Though reported cases are gross under-estimates, the figures for various crimes put sexual molestation at the top. One can also see how male crime rate exceeds female crime by a ratio of 200 to 2500 !

Though rape is sexual coercion, it is *not* perversion or a crime of passion. It occurs only within the social matrix of a patriarchal society because it is unknown in tribal societies where women have a more equal status. Rape is violation of a female's integrity and dignity as a person. Fear of rape is a pervasive instrument controlling women and curtailing their freedom. Girls are socialised to fear men and are confined, protected and escorted in the interests of safety. The fact that the violation of a woman's body within marriage is not legally defined as *rape* makes it clear that in marriage a woman is the property of the husband. Rape is analogous to *theft*. In fact in the Indian languages, it is customarily referred to as *robbing* a woman of chastity; dishonouring her. A chaste woman or girl is one who observes the codes prescribed for her—total abstinence in the case of unmarried girls, and total sexual fidelity to the married partner in marriage. Since so much store is set by woman's *purity*, rape is a dishonour, a shameful thing for a woman and maximum social stigma is attached to it. It is the one crime where the victim is the one who faces rejection and not the oppressor. Hence, definitionally an impure woman cannot be raped. The judgement in the case of the woman called Rameza-bee in Andhra Pradesh, hinged on the allegation that she was of loose character. The stigma attached to rape arises because of the notion of loss of purity; the woman or girl subject to rape is treated as soiled and hence to be rejected. It is not therefore, any wonder that rape is the most under reported of crimes as shown on pages 257 to 262.

The most vulunerable age for rape according to police reports is 16 to 20 years; the majority of rapes are on unmarried girls (78 per cent). This is proof of woman as man's property in marriage; unmarried girls are no man's property and can be *seized*. Psychologically, unmarried girls are more vulnerable, not having had any sexual experience to defend themselves or ward off attacks.[3] Rape of minor girls or single women by male relatives, very often by the father-in-law or brother-in-law, remain unreported. Though it is difficult to provide estimates of this, as this is hidden under notions of family honour, the investigation of the background of women in prostitution or protective homes

Persons Arrested Under I.P.C. Crimes by Sex during 1980

Sl. No.	*States/U.Ts./Cities*	*Rape*		*Kidnapping & Abduction*		*Dacoity*		*Robbery*	
		Male	*Female*	*Male*	*Female*	*Male*	*Female*	*Male*	*Female*
1	2	3	4	5	6	7	8	9	10
States									
1.	Andhra Pradesh	295	2	493	8	1,182	1	535	—
2.	Assam	190	3	569	20	1,548	4	707	3
3.	Bihar	634	—	1,968	67	8,312	4	2,738	—
4.	Gujarat	152	—	683	48	715	8	1,206	17
5.	Haryana	164	—	276	7	67	—	139	—
6.	Himachal Pradesh	62	1	124	5	32	—	61	1
7.	Jammu & Kashmir	177	—	594	2	168	—	72	—
8.	Karnataka	130	2	250	11	1,003	19	472	12
9.	Kerala	78	—	110	3	207	—	242	—
10.	Madhya Pradesh	1,307	—	1,661	22	2,215	—	3,245	28
11.	Maharashtra	641	7	858	48	3,012	85	3,734	79

1	2	3	4	5	6	7	8	9	10
28.	Goa, Daman & Diu	6	—	5	1	1	—	25	1
29.	Lakshadweep	—	—	—	—	—	—	—	—
30.	Mizoram	51	—	5	—	11	—	47	—
31.	Pondicherry	9	—	18	6	10	—	1	—
	Total (U.Ts.)	161	—	410	24	334	—	432	1
	Grand Total	6,781	33	16,232	520	57,006	214	27,806	182
Cities									
1.	Ahmedabad	17	—	79	13	67	7	71	—
2.	Bangalore	23	—	32	—	14	—	149	2
3.	Bombay	74	—	216	5	176	—	422	1
4.	Calcutta	26	—	160	2	179	—	574	—
5.	Delhi	75	—	328	13	214	—	300	—
6.	Hyderabad	13	—	22	2	29	—	82	—
7.	Kanpur	22	—	178	8	1,129	1	329	—
8.	Madras	18	—	16	—	5	—	88	—
	Total (Cities)	268	—	1,031	43	1,813	8	2,015	3

Crimes Against Women

Offence Section States/UTs	*Rape 376*		*Vol. per Lakh of Population*		*Average*
	1978	*1979*	*1978*	*1979*	*1978-79*
1	2	3	4	5	6
States					
Andhra Pradesh	157	173	0.32	0.35	0.30
Assam	223	244	1.21	1.29	1.22
Bihar	422	418	0.65	0.63	0.61
Gujarat	94	64	0.30	0.20	0.26
Haryana	64	78	0.54	0.65	0.60
Himachal Pradesh	23	31	0.57	0.76	0.69
Jammu & Kashmir	117	116	2.09	2.02	1.82
Karnataka	73	87	0.22	0.25	0.22
Kerala	74	53	0.30	0.21	0.24
Madhya Pradesh	858	790	1.71	1.54	1.60
Maharashtra	358	371	0.62	0.63	0.63
Manipur	5	10	0.37	0.72	0.52
Meghalaya	9	12	0.73	0.94	0.75
Nagaland	6	4	0.91	0.59	0.81
Orissa	94	115	0.37	0.44	0.36
Punjab	81	83	0.53	0.53	0.56
Rajasthan	318	202	1.02	0.63	0.79
Sikkim	10	6	4.17	3.40	2.17
Tamil Nadu	118	98	0.26	0.21	0.23
Tripura	13	4	0.67	0.20	0.54
Uttar Pradesh	812	708	—	—	—
West Bengal	495	500	0.94	0.93	0.97
Total (States)	4424	4167	0.70	0.65	0.66

(Contd.)

Crimes Against Women

Offence Section States/UTs	*Rape 376*		*Vol. per Lakh of Population*		*Average*
	1978	*1979*	*1978*	*1979*	*1978-79*
1	2	3	4	5	6
States					
Andhra Pradesh	157	173	0.32	0.35	0.30
Assam	223	244	1.21	1.29	1.22
Bihar	422	418	0.65	0.63	0.61
Gujarat	94	64	0.30	0.20	0.26
Haryana	64	78	0.54	0.65	0.60
Himachal Pradesh	23	31	0.57	0.76	0.69
Jammu & Kashmir	117	116	2.09	2.02	1.82
Karnataka	73	87	0.22	0.25	0.22
Kerala	74	53	0.30	0.21	0.24
Madhya Pradesh	858	790	1.71	1.54	1.60
Maharashtra	358	371	0.62	0.63	0.63
Manipur	5	10	0.37	0.72	0.52
Meghalaya	9	12	0.73	0.94	0.75
Nagaland	6	4	0.91	0.59	0.81
Orissa	94	115	0.37	0.44	0.36
Punjab	81	83	0.53	0.53	0.56
Rajasthan	318	202	1.02	0.63	0.79
Sikkim	10	6	4.17	3.40	2.17
Tamil Nadu	118	98	0.26	0.21	0.23
Tripura	13	4	0.67	0.20	0.54
Uttar Pradesh	812	708	—	—	—
West Bengal	495	500	0.94	0.93	0.97
Total (States)	4424	4167	0.70	0.65	0.66

(Contd.)

1	2	3	4	5	6
U.Ts.					
Andaman & Nicobar Islands	—	—	—	—	—
Arunachal Pradesh	5	7	0.85	1.17	—
Chandigarh	—	—	—	—	—
D & N Haveli	—	—	—	—	—
Delhi	—	—	—	—	—
Goa	—	—	—	—	—
Lakshadweep	—	—	—	—	—
Mizoram	—	—	—	—	—
Pondicherry	—	—	—	—	—
Total (U.Ts.)	5	7	0.06	0.08	0.07
Grand Total	2700	2865	0.42	0.44	0.43

After 1980 Research Study was not done according to Department of Police & Research Development—Home Affairs—*Source* : collected from above Department.

Crimes Against Women in 1979 (Reported Cases) (All India)

All Types	40,590
Molestation	11,614
Abduction	3,355
Rapes	4,300
Enticing with criminal intent	2,865
Procuring for Prostitution (minor girls)	917
Unnatural offences against women	73

Persons Arrested for Crimes under the Indian Penal Code in 1980

	Males	*Females*
Rapes	6,620	23 (abetting)
Kidnapping	15,822	496
Dacoity	56,672	214
Robbery	27,314	181
Immoral Traffic in women or girls	354*	
Dowry offences	149	

(*The actual figures far exceed the number of prosecutions.)

Source : Files of Dept. of Police Research, New Delhi, 1985.

reveal a history of incest and other family violence. In a research study undertaken in Vidarbha region of Maharashtra, it was found that 4 of the 400 cases studied were mostly in the age group 16 to 25 and 10 per cent were minor girls below 15 years of age. Most of them came from poor, particularly lower caste families. Rejection by family and society drives many raped women into prostitution.

In urban areas, it was found that the rapists were labourers, unemployed men and truck drivers. These were migrants who had no families with them and sought sexual outlets in places where they found unprotected girls or young women.

In rural areas, the most common offenders were landlords and government officials. It was also found that more married men than unmarried men are offenders—a significant pointer to the fact that prior experience counts for their power over inexperienced girls or women. In rural areas, as people live in a close community, rape by neighbours, acquaintances, etc., is less possible as the offender is easily identified. However, class and caste oppression is strongest in rural areas[4] and rape of scheduled caste women, agricultural workers and bonded labourers is extremely common. In parts of Bihar, even today, landlords demand 'first night' privileges. In recent years, increasing protests by the down-trodden in rural areas are met with rape of women belonging to these classes in retaliation, to intimidate and cow the men down, whose inability to protect *their* women is exposed. It is an attack on the subordinate groups of men, to dishonour them.

Government officials who wield considerable power to tyrannise the poorer sections of the village have been found to rape women—perhaps both as a show of power as well as an easy way of satisfying one's lust,[5] but most often it is the former. Tribal women are particularly vulnerable to sexual assault by employers, forest contractors etc.[6] Police repression to curb popular movements has also been increasing.[7] Another aspect of police power is custodial rape. Political prisoners, lower caste, lower-class women and girls are routinely subject to rape in police custody. The case of Mathura, a young girl, raped at a police station, hit national newspaper headlines because of the acquittal of the policemen by the High Court on the clause of *consent.* This had led to a nation wide agitation for amendment of the rape law. Officials in charge of various institutions for girls and women also quite often abuse their power. Many cases of tribal girls in ashram shalas being subjected to molestation have been periodically reported.

Public interest in rape cases is not motivated by concern for the woman victim but to make political gain. The political thrust is directed against a particular ruling party or state government. This happened in the case of a woman called Maya Tyagi in U.P. whose case was made use of by the opposition party in the State to discredit the ruling party.

Rape as revenge occurs in periods of political upheaval. During India's partition in 1947, thousands of women became victims to communal frenzy. Recently, in the riots that broke out after Indira Gandhi's death, private sources admit to the occurrence of mass rapes.

In addition to these various forms of rape, gang rapes by criminals, and others take place in several parts of the country. "Fourteen-year old girl gang raped by four jawans (soldiers) of Manipur Rifles at Imphal in a cinema house", states a newspaper report. Such cases are reported frequently. Women and young girls, returning from late cinema shows, waiting for buses or trains often fall easy victims in urban areas. Mentally retarded girls are also vulnerable to rape.

There appears to be some changes in the character of rape. In feudal settings, while upper classes routinely had access to lower class women, who were *bonded* to them or were economically dependent, this was a form of *sanctioned* power under the caste ideology. Recent cases of rapes in urban areas are confined to lower class men against lower class women, the men are generally from the neighbourhood and accessibility seems to be the main provocation, perhaps fuelled by exposure to pornography and movies. Instances of across class molestation are very rare. Upper class, educated men rarely approach lower class women as there is an acute consciousness of social distance; the exception being maid servants, where perhaps the privacy of the home and the close daily interaction reduces the social distance. In teaching establishments, we rarely hear of young college youth abusing lower class women; invariably it is the 'educated' teacher, who takes advantage of young female students, whose class background is similar. Thus though rape is the extreme exhibition of patriarchy, its manifestation in India is modified by (a) class-caste strucutre (b) the changes brought in by education (c) nature of urbanisation and migration.

The greatest hurdles in combating rapes are : (a) the social attitude towards the victim (b) the police procedure (c) the process of trial where the victim is further humiliated (d) loopholes in the law (e) attitudes of the police, judiciary and lawyers.

The law against rape has remained unchanged for over 120 years. The major provisions are such that there has to be proof that the victim did not give *consent*—in other words there have to be marks of injury etc. In the majority of cases where there is threat to life, where there is intimidation, submission becomes psychologically the most natural response. After considerable agitation by women's group, a new Rape Bill was passed which amended some clauses but did not incorporate the recommendations of women's groups and the joint select committee set up for the purpose.[8] (Details are discussed in the section on law).

Legal and police procedures are still tardy; the victim finds it difficult to undergo medical examination immediately after the traum of the assault and the family too is reluctant to bring in prosecutions.[9]

The commercial Hindi cinema has played a negative role by using rape scenes routinely as a titillating device—giving the message of rape as an *exciting sport*. It does not portray the trauma of the victim nor condems it as an atrocity in unequivocal terms. Analysis of newspaper reporting also reveals the sensationalising trend where very little attention is paid to the victim's point of view.[10]

Many anti-rape women's groups have come up in almost all major cities, who draw media attention, assist rape victims, launch prosecutions etc. But for their impact to be felt, we need intense and sustained campaigns. A sufficient study on the social background of rape-offenders has not been done. Increasing molestation of minor girls appear to be definitely associated with rapid social change. Rapid urbanisation, breakdown of social norms and controls which exist in a rural community, migration, rising age of marriage, have all taken place in a society where segregation of sexes is still very rigid, where there are no accepted modes of interaction between the sexes in non-family, non-kin set up. Along with these social conditions there is a persistence of superstitious beliefs such as virgins being a cure for venereal disease, or young girls being used in so-called tantric practices etc.

Rape crisis centres and counselling cells for victims and stringent action against offenders are necessary.

Offence : Enticing of Taking Away or Detaining with Criminal Intent a Married Woman

States	*Reported During*		*Vol. Per Lakh*		*Average*
	1978	*1979*	*1978*	*1979*	*1978-79*
Andhra Pradesh	—	—	—	—	—
Assam	7	3	0.04	0.02	0.02
Bihar	4	4	0.01	0.01	0.01
Gujarat	—	—	—	—	—
Haryana	—	—	—	—	—
Himachal Pradesh	—	—	—	—	—

(Contd.)

(Contd.)

Jammu & Kashmir	—	—	—	—	—
Karnataka	1	4	—	0.01	—
Kerala	—	—	—	—	—
Madhya Pradesh	—	8	—	0.02	0.01
Maharashtra	4	7	0.01	0.02	0.01
Manipur	—	—	—	—	—
Meghalaya	1	1	0.08	—	0.08
Nagaland	1	—	0.15	—	0.05
Orissa	1	—	—	—	—
Punjab	—	—	—	—	—
Rajasthan	6	7	0.02	0.02	0.02
Sikkim	—	—	—	—	—
Tamil Nadu	—	—	—	—	—
Tripura	—	3	—	0.15	0.05
Uttar Pradesh	2667	2817	2.65	2.74	2.68
West Bengal	3	5	0.01	0.01	0.01
TOTAL	2695	2858	0.43	0.45	0.44

(Files of Dept. of Police Research Bureau, 1985)

Procuration of Minor Girls

States/UT	*Reported During*		*Vol. Per Lakh Population*		*Average*
	1978	*1979*	*1978*	*1979*	*1978-79*
1	*2*	*3*	*4*	*5*	*6*
States					
Andhra Pradesh	3	3	0.01	0.02	0.01
Assam	9	6	0.05	0.03	0.04
Bihar	9	6	0.01	0.04	0.02

(Contd.)

(Contd.)

Gujarat	5	8	0.02	0.03	0.02
Haryana	—	1	—	0.01	0.01
Himachal Pradesh	15	6	0.37	0.15	0.27
Jammu & Kashmir	4	4	0.07	0.07	0.11
Karnataka	10	9	0.03	0.03	0.03
Kerala	6	5	0.02	0.02	0.01
Madhya Pradesh	21	23	0.04	0.04	0.05
Maharashtra	64	63	0.11	0.11	0.10
Manipur	—	1	—	0.07	0.02
Meghalaya	—	1	—	0.05	0.03
Nagaland	—	—	—	—	—
Orissa	—	1	—	—	0.01
Punjab	29	27	0.9	0.08	0.08
Sikkim	—	—	—	—	—
Tamil Nadu	7	14	0.02	0.03	0.02
Tripura	1	1	0.05	0.05	0.09
Uttar Pradesh	641	668	0.64	0.64	0.66
West Bengal	61	46	0.12	0.09	0.12
TOTAL (States)	885	916	0.14	0.14	0.14
UT					
A & N Islands	—	—	—	—	—
Arunachal Pradesh	—	—	—	—	—
Chandigarh	—	—	—	—	—
DN Haveli	—	—	—	—	—
Delhi	—	1	—	0.02	0.02
Goa	—	—	—	—	—
Lakshadweep	—	—	—	—	—
Mizoram	—	—	—	—	—
Pondicherry	—	—	—	—	—
Total (UT)	—	1	—	0.01	0.01
Grand Total	885	917	0.14	0.14	0.14

(Files of Department of Police Research Bureau)

Prostitution

Prostitution is as old as class, society and patriarchy where male dominance exists. Wherever women have been equal partners to men, rape and prostitution are unknown. The process of commoditisation of women begins with the subordination of women and the delinking of sexuality from human relationships and reproduction; it has reduced women to a tradeable commodity. The underlying approach to sexuality is the concept of sexuality as a purely physiological necessity of males only and sex as a male right. The institution of prostitution is entirely a product of male domination, sexual violence against women and their enslavement. The concept of prostitution is as affront to human dignity, a devaluation of women because it demands that women become dehumanised, cheaply available objects to appease male lust. It is defended as a social necessity. Whose necessity ? Any sexual encounter out of wedlock defiles a woman forever and hence, the prostitute like the rape victim is the one who bears the stigma, *not* the customer. A male buyer is not held accountable morally or legally for using the body of stronger for momentary pleasure, but the women who is used for the appeasement of his lust is condemned, ostracised as degenerate and can even be punished for it.[11]

In India, there has existed through centuries the tradition of courtesans but they were entertainers, accomplished in fine arts and were more like mistresses, who served rich patrons. There was no severe stigma as attached to the modern, commercialised flesh trade though they were also controlled by men. There was also the tradition of sacred dedication to temples in the South. These women were dancers and musicians and had property rights and had a high ritual status, gracing marriages and festivals. It is wrong to equate this custom to the commercialised trade, where women are completely commoditised as mere flesh-objects.

Call girls usually come from more well-to-do classes and have a higher standard of living and enter the profession voluntarily, usually due to family problems or the desire to make quick money. In India, data and reports show that women who take to prostitution do so out of economic necessity, out of helplessness that denial of educational and employment opportunities generates. Our patriarchal society classifies women as good and bad—victims of rape, incest, abandonment by lovers or husbands perceived as 'spoilt' and made to feel a deep sense of guilt. Emotionally and economically insecure women also fall easy prey to procurers.[12]

The bulk of the women found in prostitution are not voluntary entrants to a calling where conditions of earning and living are heinous. Estimates are that at least one lakh teenage girls, many of whom are minors and women in their twenties are exploited in 12,000 brothels in the city, kept like prisoners in violation of their basic human rights[13] with promises of marriage, good life or a job; young girls are lured, generally from Southern States so that they cannot communicate with others, not knowing the local language. The cases reported according to police files are only a fraction of these numbers. Over 3,00,000 girls between the ages of 9 to 20 years are transporated to India from Nepal every year by a well organised racket. Girls[14] are smuggled into and out of Uttar Pradesh, sold secretly or openly auctioned with full knowledge of the police and administration. Trafficking in women is increasing due to landlessness and chronic unemployment in rural areas.

Political power in India has always been associated with sexual licences and the private lives of politicians evoke little criticism and supplying girls to politicians and bureaucrats by business groups in return for sanctions and favours is widely prevalent.

Sheela Barse, a committed journalist has been fighting a crusade against the inhuman conditions under which women in brothels live. The major part of their earnings are cornered by pimps and lawyers who defend them: of the police and the male customers who are all implicated it can be said that they do not face any prosecution[15]. The majority of women suffer from sexually transmitted diseases (STD.). When young girls are brought in, they are routinely gang raped to break their resistance and to make their escape impossible.

There is only one law, the Suppression of Immoral Traffic in Women (1956) but though this law has existed for 26 years, it has been totally ineffective. The number of minor girls rescued are just a few hundred whereas the victims run into lakhs. (The

Vigilance Branch rescued 107 girls aged between 16 to 18 years in one year from Bombay's red light area. These girls were from Andhra, Karnataka, West Bengal and Nepal.

There have been two solutions suggested to improve the pitiable condition of prostitutes : (i) that the prostitutes must organise themselves to defend their rights (ii) legalise prostitution and provide legal safeguards against exploitations.

In Kolhapur, prostitutes have formed an organisation. *Veshya Anyay Nivaran Sangathana* for the removal of injustice against prostitutes and have asked for a separate colony to house them and demanded licensing of their trade so that brothel keepers, pimps and police stop exploiting them. In Pune, the 'Devadasis' have formed an association and the Mahatma Phule Samata Pratishthan, a social service organisation has set up a speical rehabilitation centre. In Nagpur, prostitutes have formed an organisation called *Amarapali Shakti Sangathana* and have demanded a licensing system. Several women's organisations have demanded job reservation for rehabilitating prostitutes. Another organisation called *Savdhan* works in Bombay to rehabilitate girls resuced from brotherls. Many women's groups are also demanding reform in law.

Licensing it is felt will at least ensure minimum safeguards. Both these solutions are difficult to accept as they legitimise an evil practice, and yet by not doing anything, we are condemning millions of women to a life of hell. The dilemma arises because, not to do anything will imply accepting the stigma imposed by a patriarchal culture and a means of liberation will be to do away with the stigma, to tear apart the facade of public decency, existing under a veil of indifference, a social pathology. Rape is one time violation, prostitution is continuing-rape.

When feminists talk of licensing or collectivisation, they are concerned with protecting the women from dire exploitation like excessive hours of work, bad conditions of work, their earnings being taken away, ill treatment, neglect of their health and proneness to diseases etc. and are not thinking of legitimising the practice on the specious plea that it is a 'necessary social evil'. It is an undersirable evil, not an inevitable one. Its elimination requires restructuring of the present social set up which will give greater sexual freedom to men and women with the recognition and understanding of female sexuality. It will need the abolition of the concept of woman as property of a male-guardian, sanctified by law. Education and economic independence for women will reduce women's vulnerability and bring about a change in the value system of a society that does not reward women's skills or labour but is willing to buy their bodies.

Domestic Violence

Wife beating is another private, family 'problem' never publicly acknowledged as a crime against women. It exists in all classes. In a study done in Bombay[16] it was found that the effects differed between women from the middle-class and women from the poorer class.

Women from the poorer class were frequently subject to wife beating by alcoholic husbands; the cause of quarrels was invariably the man demanding the hard earned money of the wife for his drinking. Working class women do not suffer loss of self-esteem and do not blame themselves for the phenomenon. They have witnessed violence by men—in their own families, in the neighbourhood etc. before their marriage. They attribute it to the crowded living conditions, economic hardship and so on and discuss it freely. The middle-class women are numbed with shock, and are unprepared for it and tend to view their case as an isolated incident. They are ashamed to talk about it and conceal it and attempt to keep a normal front.

In an interview with a ninety-year-old woman from Tamil Nadu, a researcher[17] was shocked to discover that this upper caste brahmin woman remembered only one thing in her life-her husband used to beat her for every little real or imagined omission or commission. It is only recently that some women are coming out with this hidden crime in middle-class families, with the help and support of women's groups.[18]

The Research Centre on Women's Studies undertook and analysis of newspaper reports of dowry deaths and deaths of married women under suspicious circumstances. We found a rising preponderance of deaths in the first few years of marriage. We tried to study these reports to see what background information was available on the family concerned but very little was reported.

Working class women who put up with alcoholism and wife

beating, when asked why they stick to men who do not even support them economically usually reply that having a man around protects them from other men--the husband is a protective fence. However bad he may be to his wife, he will guard his proprietary rights over her in case of any attempt by others to approach her. In spite of the beatings, (which the men, not having any other superiority over them, use to assert their 'superiority') the working class women remain confident and assertive.

Among the middle-class, the unemployed wife is dependent on the husband who controls the purse and yet she has the burden of keeping up middle-class standards; even if the wife earned an income she spent all of it on house-keeping and as the husband usually earns more and has a higher social, occupational status, the wife derives no authority from herbeing an economic contributor. In fact, her employment outside is seen as a threat to the authority of the husband and in-laws so beating and verbal insults are used to subjugate her.

In a shelter home run by a governmental agency[19] the manager said, "The poor women come to us for temporary shelter. They stay on, only if they have to, that is, if they have small children, thus making it impossible for them to work. They always want to get out and be independent. They will take up any job-temporary jobs in mills and factories or work as domestic servants, often staying in the homes where they work. They put the children in boarding schools or orphanages. But the women with some education, women belonging to the middle-class have more problems of adjusting themselves to an independent life. They have no qualification or experience to take up decent jobs, and they feel it below their dignity to take certain types of jobs. So they tend to stay on at the shelter home longer, the shelter becoming another place to protect them."

Some women's organisations have now come up to provide counselling for battered women, to help them become independent, to assist in divorce proceedings if they wish to separate and so on. There is also now more willingness on the part of battered women to talk about their condition.[20] In some places in Maharashtra, peasant women organised themselves against alcoholism and wife beating.[21]

TABLE 6.1

Reported Deaths of Women (1981-1984)*
(*Age-wise Classification*)

Years of Marriage	*Below 20*				*21—25*				*25—35*				*Unspecified Category*			
	81	*82*	*83*	*84*	*81*	*82*	*83*	*84*	*81*	*82*	*83*	*84*	*81*	*82*	*83*	*84*
6 months	—	—	—	2	—	1	1	5	—	—	—	—	1	1	1	2
6 months—1 year	—	1	3	5	—	—	2	3	—	—	—	—	—	—	2	8
1 year—2 years	—	—	1	2	1	—	1	2	—	—	—	—	—	—	—	10
2 years—5 years	—	1	1	3	—	—	—	8	1	—	1	2	—	—	—	12
75 years	—	1	1	—	—	—	1	—	—	—	3	—	—	—	1	7
Years of marriage unspecified	1	1	4	13	2	—	6	19	—	—	3	11	1	2	5	—
Total	1	4	10	25	3	1	11	37	1	—	7	13	2	3	9	37

*These are cases where 'dowry' is not specifically mentioned.
The newspapers available in Bombay included one or two Delhi papersthe list is given in the Appendex to this chapter.

TABLE 6.2

Reported Cases of Dowry Deaths in Major Cities (1980-1985)

Year	*Bombay*	*Delhi*	*Calcutta*	*Bangalore*	*Madras*
1980	1	1	--	--	--
1981	1	2	1	--	--
1982	2	2	1	1	1
1983	6	7	1	2	1
1984	29	57	8	7	2
1985	9	10	2	3	1

These are underestimates as they cover only newspaper reports, but even then Delhi stands out as the major offender.

Dowry Deaths

An extreme form of domestic violence is the burning of young married women by husbands and in-laws for not satisfying their excessive dowry demands. A large number of these cases are reported as suicides or accidents.

According to the Anti-Dowry Cell set up by the Police Commissioner, New Delhi, in 1983, 690 young women died in that city alone of whom 23 were burnt alive. The police records also reveal that between 1979-1983, these deaths have increased.

	Total Number of Women Burnt
1979	422
1980	429
1981	542
1982	627
1983 (Till May)	253

The dowry deaths as reported by the Minister of State for Home Affairs in the Parliament :

	1981	*1982*	*1983*
Delhi	24	40	42
West Bengal	2	7	9
Andhra Pradesh	2	4	4
Karnataka	7	8	31
Tamil Nadu	2	5	5
Assam	1	--	--
Haryana	28	42	42
Punjab	35	40	40

These are gross underestimates as the majority of cases go unreported or the victims give a dying declaration absolving the husband and in-laws under duress. In 1985, if we include not only dowry deaths but harassment due to dowry, the number of reported cases were 138. Rajasthan, Bihar and Orissa also reported a number of cases of suicide/murder due to dowry and suicide due to general harassment by husband and in-laws.

Dowry deaths are difficult to prove and prosecution therefore, becomes impossible. A major reason for the occurrence of this violence is the unwillingness of parents of the girl to take her back when she complains of harassment. They grieve after the girl dies, but take no action to protect her when she can still be saved. Notions of dishonour if a married girl returns to her parental house and reluctance to support her after she has been settled and the generally idea that a girl is a liability, all condemn the girl to face the harassment and give her no means of escape. Even after it is known that a man's wife died under suspicious circumstances, parents are ready to offer their daughter for remarriage to the man. Often the daughter does not even complain to her parents, socialised as she is to being submissive. It could also be that adequate communication and frankness does not exist between parents and daughters.

There have been several organisations that have come up to resist dowry and to seek justice in cases of dowry murders but a great deal of community and neighbourhood support is necessary to make them effective.[22, 23, 24, 25] There are no proper studies on the social background of offenders, but sundry evidence seems to suggest that they belong mostly to petty shop-keepers and aspiring men from business castes, but an increasing number of cases are reported from the propertied classes and professionals. There are a large number of unnatural deaths of young, married women which get reported as suicides or accidents but could well be suicides due to harassment by the family or even outright murders. An exceedingly large number of burn cases among women aged 16 to 30 seem suspiciously convenient kitchen accidents-Malini Karkal's study on Colnorie's reports in Bombay appear to point to increasing violence against young married women.[26, 27]

Pornography

This is another form of exploitation of women, but often this is defended as freedom of expression. The interviews reported here represent two points of view which are fairly typical : (a) it is unhealthy and degrading (b) that it is freedom of expression.

The freedom of expression view forgets that an individual's actions affect others. Secondly, it fails to take note of the ways the so called *individual* choices are really learned behaviour and there is little real freedom in it. It is difficult to estimate the circulation of pornographic literature as it is an underground activity. According to newspaper reports there has been a proliferation of such literature, sold openly in shops and street corners. A new addition is the screening of blue movies surreptitiously in video parlours.

Why do feminists disapprove of pornography ? First of all much of it is anti-women; Secondly it includes a lot of violence against women; Thirdly it dehumanises the relations between the sexes.

It is often argued that the line between erotica and pornography is very thin. The definition of pornography according to law is that it *debases*. The level of tolerance of a society for what is considered *debasing* varies. The greater the permissiveness, the greater the level of tolerance.

The following two points of view reported in a journal are typical of the arguments for and against. It is not true that *pornography* is harmless. What people mean when they talk of it being harmless is that it does not necessarily result in violence or sexual perversions, but we really do not have enough facts to prove or disprove this. However, it is undeniable that it alters the consciousness of the reader, and influences how sexuality is perceived. In the absence of proper and balanced sex education, adolescent boys derive their information mainly from pornography.

Feminists have recently been questioning the very construction of sexuality exclusively from a male point of view.

Conclusion

Violence againt women has been increasing--but such violence has existed for centuries and has never been questioned but accepted as part of the patriarchal structure. It has been the more visible aspect of coercive male power and family oppression. Hence there has never been any shock or indignation expressed over it by any group in society. This total desensitising attitude on the part of both the victim and the oppressor is responsible for failing to treat such violence as a *crime* rather than as something that men are entitled to. Only recently has some consciousness emerged among women, that this state of affairs is unjust. The instruments of law and order and the various minions of justice still dismiss these acts of cruelty lightly. A major effort at eradication of these brutalities will first lie in increasing the sensitivity of people and society to these crimes.

Impact of Media on Women

Media plays a crucial role in the functioning and change of any society. Both the forces of change and of opposition utilise different forms of media to suit their needs. Modern technology has vastly increased the outreach of media and made its centralised control possible. One has to be more concerned about not merely the direct reach of the media but also its indirect influence. By gradually shaping, public opinion, personal beliefs and even people's self-perceptions, media influences the process of socialisation and shapes ideology and thinking.[28] One of the prominent women's groups, Vimochana, in an open letter to the producer of a television programme entitled *It's a Woman's World* remarks : "The communication media has after all always been an integral part of society's myth making machinery consciously or unconsciously recording, defining, channelising and reinforcing attitudes and value structures, the *status quo* in short. The images have fluctuated between the much maligned and (disrobed) vamp to the over glorified mother, sister, daughter or wife."[29] The established media portrayal of women is one more evidence of ideological violence on women, both through explicit scence of wife beating, rape and other forms of sexual harassment wherein it is possible to project simultaneously a provocative exhibition of woman's body, projecting her as docile, self-suffering, naive, and devoted. In fact the media provides a particularly appropriate evidence of the interwining of patriarchal attitudes with a profit oriented commercial society--an enmeshment that debases women. Before we describe the projection of women in various media, it would be useful to know the relative significance of different media in the Indian context.

With a vast illiterate population and a background of two thousand years of cultural transmission through the oral tradition, the print media has a very limited impact on the mass of people. Audio-visual media such as broadcasting, cinema and now television have a deeper impact on people. The UNESCO in 1978 set up a few norms suggestive of the out reach of different media in third world countries.[30] The differential significance has not only substantially not changed but with the spread of television it has been re-inforced.

Sl. No.	*Medium*	*UNESCO norm per 100 persons*	*Indian situation*
1.	Daily newspaper	10 copies of daily	One copy of newspaper (press reaches barely 37 per cent of the urban and 7 per cent of the rural population).
2.	Radio set	5 radio sets	About one set
3.	Cinema	2 sets	About two cinema seats.
4.	T.V.	About 2 T.V. receivers.	--

As reported in the annual report, 1984-1985, of the Ministry of Information and Broadcasting at the completion of sixth plan projects : "Coverage by AIR would increase to 95 per cent of the population and 86 per cent of the area and TV coverage to 33 per cent of population and 17 per cent of the area."[31] Recently it has been reported that a social TV expansion plan has been launched to cover 70 per cent of the population and the starting of second channels from various centres to make up for the limited time available on the present channel. Against an overwhelming poverty this figure appears to be mere wishful thinking. Undoubtedly, radio today reaches more listeners than newspapers, the number of radio sets an estimated 20 million being more than double the combined circulation of all the daily newspapers.

Similarly, in 1984, 833 feature films were certified. The language-wise distribution is revealing; Telugu (170), Hindi (165), Tamil (148) and Malayalam (121) ; the remaining 229 films are produced in the other 19 languages.[32]

A very significant feature of the media in India is that Broadcasting and Television are in the public sector while newspapers, cinema and advertising are predominantly privately owned media.

For the privately owned media profit and marketability are the major considerations. Objectives like information, education, improvement of the economy or value change are given significance so long as they serve the purpose of profitability, while the publicly owned media could be expected to impart information, generate motivation for attitudinal change as well as entertain. This dual system of ownership creates an illusion that the function of the public sector owned media is to educate while the private sector entertains. In reality, as the public sector media depends heavily on the private sponsored programmes for increasing revenue, the distinction is marginal. For instance, on the radio a separate programme of *Vividh Bharti* is largely fed by cinema songs, skits and commercials supplied by advertising companies. Similarly, TV software like feature films, sponsored programmes like soap operas and sitcoms and film-based programmes predominate without any protect from any quarter--either the promoters or critics or viewers.

The report of the working group an autonomy for Akashwani and Doordarshan established in 1977, headed by Shri B.G.

Verghese and of the working group on software for Doordarshan formed in 1982, headed by Dr. P.C. Joshi, are significant documents not only in providing information but also a valuable critique on the directions in which the public sector media is at present moving and ought not to move. The Verghese Committee analyses succinctly *Vividh Bharti* programmes which forms the largest chunk of the entertainment component. It is operated for 12 hours and 45 minutes on week days with a half hour extra on Sundays and holidays. The *Vividh Bharti* channel carries two news bulletins each of five minutes. Other spoken word announcements, talks, plays, short stories and poetry recitals account for ten per cent of the total transmission. The remaining 90 per cent consists of music; classical and light music 16 per cent, folk and regional music 10 per cent and devotional and patriotic music 4 per cent, taking up a total of 30 per cent of the transmission time. The remaining 60 per cent is devoted to film music.[33] Thus it has ceased to be a variety programme but has become an essentially repetitive film disc programme.

Similarly, the Joshi Committee scathingly criticises Doordarshan for depending upon commercial films for entertainment. A content analysis of Delhi Doordarshan's offerings in 1983, showed : "Feature films and film related programmes occupied the largest single chunk of the telecast time (21.1 per cent). For TV also the order of priorities seems to be entertainment, information, education. The Committee also bemoans the fact that the middle-class regards the purchase of a TV set as a wholesale investment in movie entertainment which obviated the bother and expenses of going to a cinema house and queueing up for tickets."[34]

Radio and TV media have been further depleted of their educational or value change objective by the massive use of sponsored programmes. Besides commercials which yield revenue to these media, the sponsored programmes have been introduced in the TV since 1983, with two-fold objectives : (i) widening the programme production base by tapping the talent base from outside, (ii) increasing Doordarshan's commercial revenue.[35] For advertisers to give advertisements in the radio or TV is very profitable. Verghese report's comments on intermedia comparisons are quite revealing: "Inter-media comparisons indicate that the cost per thousand (CPM) for reaching all adults in household with over Rs. 500 per month incomes in Bombay-Pune-Nagpur-Vividh Bharti stations : Rs. 7.77 for a 30 second television commercial; Rs. 13.20 for a quarter page advertisement in Bombay's leading English language newspaper and Rs. 21.60 for a 30 second black and white film strip in a top rate cinema."[36] It is obvious that this situation has led to a mushrooming in production of sponsored programmes. What is more depressing is the fact that sponsored programmes thrive on soap operas. Joshi Committee's remarks are quite justified : "Dominated by the commercial formula-film, film-based programmes and its own film imitative culture, Doordharshan emerges from this analysis as succumbing to the role of a hand maiden of the vested commercial/consumerist interests that exploit the female form to titillate and/or by their socially insensitive approach, simply trivialise and debase the image of womanhood."[37]

Having provided a brief background to the different media we will disucss the projection of women in the media.

Portrayal of Women in Different Media

In order to evaluate the media portrayal of women, we will take all media forms together. Excepting the advertisement, media portrayal of women comes in two ways; firstly there are special women's programmes as in TV or broadcasting, and women's pages in the newspaper or women's journals. Secondly by using other media forms like advertisement or feature films, reactionary values get perpetuated.

In radio for instance, all stations broadcast two to three times a week programmes on women in regional languages. They form 1.4 per cent of the total broadcasting time. Half an hour or an hour devoted to women's programmes is filled in with 60 per cent for entertainment through songs, drama, skits etc., 20 per cent education and 20 per cent information. Songs selected are by and large on religious themes or depicting themes of coy young women waiting to be married; plays convey the message of the ideal woman who is a housewife and mother. If she is employed, then surely she must be neglecting her home and children : Often in the guise of making a programme light and entertaining, some of the stereotypes are reinforced. A woman is a gossip-monger. She cannot hold a secret; she is a flippant creature who loves to go to 'sales' and ultimately gets duped. In short these programmes seem to be for the education of women; but focus on issues of women which are limited to imparting instructions on sewing, cooking, knitting and the like. Advice is generally given as to how to become a good wife, good mother and improve one's looks. At times, there is a lot of talking down to women.

In spite of the fact that 36 per cent of the agricultural work force is provided by women, in producing rural development programmes, it is the rural woman who is missing in TV or radio! Most training, information and resources for the development of agriculture, horticulture, animal husbandry are given to male farmers. A rare appearance by women in this programme is usually either as folk dancers or as health advisers for pregnant mothers.

Going to the cinema in a poor country like India, is the cheapest means of entertainment. As an industry also it is one of the largest, having Rs. 720 million invested capital and employing 200 thousand persons. The government controls the release of all films, through the Censor Board, and as a regulator it affects cinema industry through the measures of licences and import of raw material. Big money is the bane of this industry. Producers and financiers are not worried about the message of change, aesthetics or content of the films. They themselves see women as sexy, glamourous and empty headed.

The formula film preaehes respect for elders, sacrifice for the family, reaffirmation of the value of self-effacement, devotion, acceptance of the subordinate position of women and censure for women who opt for a less traditional life. Over and above these traditional patriarchal values, these films depict violence in such a stark manner that it dehumanises the individual. Wife-beating and insults to women are a part of this genre of films. Various studies on the projection of women in films have pointed out that the mainstream cinema presents woman as an "ideal Sita" acquiescing unquestioningly in her husband's rejection of her. The average woman is not viewed as anything more than wife, daughter, mother. She has to be subjected to men in one form or the other. These women hardly exhibit a capacity for rational and logical thought. This theme is repeated and reiterated in film after film. The films also highlight the fact that women's only hope for gaining status is in becoming a mother of sons. Along with the Sita model, films also project women as a vamp who either lures men from their right path or provides solace to them from a supposedly 'unhappy' life. It is interesting to note that in an account of the film-hit parade from 1950 to 1980 of a dozen films, not a single film contained a projection of woman which showed her possessing dignity or self-esteem; nor did any of the films expose the social evils corroding the Indian social structure.[37a]

It is not an exaggeration when we say that wider movements, both of women and in general, during the last decade have made some impact on the film industry. A few committed producers in their films try to depict a woman leading her own independent life in the event of marital crisis; or she may decide to prefer a career to stressful family life; she is also projected as an angry woman exposing the dual morality structure. She is also depicted as a companion to her husband and a dignified individual in her own right. Of course, this parallel cinema is patronised by a small section of the society.[38]

The advertisement medium is very blatant and openly anti-woman, treating her only as a sex symbol. The studies on the projection of women in advertisements have shown that whether a woman is used for advertising cosmetics, fabrics, jewellery or domestic gadgets or suitcases, scooters or stationery, she has to be glamorous and enticing. The feminine mystique has created a ready market for products like cosmetics, fabrics, jewellery. They sell a mysterious *feminity* preserved in perfume jars and packaged in flimsy nightwear. Another trend that one sees even in the advertisement of men's clothes is the invariable use of admiring women by the side of men which would create the impression that all a woman desires is a man dressed in sophisticated garments. Emphasis on the macho image of man, and woman as the enticing object are the predominant themes. The woman is invariably in the kitchen, cooking food which is approved by her mother-in-law, washing a bucketful of clothes and yet very charmingly, bandaging children's bruses and feeding her husband and children.[39]

Analysis of various types of advertisement on the radio indicates that more than 25 per cent of advertisements are on cosmetics, food products, beverages and fabrics. These are the goods where a woman could be shown as a glamourous as well as a submissive, brainless consumer.

Purnima Mankekar refers to a study conducted in 1983 by the Indian Institute of Mass Communication entitled. "Advertising and Social Responsibility" which highlights some of the glaring features which reveal the perception of woman either as a sex symbol or as a dud. One out of every five advertisements features a woman irrespective of her relevance to the product being sold. It is interesting to note that an equal number of respondents agree with both views--one that woman is represented as a sex object and the other as a progressive and modern person. This in itself is a pointer to the ambivalence of viewers about the image of women in society. When about 48 per cent of respondents feel that there is no specific role portrayal of women, it really is a very sad commentary on the status of women in society.[40]

As mentioned earlier, TV relies considerably on commercial cinema and advertisements hence the stereotyped image of woman is reiterated. Many of the TV programmes are produced on contract basis. This feature leads to unevenness in perspective. A feminist producer might be discussing the serious dowry problem or the impact of harmful drugs on women's health. Soon after this in other programmes like drama, dance or other discussions, the traditional role of women is glorified, thus nullifying what has been said earlier. As mentioned previously, with the growing reliance on sponsored programmes, TV has opened its doors wide, to the big, unscrupulous financiers, with the result that the dull grey propaganda of the government activities is replaced by the more seductive, slick, glamorous, tinselled world of advertisements. The stereotype of a woman who is a devout, silent 'Sita' or a quarrelling mother-in-law or a 'modern' naughty opinionated woman, is a marked feature of most of these programmes.

Coming to the print media, there are special women's features in the newspapers which generally confine themselves to the image of woman as a consumer, glamour loving and confined to her wife and mother roles. Women's magazines particularly in English and specifically those which are part of the newspaper chains or journals, give a mixed bag of recipes, tips on beauty aids, a romantic story, a feature article on some current issue like rape or dowry death, a Supreme Court judgement on maintenance or on restitution of conjugal rights and sometimes a serious discussion on gender problems. The content of the journals is so heterogenous that one wonders whether there is any serious message regarding woman's status or problems.

Recently, for newspapers and journals some of the issues concerning women like rape, dowry, sexual harassment, have become news worthy. Ila Pathak, while discussing the handling of rape news by Gujarati language newspapers in a content analysis conducted in 1980, remarks angrily : "Why do journalists see rape cases as merely spicy stories ? Whenever I read such reports I wondered why the journalists treated the case of helpless women as merely opportunities to titillate their reader and sell their journals better ? Why could not their attitude be more healthy, more sympathetic towards women."[41]

In the *Sunday Review* section of the renowned *Times of India*, dated 15th June 1983, a discussion on rape by leading men and women is reported with a heading *Sex-an instrument of Oppression*. Almost the whole upper half the page is filled with two large photographs of seventeenth century paintings on rape.[42] Rape scenes from Indian films are used by the journals. Thus, the attempt seems to sell violence on women as a *worthy commodity*.

A few feminist journalists in the mainstream print media are utilising various columns to project positive images of women and raise issues of gender justice. There have been protests against media portrayal of women, which we will discuss in later sections. These are hopeful signs.

Notes and References

1. "Report of a seminar on violence", Department of Sociology, South Gujarat University, *Economic and Political Weekly*, Vol. 20, No. 12, 23rd March, 1985.
2. Madhu Kishwar, "Gandhi on Women", *Economic and Political Weekly*, Vol. 20, No. 40, Oct, 5, 1985 and No. 41, Oct. 12, 1985.
3. Seema Sakre, "Analytical Study of the Recent Rape cases in Vidarbha Region of Maharashtra State in India," Paper, Second National Conference on Women's Studies, Trivandrum, 1984 (mimeo).
4. Vimla Farouqi, *Women--Social Victims of Police and Landlord Atrocities*, National Federation of Indian Women, New Delhi, 1980.

5. Sudesh Vaid, Amiya Rao, Monica Junje, *Rape, Society and State*, People's Union of Civil Liberties, New Delhi, 1983.
6. Sujata Gathoskar, *Politics of Rape*, Paper, First National Conference on Women's Studies, Bombay, 1981.
7. Stree Sangarsha, "Mass Rape in Santhal Parganas--Police Repression against Tribal Movement to Reclaim Land--An on the Spot Study," *HOW*, Vol. 3, No. 5, May 1980.
8. *Rape and the Law*, Committee for Legal Literacy, Bombay, 1983.
9. Anjali Deshpande, "Post rape Ordeal of a Victim", *Mainstream*, Vol. 21, No. 33, April 1983.
10. Ila Pathak, "The Handling of Rape News by Newspaper", Ahmedabad Women's Action Group, Ahmedabad (mimeo), undated.
11. Maithreyi Krishna Raj, *Newsletter* of the Research Unit on Women's Studies, S.N.D.T. Women's University, Vol. 4, No. 3, August 1983.
12. Sheela Barse, "Flesh Trade in Bombay--Shocking indignities on Minors", *Indian Express*, 7 July, 1983.
13. Dr. Ishwarprasad Giladia, "Prostitution in Urban Centres' Study : Perspectives and Positional Problems for Social Intervention", Survey by the Indian Health Organisation, June 20, 1982 (mimeo) (Presented at the Forum '85 at Nairobi, July 1985).
14. Sheela Brase, "Judged without a Hearing", *Indian Express*, 20 August, 1983.
15. Promilla Kapur, *Life and World of Call Girls in India*, Vikas Publication New Delhi, 1978.
16. Flavia D'Mello, "Domestic Violence : Difference Between Working class and Middle class",*ISRI*, Bombay, 1980.
17. C.S. Lakshmi, "Non Textual Methods of Research in Women's Studies", (mimeo). Seminar Abstract, Research Unit on Women's Studies, SNDT Women's University, Bombay, 1983.
18. Madhu Kishwar, "Making Life More Meaningful--An Interview with Rinki", *Manushi*, Vol. 4, No. 5, July 1984.
19. Flavia D'Mello, "Our Fight Against Wife Beating", Paper, Conference on Research and Teaching Related to Women held at Concodia University Canada, 26 July-4 Aug., 1982.
20. Flavia D'Mello, *Domestic Violence*, Women's Centre Publication Bombay, Nov. 1984.
21. Gail Omvedt, *We will smash This Prison*, Orient Longman Ltd., 1979 (Bombay) (by arrangement with Zed Press, London).
22. Monica Junjee and Sudesh Vaid, "Delhi Women Protest Dowry Deaths", *Alternate News and Features*, Jan. 1980.
23. "Rape and Dowry Deaths", Saheli (mimeo), New Delhi, 25 Nov., 1983.
24. *Voices of the Working Woman*, Vol. 3, No. 4, July 1983.
25. "Women Lecturers Mobilise Against Dowry Deaths",*Manushi*, Vol. 2, No. 12, Nov.-Dec. 1982.
26. Malini Karkarl, "How the Other Half Dies", *Economic and Political Weekly*, Vol. 20, No. 34, 25th Aug., 1985.
27. Sujata Anandan, "Marriage or Murder", *Illustrated Weekly of India*, 15th Aug., 1982.
28. Kamla Bhasin and Bina Agarwal (Ed.), *Women and media*: Analysis, *Alternatives Action, Kali for Women*, Delhi, 1985, p. 9.

29. An open letter to Simi Grewal, Producer "It's a Woman's World", a Doordarshan programme written by Vimochana, *Forum for Women's rights*, Bangalore, May 1985.
30. Roberge Gaston, *Chitra Bani*, Rafi Ahmed Kidwai Road, Calcutta, 1974, p. 20.
31. Ministry of Information and Broadcasting, *Annual Report*, 1984-1985, p. 10.
32. *Ibid.*, p. 87.
33. *Verghese Committee Report*, Vol. 1, p. 153.
34. *Joshi Committee Report*, Vol. 1. p. 159.
35. *Annual Report*, op. cit., p. 31.
36. Op. cit., p. 87.
37. Op. cit., p. 141. It is important to note that at the termination of one of the most popular sponsored serials *Hum Log* which ran into 156 episodes, there was lot of emotional outburst. A section of viewers do feel that this family drama was so appealing as it reinforced the existing stereotypes and values.

37a. A telling instance of an Indian woman on the screen being modelled as the great mythological character Sita could be seen in a film entitled *OH BEWAFA* (Oh Disloyal). In this picture at one stage the wife of a disloyal person is addressed by a well wisher who himself has a concubine thus, "As she circles the fire seven times during her marriage behind her husband, every Hindu woman vows to follow him wherever he goes, whatever he does. Only at the last moment, does she step in front of him, this implies that when death comes, she will go first."

38. To name a few significant films which not merely depict alienation of man (when a woman is merely an appendage) but dominated or supported equally by woman are *Ankur*, *Akrosh*, *Chakra*, *Subah* and *Paar*. Besides the two extremes of films viz. formula and new wave there are some in between films which attempt to combine a bit of both. The wife is shown having some independent life, opinion, courage. Some of these films are *Artha*, *Andhi*, *Lajvanti*, *Kora Kagaz*.
39. Pathak and Amin, "Media and Sex roles", mimeographed, Ahmedabad Women's group (*AWAG*); Advertisement of *Maggi*, *Lyril Soap*, *Dalda*, *Refined Oil*, *Surf*, *Soap*, *Burnol*--all give this message.
40. J.S. Yadav and Abhilasha Mohnet, *Advertising and Social responsibility*, Indian Institute of Mass Communication, 1983, Vol. 2, p. 70, Vol. 1, p. 73, 75.
41. Pathak Ila, "The survey of the handling of the rape news", by Journalists in the *Dailies* of Ahmedabad, mimeo, p. 2.
42. ibid., p. 5.

APPENDIX

The list of Newspapers and Magazines referred to for dowry deaths

Hindustan Times	New Delhi
The Times of India	Bombay
Deccan Herald	Bangalore
Indian Express	Bombay
The Telegraph	Calcutta
Daily	Bombay
Mid Day	Bombay
Evening News	Bombay
Free Press Journal	Bombay
The Statesman	Calcutta
Hindu	Madras
Sunday Observer	Bombay
Eves Weekly	Bombay
National Herald	Delhi
Onlooker	Bombay
Femina	Bombay
Blitz Weekly	Bombay
Free Press Bulletin	Bombay
New Age	Delhi
Sunday	Calcutta
Economic Times	Bombay
Nav Kal	New Delhi
Sunday	Secunderabad
Probe	New Delhi
Patriot	New Delhi

7

Action for Change

The diversity of situations and problems arising out of the interplay between the political economy and patriarchal value system has not always been meekly accepted. Various strategies have been adopted to usher changes in sciety, which would provide the basis for an egalitarian social structure, a structure that would ensure gender justice.

In this chapter, we have divided the discussion on social action in to two broad divisions. Firstly, there are efforts made by the government, for instance the establishment of a democratic government providing opportunities to women for participating in the formal process of gaining political power. Further, law is used as an instrument of social change in many Third World countries. Changes in law backed by legislative action are steps forward towards change. Finally, in the last four or five years the government has taken some positive policy measures to protect interests of women.

Besides government action, of equal importance have been non-governmental efforts to initiate change. In this respect, the emergence and functions of women's organisations as well as the role of media, not only to counteract the distorted projection of women in the established media but also to evolve a counter culture, are significant.

We will start with the discussion on political participation of women.

SECTION 1

POLITICAL PARTICIPATION OF WOMEN

If democracy is the rule by the people, the question arises as to who participates in political decisions, which is one of the most fundamental questions of democracy. It is the will of the people, men and women, which decides who should rule and what are the goals. Citizens use participation as a way to communicate their needs and aspirations and a technique to maximise the allocation ofbenefits. Lack of ability to participate implies lack of full membership within the system. The government takes important decisions not only on important national and international issues but also on matters which affect women's lives directly like maternity, child care, nutrition, economic and social discrimination. Though women have a large stake in politics, as large as that of men, they are conspicuous by their meagre number in decision-making bodies in India. Very few Indian women really wield political power. History is resplendent with examples of powerful women rulers like Lakshmibai or Razia Sultana, and the glaring fact cannot be overlooked that women never wielded political power through recognised channels.

Till the end of the nineteenth centruy, women in India were crushed under the weight of evil customs like infanticide, child marriage and *Sati*. They were socially weak, economically dependent and politically powerless. Even when they entered the elite national organisation like the Indian National Congress, the feeling which prevailed initially was that women *should be seen and not heard*. Though the women delegates of those days reacted sharply against it by asking men to *have some pretty wax figures nicely dressed on the platform*, the history of the Congress bears ample testimony to the fact that most of the women who attended the Congress sessions worked as volunteers and took the lead in singing the national anthem and, barring a few, did not actively participate in the deliberations.

Though some powerful women like Sarojini Naidu and Indira Gandhi achieved glory and fame in political life, the political arena largely remained a field unploughed by women. Again, if a woman rose to the highest seat of power, the norms and values were not considered to be threatened; rather it was ascribed to the Indian tradition, which accords a high place to women. Sarojini Naidu saw, in her election as Congress President in 1925, only a reversion to an old tradition and restoration to Indian womanhood, the classic position she once held symbol and guardian alike of the hearth-fires, the alter-fires and the beacon-fires of her land.[1]

The demand for franchise before Independence was pressed for by the elite women, who were conscious of their political rights and who were influenced by the democratic values and ideals. Annie Beasant, Margaret Cousins, Sarojini Naidu, Heerabai Tata and other educated women in women's organisations worked actively for generating political consciousness among women. A deputation of women met Montague in 1917 to demand the *right to vote for women*. The Government of India Act, 1919, laid down that the question of franchise could be settled by the provinces. The province of Madras took lead in the matter and Dr. Muthulakshmi Reddi became the first woman legislator. By 1926 women secured equal position in franchise, so far as the election to the provincial legislatures was concerned. The Government of India Act, 1935, extended franchise to six million women. In 1937 elections, eight women were elected from general constituencies and forty-two from reserved constituencies. Vijayalakshmi Pandit became the minister for local self-government in U.P. Later, Anasuyabai Kale was appointed Deputy Speaker in M.P. and Hansa Mehta became Parliamentary Secretary in Bombay. Some women like Sucheta Kripalani, Ammu Swaminathan and Sarojini Naidu contributed their political acumen and experience as members of the Constituent Assembly.

During the pre-Independence days, it was Gandhiji who played an important role in mobilising women. According to him. "My contribution to the great problem (of women's role in society) lies in my presenting for acceptance of *truth and ahimsa* in every walk of life, whether for individuals or nations. I have hugged the hope that in this woman will be the unquestioned leader and, having thus found her place in human evolution, will shed her inferiority complex."[2] He appealed to women's noble sentiments, to their higher self and to their moral force.

Women responded to his appeal by coming out of their sheltered houses to contribute to his constructive programme. They sold *Khadi,* held meetings, organised processions, did vigorous pick-etting before the shops selling foreign cloth and liquor, faced the police and courted arrest willingly. Commenting on the magnificent role played by them, Kamaladevi writes, "Women turned every home into a sanctuary for the law—breaker. They lent sanctity to their act by their purity of spirit. Even the mightiest military power cannot cope with a struggle that has its being in the sacred precincts of the home."[3]

The Constitution of an Independent India gave women equal opportunities of political participation with men.

Political participation, according to Sidney Verba and others, refers to "acts by those not formally empowered to make decisions—the acts being intended to influence the behaviour of those who have such decisional powers".[4] Yet as Verba notes, successful participation refers to those acts that have (at least in part) the intended effects.[5] This brings out two meanings of the term *political participation.* In a conventional analysis, it means voting, attending party meetings, campaigning, supporting pressure groups, active membership of a political party, holding party offices, contesting elections, raising party funds and communicating directly with legislators, Thus, in a limited sense it refers to those activities designed to influence decision-making carried on within the framework of a political system. And yet, this meaning has serious limitations, especially in the context of political participation by Indian women. The available data on women in the political process bears evidence to this fact due to a curious combination of some social, economic and political variables. Women are left on the periphery of the political process and political participation remains elusive for most of them, in spite of their voting rights and capturing a few positions of power. One is tempted to apply the definition of political participation in a broader context. According to Myron Weiner : "The concept of political participation refers to any voluntary action, successful or unsuccessful, organised or unorganised, episodic or continuous, employing legitimate or illegitimate methods intended to influence the choice of public policies, the administration of public affairs, or the choice of political leaders at any level of government, local or national."[6]

Now let us analyse the political participation of women in the voting activities of the parties and exercise of power.

Voting is the most important and basic means by which citizens are assimilated in the political process and learn the art of exercise of power. When India decided to hold the biggest experiment of democracy by granting adult franchise, millions of men and women participated in the political process for the first time in the history of the nation. It is disappointing that initially enough care was not taken to compile the data and statistics pertaining to women. The following table shows the number of men and women as voters and electors during the last seven general elections.

TABLE 7.1

Voters and Electors (1957-1980)

Year	*Total Voting Percentage*	*Percentage turn-out of men voters*	*Percentage turn-out of women voters*
1957	47.74	55.77	38.77
1962	54.76	62.05	46.63
1967	61.33	66.73	55.48
1971	55.35	61.00	49.15
1977	60.49	65.63	54.96
1980	56.92	62.15	51.22

In the very first election, thousands of women were left out, as their names were not properly registered. The reason for this lies in the traditions of the land, where a woman is known mainly by her relation to a man as father, husband or son. These women naturally could not grapple with the reality that giving one's name precisely is the first step in the process of exercising political power.

The striking fact about the male and female turnout in voting was the astoundingly low figure for women in the initial years. A redeeming fact, however, is the gradual increase in the exercise of their franchise.

Female turnout is low in states like Orissa, Madhya Pradesh, Rajasthan, Uttar Pradesh and Assam, but relatively high in

States like Tamil Nadu, Haryana, West Bengal and Maharashtra; throwing light on the fact that places showing greater mobilisation of women are socially, politically and economically less backward. Again, factors like exposure to western influence a cosmopolitan cultural outlook, industrial base and urban character play an important role. It has to be also noted that there is a state like Kerala which has traditions of a matrilineal society which ensure a relatively dominant place to women.

The close relationship between literacy and voting is generally accepted. The states and union territories having the maximum mobilisation of women voters have a high female literacy rate. In 1960, Keralite women exhibited unprecedented interest in politics and according to a correspondent, they were responsible for the defeat of the communists.[7] Still it will be wrong to assume that literacy always stimulates political awareness. There is no dearth of evidence that educated women are often apathetic to voting.

Women's vote has been found to be more conservative and prone to the influence of religion than that of men. This is so in almost all parts of the world, but in a country like ours, bound by traditions and dominated by religion, there are greater possibilities of the votes being influenced by religion or religious leaders. Though ours is a secular State and most political parties vie with each other in swearing by secularism they appeal to the religious sentiments of women voters, and make clever use of religious festivals for mobilising women voters belonging to a particular religious community.

How religious minded women voters are, can be illustrated by an example from Bombay. In the second general election, an old orthodox Hindu woman went to the polling booth to register her vote. The polling officer got worried as she did not come out for a long time. When he looked into the booth, to his utter surprise, he found that the old woman was offering prayers before the box having the Sun—the symbol of the Ram Rajya Parishad. On talking to her, he found that she believed that not only was it necessary for her to vote but also to propitiate the Sun god before performing her sacred duty.

Another common belief regarding women's voting behaviour is that they are influenced by the male members of their families. Most of the surveys in India lend support to this hypothesis. The tendency of women voters to consult their husbands seems to be a worldwide phenomenon prevalent in Norway, the Netherlands and France.

Consciousness regarding caste and class also affect and influence the voting behaviour. According to a study of the first general election in Uttar Pradesh, the middle and the upper middle-class women considered it below their dignity to go and vote in the open. The working class and backward caste women were inspired to imitate this trend.[8]

Again, having candidates of thier own sex or women's issues at stake also do not always motivate women on a mass scale. One great difficulty about the Indian political setup is that it is impossible to generalise about the inter-relationship between any single factor and political behaviour. Patterns of political behaviour from different regions show different relationships, influenced as they are by inter-related factors like the social status of women, their economic position, the cultural norms and the above-all regional outlook towards women's participation in the wider society.[9]

There are some election surveys showing that as compared to men, more women give *no opinion* or *no information* responses indicating that women lag behind men in matters of political awareness and their knowledge about political issues. Though women do not indulge in political discussions as much as men do, and they are not much interested in the election propaganda carried on through mass media, it will not be correct to say that they are completely unaware of the issues. But they seem to be more concerned with issues which affect them directly like price rise, family planning, scarcity of water, housing problem and adulteration.

On the whole, women are more likely to abstain from voting than men. This seems to be the universal trend found in the UK, the USA, West Germany, Australia and Yugoslavia. N.D. Palmer finds that in almost all elections in almost all parts of India and Sri Lanka, men have voted more often than women, especially in rural areas and among low caste groups. This would be particularly expected in India, where social conventions and taboos, as well as relative of literacy, have tended to keep women more aloof from public activities.[10]

Views on public policy issues are crystallised in their manifestos by political parties. It is interesting to know what different parties promise to women. The Indian National Congress had accepted equality in franchise as early as 1917 and made a historic declaration of its policy to women in 1931. It was evidently influenced by Gandhi's views and by women's contribution to the nationalist movement. In 1952 it promised to remove disabilities in the path of women so that they may contribute to the nation's social and economic progress, and to give them opportunities in jobs, social work and legislatures. In 1977 it showed its concern for the issue affecting women. In 1980 it promised to resist all attempts to abridge the rights of women and to initiate certain steps such as equal minimum wages, special educational opportunities and increased representation in various avenues of public activity. The Congress (O) had some references for betterment of women in its 1971 manifesto. In 1980 it promised women all opportunities for increased participation in the administrative, economic and political life of the country, and implementation of the principle of equal wages for equal work, adequate care for expectant mothers, fight against dowry and special schemes for earning a livelihood.

The Communist Party from the beginning has promised to remove obstacles in the path of social and economic progress among women, equal pay for equal work and fully paid maternity leave. To all these were added promises of support to inheritance rights, benefits for social welfare and removal of restrictions on married women for doing certain jobs. The same were repeated in 1962 and 1967. In 1967, even after the split, both CPI and CPI(M) continued to have the same stand on the problems of women. They reiterated their promise in subsequent elections to guarantee women the right to participate fully in the socio-economic life of the country and to remove all their disabilities.

The Socialist Party promised equal pay for equal rights and common Civil Code in 1952. It repeated its earlier promises and came out with a programme to fit pumps on wells in villages and other schemes to reduce the drudgery of women. In 1962 the Praja Socialist Party realised that there was no major improvement in women's position after Independence and serious efforts were needed to bring equality between men and women.

TABLE 7.2

Women Candidates Put up by Political Parties for Elections to the Lok Sabha

Year	*Cong. (I)*		*Congress*		*C.P.I.*		*C.P.I. (M)*		*Swatantra*		*Janata*		*Independent*		*Others*		*Total*		*Per-centage*
	1	*2*	*1*	*2*	*1*	*2*	*1*	*2*	*1*	*2*	*1*	*2*	*1*	*2*	*1*	*2*	*1*	*2*	
1957	—	—	26	23	4	2	—	—	—	—	—	—	7	—	5	2	42	27	5.4
1962	—	—	33	27	2	2	—	—	9	5	—	—	8	—	13	—	65	34	6.7
1967	—	—	33	23	3	—	1	1	2	2	—	—	10	3	13	2	62	31	5.9
1971	21	15	14	—	3	1	2	1	2	1	—	—	29	1	11	3	82	22	4.9
1977	22	6	—	—	3	1	2	2	—	—	15	8	24	—	4	2	70	19	3.4
1980	32	20	10	—	2	1	3	2	—	—	20	2	60	—	15	3	142	28	5.1

Figures 1 and 2 below Political Parties denote :
1=No. of Contestants
2=No. of Successful Candidates

It promised free education for women at all levels and special jobs for them at the local level. It repeated its stand in 1967. It promised free education for women at all levels and special jobs for them at the local level. The Lohia Group promised 60 per cent reserved places for women, Shudras, Harijans, Adivasis and minorities and announced certain relief measures for these sections. In 1967 it asserted its promise for implementation of women's rights in marriage, adoption and inheritance and a Common Civil Code. In 1971 the Praja Socialist Party and the Samyukta Socialist Party came out with a scheme to liberate women from helplessness specially in rural areas.

Jan Sangh in 1957 regarded the relation between husband and wife as the basis of Hindu society, taking its stand against the Hindu Code Bill and the Hindu Inheritance Law. Still it promised to remove some disabilities in the way of social, educational and economic progress of the women, and recognised the woman's rights of property in her in-law's family. In 1962 it again declared its commitment to liberty of women without disturbing the overall social framework. In 1967 it went a step further and promised a Common Civil Code, and in 1971 it spoke of equal opportunities for women, equal wages for equal work and some schemes.

In 1977 the Janata Party declared its policy to strengthen women's capacity to contribute to national life and in 1980 it promised to provide special support to them as mothers and home-makers, breadwinners and decision makers, and deprecated the system of dowry. The Lok Dal in 1980 declared its policy to promote girls' education and to lighten the burden of women in rural areas by some schemes such as smokeless chulhas and lavatories. It promised to abolish dowry. Jan Sangh in 1980 declared its commitment to a common civil and marriage law. Bharatiya Janata Party pledged itself in 1980 to restore to women the position of equality with men that the Indian tradition accepted. It made its anti-dowry stand clear and emphasised launching of programmes for organising women for their defence, their employment and general welfare.

Almost all the parties vie with each other in attracting the votes of women at the time of the election. But the record of most of the parties is poor so far as women are concerned. Though exact figures are not available, it can be safely presumed that membership of women in any party does not exceed 10 to 12 per cent of its total membership.

Women of different parties actively participate in campaigning and organising meetings at the time of elections. But very few get to fight in the arena of elections. Almost all the parties hesitate to field women candidates. So the number of successful women is naturally very low. Tables 7.2 and 7.3 make this position clear.

TABLE 7.3

Women Ministers

Year	Cabinet-rank Minister	Deputy Minister	Minister of State
1957	—	3	—
1962	2	5	2
1967	1	3	2
1971	1	2	2
1977	1	—	3
1980	2	2	2
1985	1	—	4

It is obvious that the number of women candidates has always been very low as compared to that of the population. Statewise, the number of successful candidates has been greater in Uttar Pradesh Madhya Pradesh and Uttar Pradesh have sent women representatives to the Lok Sabha in every election. As against this, no woman was elected from Orissa, Haryana and Manipur.

Some members came with the experience of participation in the Nationalist Movement. Among them were Sucheta Kripalani, Vijayalakshmi Pandit, Sushila Nair, Amrit Kaur and Renuka Ray. Others like Gayatri Devi and Vijay Raje Bhosale came from princely families, while some were the *daughters of the soil* like Maniben Patel, Laxmibai and Sahodarabai. A few women became seasoned politicians as they contested elections three to five times. Subhadra Joshi, Minimata Ajam Das Guru and Jyotsna Chanda were elected to the Lok Sabha five times.

Indira Gandhi was a powerful Prime Minister. Sucheta Kripalani, Nandini Satpathy and Shashikala Kakodkar have shown their political acumen while administering the affairs of their states as Chief Ministers. In spite of the ability in administration and the art of political articulation, very few women have captured the seats of power as cabinet ministers like Amrit Kaur and Sushila Nair did in the Health Ministry. Others who could make it to the council of ministers remained deputy ministers or Ministers of State, as Lakshmi Menon, Tarakeshwari Sinha, Nandini Satpathy, Phulrenu Guha and Sarojini Mahishi. Such women could take the burden of heavier ministries, but were generally given portfolios not demanding special verve and vigour. The pattern of the State Assemblies also is not very different in the representation of women and their inclusion in the council of ministers.

Almost all the parties have a women's cell or wing. But they work more or less as ancillary bodies. However, a few women leaders reach the position of party president or leader of the legislature party as did Premila Chavan, Prabha Rao (Cong. (I) Maharashtra) Mohsina Kidwai (Cong. (I) Uttar Pradesh) Chandravati (Janata, later Janata (S), Haryana) and Rajmata Vijaya Raje Scindia (Vice President, Bharatiya Janata Party).

Women contestants are generally Hindus belonging to the upper class. However, other parties and the Congress have fielded some candidates from scheduled castes, scheduled tribes and Muslim sections. But this too has been attempted cautiously, as in the case of Rani Kesar Kumari Devi from a Scheduled Tribe Constituency in Madhya Pradesh and Begum Mofida Ahmed in Assam.

The background of elite and politicised families always helps women to have a smooth entry in politics. Sometimes women enter politics because of the connections of husbands or brothers as in the cases of Begum Abida Ahmed and Tarabai Sathe. Accession to power by widows is not an uncommon event in India, Sri Lanka, Argentina or even the U.S.A. Some women have played supportive roles in politics to the male members in the family like Indira Gandhi (as Nehru's daughter), Maneka Gandhi, Maya S. Ray or Kamala Bahuguna. Often they came out of these to carve out their own political career as did Indira Gandhi and Maniben Patel. Again, it is not unusual in the Indian political arena to have some couples engrossed in politics in their individual capacity, such as Acharya Kripalani and

Sucheta Kripalani, Madhu Dandavate and Pramila Dandavate, P.K. Gopalan and Sushila Gopalan and Pheroze Gandhi and Indira Gandhi. In each of these cases, the woman has emerged as a powerful leader in her own right. There is also the case of Gauri Thomas and her husband who worked in different parties in Kerala.

Many factors are important in the election of women candidates such as literacy, family background, family financial position, involvement in politics, local conditions, campaign strategy, pull within the party and personality. The combined result of all these factors is that very few women are given party tickets or can fight elections as independent members and out of them naturally even fewer can get seats in the legislature.

Now let us analyse the reasons for this low political participation of women in India. When we glance at the political activities of women in other countries, we find that low participation is a universal phenomenon. Attempting to exercise political influence is a special kind of political investment, one which a female citizen finds very hard to engage in.

In India women's traditional role demands full attention to home, husband and family. Women in the rural areas have the additional burden of working in the fields and women in the urban areas have to face the day-to-day hassles of queues for rations, water and kerosene. Added to these are age-old ideas of modesty and submissiveness as virtues. Such a social environment naturally results in a low level of political participation as a woman does not think at all in terms of political effectiveness. Social environment is vital for effective political participation, because political participation has to be learnt through groups, various associations and discussions. The Indian woman remains far from such activities. Gandhi could mobilise women's participation essentially because without giving any jolt to the social set up, he revived the ideal of the self-effacing and fearless woman, who was superior to man by her moral strength. This message reached even the humble abodes of villagers and an ordinary woman could understand Gandhi's language. When she broke the Salt Law, she could feel that she was involved in a sacred work for her nation.

As Gail Minault notes, Indian women in the nationalist movement followed strategies derived from their family roles, not only because they were familiar but also because they were effective, whether in aiding the nationalist effort or in gaining greater acceptance for increased roles and rights for women. The extended family provided a metaphorical construct for the expansion of women's reach beyond the home into arenas of public activity in the context of the Indian national movement. Men and women both used this metaphor when articulating their thoughts about women's political participation. Liberals regarded women's political concern as a legitimate extension of their nurturing roles. Radicals accepted women in public roles to the degree that they symbolised resistance to foreign cultural as well as political domination. Women identified with these and other ideological persuasions and used the metaphor of the family to justify their action to the public and to themselves.[11]

When the Constitution of Independent India granted eqquality to women, it remained a rather vague and distant concept. When they were involved in the freedom struggle, women had the feeling of doing their sacred duty and participating in *Yajna* (a sacrifice). They hardly considered themselves as separate individuals. They saw themselves as units of the family or community. Independence ushered them into the era of equality, liberty and democracy—ideals vast as the ocean and open as the sky. They lost their links with the participation of the freedom struggle and were unable to locate their place in competitive male dominated politics. Suddenly the compatibility of private and public roles of women was disturbed.

Again, political participation has a relation with some psychological elements. It is often viewed as a way to give relief to a man's intra-psychic tension. But for the Indian women generally the home gets the top priority. Even her psychological frustrations can be channelised into work for the family or community. Political activity is not on her priority list. The reaction of the happily married Indian wife to her being considered for a party ticket was that politics was a good pastime for those women who do not get on well with their husbands and wanted to avoid domestic responsibilities; but certainly not for women like her who derive satisfaction from performing their duty to husband and children. Many active women leaders and members of political parties feel that the main reason why women are reluctant to contest the elections is the deliberate discrimination on the part of men who lead political parties and wield a decisive influence in the selection of party candidates. Of course, members of leading political parties deny this charge and assert that it is difficult to get sufficiently qualified women candidates. Many parties allot some seats to women candidates only as a token and for some propaganda of their egalitarian attitude.

Other deterrents in the way of women wanting to participate in politics are economic dependence, prohibitive election expenses, a low level of public life for women at all levels, threats of violence and character assassination. A woman who enters politics does so at the risk of tarnishing her femininity.

As Vina Mazumdar points out, traditional values and behavioural norms bred through thousands of years inhibit them (women) in asserting themselves as individuals except in very limited contexts. The more complex the process becomes, the greater is the communication gap and the difficulties in women's effective participation in the political process. This is borne out by the experience of women in the most developed countries where in spite of higher educational levels and better developed communication systems, women's effectiveness in politics has remained limited.[12]

It also happens at times that women desirous of some participation in political parties get deterred by the connotation of the world *political.* It conveys dirty game and sometimes intellectual discussions and seminars organised by parties means stimulation only for some educated person at the theoretical level.

Gandhi had hoped and worked for feminising the political process. He had a vision of clean and unsullied politics with women's participation in it. But the experience after independence does not lend support to this. Women in the Parliament could not keep themselves confined to the issues of women only. Most of them feel that they represent both men and women of their constituency. Over the years they could not evolve *women's politics* or indigenous political tools to influence the decisions. Like men they also were drawn into the game of power with all its ruthlessness. It cannot be said though that women's approach to politics is identical to that of men. This is more so at the local level. A woman member in a village *panchayat* in

Maharashtra expressed it beautifully when she said that unlike men who have hearts of cement concrete, women have hearts of clay and are more suited to the art of administration.

It is important to note that the question of reservation of seats for women does arise on some occasions, and this was the only issue on which the Committee on Status of Women in India could not achieve unanimity.

The question of reservation of seats for women has been a ticklish one. Arguments in favour of reservation are that it will broaden the base of women's political participation and will help to strengthen women's faith in the political process which is otherwise dominated by men. It will help women to reach the level of equality with men in due course of time. As against this, it is argued that women have opposed reservation even during pre-independence days and to accept it now would be a retrograde step.

The Committee on Status of Women has rejected the proposal mainly because women's cause has been championed by all progressive forces, and women's interests cannot be isolated from other social and economic groups in the society. Moreover, experience has shown that once granted, it will be extremely difficult, if not impossible, to withdraw such a privilege, and women have given a good account of themselves in pre and post-independence days. However, it suggested some reservation at the local level.

Thus, when we analyse the political participation of women at the levels of exercise and acquisition of power, we realise that there is a disparity between the formal idea of women's political participation and their meaningful use of power. Women's votes have never been considered of such consequence either by political parties or by women themselves. They have never emerged as a potential voters' bloc. Naturally political parties have also not appreciated the full value of women's votes. If a party organises half the nation, its chances of winning the election will improve considerably. However, at local and state levels sometimes political particiaption does raise issues touching the day-to-day life, and thereby attracting women's votes. Charismatic personalities of leaders like Indira Gandhi or Rajiv Gandhi proves to be a pull for women's votes, when there is identification with the personal tragedies in the lives of such leaders, e.g. in the 1984 election women's sympathy vote was supposed to be a big factor in the victory of Rajiv Gandhi's party.

Though voting is the most important indicator of political participation, it is also the most unsatisfactory indicator. India appears to be an example par excellence of a political system where the act of voting is not an integral part of the *participant syndrome*, reflects little psychological involvement, motivation, or concern about public life, and is closely associated with partisan attachment.[13] Though the Indian voter is mature and has shown political acumen and understanding at the time of elections, it has to be taken into consideration that voting requires the least initiative and internal motivation. This is more so with women, for whom election day is a festival, a day to experience some unusual excitement and entertainment.

Voting has its own strength and weakness as an indicator of political participation for women in India. It has its strength in the sense that it serves as a tool of political equality. Millions of women could be absorbed in the political process with men only through the franchise. It has a tremendous equalising and mobilising effect on women. Still the act of voting itself does not yield the desired end of equality. In a nation where the rate of female literacy is 24.82 per cent even in 1981, political equality does not have much meaning.

Discussing the dynamics of elections, Palmer feels that on the whole, one might say that elections are essentially *modern* political institutions, and have had a *modernising* impact on Indian political behaviour; but it would be almost equally true to add that far from contributing to the increasing *modernization* of Indian politics on a steadily accelerating scale, elections show some signs of becoming more traditionalised in the Indian setting.[14] Studies by some Indian scholars lend support to this view. It is worth noting that Samuel P. Huntington believes that the extension of the suffrage to the rural masses in a society which otherwise remains highly traditional, strengthens and legitimises the authority of the traditional elite.[15] These views become more relevant while analysing political participation of women in India. The women remain more or less on the periphery of the political arena. Using Milbrath's model of hierarchy of political involvement,[16] it can be said that women are concerned more with *spectator activities*, little with transitional activities and very little with *gladiatorial* activities. It is again not unusual for them to be apathetic.

Very few women can capture seats of power. Obviously, the number of women who can make their presence felt in the legislature is very small. Evidence is not lacking to prove that women legislators are aware of the problems of the people in general and of women in particular and have proved their worth in spite of constraints of rules of the house and party. It seems that traditional indicators of political participation are inadequate to evaluate the performance of women.

Traditionally, politics and quest for power are considered incompatible with a woman's personality. A woman is to be confined to the private world of the family and domestic life, playing the roles of a wife and a mother, and a man goes out in the public world of power and politics. In recent years this conventional concept of politics is being criticised. Kate Millett refers to politics as "power-structured relationships, arrangements whereby one group of persons is controlled by another."[17] Lynne B. Iglitzin charges that political science, reflecting society, has made women apolitical by definition because the politics, defined as power and goverance, has been sex-stereotyped as belonging to the masculine domain.[18]

Now the conventional concept of the public-private divide is being challenged. Increasingly, women do not accept the prevailing notions about parameters of the public and the private spheres. Results by use of measuring devices for determining power or influence are also shrouded by doubt. As Marianne Githens points out, using power to measure the performance of women in the political elite is analogous to using winning as a measure of performance in a race between an Olympic runner and a person with one leg: regardless of practice or effort expended, the legless runner is bound to lose the hundred yard dash.[19]

Women's nature does not imply social passivity and indifference. Women have been active in times of crisis as well as in those of peace. Their activities range from movements for peace, child welfare and trade unionism to protests against rape, dowry, domestic violence, food adulteration, price-rise and deforestation. They are raising their voice against discrimination and injustice in social, economic and political spheres.

Politics for them means only the activities of governing, using power and electing representatives. It also includes efforts of educating, raising consciousness and changing the status quo for the better. Consciousness raising and change oriented actions and movements at grassroot level become of paramount importance in this context.

SECTION 2

WOMEN AND LAW

One of the most basic causes for the woman's inferior status is the inadequacy of the legal system to keep pace with the changing needs and times and to provide her with the framework which would enable her to contribute her ability fully to society. Discrimination between sexes may stem from attitudes, customs, traditions and cultural norms. The victims of discrimination look upon law for equality and justice. Law includes not only the provisions of the Constitution and legislation but also the judgements and governmental decisions and actions.

Independent India inherited a legacy from the British period—a legacy of confirming an inferior position to a woman. Apart from suffering inequities in economic and political matters, she had no right in the family set-up, in the matters of marriage and property. The British rule perpetuated a system by which each community remained governed by a different system of law. It never intervened in the sphere of personal law on the ground that it was religious. As a result, different communities continued to be governed by different personal laws. Indian women suffered from a double discrimination resulting from colonial rule and social prejudices. Still, some legislation banning female infanticide and the practice of *sati* were enacted in the early part of the 19th century on humanitarian grounds under pressure from social reformers. The Hindu Widows' Remarriage Act was passed in 1856. Other important steps taken were the passing of the Age of Consent Act, the Child Marriage Restraint Act, and the Hindu Women's Right to Property Act. The Shariat Act, 1937, brought all Muslims under the Act and Muslim women got the right to divorce in 1939.

The demand to improve the social and legal status of women became intense because of untiring efforts by social reformers and women's organisations. Impressed with the massive participation of women in the freedom struggle, Gandhi continued to stress the need to remove social and legal disabilities of women. Women had all the attributes of a minority suffering from social and economic inequality. But throughout the struggle for independence, they themselves resisted any idea of being given special privileges. The Constitution provides a framework of equality and justice, but even then the roots of the concept of inherent inferiority of women are so deep in our social and cultural structure that any attempt aimed to bring change is met with formidable resistance. Even after independence, passing of laws for betterment of women has never been easy. An effort is made here to take a bird's eyeview of the laws affecting women.

Marriage

Equality cannot be a reality for a woman unless her legal rights in the family are secured. The sufferings of an Indian woman are immense due to oppressive customs and traditions. An attempt to improve the legal status of women was made by the Hindu Code Bill. But the Constituent Assembly which passed the equal rights clause in the Constitution without any debate, later functioning as the Central legislature, could not agree on passing the bill which had to be passed piecemeal. The first important legislation in the series was the Hindu Marriage Act, 1955. Before this law was passed, a Hindu man could marry more than once. This practice had naturally generated abysmal miseries in women's lives. Now this law has brought the much desired social change by establishing the principle of monogamy for all Hindus, including Buddhists, Jains and Sikhs. Now bigamous marriage is illegal and involves criminal liability. Bigamy is prohibited among the Christians and Parsis also. However, among the Muslims men and women are not on the same footing as a man can have four wives at a time.

The minimum age of marriage for girls is eighteen years and for boys twenty-one years. Violation of this leads to penal consequences.[20] But as under the personal law, in no Indian community a child marriage is void, this rule is often violated.

All personal laws have provisions prohibiting marriage on account of relationship of blood or affinity. They all have different rites or ceremonies to solemnise marriage, e.g. the Hindu rite requires the taking of seven steps jointly by the bride and the groom before the sacred fire. The registration of marriage is compulsory among the Parsis and Indian Christians but not among the Hindus. According to Muslim law, a marriage is a contract with the purpose of procreation and legitimisation of children. Consent of the parties to marriage is essential. A wife is entitled to have dower or mehr which is the amount of money or property to which a wife is entitled in consideration of marriage. Under the Special Marriage Act, 1954, the parties are required to give notice to the marriage officer of at least thirty days.

Divorce

When the idea that marriage is indissoluble generally lost ground, the right of divorce was introduced in all legal systems of India. Most laws are based on the fault theory, i.e. the principle that one of the spouses was guilty of a matrimonial offence and, therefore, the aggrieved spouse was entitled to divorce. However, the Special Marriage Act and the Hindu Marriage Act now permit divorce by mutual consent.

The main grounds of divorce for Hindu men and women[21] are adultery, cruelty,desertion for two years, insanity, incurable leprosy or venereal disease, not being heard of as being alive for seven years[22] and conversion to another religion or renunciation of the world. In addition a wife has two more grounds: (1) if the husband has more than one wife living, or (2) if he has been guilty of rape, sodomy or bestiality.

Among the Christians, the husband can ask for divorce if the wife is guilty of adultery. But the wife must have an additional ground, as incestuous adultery, bigamy with adultery or cruelty with adultery.[23] The Parsi men and women can ask for divorce on some specified grounds such as insanity, adultery or desertion. In addition, the wife has a right to seek divorce if she is forced into prostitution by the husband.[24]

Under the Muslim law the husband has an absolute right to divorce his wife; hence the position of the wife is very weak. Still she has some grounds for divorce spelt by law,[25] such as cruelty, husband's imprisonment for seven years, and failure of the husband to fulfil his marital obligations for three years. Moreover, a girl can repudiate her marriage on attaining the age of eighteen years, if she was married before fifteen years of age by her parents or guardians and provided the marriage was not consummated.

Family Courts

The latest legislation introduced during the International Women's Decade was the Family Courts Act, 1984. It provides for setting up family courts to deal with disputes relating to marriage and family affairs. It also empowers the Courts to seek the help of medical experts and social workers in discharging such functions.

Dowry

The Dowry Prohibition Act, 1961 was passed to curb the social evil of dowry which affects the dignity of women. Dowry is any property in cash or kind given by the bride's family to the bridegroom's family. It may be given before, or after marriage by one party to another as *consideration for the marriage*. This law remained a paper tiger for many years, and the number of deaths of young brides continued to rise. Then in response to insistent demands by the women's organisations another attempt was made by the government. The Act was amended in 1984 and the words *as consideration for the marriage* have been replaced by the words *in connection with marriage*. The Act also provides that presents given at or about the time of marriage must be entered in the list maintained according to the rules. Such gifts must be of a customary nature and their value must not be excessive having regard to the financial position of the parties. Under the Act, the aggrieved persons themselves or a recognised welfare institution or organisation can file a complaint. A fine in addition to the sentence of imprisonment can be imposed on the offender. The offences connected with the dowry were non-cognisable, but the Act after amendment provides that such offences are cognisable for the purpose of investigation.

Another attempt to curb the rising rate of dowry deaths is made by amending the Criminal Law.[26]. When a woman commits suicide within seven years of her marriage and when it is shown that her husband or his relatives had subjected her to cruelty, the suicide is presumed to have been abetted by the husband. Cruelty is defined as wilful conduct of such a nature as is likely to drive a woman to commit suicide or cause physical or mental injury to her. It also means harassment of the wife by making unlawful demand for property or valuables. The Act however provides that no court shall take cognisance of the offence except upon a police report or a complaint made by the victim's family.

Abortion

The demand for making abortions legal had been there for many years. The government passed the Medical Termination of Pregnancy Act in 1971 to this effect. The Act allows termination of pregnancy if the continuance of pregnancy would be of grave injury to the woman's physical and mental health; or, if there is substantial risk that the child, if born, might suffer from physical or mental abnormalities. Apart from health reasons, abortion is permitted if pregnancy is caused by rape or by the failure of any contraceptive method used by the woman or her husband.

Guardianship

There is no uniform law in this sphere of family law also. For the Hindus, the Hindu Minority and Guardianship Act, 1956 has codified the law, but has retained the superior right of the father. It lays down that a child is a minor till the age of eighteeen and the natural guardian for both boys and unmarried girls is first the father and after him the mother. The prior right of the mother is recognised only to custody in the case of children below five. In the case of illegitimate children, the mother has a better claim than the father. The Act directs that while deciding the case, the Courts must take the welfare of the child as of paramount consideration.

The Muslim law distinguishes between guardianship and custody. Guardianship is related to the minor's property and custody to the minor's person. The father is the natural guardian and has control over both the property and person of the child. The mother can never be the natural guardian, but the father may appoint her as testamentary guardian. However, in the matter of custody of minor children, the mother has definite rights. Both the Sunni and Shia schools agree that in case of a minor married daughter, the mother must retain custody until her daughter has reached puberty.

The Guardians and Wards Act, 1890, which governs the communities other than the Hindus and the Muslims, lays down that the father's right is primary, and no other person can be appointed unless the father is found unfit. However, as in Hindu law, the Act provides that the Court must bear in mind the welfare of the child.

Adoption

In India, the only personal law which recognises adoption in the true sense is Hindu Law. The object of adopting a son was to ensure spiritual benefit by performing the last religious rites and to continue the line. So Hindu law did not recognise the right of a Hindu to adopt a girl. The Hindu Adoption and Maintenance Act, 1956 changed the whole basis of adoption. A Hindu can adopt either a son or a daughter since the religious purpose has given place to a secular one and the husband can no longer give or take in adoption without the consent of the wife. Moreover, a woman can now adopt a child if she is unmarried, widowed or divorced. A married woman also can adopt a child in case her husband has renounced the world or has ceased to be a Hindu or has been declared by the Court to be of unsound mind. The Adoption Bill, a secular law, which would have enabled any citizen to adopt a child was introduced in 1972, but the law has not yet been enacted. Women's organisations concerned with rights of children and the desire of women from non-Hindu communities to adopt a child, have made several recommendations for expediting this law.

Maintenance

The right to maintenance forms a part of personal law and hence is not uniform. Among the Hindus[27] an alimony can be claimed by the husband or the wife who does not have any independent income to support him or her. The amount is determined by the Court taking into consideration the income and property of the respondent and that of the applicant. Apart from this, the Hindu wife has certain special rights of maintenance.[28]. In assessing the amount of maintenance, the Court takes into account various factors like the position and status of the parties, the reasonable needs of the claimant and the obligations and liabilities of the husband. But the wife loses her right if she is unchaste. The Special Marriage Act provides for the payment of permanent alimony to the wife only.

The Parsi and the Christian laws recognise only the right of the wife to maintenance. Under the Muslim law the maintenance of the wife is the highest obligation of the husband. Her right to maintenance lasts so long as she remains a wife.

Apart from these provisions of maintenance in the personal laws, Section 125 of the Criminal Procedure Code makes provision for right to maintenance. Under this section, a wife can get maintenance allowance not exceeding Rupees five hundred per month, by an order of the Court if she is unable to maintain herself and the husband, having a sufficient income, refuses to maintain her or neglects her.

Inheritance and Succession

The woman remains in an inferior position so far as her rights to property and inheritance under different laws are concerned. The Hindu Succession Act, 1956 brought far-reaching changes by giving the woman the same rights in the matter of succession as a male. A Hindu woman cannot acquire, hold and dispose off property in the same manner as a male. Still, the differentiation between sons and daughters becomes evident in the context of joint family property. Under Hindu law joint families follow two schools. The Dayabhaga School gives importance to the father and holds that during the father's life, the sons, grandsons and great grandsons who constitute the joint family together with the father have no right to property and their right remains only one of the expectancy. According to the Mitakshara School, the joint family has a small nucleus, known as coparcenary, of which no woman can be a member, and it is composed of the father and his descendants of male line. The right of a member of the coparcener is a right by birth. So a son, grandson or great grandson has the same right to joint family property as the father. This right by birth hampers the attainment of equal rights. If a person dies leaving a dwelling house and the house is occupied by the other members of the family, the daughter has the right to residence. The right of residence is given to a daughter if she is unmarried, widow or deserted or separated from her husband.

The Muslim law specifies different types of heirs: sharers, residuaries and uterine relations. The share of each heir is specified, the female heir receiving a share half the size of the male heir's. Women are benefited by a provision of restriction on the right of a person to will away or give away his property. Under Muslim law there are two schools of inheritance practice—the Sunni (or Hanafi) School and the Shia School.

The Government of India had enacted a law, the Indian Succession Act 1925, to consolidate different laws governing succession of groups other than those governed by Hindu or Muslim law. The Act contains two schemes, one to govern succession law of those who are not Hindu, Muslim or Parsi and the other to govern Parsi Succession. The Christians are governed by the first scheme which provides for succession rights of both widows and daughters. In addition, the Christians of Travancore and Cochin are governed by each group's respective laws. The Parsi law has two schemes for distribution—one governing the property of men and another of women.

Prostitution

Buying and selling of girls under eighteen for the purpose of prostitution is prohibited by the Indian Penal Code. Kidnapping, abducting or inducing a woman to compel her to marriage or illicit intercourse is an offence. The Suppression of Immoral Traffic in women and Girls Act, 1956, sought to bring uniformity in the laws, meant to curb prostitution. According to the Act, prostitution is banned within a distance of two hundred metres of any public place of religious worship, educational institution, hostel, hospital and nursing home. Moreover, keeping a brothel, living on the earnings of prostitution and procuring or inducing a woman or girl for the sake of prostitution are offences.

Labour Laws

There are laws regulating employment of women in dangerous operations. The Factories Act, 1948 prohibits women's employments in certain areas. They are not allowed to clean or adjust heavy machinery while in motion and to handle excessive heavy weights. The Mines Act, 1952 prohibits employment of women underground. Employment of women between 7 p.m. and 6 a.m. is prohibited under certain Acts.[29] Under certain circumstances in some industries this time limit can be relaxed.

The Maternity Benefits Act, 1961 is applicable to establishments which fall in the category of factory, mine and plantation and which are not already covered under the Employees State Insurance Scheme. Under this Act, the woman has a right to maternity leave upto twelve weeks i.e. six weeks before the date of delivery and six weeks after the delivery. The maternity benefit consists of payment of average daily wages and provision regarding nursing breaks.

Creches are to be provided under the Bidi and Cigar Workers (Conditions of Employment) Act, 1966 and the Plantation Labour Act, 1951 in an establishment employing more than fifty workers. The Factories Act, 1948 provides for the setting up of a creche in an establishment where the number of employees is thirty. In case of mines, creches are to be provided even if a single woman in employed. Separate latrines and urinals are to be provided under the relevant laws for women in every factory or mine or plantation.

The Equal Remuneration Act, 1976, was a long awaited legislation, which was at first issued as an ordinance in 1975. It provided for the payment of equal remuneration to, men and women workers and prevention of discrimination against women on grounds of sex in matters of employment. The Act also provides for the setting up of Advisory Committees which will tender advice keeping in view the conditions of work, suitability of women for employment and need for providing increasing employment opportunities to women.

Criminal Law

Many sections in the Indian Penal Code reflect women's inferior position. However, recently there have been some changes. Insulting the modesty of a woman by word, gesture or act is a punishable offence. Offences of assault and the use of criminal force with intent to outrage the modesty of a woman, and criminal intimidation with a threat to impute unchastity to a woman carry heavy penalities. Adultery and enticing a married woman with the intent that she have illicit intercourse with another person are offences against the marriage, and place the husband in superior position. The husband has the right to prosecute the man who has engaged in sexual intercourse with his wife, but the wife is not liable to be punished even if she is an abettor to adultery. However, a wife, similary situated as the husband, has no corresponding right to prosecute the offence.

The worst offence affecting the person and dignity of the woman is that of rape. The law pertaining to rape was very harsh to women, who would be victims of physical and mental trauma. The Mathura case[30] triggered off the debate on the issue. Women's organisations and academics highlighted the inadequacy of the existing law, and agitated for an immediate amendment.

A major change was brought by the Criminal Law (Amendment) Act, 1983. It contains provisions prohibiting publicity and conducting the proceedings of the courts in such cases in camera. A man is said to commit rape if he has sexual intercourse with a woman without her consent, or with her consent, but having obtained it in state of insanity or intoxication or by putting her or any person in whom she is interested in fear of death or of hurt or when she is below sixteen years of age. (Sexual intercourse by a husband with his wife who is above fifteen years of age is not rape.) The Act also introduced categories of offence of sexual intercourse by persons who take advantage of their official positions in custodial situations such as superintendents of remand homes and hospitals, a police officer or a public servant. In any situation of custodial rape, if the victim gives evidence that she did not consent, the court would assume that she did not consent.

Granting of fundamental rights and passing of some progressive legislation has not paved the way for an egalitarian society. Even now, after so many years of independence, women suffer problems of inequlity and discrimination of dependene and domination. Some individual women have achieved stupendous success in some fields such as politics or education. But the majority of women are lost in the darkness of ignorance.

The fact remains that India is a nation where people belonging to different religions live and practise their own way of life. The Constitution did not establish a Common Civil Code, and personal laws of different communities remain operative. It is unfortunate that in a democratic and secular state like ours, all the women are not on the same footing. According to A.R. Desai, while the Constitution of India lays down the norm of the family as equalitarian, conjugal and nuclear family of husband and wife who have entered into wedlock of their choice, the numerous acts, particularly dealing with personal laws give legal validity to various religious communities. These enactments pertaining to personal laws, permit patriarchal, monogamous, bigamous families which not only shape different structures of families but also provide diversity and contradictions in rights and obligations of various members within the family, as well as differentiation with regard to succession, descent, inheritance, and other aspects of family.[31]

Though polygamy is punishable by law, bigamy is not extinct. Under unpleasant circumstances, the wife accepts it as protest against it would leave her without any protection for practical purposes. Under the present law only an aggrieved person can go to the court. In the case of the wife, the complaint may be made on her behalf by one of the family members. Very often it is difficult for the wife to go to the court because of lack of education or knowledge, financial dependence and social pressure. There is another hurdle in the sense that bigamy is not proved unless it is established that the second marriage is celebrated with proper ceremonies and due form. The provision regarding the age of marriage is frequently violated and child marriages are not uncommon and the law loses its meaning in absence of proper implementation. There are large-scale violations of the Act specially in rural areas. The non-cognizable character of the offence makes the law toothless.

The Act prohibiting dowry has failed miserably. Some blood curdling tales of dowry deaths which have surfaced in recent years throw light on the current treatment meted out to women. The provision regarding the gifts hits at the very object of the Act, as dowry is given in the form of gifts. There is no way of determining whether the gifts or presents are of customary nature or of excessive value. Another hindrance to the implementation of the Act is reluctance of the police to investigate dowry deaths and a tendency to look upon them as cases of suicide relating to domestic disputes.

The policy of making the offence non-cognizable defeats the very purpose of the Act. The loopholes in the law make it easy for the party concerned to evade it, as in a case[32] where the husband was convicted by the Sessions Court and the High Court for the murder of his wife by poison, but the Supreme Court held the view that both the courts had erred as there was a possibility that the wife had committed suicide. However, some judgements of the Supreme Court reflect a progressive outlooks as in a judgement in the case involving the violation of the Dowry Prohibition Act, the Supreme Court came out with a remarkable judgement that the very demand for dowry is an offence, notwithstanding that the dowry was not paid.[33]. Again the Supreme Court judgement on *Streedhan* (Woman's Property)[34] is a landmark in the field where it held that it can not be said that upon a woman entering her matrimonial home, the ownership of *Streedhan* property becomes joint property with her husband or his relatives. If *Streedhan* is placed in the custody of the husband or in-laws by a woman, they must return it if and when demanded by her as their position is that of trustees.

Divorce is still a social stigma, and a divorced woman has to face social and financial problems. Though recently rules for divorce have become less rigid, it is to be noted that in 1981, a Bill providing for an amendment of the marriage laws by introducing irretrievable breakdown of marriage as a ground for divorce could not be passed. Many organisations including women's organisations protested against it, reflecting the traditional outlook and values. In divorce cases, it is usually the woman who suffers from financial insecurity and emotional trauma.

So far as although family courts have been set up, there is a danger that reconciliation between a husband and a wife will be brought at the cost of the interest of the wife. It is usually the woman who can be pressurised with arguments about the *sanctity of marriage and welfare of children*. According to Indira Jaising, what is totally overlooked is the fact that the so called preservation of the institution of marriage is achieved at the cost of the woman, who remains a prisoner within it and is subjected to extreme mental and physical cruelty.[35]

Muslim law gives the husband an absolute right to dissolve the marriage making the wife totally helpless. Men from other religions also take advantage of the provisions of the Muslim law concerning marriage and divorce to suit their convenience.

The Courts are often faced with the difficult taks of delivering judgements on sensitive issues. The Andhra Pradesh High Court, giving an historic judgement on the restitution of conjugal rights,[36] held that section 9 of the Hindu Marriage Act, to the extend that it provides for the passing of a decree for restitution of conjugal rights on the petition of a husband, was unconstitutional, as it violated the fundamental right guaranteed by the Constitution. Unfortunately, later, the Supreme Court differed from this.[37]

So far as the question of maintenance is concerned, the Report of the Committee on Status of Women rightly points out that the common problem faced by most women even among the very few who know of their rights, is the expense and delay in first getting an order from court. Often a counter claim is made by the husband for restitution of conjugal rights in order to defeat or at least dealy her right. Even when the order for maintenance is made, the husband very often fails to pay after a few months and this entails the wife going again and again to the court, suffering tremendous delay and expense.[38]

There is discrimination between the Muslim and other Indian women in the matter of maintenance. The right to maintenance of a Muslim woman lasts only as long as she remains a wife. If she is divorced, she loses her right of maintenance and is only entitled to it for three months. After this period, she has no further claim. However, a recent judgement of the Supreme Court[39] has stirred a hornet's nest. Pointing out the necessity of uniform Civil Code, it stated that the Muslim husband is liable to provide maintenance for a divorced woman who is unable to maintain herself.

As reported in the well known journal *The Illustrated Weekly of India*, 29th December 1985: "Almost overnight Shah Bano Begum, a 75-year-old Muslim woman from Indore became a national celebrity. Praised and reviled in equal measure, Shah Bano's petition for maintenance allowance from her wealthy lawyer husband who had divorced her after 43 years of marriage was upheld in a landmark judgement by the Supreme Court on April 23." Conservative Muslims denounced the Court's interference in their religion, insisting that the verdict was against the Shariat which govern the Muslims, while the progressive Muslims welcomed the judgement—the counter action has been so vehement and powerful that Shah Bano asked the Supreme Court to revoke the judgement if it is going to lead to bloodshed. The impact of the fundamentalists 'backlash on the women's groups' position has been rather disturbing as some of them are now seriously rethinking whether it is expedient at all to demand a common civil law in such a sensitive situation. This could well divide their ranks and postpone the feasibility of a long cherished goal.

So far as the guardianship of minor children is concerned, it is usually the father who has more rights. Equality of sexes is relegated to the background when it comes into conflict with traditional attitudes regarding the father as the natural guardian of the child.

The Hindu Succession Act of 1956 has not been able to bring the desired results in equalising the women with men. As the Report of the Committee on the Status of Women points out, Mitakshara coparcenary with its basic principle of right by birth of a male coparcener is the cause of unequal rights between the male and female heirs, though the Act accepted in principle the equality of the sexes. Again, another provision in the Act which contributes both to the lack of uniformity as well as continuation of discriminatory treatment of female heirs is the provision excluding the devolution of tenancy rights under the legislation of the States from the scope of the Act. Another provision of the Act going against the interest of the women is that pertaining to the right of inheritance to a dwelling house. Female heirs of a Hindu are entitled to only the right of residence, and even that also is restricted to unmarried, widowed or deserted daughters.[40]

There is an urgent need to protect woman's rights of inheritance, because ordinarily she is dependent on the family. Many times a daughter waives her right in favour of a brother for fear of alienation from the family. Better property rights would give her a sense of security and a strong position. There is need to recognise a woman as joint owner to property acquired during the existence of marriage.

The Suppression of Immoral Traffic in Women and Girls Act, 1956, has not eradicated the vice of prostitution. It makes the prostitute a criminal but her male partner is not made a party to the crime. The law remains a paper tiger because of difficulties in its implementation, like the facade of decent houses for prostitution, inadequate punishment and the provision demanding witnesses, which lays down that Special Police Officers conducting the search without warrant shall call upon two or more respectable inhabitants, at least one of whom shall be a woman of the locality in which the place is situated to attend and witness the search.

The provisions of the labour laws do not reach all women workers and are not properly implemented. The Equal Remuneration Act has not brought equality for women in the field of employment. Legal prohibition of night work and under-ground work and employment in hazardous occupations have affected women's employment adversely. Specific welfare measures for women are not implemented by many employers. Many times an adequate number of women is not employed, so that the establishment is not bound to provide facilities, such as creche. Again, women workers who have been suppressed for a long time, themselves think twice before lodging a complaint, giving the employer an opportunity to take advantage of the situation.

Though it is one of the duties of an Indian citizen to renounce all practices derogatory to the dignity of women, women are often subjected to atrocities like rape or physical assault. Trade in human flesh is still prevalent. Women are bought and sold like commodities.[41] Rape victims suffer from tremendous trauma and damage to their personalities. As Nandita Haskar points out, rape, adultery, kidnapping and seduction are offences. They have been so made to protect the rights of the man against violation by other men. They are not designed to protect the person of the woman. For society looks upon woman as the property of a man whether he is father or husband.[42] However, the Supreme Court has shown a sensitive attitude in a case in 1983 in an appeal which went to the Supreme Court on a conviction for rape.[43] The accused argued that in the absence of corroboration of the evidence given by the woman raped, the convinction should not be sustained. Rejecting the argument, the Supreme Court held that the evidence of the victim of a sexual assault stands on a par with the evidence of an injured witness. Still it is to be noted that marital rape is not covered by the law. Moreover, the provision making publication of the name of the rape victim on any matter likely to identify her an offence, prevents motivation for debate and social pressure on the issue.

Treatment of the offences of adultery brings out the traditional value that respected the dominant position of the husband and regarded the wife as his property. Moreover, adultery is a matrimonial and not a criminal offence. The aggrieved person is free to seek a remedy in divorce. Treating adultery as a criminal act, apart from reflecting the outmoded values sometimes deters persons of the opposite sex from giving help to a woman oppressed by her husband.[44]

It is unfortunate that even after so many years of independence, a Common Civil Code is still a distant dream. Some Acts like the Indian Christian Marriage Act, 1872 which are more than a century old remain operative even today. In spite of India being a democratic secular state, women suffer because of discriminatory personal laws. Women have been protesting against it. Shehnaz Sheikh has filed a petition in the Supreme Court which challenges certain provisions of the Muslim Personal Law, as being discriminatory against women. There is a growing awareness of discrimination against women. Some change is noticeable in the attitude of the judiciary where some progressive judgements have been delivered relating to conjugal rights, property rights, employee rights etc. Information regarding legal measures to all sections of society can accelerate it. In this connection, it should be noted that the National Committee on Legal Aid has been engaged in the promotion of legal literacy among women through publication of booklets and pamphlets by various voluntary organisations as well as professional bodies. It has framed a national plan for legal literacy and has initiated measures to incorporate the legal rights of women into adult education, workers education and national social service programmes.

Reviewing the position of the women under the Indian Constitution, Upendra Baxi feels that women have not been perceived by the Founding Mothers as a specially deprived and disadvantaged community like the scheduled castes, tribes and other backward classes. Women of even these scheduled groups—who are doubly oppressed, first as women and second as women within the scheduled groups—have also not been seen as special constituencies within the scheduled groups. The Constitution does not see patriarchy as problematic; it perceives it as natural. Pointing out the basic weaknesses of laws like the Hindue Code Bill and Dowry Prohibition Act, he further argues that even after the independence, efforts to combat the patriarchal ideology of the law (never consciously perceived as such) have not led to even the blunting of the edge of male domination.[45]

Merely reforming the legal procedure and passing of laws which become worn out will not solve the problem. What is required is the orientation of attitudes of all persons connected with the law, relating to the principles of social justice. As stressed by Neera Desai and Vibhuti Patel, it is very important that women's organisations, sensitive lawyers and judges and democratic rights organisations work together for legal reforms and their enforcement.[46]

SECTION 3

GOVERNMENT POLICY

On 15 August, 1947 India kept her tryst with destiny after a unique struggle for independence in which Indian women fought shoulder to shoulder with men. The Constitution implemented from 26 January 1950, included a promise to the men and women of India, that the government of this free nation would rebuild their society with new values based on the principles of social, economic and political justice. The Preamble assures equality of status and opportunity. Article 14 promises equality before the law and equal protection by the laws. Article 15 prohibits discrimination on grounds of religion, race, caste, sex or place of birth. The same Article provides that the State may make special provisions for women and children, and that such provision may not be an unconstitutional violation of the equality principle. Article 23 prohibits traffic in human beings as well as forced labour. Fundamental rights as guaranteed by the Indian Constitution remove social, political and legal disabilities and inequalities from which the Indian women had suffered through centuries.

The Directive Principles of State Policy also have some provisions in relation to women. According to Article 42, the State must provide for just and human·conditions of work and maternity relief. Article 39 directs the State to have a policy of equal pay for equal work for both men and women, and asks the State to see that the health and strength of man and women workers is not abused. According to Article 44, the State shall endeavour to secure to all citizens a uniform Civil Code. a provision incorporated by the 42nd Amendment in 1976, specifically makes it a duty of the citizen to renounce practices derogatory to the dignity of women.

In the Constituent Assembly, the women members themselves felt that there was no need for any special reservation of seats for women; deserving women would always rise to high positions on merit alone. The Indian National Congress, the political party which formed the first government, had a record of resolutions supporting women's rights and acknowleding their contribution to the freedom movement. It seemed in 1950, on the whole, that India had been ushered into a new era of liberty and equality where women were equal to men.

The immediate problem the Government had to face was the rehabilitation of people, specially women in large numbers whose sufferings were beyond description. India started the journey on the road to progress after the consequences of partition. Framing of five-year plans was the first major step taken in the direction of realising the ideal of a Welfare State. Jawaharlal Nehru was aware of the need to have a special policy towards women. In his opinion: "We talk about a welfare State and direct our energies towards its realisation. That welfare must be the common property as it is today. If I may be allowed to lay greater stress on some, there would be the welfare of children, the status of women and the welfare of the tribal and hilly people in our country. Women in India have a background of history and tradition behind them, which is inspiring. It is true, however, that they have suffered much from various kinds of suppression and all those have to go so that they can play their full part in the life of the nation."[47]

The Central Social Welfare Board is a national body involved in women's development at three levels—policy, programmes and implementation. The Board frames policy's at the central level through links with voluntary women's organisations, makes its own development programmes for women on the basis of funds given by the government, and implements programmes through is Welfare Extension Projects which reach remote areas of the nation.

The Union Government established the Board in 1953 to promote welfare and development services for women, children and other underprivileged groups. State Social Welfare Boards were also established for the same purpose. Agencies administering programmes for women's developments are scattered in different departments and agencies of the government at the Centre, the State and the local level. At the Centre level, the Planning Commission, Ministry of Education and Socail Welfare, with its two specialised agencies, the Central Social Welfare Board and the National Council for Women's Education, Ministry of Health and Family Planning, Ministry of Home Affairs and Ministry of Labour and Employment, usually share the work of implementing such programmes. They are diffused in many departments like Health, Education, Family Planning, Agriculture and Community Development and Local Self Government. Some States also have separate directorates for Women's Education or Women's Welfare.

The Planning Commission defined three major areas in which they have paid special attention to women's development: Education, Social Welfare and Health. The first Plan stressed adequate services which need to be promoted for welfare of women, such as school feeding schemes for children, maternity and child health centres and family planning. The special focus of the Second Plan was on the problems of women workers. The Third Plan emphasised the expansion of education for girls. The Fourth Plan emphasised women's education and allowed the voluntary sector to operate programmes of social welfare. The Fifth Plan gave priority to training women in need of care and protection, women from low income families, needy women with dependent children and working women.

An examination of these Five Year Plans reveals that in spite of the policy emphasis on welfare or investment in human resources, the share of investment in the social services in terms of the actual allocation has been steadily declining in successive plans. The stated objectives as well as the share of allocations indicate that among programmes specifically designed for women's development, the order of priorities up to the Fourth Plan has been education, then health, and lastly other aspects of welfare, because it was generally assumed that all other programmes will benefit women indirectly, if not directly.[48]

The Report of the Committee on the Status of Women in India, notes with surprise, that with the exception of the Second Plan, all the others have confined their concern for women's development to education, health and welfare. Conspicuous by its absence is any reference to the need for generating and improving employment of women. Even the Fifth Plan which gives the highest priority to employment generation, appears to accept the present low representation of women in the labour force as part of the natural order of things which will continue unchanged in the years to come. This expectation appears to be in direct contradiction to the Planning Commission's own view that utilisation of idle manpower would be a tremendous force to speed up the process of development. It is also a denial of the Government of India's stated objectives regarding the total involvement of women at all levels of national development.

The Government had appointed the Committee on the Status of Women in India in 1971, to undertake a comprehensive examination of all the questions relating to the rights and status of women in the context of changing social and economic conditions in the country and new problems relating to the advancement of women and to suggest further measures which would enable women to play their full and proper role in the building up of the nation. The Committee submitted its historic Report entitled *Towards Equality*,and pointed out that the dynamics of social change and development had affected the majority of women adversely, and had created new imbalances and disparities. The Report stressed that disabilities and inequalities imposed on women have to be seen in the total context of the society where large sections of the population—male and female, adults and children—suffer under the oppression of an exploitative system. It is not possible to remove these inequalities only for women. Any policy or movement for the emancipation and development of women has to form part of a total movement for removal of inequalities and oppressive social institutions, if the benefits and privileges won by such action are to be shared by the entire women population and not to be monopolised by a small minority. After a debate on the Report, Parliament adopted a unanimous resolution urging the Prime Minister to initiate a comprehensive programme of legislative and administrative measures aimed at removing, as far as possible, the economic and social injustices, disabilities and discriminations to which Indian women continue to be subjected.

Slowly there occurred a change in policy from viewing women as targets of welfare policies, to recognising them as critical groups for development. It also started becoming evident that women as a group are adversely affected by the process of economic transformation. This recognition is reflected in the Sixth Five Year Plan which contains, for the first time, a chapter on women's development.

After the mandate from Parliament on the Report, the Government framed a National Plan of Action for women based on its suggestions and on the U.N.'s World Plan of Action. It was endorsed by a National Committee, under the chairmanship of the late Prime Minister Indira Gandhi. It was appointed in 1976 to ensure "a fair deal for women" and as an alternative to the National Commission recommended by the Committee on the Status of Women in India and the U.N. World Plan of Action. A Women's Welfare and Development Bureau was established in the Ministry of Social Welfare to act as the nodal point within the Government, to co-ordinate policies and programmes and to initiate measures for women's development. It was backed by an inter-ministerial standing committee. Special Cells for women were also established in the Ministries of Labour and Employment and of Rural Development.

During 1977-1978, when exercises began for the Sixth Five Year Plan, the Planning Commission appointed a Working Group on Employment of Women, and encouraged the Ministries of Agriculture and of Rural Development to review their programmes and politices. Simultaneously, the Ministry of Education, busy with the promotion of the National Adult Education Programme, appointed a special committee to advise the Adult Education Programme for Women. The Ministry of Industrial Development also appointed a Working group on Self-Employment for Women. All these groups included Government representatives, researchers and persons from Women's organisations.

The Sixth Five-Year Plan emphasised economic independence, educational advance and access to health care and family planning as essential for women's development. It notes that the main drawbacks in women's development have been mainly the pre-occupation with repeated pregnancies without respite, the physical workload, lack of education (formal and non-formal), and a preponderance of social prejudices along with lack of independent assets. So the strategy has to be three fold: of education, employment and health. They are interdependent, and dependent on the total development process.

The national machinery set up in India in 1975 consists of: (a) a National Committee, which advises the Central and State Governments on the legislative and administrative measures necessary for removing discriminations against women and reviews the progress of programme implementation; (b) a Steering Committee of the National Committee, which identifies the fundamental questions and demarcates the roles of government, political parties and women's organisations; (c) an inter-departmental co-ordination committee, constituted on the recommendations of the Steering Committee, which provides analysis of the bureaucratic framework in terms of women's development programmes and their implementation; (d) a Women's Welfare and Development Bureau, which plans financial and physical targets for the implementation of the national plan of action. This also necessitates the collection and analysis of data and the coordination of development programmes for women in different sections and through State Governments.

After the recent elections in 1984, a special Ministry for Women and Child Development was formed at the Centre. The Prime Minister has been referring to the development of women as a priority issue. Other important steps taken by the Government include a National Plan of Legal Literacy and setting up of Special Cells to help women in distress. The Government provides financial assistance to voluntary organisations for women's welfare. It has launched many programmes for women, but sometimes they do not reach the women for whom they are intended: sometimes they are not able to change their socio-economic status. As pointed out by Neera Desai and Vibhuti Patel, most of our progressive development policies have resulted in one step forward for men and two steps back for women.[49]

SECTION 4

WOMEN'S ORGANISATIONS

A striking phenomenon in recent times is the emergence of various types of women's groups and organisations, pressing for removal of disabilities, fighting for establishment of justice for women and drawing the attention of society on some of the burning problems women suffer from. There is a feeling that a new era in the women's movement has begun. In fact the emergence and growth of women's organisations has been one of the important stages in Indian women's history. Besides women's organisations, support to women's cause has come from grass-root organisations like left political parties, trade unions, peasant groups, non-party organisations working for deprived sections of society, civil rights groups and others. In these groups the focus is not on women's issue *per se* but a common problem or a condition that also affects women. Women as an integral part of all these organisations, have been working in them in various capacities. The relationship of women's organisations with wider struggles has aroused a serious debate both among the feminists as well as grass-root organisations on whether this will deflect attention from women's issues. Before we describe various types of women's organisations, the issues taken and strategies evolved, a brief look at the historical antecedents of women's movement will be useful.

Emergence of Women's Organisations in Pre-independent India

The social reformers of the nineteenth century were the pioneers in raising discussion on women's issues like child marriage, prohibition of widow remarriage, *purdah*, denial of education to women etc. They felt that opening of educational opportunities to girls, legal reform and creation of awareness to the disabilities faced by women will help bring about social transformation. The social reform movement did not challenge the patriarchal value system, nor did it argue for wider participation of women. In fact the wife and the mother role was re-emphasised by the social reformers, with a proviso that these roles be performed more efficiently. Raja Ram Mohan Roy's crusade against *Sati,* Ishwarchandra Vidyasagar's fight for widow remarriage, Ranade, Karve and other social reformers in Western India making a vehement plea for educating women were issues primarily affecting women of the upper castes. Yet in highlighting them the reform movement played a crucial role in creating awareness of the general oppression of women in nineteenth century society.

Similarly, the growth of the nationalist movement, particularly the new direction, strength and inspiration provided by Gandhiji after the 1920's created a space for women in public life. The forms of political organisation and protest adopted by Gandhiji, viz. the use of homespun cloth (*khadi*) and of observing *Swadeshi*, through boycott of foreign goods, picketting at liquor shops, civil disobedience against injustice etc. were styles that suited women. The fact that they were also tinged with moral overtones, advocating 'duty' towards self and nation, provided legitimacy for women of various classes for social action and participation in non-familial activities. Women in thousands participated in Bardoli Satyagraha of 1928, the Civil Disobedience Movement of 1930 and Quit India Movement of 1942. Examples of unsophisticated rural women as well as educated urban elite women courting arrest in large numbers though unprecedented, provided a new role in women's lives. In fact Jawaharlal Nehru remarked, "many strange things happened but undoubtedly the most striking was the part of women in the national struggle".[50]

Maharshi Karve once said that what Social Reform Movement could not achieve for women after decades of work, Gandhi's movement helped attain the same in a matter of years.

Thus the Social Reform Movement created a climate of acceptability for improving women's social status, while the Nationalist Movement provided an opportunity for women to take part in extra familial and non-caste activities giving them a new sense of power and self-image.

Nature of Women's Organisations in the Pre-independence Period

The establishment of institution for promoting the cause of social reform as well as religious reform, was a special feature of late nineteenth century-reformers. A National Social Conference was also established in 1886 as an apex body to coordinate reform activities in various parts of the country. Forming women's organisations was also a part of this programme. There have been quite a few women's organisations started in 1880s and some of them have already celebrated their centenaries. Many of them were dominated by benevolent men reformers, and concentrated mainly on providing education and organised debates on social reform topics. Beginnings were also made in establishing rescue homes providing shelter to distressed women.[51] None of these organisations challenged the religious or social system.

With the formation of the All India Women's Conference (AIWC) in 1927, a new trend set in. A product of the nationalist ferment, AIWC was inspired, formed and dominated by women, unlike previous women's organisations which owed much to male leadership. It began with the modest objective of promoting education for women and creating awareness about evil social customs. Though many of the leading women of this organisation had participated in the nationalist struggle it formally declared itself a non-political body, may be because it initially received the patronage of royalty and of families of pro-British officials. Its constitution declared that it would be guided in its work by principles of justice, personal integrity and equal rights and opportunities for all. It was a deliberative body and as an affiliating organisation it attempted to carry on programmes of women's uplift through its various branches all over India.[52] In its earlier years the AIWC emphasised the role of mothers and harped upon women's distinctive values and qualities; traditional feminine values, selflessness, love—were urged on women as guides to their efforts in the development process. Women who identified with quite diverse political and class interests, showed commitment to women's uplift, making appeals which invoked tradition, Gandhian programmes, and Western liberalism. From the 1930's the AIWC talked in terms of equality between the sexes as a necessary condition of social development. including the use of Indian made goods and women's employment. As a deliberative body it condemned a range of social practices which hampered the growth of women. Margaret Cousins, one of its founders, once said, "All women's struggles for reforms when analysed are our expressions of revolt against a double standard."[53]

It also played a very important role in creating a favourable climate for new social legislation. The Sarda Act (1929) forbidding child marriage, the Dissolution of the Muslim Marriage Act (1939), the bill for the better supervision of orphanages, rescue homes and marriage bureaus (1940) were all made possible because of AIWC pressure. It was successful in drawing attention to the need for reform in family law by various means, including persistent lobbying on the Hindu Law of Marriage and Succession until its eventual passage in 1955. In the 1930s it advocated the appointment of a committee to investigate the success of legislation on the age of marriage. AIWC played a leading part in the Hindu Code debate for twenty years in the face of the British Government's lukewarm attitude and later because of the influence of conservative forces within the ruling party, the Congress.[54] Credit goes to AIWC for whatever limited reform has been achieved through the enactment of Hindu Law of Marriage and Succession, 1955 and 1956.

During the pre-Independence phase various state-level and local organisations were also founded, some by different castes and communities. Their programme reports, however, show a dull uniformity in their activities. Mostly concerned with educational programmes, they organised craft classes to increase members' chances of employment or to enrich their personalities, or Hindi and English classes so that women's knowledge was not limited to their own regional languages. Some of the women's organisations did set up rescue homes providing shelter for women oppressed by their husbands or joint family members. Women's Aid Centres had existed in India since the 1930s, but although these provided a shelter for women, they made no attempt to conscientise them to the roots of their suffering.

A very important aspect of these women's organisations was that is leaders served as role models for women who wanted to take part in activities outside the home. The organisations' leaders were very frequently involved in political activities, many times they courted arrest, wore simple dress and in addition, as many of them came from the upper class, and upper castes, easily commanded respect.[55,56]

Though women's organisations were not direct wings of political parties, some of the women were members of political parties and took part in political activities. Kamaladevi Chattopadhya, for instance, was the founder member of Congress Socialist Party and yet was an active member of AIWC. Similarly, some of the Communist Party members also were under the roof of AIWC.[57] It has been contended that though AIWC demanded equality it was not anti-men, and that the women's movement it propagated was not separate from the larger mass struggles, and that therefore the women's movement became a broad based social force. Kamaladevi remarks, "It (women's movement) was in fact part of a great social upsurge for deep changes, which provided it with a healthy core and a rational demeanour. Society was not divided into two warring parties—women versus men."[58] It was further asserted that feminism and nationalism were closely inter-linked. A similar debate regarding the relationship between the wider struggles and feminist movement has been in sharp focus in recent times.

Post-Independence Developments

Before we describe the nature of the women's movement in contemporary times, it will be useful to examine some of the features of the women's movement till the seventies.

India achieved freedom in 1947 and with that event ushered in a new era of hope and buoyancy. Indian rulers, under the leadership of the Indian National Congress adopted the policies of planned social change to be realised through the path of development based on mixed economy. As mentioned earlier, equality of sexes was established through the Constitution of free India, which at least formally terminated the centuries' old unequal status of women. By adopting the principle of adult franchise, the government sought to establish a democratic republic.

The view that Indian economic policy is based on progressive capitalist strategy made the left parties particularly, the Communist Party of India, rally together for the purpose of setting up a national democratic front to stem the further growth of big and monopoly capital.

Finally, with the creation of a Central Social Welfare Board (CSWB) in 1953, (to improve and expand existing welfare programmes by providing financial assistance and professional advice to existing voluntary organisations), an important step that was to have serious implications for growth of women's organisations had been taken. A number of organisations dependent on CSWB not only proliferated but by becoming target oriented, the women's organisations lost their earlier dynamism and sensitivity to women's issues. Similarly, the establishment of *Mahila Mandals* (Women's groups) in the rural as a part of community development under government sponsorship have no doubt generated a mushrooming of *Mahila Mandals*. It is estimated that we now have about 50,000 of them in the whole country. However, various studies of these organisations have indicated that they are more or less defunct and wherever they do exist they have not reached the masses of women.

In short upto the late sixties many women's organisations were paper organisations. The more serious among them tried to bring some economic relief to their members by organising income generating activities. As far as leadership was concerned, particularly in AIWC, many lending personalities got recognition through the appointment to offices in various central and state power structures. As formal equality has been achieved, these women tended to see the problem as one of the implementation only.

The veteran woman leader, Kamaladevi expresses her concern at the decline in the women's movement, thus "The vast concourse of women who had poured into the freedom arena, had slipped back into their old grooves... The women leaders too had got settled in, though in new social grooves of power and position that independence had thrown up. They forged no links with the wide mass of women who are only approached briefly at voting time to secure their ballot papers."[59] Many studies which have been done on women's organisations have invariably referred to the acquiescene and cooption of leadership and absence of dynamism among the women's organisations.[60]

The Planning Commission also till the late sixties, did not seriously focus on women's issues and worked on the belief that welfare programmes will automatically reach women.

Whereas this was the scenario of the power holders, the condition of the mass of people was deteriorating. The period from the late sixties has been marked by economic crisis and stagnation, rising prices, increasing landlessness and generalised discontent both in rural and urban areas. Politically the left was fragmented by the break up of CPI into three separate parties, CPI (pro-Soviet Russia), CPI-M (Marxists) and CPI-ML (Marxist Leninist). What was significant during this phase was that though women's issues were not taken up, women were mobilised in large numbers and they participated in the general struggles of the rural poor, tribals and industrial working class. Vibhuti Patel, a feminist activist, refers to the developments thus "The Crisis of the mid and late 1960s gave rise internationally as well as in India, to a radicalization process of the masses of the struggling working class".[61] A major source of radicalization of women during the 1960s, according to Patel, was the *Naxalbari* movement which affected the women of West Bengal, Andhra Pradesh, Bihar and Kerala. When there was military repression in Burdwan district, two thousand women of that area fought back. In the first clash between CRP and the masses, during the *Naxalbari* movement in 1966, seven women died, in what came to be known as the *Saptakanya* (Seven Women's) martyrdom. Tribal women in Bihar and Madhya Pradesh, participated in the fight against landlords.[62] In Maharashtra, in Dhulia district, in 1972 along with the struggle against landlords and corrupt officials, women's issues were also highlighted. The agitations against rape of tribal women by the rural rich, and on issues like alcoholism and wife beating were able to draw hundreds of women.

Similary, the anti-price rise movement of early 1970s which mobilised women of the middle classes and in real sense was a United Front composed of women from the CPI(M), Socialist Party, Congress and non-party middle class housewives. It agitated against the 'empty hearths' and scarcity of essential goods.

The left parties like CPI and CPI (M) had recognised the need of mobilising women for serving their own political goals. Hence, in 1954, CPI established a National Federation of Indian Women (NFIW) affiliated to the Women's International Democratic Federations (WIDF) composed primarily of women from socialist countries.

Thus by the late sixties and early seventies, though the mainstream women's organisations were busy carrying programmes of cultural activities, craft classes, beauty shows, the poor women were getting entrenched in the wider movements. The left political parties in their mass movements were mobilising women, and at certain points of times, women took the leadership and along with other demands focussed attention on women's isues.

Before we discuss the nature of women's movement in the post 1974 phase, a brief reference to the famous Chipko movement will be relevant. It is an example of significant women's participation and the ways in which women were involved in it as well as the consequences of that involvement, have a bearing on the women's issues and the larger struggles. The Chipko movement is an ecological movement concerned with preservation of forests and the maintenance of the eco-balance in the sub-Himalayan region. The forest policy of both the British government and the present government has negatively affected the ecological balance, leading to the uprooting of the indigenous people who depend on forests for their survival. Women shoulder the major burden and the drudgery of bringing fuel and fodder and water from long distances.[63] In 1973 a non-violent agitation against deforestation took place in Garhwal to protest against the exploitative, commercial policies of the government. In 1974 when forest officials, contractors came to fell trees women literally hugged the trees to prevent their cutting. This action of women brought home the point that women have a high stake in protecting the forests, and they can also show initiative and militancy.

The Chipko movement, and the women's part therein, has thrown up some of the vital issues concerning women's involvement in wider struggles. Women are generally treated as supporters but not initiators of any movement; when they do take the initiative, male ego is considerably hurt. Women's participation is looked upon more as mobilisation i.e. adding support by their presence in large numbers rather than sharing in the decision making process. Women's participation in the Chipko movement has introduced changes in perceptions of the women that could also lead to possible changes in gender relationships in the Garhwali society.

Women's Movement in the Last Decade

The last decade in the women's movement has been of significance in more than one way. The year 1975 heralded two or three crucial events. It was in the early part of the year that the Committee on the status of Women in India (CSWI) presented a powerful document entitled *Towards Equality* which pointed out some of the glaring inequalities existing in Indian society and the worsening position of women in Indian society. The findings literally shook both men and women from their complacencies. 1975 was the International Women's Year (IWY), which was later extended to a decade. The decade not only provided an opportunity for drawing attention to women's issues but it also stimulated the growth of new women's groups. Finally it was the year when the Indian government declared an emergency, when for nearly two years, women's organisations, were unable to function. It is worthwhile to remember that it was during this year that for the first time, March 8th was celebrated as International Women's Day, when a huge United Left conference of women of all classes and castes was held in Pune and another conference of Left scholars and activists in Trivandrum was convened. These were indications of new style of women's organisations.Besides mainstream organisations, women's organisations could be divided into six or seven categories. They are as follows:

(i) Agitational, propagandist, consciousness raising groups which may be termed autonomous groups.

(ii) Grass-root or mass based organisations like trade unions, agricultural labourers organisations, democratic rights groups, tribal organisations etc. Women participate in these large organisations; but often when women's issues like wife beating, sexual violation, harassment by the landlords, alcoholism of men and witchcraft etc. have been taken up for action they have served as important instruments for mobilising and launching mass struggles.

(iii) Groups that concentrate on providing services, shelter homes etc. to needy women.

(iv) Professional women's organisations such as doctors', lawyers', scientists', researchers', journalists' etc. that seek to agitate against discrimination more often create alternate channels for professional activity.

(v) Women's wings or fronts of the political parties.
(vi) Groups involved in research and documentation on women's issues wherein both academics and activists are members of these groups.

The emergence of autonomous groups that exist independently of any political party is a noteworthy phenomenon, as they provide an alternate pattern of working for women's cause. These groups and organisations take up women's problems, its members are only women and they are run by women without any interference from any party. Individual members may retain their individual political affiliations, but these organisations are not like women's wings of parties. Their major concern is fight against oppression, exploitation, injustice and discrimination.[64] The Western feminist movement through its literature, its style of functioning and the nature of issues raised who affected Indian women's groups considerably. Many of the members claim themselves to be socialist feminists. These groups are found in almost all the urban areas. In a recent National Conference on Perspectives for Women's Liberation Movement in India, held in Bombay during Dec. 23-26, 1985, nearly 400 delegates from almost all parts of the country representing more than one hundred groups participated. It is interesting to see how very different they are from the established women's organisations. The members in the new group come from educated middle class urban sections of the society, and belong to all shades of political ideology from Sarvodaya to Socialist Feminism. They are young, very often single, are informal in dress and behaviour. They strongly believe in not having a hierarchical structure of organisation, and adopt the collective as an alternative style. They have interesting names which suggest feminist solidarity, e.g. *Saheli* (female friend), *Sahiyar* (comrade), *Maitrini* (female freind), *Manushi* (woman) etc. Some of them have also adopted names which suggest woman power like *Stree Shakti, Nari Samta Manch* (equality for woman association), *Vimochana* (liberation), *Chingari* (spark) *Mahila Sangarsh Samiti* etc. (women's struggle association).

All these groups have taken up various issues like atrocities against women, rape, alcoholism, wife-beating, dowry harassment and murder, violence in the family, problems of working women, traffic in women, oppression of lower class, lower caste and minority women, media distortion of women's image, personal laws, health issues, problems of women in slums etc. Of course there are regional differences with regard to the priority of issues.

Various strategies have evolved to mobilise public opinion, depending on the issue involved. They issue pamphlets, leaflets, collect signatures to support a demand, organise protest rallies, sit-ins and demonstrations. They also organise street corner meetings, street plays, skits and songs and poster exhibitions. Newsletters in regional languages and journals are published and reach out to a large number of people. There are special interest groups working in the field of health, media, law, violence against women etc.[65]

Besides general awareness towards women's issues, these groups have been successful in exposing the conservatism of the judiciary as in the Mathura Rape case, in stopping the T.V. screening of a programme called "Its a woman's world' which portrayed a grotesquely caricature in removing the bill boards which showed obscene scenes or stopping stage shows of plays that use women as sex symbols.

While the new women's groups have emerged on the Indian scene with youthful enthusiasm, the established institutions are also slowly coming out of their quiet existence. Particularly in the last few years of decade, these organisations are trying to reach out to the lower sections of the society; and they are also organising meetings round issues of dowry, rape, personal law etc. AIWC, YMCA and NFWI are national women's organisations that are sensitively reaching to the new need. In 1980, they jointly issued a 'Development Perspective for Women in the 80's and in 1985 organised a joint Decade Review Conference.

Similarly, the political parties and particularly the far left groups earlier gave priority to mass work and general political issues, as they feel that the problem of inequality will be solved after the revolution succeeds, otherwise it may lead to division in the masses. These groups are now recognising the need of special attention to women's issues. The thawing of the earlier rigid party position of the women members of these groups is a healthy sign. It has provided at the same time evidence of the patriarchal nature of the functioning of most political groups. Many women members have experienced gender subordinate while working in the party or groups.

For the autonomous groups it is not always a success story. They face many dilemmas. This came out in the choice of subjects (theoretical and practical) chosen for the recently held National Conference. To illustrate : Participation of women's organisation in mass and other organisation; relationship between consciousness raising and support to individual women; politics of personal growth; structure, methods and intra-group dynamics of women's group—these were the topics for discussion.[66]

As articulated by Vibhuti Patel, "To establish linkages between women's movement and broader socio-political movement is the major challenge faced by women's groups. They have to address themselves to questions like casteism, class issues, communalism."[67]

We will close this section by briefly mentioning the emergence of groups involved in research and documentation. A growing academic interest in women's issues is one of the striking features of the Decade. The establishment of the Indian Association of Women's Studies in 1981, has been a landmark in the development of women's movement. In these conference sessions varieties of themes are discussed by academics and activists. Effort is directed to start a debate on some of the fundamental issues facing women's movement and to generate more Indian data. Economists interested in women's Issues Group held seminars focussing on technical problems of the women and work, women and poverty, and women and technology. Similary, the International Workshop on Women and Household discussed some of the theoretical issues like definition of household, structure of production, kinship systems, role of the state etc. Several seminars and workshops on current as well as basic issues were organised by women's studies centres and university departments.

All these activities have encouraged both activists and researchers to produce material on women. In fact the latter part of the decade is marked by a number of publications on women in the form of books, journal articles, pamphlets.

With all these developments there is a growing feeling that we need to understand feminism in an Indian context because Third World reality is different. Societies that had experienced colonial rule, now find themselves in a situation where the modern industrial development incorporates many pre-modern relations to create a contradictory socio-cultural mix. The sheer magnitude of the struggle for survival, the high level of illiteracy, the hold of obscurantist culturtal values submerge the mass of Third World women in a helpless situation, creating a difference in fighting against gender discrimination and oppression. Therefore, for Indian feminists the linkage between their struggles and wider movements of oppressed classes becomes very crucial. As the sufferings of both men and women are severe, organising joint actions become a necessity. In the absence of state relief services, the family remains the sole supportive institution and women's allegiance to the family is also another imperative, and challenges to the oppression within the family becomes difficult.

To conclude, the development of the women's movement in India is a significant element in actions for bringing social change in society. However, it has also raised some fundamental issues in the process.

Section 5

ALTERNATE MEDIA

One of the encouraging signs in the field of media action is not only protest against negative portrayals of women, but also the creation of alternatives. As mentioned earlier, both these above mentioned actions have very close links with the women's movement and/or with other progressive movements for social change. Since we have discussed the protest actions against the media in the earlier sections we will focus our attention on the issue of alternate media here.

The editors of a very valuable work on media mention alternatives in the following senses:

"in their being initiated and managed (with the exception of CENDIT) primarily or solely by women, thus transforming women from being passive consumers of sexist media, to being active agents in media creation;

in their content which presents an authentic and sympathetic portrayal of women and their problems; in particular, they reach out to the poorer women in rural areas, who have generally been ignored by the urban, middle-class biased media;

in their form: in, for example, the use of street theatre, jalsas, etc. in the motivation and commitment of the groups who are working for social change, not profit;

in their method of functioning: most groups have evolved and seek to function through a participatory and non-hierarchical interaction among the group members;

in their method of ineraction: their seeking to dissolve the division and distance between spectators and performers, between those watching and those creating, by actively involving the communities who are subjects in a participatory way, and even teaching them how to handle the technology."[68]

Thus, during the last six to seven years, many women's groups realised that protest action against using woman as sex object is the first step. But it is necessary that women should have their own media, highlighting both negative and positive aspects of a woman's life. While starting "One Woman" a programme of screenings and seminars of women's films, Meera Dewan a feminist film maker justifies her action by mentioning that consciousness raising exercise among women is essential as it is necessary to expose them to different portrayals of women as those who are participating in the economy and in protesting, building up organisations etc. in ways that would provide strength to women.[69] Women's groups have shown considerable creativity in the use of street theatres, exhibitions, posters, new kinds of leaflets in all their campaigns. Efforts are being made to create woman's cinema, women's literature, feminist songs, depicting both struggles and joys of women. Many workshops are organised on regional and national levels for developing skills to produce alternate media. This activity has given opportunities for sharing experience, creating a new image and building up a sense of identity.

Alternate media like street plays or songs are not to be viewed merely as alternate depiction of stark reality but also as alternate kind of politics, i.e. consciousness raising by appealing to both emotion and reason. Amrita Chhachi who has been actively involved in street theatre movement since 1979, describes vividly how the play 'Om Swaha' became an instrument of politics. She says: "Emphasis on lack of specialisation, on flexibility, on a decentralisation in that the aim was not to recruit a 'mass base' but help the formation of autonomous community or women's groups, not to give solutions but to pose questions in order to develop a critical consciousness, all these embodied the basic politics of the women's movement. The play thus was not a form used to sell a message but both in its form and content, and alternative."[70]

Since then, there has been a spurt of activities in the production of plays, poster exhibitions, slide-tape presentation etc., depicting the lives and struggles of working women, reproductive cycle, dowry, suicide, strains of dual burden for a middle class working woman and such other themes. Songs written by women either adapted to old tunes or given new content have been an essential part of the movement, whether at a meeting, demonstration or just a form or greeting.[71]

A successful effort was made to go in a group touring around the region, mobilising women and giving them the message of change. A group of fifty women toured in some of the major districts of Maharashtra, staging plays, singing songs, selling literature, organising discussions on crucial issues on women. Nearly ten thousand people attended these programmes.

In the alternate media, special mention must be made of the emergence of newsletters, journals and even book production with feminist perspective. Alternative to glossy women's magazines, 'Manushi' is the only feminist journal which has become a forum for women to speak out, to share their experiences to get expression of their creativity. 'Samya Shakti' an annual journal of Centre for Women's Development is another significant addition of course, its focus is more academic discussion. A very encouraging trend has been the spurt of regional language journals or newsletters, attempting to present a positive feminist approach. In the print media, a noteworthy step has been taken by establishing a feminist publishing house, called "Kali for Women" which is engaged in publishing books on women and by women.

Conclusion

The mainstream media has been projecting a stereotyped view of women. Women's organisations as well as other progressive groups resenting this distorted portrayal have adopted various ways of combating this trend. Protest actions against offending advertisements in newspapers, cinema, TV programmes, have been organised. Legal action against pornographic films have been launched. Objectionable bill boards have been blackened.

Besides the resistance movement, efforts are made to create an alternate image through not merely surfacing sufferings and trials of women but providing positive aspects of women's life and emphasising the need to meet the obstacles through solidarity.

Amrita Chhachi's caution is worth noting. In creating an alternative image of empowered woman (*Shakti*) one has to be alert with regard to the symbol one uses. Promotion of religious symbols, of mother goddess of Kali or that of Durga tend to encourage revivalism, fundamentalism and cooption.[72] Building up of a counter culture is a very complex task and can be accomplished gradually. We have to be very vigilant when dealing with this sensitive, creative aspect of reality.

Notes and References

1. A.M. Zaidi and Shaheeda Zaidi, *The Encyclopaedia of the Indian National Congress*, Vol.9, p.29, S. Chand and Co., New Delhi, 1980.
2. *Harijan*, February 24, 1940.
3. Kamaladevi Chattopadhya, "The Struggle For Freedom," p.19, in *Women of India*, (Ed.) Tara Ali Baig, Govternment of India, 1958.
4. Verba Sidney, "Democratic Participation", p.55, *The Annals of the American Academy of Political and Social Science*, CCCL 23, Sept. 1967.
5. Ibid.
6. Myron Weiner, "Political participation: Crisis of the Political Process," p.164, Chapter in *Crisis and Sequences in Political Development*, Leonard Binder et al., Princeton University Press, Princeton, 1979.
7. K.P. Bagat, "The Kerala Mid-Term Election of 1960: The Communist Party's Consquest of New positions", Quoted in *Symbols of Power*, p.74, Vina Mazumdar (Ed.), Allied Publisher, Bombay, 1979.
8. Lakshmi, N. Menon, "Political Rights of Women in India," UNESCO Seminar, No.4, Quoted in *Symbols of power*, Vine Mazumdar (Ed.), p.31, op.cit.

9. *Towards Equality* The Report of the Committee on the Status of Women, p.287-288, Govternment of India, 1974.
10. N.D. Palmer, *Elections and Political Development · The South Asian Experience*, p.72, Vikas Publishing, 1976.
11. Gail Minault (Ed.), *The Extended Family : Women and Political Participation in Indian and Pakistan*, p.13-14, Chanakya Publication, New Delhi, 1981.
12. Vina Mazumdar, op.cit., p. 18-19.
13. N.D. Palmer, op.cit., p.77.
14. Ibid, p.24.
15. Samuel P. Huntington, *Political Order in Changing Societies*, p.444, Yale University Press, New Haven, 1968.
16. Lester W. Milbrath, *Political Participation*, p. 18, Rand Mc Nally & Co., Chicago, 1965.
17. Kate Millett, *Sexual Politics*, p.23, Abacun, London, 1972.
18. Lynn B. Iglitzin, "The Making of a Apolitical Women : Feminity and Sex Stereo typing in Girls," p.25-36. *Chapter on Women in Politics*, Jane Jaquette (Ed.), *Women in Politics*, John Wiley, New York, 1974.
19. Marianne, Githans, :Women and State Politics : An Assessment," Chapter in *Political Women*, Jannet Flammang (Ed.), p.54, Sage Publication, Beverly Hills, 1984.
20. *The Child Marriage Restraint Act, 1929, 1978.*
21. *The Hindu Marriage Act, 1955*
22. *The Grounds for divorce under the Special Marriage Act, 1954.*
23. *The Indian Divorce Act, 1969.*
22. *The Parsi Marriage and Divorce Act, 1936.*
25. *The Dissolution of Muslim Marriage Act, 1939.*
26. *The Criminal Law, Second Amendment Act, 1983.*
27. *The Hindu Marriage Act, 1955.*
28. *The Hindu Adoption and Maintenance Act, 1956.*
29. *The Factories Act, 1948.*
The Plantation Act, 1951.
The Mines Act, 1952
The Bidi and Cigar Workers (Conditions of Employment) Act, 1966.
30. *Tukaram Versus The State of Maharashtra*, AIR 1979, Sc. 185. Mathura was a tribal girl raped in police custody, and the supreme court did not believe the evidence of the woman that her consent was not a free consent.
31. A.R. Desai, *Urban Family and Family Planning in India*, Popular Prakashan, Bombay, 1980.
32. *Sarda Birdhichand Sharad* Versus *The State of Maharashtra*, AIR *1984, Sc. 1622.*
33. *L.V. Jadhoa Versus Pawar*, AIR, *1983 Sc. 1219.*
34. *Prathiba Rani Versus Surat Kumar*, AIR *Sc. 628, 1985.*
35. Indira Jaising, "Evaluation of Changes in the Law relating to women during the decade 1975-1984", a paper presented at the National Seminar on≤"A Decade of Women's Movement in India": *A review of achievements and issues, SNDT* University, 8-10 January, 1985.
36. *T. Sareetha Versus Venkata Subbiah*, AIR, 1983, Andhra Pradesh 356.
37. *Saroj Rani Versus Sudershan Kumar Chadha*, AIR 1984, 1562.
38. *Towards Equality*, op.cit., p.131.

39. *Mohd. Ahmed Khan Versus Shah Bano Begum*, AIR 1985, Sc. 945.
40. *Towards Equality*, op.cit.,p.136.
41. *The Supreme Court ruling on the Kamla Case in 1981*. This case had generated agitation and shock throughout the country. Kamla was a woman brought by a reporter in Indian Express. A Petition was filed praying for an investigation into the business of buying and selling women. Later Kamla was found missing and has not been found till today.
42. Nandita Huskar, "Dominance, Suppression and Law," a paper presented at second National Conference on Women's Studies, 9-12 April, 1984, Trivandrum.
43. *B.B. Hirjibhai Versus State of Gujarat*, AIR, 1983, Sc. 753.
44. *Towards Equality*, op.cit., p.144.
45. Upendra Baxi, "Patriarchy, Law and State : Some Preliminary notes," a paper presented at Second National Conference on Women's Studies, 9-12 April 1984, Trivandrum.
46. Neera Desai and Vibhuti Patel, *Indian Women's Change and Challenge in the International Decade, 1975-1985,* p.49, Popular Prakashan, Bombay.
47. Jawaharlal Nehru, "Towards Freedom," Beacon Press, Boston, 1958, p. 161-162, *Foreward to Social Welfare in India, the* Planning Commission, New Delhi, 1955.
48. *Towards Equality* op.cit., p.308.
49. Neera Desai and Vibhuti Patel, op.cit., p.308.
50. Jawaharlal Nehru, *Towards Freedom*, Beacon Press, Boston, 1958, p.161-162.
51. Neera Desai, *Women in Modern India*, Vera and Company, Bombay, 1977, Chapters I and IV.
52. Kamaladevi Chattopadhya, *The Women's Movement : Then and now Indian women*, ed. Devaki Jain, Ministry of Information and Broadcasting, Govt. of India, 1975.
53. *AIWC Proceedings, 1936*.
54. Jane Everett, *Women and Social Change in India*, Heritage Publishers, New Delhi, 1975.
55. Vijaya Agnew, *Elite Women in Indian Politics*, Vikas Publishing House Pvt. Ltd., New Delhi, 1979, p.80-90.
56. To name a few, the women of the Nehru family, Mrudula Sarabhai, Sariadevi, Sarabhai Indumati Sheth, Mituben Petit, Khurshedben—granddaughter of Dadabai Naoroji, Parvati Devi, Lala Lajpat Rai's daughter, all of them came from important upper class families.
57. Renu Chakravarti, *Communists in Indian Women's Movement*, ch. 14, People's Publishing House, New Delhi, 1980, p. 45-46; also refer to Gail, Omvedt Rural Origins of Women's Liberation in India, *Social Scientist*, 1975, Vol.4, No.415, Nov.-Dec., p.45-46.
58. Kamaladevi Chattopadhya, op.cit., p.29-30.
59. Ibid., p.33.
60. Kalpana Shah, *Women's Liberation and Voluntary Action*, Ajanta Publications, New Delhi, 1984.
61. Vibhuti Patel, "Emergence and Proliferation of Autonomous Women's groups in India, 1974-1984," 1985 mimeographed.

62. Vibhuti Patel and Rajni Baxi, "The Women's Movement in India—A Historical Perspective," mimeographed, 1982.
63. Kumud Sharma, *Women In Struggle : A case Study of Chipko Movement. Samya Shakti*", Vol.I, No. 2, 1984; Shobhita Jain, "Women and People's Ecological Movement," *Economic and Political Weekly*, Vol.XIX, No. 41.
64. Vibhuti Patel, op.cit., 1985, p.2.
65. Neera Desai and Vibhuti Patel, op.cit., p.62-73.
66. For details ref. paper of National Conference on Perspective on Women's Liberation, "Forum Against Oppression of Women", Bombay, Dec. 1985.
67. Vibhuti Patel, op.cit., p.10.
68. Kamala Bhasin and Bina Agarwal (ed.), *Women and Media Kali for Women*, in collaboration with ISIS International and PAWF.
69 *Cine Woman*, Feb.-March, Vol. I, No. 1, p.4, 1982.
70. Amrita Chhachi, *Media as a political statement in Women and Media*, op.cit., p.95.
71. Ibid., p.99.
72. Ibid., p.100.

Appendix

SUGGESTED FURTHER READINGS

(There are some extensive bibliographies available in different places, but we have selected a few books that in a broad way indicate different aspects, so as to give some flavour of the subject. This short list may stimulate them into foraying further).

1962

The position of Women in the Hindu Civilization : From pre-history to The Present Day, A.S. Altekar, Motilal Banarsidas, New Delhi (3rd Edition).

Altekar's work is a classic text on the status of Hindu women from pre-historic times to the present day. The treatment of the subject is both chronological and thematic and provides a detailed picture of the various social, cultural and economic status of women in India at different times. Moreover, the work presents some hypotheses regarding the gradual decline in the status of women over a period of time.

The exposition is based on meticulous research on sanskritic texts and a deep knowledge of Indian cultural histories. It includes a comparative study of the status of women in various civilizations of the world at a particular point of time.

The scope is however limited, as the analysis of the status of women is restricted to the elitist sections within the Vedic Aryan traditions. Being clearly an upper caste, upper class account it makes no attempt to take into account the regional variations and class/caste differences.

1966

Education of Women in India 1921-1966, by Lakshmi Mishra, Macmillan, Bombay.

"Education of women in India 1921-1966" provides the necessary historical data regarding the growth of women's education.

1921-1966 is an eventful period for women's education. Literacy was spreading and norms governing education of women were changing. More and more avenues of learning were thrown open to women, after a lot of debate on the type of education necessary for women.

This book gives us the background material on the conditions and forces that influenced the education of women before 1921. There is also a detailed statistical account of the progress of education for women. It also touches on the contemporary forces moulding women's education.

The author discusses the basic problems and issues of women's education—a useful addition to the discussion on the persistent inequality in education between men and women.

1972

Social Status of North Indian Women, by Ila Mukherjee, Shivalal Agarwal and Co., Agra.

Ila Mukherjee's work studies the status of women during the period of the Mughals in India. Scholars generally feel that during the *Vedic Period* women enjoyed a high status, but during the subsequent periods there was a steady decline in the status of women. This decline is generally held to have reached its nadir during the Muslim period.

We get here a graphic picture of the position of women during the two hundred years of Mughal rule and the condition of woman in all phases of her life. We get some ideas on the social laws customs and traditions which governed their lives.

The study is mainly based on the written text of contemporary vernacular literature—mainly Hindi, Bengali and Oriya and accounts of foreign travellers. The discourse is restricted to certain domains only. The detailed account of women's contribution in various fields of art and literature during the period and their dress and jewellery makes interesting reading.

The book is useful to fill in the gaps of *her story* in the mainstream of *history* but is not very useful in understanding women's subordination.

1973

Modernisation of Indian Traditions : A Systematic Study of Social Change, by Yogendra Singh, Thomson Press India Ltd., Delhi.

Yogendra Singh's book on social change is considered one of the standard works of sociology. It provides the sociological perspective on the processes affecting Indian Society and analyses the structural/historical factors which facilitate or hamper social change.

The author critically evaluates the concepts, such as sanskritisation and westernization; universalization and parochialization; little and great traditions etc.

This is of use in grasping the cultural diversity of India and the various factors and norms which influence the status of women, for instance how the small traditions of India differ greatly from the *great traditions*, how the context affects the text. A focus exclusively on the great tradition has led often to sweeping generalisations resulting in many inaccuracies because the specifics of gender injustice differ greatly in different strata of society. The social norms of the great tradition controls women's sexuality and participation in the economic and decision making processes of society. In the small tradition women's oppression takes on a different dimension and is compounded by poverty, caste system, limited access to economic resources.

The process of sanskritisation again affects the status of women adversely, because when there is economic betterment in the family, social aspirations makes them adopt sanskritic norms and women withdraw from productive employment. The economics of the dowry system, too, fits into the broad conceptual framework of sanskritisation and the malaise of dowry now affects the communities which previously practised bride price.

This is a useful introduction on social change in India for the students of women's studies.

1976

Role Conflict in Working Women, by Kala Rani, Chetna Publications, New Delhi.

Indian society continues to be governed by the traditional value system and the role expectation of the past, wherein women were clearly assigned the roles as wife and mother. She was not expected to participate effectively in the larger affairs of the society.

However, changes in the socio-economic conditions of modern life and the spread of education has led to the emergence and participation of a large number of middle class women in different spheres of activity.

Kala Rani's work is an attempt to analyse the nature and dimension of the role conflict among the educated married working women.

1977

Scheduled Caste Women : Studies in Exploitation, by Harshad Trivadi, Concept Publishing Company, New Delhi.

Harshad Trivadi's works is based on two major studies—one of which was commissioned by the Indian Council of Social Science Research. It seeks to study the status of women with reference to ignorance, poverty and superstitution and deals specifically with data collected from a few states and not from all the states.

It focuses on the exploitation of the scheduled caste women for prostitution. The regions studied include Bijapur in Karnataka, Raipur in M.P. and Uttar Kashi in U.P.

This documentary-cum empirical study is made up of historical and ethnographic accounts, case studies and sample surveys.

Among other things the status of women and the economic and occupational life of the family are covered and the book provides a comparative assessment of the change in status of scheduled caste women. There are some very useful statistics appended to the chapters.

Women in Modern India, by Neera Desai, Vora and Co. Publishers, Bombay (2nd Edition).

"Women in Modern India", is a pioneer work on Indian women from a feminist perspective. It studies the changing position of women in India in various historical epochs and explores some of the fundamental factors which affects the status of women in the modern age.

It also brings out vividly the complex interrelationship between the process of tradition and modernisation and the extraordinary energy and skill with which ideas from the West have been tested and either rejected on assimilated.

The work has been widely used as a standard beginner's text in women's studies courses.

Law and the Status of Women in India, by Lotika Sarkar, Chapter from *Law And The Status of Women; International Symposium*, Centre for Social Development and Humanitarian Affairs, United Nations, Columbia Human Rights Law Review, U.S.A.

In her essay "Law and the Status of Women in India" Lotika Sarkar explains how the legal system, which is a legacy of the colonial period affects the status of women; for instance, as a part of the British *divide and rule* policy separate personal laws were instituted. This has made it difficult to bring changes in the status of women, as laws affecting women come under the purview of personal law.

These factors have made it difficult for the secular government to institute change through social legislations. It also discusses the various laws pertaining to marriage, inheritance, divorce, guardianship, the penal code and examines its effect on the status of women.

The Letters and Correspondence of Pandita Ramabai, by Sister Geraldine, (Ed.) A.B. Shah, Maharashtra State Board for Literature and Culture, Bombay.

To understand the beginning of the feminist ferment in India today, we must know something of the role played by 19th century women leaders and feminists. The material included in this book contains the selected writings from the eight note books compiled by Sister Geraldine.

It provides a useful and intimate knowledge of Pandita Ramabai, one of the greatest women produced by modern India. This autobiographical material brings to us first hand, the kind of hardships and opposition she had to face in championing women's rights. We also get glimpses of Ramabai's pioneering work for women's education and upliftment of widows.

1978

Hindu Women : Normative Models, by Prabhati Mukherjee, Orient Longman Ltd., New Delhi.

Prabhati Mukherjee has attempted to understand the normative structure governing women in Hindu society and the roles and status assigned to women in it. It includes a detailed analyses of the various Hindu traditions wherein women are devalued, and shows how the *pativrata* dharma was glorified, so that women ended up as pale shadows of their men.

It shows how the images of independent, heroic women like Sita and Draupadi were distorted and made into role models to control women's individuality and sexuality so as to serve the patriarchal ideology of society.

1979

Women and Social Change in India, by Jana Matson Everett, Heritage Publishers, New Delhi.

This is a comparative study of the historical development of the Indian women's movement in the late 19th and the early 20th centuries with the feminist movements of the West, based on secondary sources.

The author has sought answers to the question : to what extent can the origin, ideology, success and failure of the Indian women's movement be explained by the same factors which explains the course of the movement in the West and to what extent by factors specific to the Indian experience.

The work also seeks to examine the question why the campaign for political representation in India did not provoke the type of hostility experienced in Britain and America.

It also brings out the weak characteristic of the women's movement in India and the West and their inability to affect mass mobilization.

Symbols of Power : *Women in changing society*, Ed. by Vina Majumdar (Ed.), S.N.D.T. University, Bombay, Allied Publishers.

'*Symbols of Power*' is a collection of research studies on the political status of women in India. The book helps to shatter some of the comfortable myths regarding the status of women in Indian society and shows that the fact that women have been granted formal political rights and that quite a few of them are occupying positions of power tends to cover the stark reality of the situation of gender injustice.

The essays include an analysis of women's participation in the electoral processes of the country, the politicalisation of women in India—this is a specific study of women in Gujarat and Maharashtra and finally a study of women's position in state politics.

1980

Her Gold and her Body, by Jamila Verghese, Vikas Publishing House, New Delhi.

This is an effort at consciousness raising against the evils of dowry by bringing home to the reader the horrors of dowry deaths.

Tracing the historical, social, economic and political reasons for the secondary status of women and the origin of dowry, the author shows how a gift of affection degenerated into a system of exploitation.

Although the book is based on facts drawn from newspaper reports, documents, records and interviews, the style of presenting is partly that of fiction and partly that of a human interest story and hence, readable. A useful book for classroom discussion!

We will smash this prison, by Gail Omvedt, Orient Longman Ltd, New Delhi.

Many political activists testify that women are most ready to fight, the first to break through political lines and the last to go home. Yet their contributions are often ignored or over-looked, this is because men are the organisers.

Gail Omvedt seeks the answers for these questions in her book *We will Smash this Prison* which is a first person account of a feminist activist. It records the awakening of the women's movement in India specifically in Maharashtra.

The book emphasises that women are oppressed many times over; firstly, by the acute poverty and the larger social issues which affect the whole community like caste system etc. Secondly by the fact that as women they have to face gender inequality of society, which denies them access to resources and thirdly as women again they have to carry the ultimate burden of providing for the family.

Women's Quest for Power : Five Case Studies, by Devaki Jain, Vikas Publishing House, New Delhi.

Devaki Jain describes the growing awareness of women and provides as much as five detailed examples of women's efforts to organise, participate and vocalize their demands for better food, clothing and shelter.

The organisations studied include : a trade union formed by the unorganized self-employed in Ahmedabad (SEWA), the milk producers of Kaira (Amul), the pappad rollers of Lijjat, i.e. Shri Mahila Griha Udyog Lijjat Pappad and finally the painters of Madhubani.

This is an excellent documentation of women oriented development projects. The experiences presented, analysed and evaluated are useful for debates on the role of women in the development process and carries, therefore, a message of hope rather than that of helplessness.

1981

The Extended Family : Women and Political Participation in India and Pakistan, Gail Manault (Ed.), Chanakya Publications, New Delhi.

This volume is an important contribution to the study of the Indian women's movement. The collection of articles here examines the participation of women in the sub-continent, in a historical perspective, starting from the onset of the reform movements of the 19th century since the freedom movement onward to the contemporary period.

This three sections of the book deals with three related areas: the first examines the involvement of women in public life; the second discusses the relationship between the freedom movement and women's movement and shows how each of these parallel events facilitated the other. The third part of the book studies women's political and economic rights in relation to their political participation after independence.

These articles and the research on which they are based represent an interdisciplinary approach to the study of social change.

1982

My Reminiscence : Social Development During the Gandhian Era, by Renuka Ray, Allied Publishers, Bombay.

The author is a well known political figure whose autobiographical account provides a realistic picture of the most important period of Indian history which witnessed the rise of Nationalism right down to far-reaching changes in post Independence India.

While the recurring theme of the book is the status of women in our society, the focus is also on detailing the level of women's rights which has led to the passing of bills seeking to improve the status of women in Indian society.

A major problem even today is how to enhance the involvement of women in the political process of the country. And the first-hand experiences of participants like Renuka Ray provide some clues.

Feminism and Nationalism in the Third World : In the 19th and early 20th centuries, by Kumari Jayawardane, Institute of Social Studies, The Hague, Netherlands.

These form a part of a series of lectures on the history of the women's movement in 1980 as a part of the Women and Development Programme of the Institute of Social Studies. The present book is the second in the series.

These lectures cover the history of active and militant feminism, in the Third World countries as well as the early movement for women's emanicipation. It also highlights women's participation in revolutionary and democratic movements within their countries because most history books tend to overlook the part played by women in these movements.

Chapter V deals specifically with the rise of nationalism, social reforms and women's uplift in the Indian context.

The lucid style of the book helps us to understand the meaning of feminism in the Asian context and provide the historical facts of the women's movement in India and other Asian countries.

Indian Family in Transition, (Ed.) by S. Augustine, Vikas Publishing House, New Delhi.

Changes take place at all levels of society, while it is clearly discernible at the macro level, it may be imperceptible at the macro level of society, for instance, family.

The authors attempt to point out and understand the changes taking place at all levels of society namely rural, urban, Christian, Muslim, tribal etc.

The book provides us with various facets of the family, including the inter-dependence with in it. There is some treatment of the status of women and how it is affected by the mobility of the family and also a review of marriage and role adjustment compulsions in Indian families.

1983

Women's Studies in Asia and the Pacific : Occasional Paper Series, by Bina Agarwal, Programme on Women in Development, Asian and Pacific Development Centre, Kuala Lumpur, Malaysia.

Bina Agarwal reviews women's studies in a few selected countries of Asia and the Pacific and provides an adequate overview of the trends in research, the gaps in research and also some of the issues concerning methodology.

Regarding India, for instance, she points out how there is in recent years a shift in research interest from pre-occupation with women's roles in the family, marriage and kinship network to their participation in the economic structure of society.

She mentions the usefulness of many research studies and points to the general limitations of these studies. She also refers to areas where research needs to be undertaken. It's indeed a bird's eyeview of women's studies in the region without consuming more time.

Glimpses of Women in India, by Shanta Krishna Swamy, Ashish Publishing House, New Delhi.

This is a study of women perceived in Indian fiction in English, between 1950 and 1980, as reflected in the novels of six major writers of Indian fiction—they are Raja Rao, R.K. Narayan, Bhavani Bhattacharya, Kamala Markandaya, Amita Desai and Ruth Pawar.

The author traces the changes in the images of women and the growing sensitivity to the portrayal of women reflected in the Indo-English literature.

In this age of conflicting values the woman's question serves as a rallying point for the artists' dissatisfaction with the status quo. The women in fiction now reflect the subtle shifts taking place in the sensibility of the writers and readers, and becomes the artists' expression of their awareness of the cumulative pressures of social experience.

Indian Women's Battle for Freedom, by Kamaladevi Chattopadhya, Abinav Publication, New Delhi.

Kamaladevi Chattopadhya needs no introduction to Indians. Here we get a chance to hear the story of women's battle for freedom from the late 19th century to the present day in her own words and is a valuable record of the progress in the struggle for women's liberation in the country.

It brings out vividly the pathos of the lives of women treated as inferior and exploited in every way. It highlights the much ignored facet of history, namely the role played by pioneering women and the tremendous odds they faced in bringing it about.

Women and Rural Transformation : Two Studies, by Rekha Mehra and K. Saradamoni, ICSSR Programme of Women's Studies, Concept Publishing Company, New Delhi.

The two studies in the book *Women and Rural Transformation* provides a critical view of rural development programmes and planned policies for social and legal change.

Both the studies start with the premise that the policies for rural development and other social, legal changes, necessary for the *take off stage of development* are invariably based on middle class male criteria. In operation, therefore, the policies fall to effect any change in the socio-economic lives of the women, or when it does so, it's for the worse.

1984

Women and Media : Analysis, Alternatives and Action, by Kamala Bhasin and Bina Agarwal, Produced and Published by Kali for women, New Delhi, in collaboration with ISIS, International and PAWF.

This ISIS International issue depicts the ways in which women have been portrayed in the media to arouse awareness of the sexist distortions in the media portrayals of women across the non-socialist countries, both developing and develped. The focus is mainly on the Asian and the Pacific regions.

The study is divided into two sections. The first one shows the way in which women are portrayed in different medias and the second one focuses on the attempts made by various women's groups to protest against the existing negative portrayals and their struggles to create alternatives.

Written in an easy readable style, it shows how the male-dominated media strengthens sex stereo types; leads to distortions in women's self image and contributes to the invisibility of women and their work in society.

Women in Focus : A community in search of equal roles, by Kumud Sharma, Sangam Books, Hyderabad.

Kumud Sharma's work is based on data collected from two small districts in Uttar Pradesh. It explores the various experiences of being a woman and the broader aspects of sex role differentiation built into the social structure characterised by the inequalities of class and caste.

It focuses on the development strategies and the marginalization of women in the perceptions and attitudes of the policy-makers and the way the imbibed self-perception of women acts as additional barriers.

Rakku's Story : Structures of Ill Health and the Source of Change, by Shiela Zurbrigg and George Joseph, Sidma Offset Press, Madras.

Health is not merely a matter of medicines. If has more to do with social relations. Rakku's story analyses the social structure of all health in India. It is written in four parts.

The first part, 'Rakku's story' is a narration of the pathetic struggles of a village woman battling against the insurmountable odds of poverty, ignorance, lack of medical facilities, and employment conditions to save the life of one of her children and, when she fails, she has no time for grief, but is forced by circumstances to continue the struggle for existence. Her story is not an isolated instance of a mother's grief, but the widespread reality in the lives of all the labouring poor in the Indian villages, where life is a daily battle for existence, and infant mortality due to easily controllable diseases like diarrhea is very high.

Rakku's story is used as a stepping stone to understand the underlying causes of ill health. The subsequent chapters analyse step by step the very structure of society and the exploitation within the Indian social system.

Women's Liberation and Voluntary Action, by Kalpana Shah, Ajanta Publications, New Delhi.

The Akhil Hind Mahila Parishad, started in 1927 is considered as one of the important voluntary organisations of the country with its branches in almost all the states and many districts.

This volume attempts to understand the working of the AHMP in its historical as well as in all India perspective.

At a larger level the author seeks an analysis of the relationship between ideologies, leadership and programmes of the women's movement.

She further examines the central issues of development and explains how the welfare programme undertaken by a middle class women's movement unwittingly strengthens the traditional image of women and, therefore, performs a very restricted and perhaps even a regressive role.

Feminism in a Traditional society, by Manjushri Chakki Sircar, Shakti Books, Vikas Publishing House, Ghaziabad, U.P.

India is a vast sub-continent and there are wide variations in her cultural patterns across the nation; while the mainstrean experiences receive attention, this cultural plurality must be recognised if we are not to generalise too quickly or make facile assumptions.

By this study on the high status of women in the Meitis society in the Manipur valley, Ms. Sircar has added to our understanding of the plurality. Although the Meitis society is basically a patriarchal one and has been influenced by Brahminical ideologies, the society continues to have distinct overtones of female power and independence.

This anthropological study brings out vividly the mutual partnership and respect between the two sexes and the individual self-reliance and sisterhood among these women of Manipur valley.

Men and Women perform their assigned roles in their respective sphere and the collective power of the women emerge as an intergal part of an otherwise patrilineal society.

The Face Behind The Mask : Women in Tamil Literature by C.S. Lakshmi, Vikas Publishing House, New Delhi.

Here is an interesting book which brings out forcefully and humourously how literature is used to enforce the traditional role of a wife and mother. In a male dominated society women are valued only for their physical attributes and their roles as a wife and mother, while to men are accorded the superior position of thinkers and decision-makers of society.

Tamil literature continues to perpetuate traditional roles for women. It glorifies the home, the sacrificing wife, and mother and considers liberated working women as deviants. A woman working outside the house out of economic necessity is sympathised with, but otherwise there are subtle and not so subtle insinuations against working women. The books brings out to the readers the pathos of the lives of the women forced into a mould and shackled with unreasonable expectations.

It critically dissects the contribution of women writers and seeks to understand the persons behind the mask, the limitations and restrictions under which they write. Although the subject deals specifically with Tamil literature, the facts highlighted are equally applicable to the literature of all the regions and languages of India in so far as they share the same culture.

1985

Indian Women : Change and Challenge in the International Decade 1975-1985, by Neera Desai and Vibhuti Patel, Popular Prakashan, Bombay.

This monograph is a country wide report on the impact of the International Decade for Women on the Indian women with the view of examining the achievements and limitations. It takes into consideration the various aspects of Indian women like their lives, status and struggles; and studies it with reference to the changing socio-economic and political reality. It critically reviews the demographic, employment, unemployment situation, socio-cultural and mass media and critically evaluate the policies and programmes of development for the welfare of women. It also examines the various trends of women's groups and organisations.

While the authors have attempted to give as balanced as possible a view of the decade, it hopes to build an awareness of women's problem.

Development Crisis and Alternative Vision : Third World Women's Perspectives, by Gita Sen and Caren Grown, for the Project Development Alternatives with Women for a New era, Dawn Secretariat, (at present located) Institute of Social Studies Trust, New Delhi.

Gita Sen and Caren Grown discuss the major issues of development, social and economic crisis at the vantage point of the poor and oppressed women.

The reason why these women are chosen as protagonists for discussion on the development question is because women constitute the majority of the poor and the downtrodden. They are socially disadvantaged in most societies and carry the additional burden imposed by gender inequality. If, therefore, the development question is based on the premise of the improved standards of living, removal of poverty and social inequalities, women must necessarily become the protagonists for the discussion.

The book focuses on the built in inequalities of a patriarchal society and how women's economic deprivations were aggravated by the colonial system and how social norms, fear of rape etc., restricts women's movements in society and access to resources, while at the same time they carry the ultimate burden of providing for the family.

It points out how the present global economic and political crisis have acutely affected women in Third World countries. It also proposes strategies which could lead to redistribution of power, economic resources and help to break off the existing tall hierarchies in societies.

Women's Oppression : Patterns and Perspectives, (Ed.) by Susheela Kaushik, Shakti Books, Vikas Publishing House, New Delhi.

An attempt is made here to analyse the status and position of women in developing countries and pinpoint the gender injustice within the household and in other important fields such as employment, education and wages. Viewing women's oppression in a historical, social cultural perspective it points out that the oppression lies in the patriarchal system of society.

It also discusses crucial questions regarding the criteria for development strategies and emphasises the need to utilize both men and women in the development process.

Tyranny of the Household : Women in Poverty, by Devaki Jain and Nirmala Bannerjee, Shakti Books, Vikas Publishing House, New Delhi.

This is a collection of essays on women in the poor households. The essays bring out the harsh realities of the gender based inequalities within the household by empirical findings and shows how the inadequate recognition given to women's work within the household has been an important factor contributing to their low status.

The major thrust of these essays is that, there is need to quantify, reveal and analyse the inequality in nutrition, energy outputs and inputs in the work loads that exist within the household, in order to understand how these enmesh with each other—in other words factors treated exogenously need now to be understood as endogenous and built into the framework of analysis not as stray factors that influence outcome.

Journals that carry scholarly or research based articles :

1. *Social Scientist*,
   Indian School of Social Science,
   Post Box No. 116,
   Trivandrum-695 001,
   Kerala
   —Monthly
   (often has special issues on women)

2. *Economic and Political Weekly*,
   SKYLARK,
   284, Shahid Bhagat Singh Road,
   Bombay-400 038
   —Weekly
   (Has since 1985 begun a biannual *Women's Studies Review Supplement*)

3. *Mainstrem*,
   Perspective Publications Private Limited,
   F-24, Bhagat Singh Market,
   New Delhi-110 001
   —Weekly

4. *Samya Shakti and CWDS Bulletin*,
   Centre for Women's Development Studies,
   B-43, Panchasheel Enclave,
   New Delhi-110 017
   —Samya Shakti 1 per year.
   CWDS Bulletin Quarterly

5. *Roshni*,
   All India Women's Conference,
   Central Office AIWS,
   6, Bhagwandas Road,
   New Delhi
   —Bimonthly

6. *Stree Sangharsh* (Hindi),
Aajivika Press,
B.M. Das Road,
Patna-800 004

7. The Voice of Working Women,
All India Coordination Committee,
of Working Women (CITU),
Talkatora Road,
New Delhi-110 001

—Bimonthly

8. *Manushi : A Journal about Women and Society*,
C1/202, Lajpat Nagar,
New Delhi-110 024

—Monthly

It is brought out one month in Hindi and one month in English.

9. *Social Change*,
Journal of the Council for Social Development,
Sangha Rachana,
53, Lodi Estate,
New Delhi-110 003

—Monthly

10. *Social Action*,
Indian Social Institute,
10, Lodi Road,
New Delhi-110 003.

SOME BIBLIOGRAPHIC AND DATA SOURCES

ICSSR, Southern Regional Centre : *Selected Bibliography on Indian Women-1982.*

Sakala, Carol, *Women of South Asia : A guide to Resources*, Krans International Pub., 1980.

Burmic, Mayra, *Women and World Development : An Annotated Bibliography*, Overseas Development Council, Washington, 1976.

Rihani, May and Joy, Jodi, *Development as if Women Mattered: An Annotated Bibliography*, Overseas Development Council, Washington, 1978.

Das Gupta Kalpana (ed.), *Women on the Indian Scene : An Annotated Bibliography*, Abhinav Publications, New Delhi, 1976.

Khandwala Vidyut (ed.), *Education of Women in India 1850-1967 : A Bibliography*, SNDT, Bombay, 1968.

ICSSR, *Volumes of Dissertation Abstracts*, New Delhi.

India, Ministry of Social Welfare :

(a) *Women in India : A Statistical Profile-1978.*
(b) *Handbook on Social Welfare and Statistics*, New Delhi, 1983.

ISIS, *Women in Development : Resource guide for Organisation and Action*, Geneva, 1983.

India, Ministry of Labour and Rehabilitation : *Statistical Profile on Women Labour* : Department of Labour, Labour Bureau, Simla, 1985.

ISST, *Women at Work—India : A Bibliography*, Compiled by Suchitra Anant, S.V. Raman Rao, Kabita Kapoor, Sponsored by the Ministry of Labour, Government of India, Sage Publication New Delhi, 1986.

Bibliographical References

Acharya, Sarathy, *Employment of Women in India : A Historical Review 1901-1951,* Vol. 22, No.3, October, 1979.

Acharya, Sarathy, "Transfer of Technology and Women's Employment in India", ICSSR (unpublish mimeo), 1979.

Agarwal, Bina, "Work Participation of Rural Women in Third World : Some Data and Conceptual Biases", *Economic and Political Weekly*, Vol.XX, No. 51 and No.52, 21 and 28 December, 1985.

Agarwal, Bina, *Agricultural Modernization and Third World Women Pointers from literature and an Empirical Analysis,* WEP I 1-0, Geneva, 1981.

Agarwal, Bina, "Reports on the Current Status and Needed Priorities of Women's Studies in Asia and the Pacific", APDC, Kuala Lumpur, 1983.

Agarwal, Bina, "Women, Poverty and Agricultural Growth", *Journal of Peasant Studies,* Vol. 13, No. 4, July, 1985.

Agarwal, J.C., *The Progress of Education in Free India,* Arya Book Depot, New Delhi, 1984, p.395-396.

Agnew, Vijaya, *Elite Women in Indian Politics,* Vikas Publishing House, New Delhi, 1979, p.80-90.

AIWC Proceedings, 1936

All India Law Reporter : 1979 Sc 185; 1984 Sc 1622; 1983 Sc 1219; 1985 Sc 628, 1983, Andhra Pradesh 356; 1984 Sc 1562; 1983 Sc 753.

Allen, B.C., "Monograph on the Silk Cloth of Assam", Assam Secretariat 1899, Navrang, New Delhi, 1974.

Altekar, A.S., *The Position of women in Hindu Civilization*, Motilal Banarsidass, New Delhi, 1962.

Ambannavar, J., "Changes in Economic Activity of Male and Females in India", *Demography India*, No. 42, 1975.

Ambarassankar, Karkaruna, *Factors influence, the Role and Status of Fisher-Women : A Study of three villages in Chingleput District*, Tamil Nadu, MID, 1984.

Anandan, Sujatha, "Marriage or Murder", *Illustrated Weekly*, of India, 15 August, 1982.

Anonymous, "Bidi Workers of Nipani", *Economic and Political Weekly*, Vol. XIII, No. 29, 22 July, 1978.

Bannerjee, Nirmala, "The Bengal Experience Seminar Paper : Technical Seminar on Women's Work and Employment", ISST, New Delhi, 1982.

Bannerjee, Nirmala, "The Role of Women in Export Industry", ICSSR, Indo-Dutch Project, 1983.

Bannerjee, Nirmala, "Women in the Unorganised Sector, The Calcutta Experience" Hyderabad, Orient Longman, 1984.

Barrett, Michele, *Women's Oppression Today : Problems in Marxist Feminist Analysis*, Virgo Publication, London, 1980, p. 43-47.

Barse, Sheela, "Judged Without a Hearing", *Indian Express*, 20 August 1983.

Barse, Sheela, "Flesh Trade in Bombay Shocking Indignities on Minors", *Indian Express*, 7 July, 1983.

Basu, Aparna, "Gujarat, Women's Response to Gandhi 1920-1942", *Samya Shakti*, Vol. 1, No. 2, 1984.

Batliwala, Srilatha; Daswani, Mona and Leena, Bakshi, "Sex Bias in Modern Medicine : Gender Descrimination in Health Training Delivery and Personnel", *Social Action*, Vol. 35, July-Sept., 1985, p. 241-253.

Batliwala, Srilatha, *The Energy, Health and Nutrition Syndrome in Women and Poverty*, (Ed.) Devaki Jain and Nirmala Bannerjee, op. cit., 1985.

Batliwala, Srilatha, Women in Poverty, "The Energy, Health and Nutrition Syndrome", **Chapt in** *Tyranny of the Household Investigative. Essays on Women's Work*, (Ed.) Devaki Jain, Nirmala Bannerjee, Shakti Books, 1985.

Baxi, Upendra, "Patriarchy, Law and State—Some Preliminary Notes". A Paper presented at the Second National Law Conference on Women's Studies, 9-12, A.P., Trivandrum, 1934.

Bhagat, K.P., *The Communist Party's Conquest of New Positions*, Popular Prakashan, Bombay, 1960, p. 123.

Bhagwati, Jagdish, "Education, Class Structure and Income Equality", *World Development*, Vol. 1, No. 5, May, 1973.

Bhan, Susheela, "The National Adult Education Programme", in A.B. Shah and S. Bhan's (ed.), *Non Formal Education and the NAEP*, Oxford University Press, New Delhi, 1978.

Bhandari, R.K., *Educational Development of Women in India*, Ministry of Education and Culture, New Delhi, 1982, p. 36.

Bhargava, Hitesh, Karma, S. and Pant, Nirmal, "Perinatal Mortality", *The Journal of Obstetrics and gyneacology of India*, Vol. 31, No. 4, 1981, p. 584-592.

Bharin, Kamla and Agarwal, Bina, "Women and Media : Analysis, Alternatives and Action, Kali for Women", ISIS International and PAWF, 1984.

Bhattacharya, Sukumari, "Women in Mahabharata", A Paper presented in a Seminar on Women and Culture, organised by the Indraprastha college, 1981, p. 1.

Bhatty, Zarina, "Economic Role and Status of Women—A case study of Women in the Beedi Industry in Allahabad", *World Employment Programme*, ILO Working Paper, 1980.

Birdwood George, C.M., "The Industrial Arts of India", Idarah-I-Adabiyat I, Delhi, 1974.

Borthwick, Meredith, *Changing role of women in Bengal*, 1849-1905, Princeton University Press, Princeton, 1984.

Boulding, Elise, *et ae.*, *Hand Book on International Data on Women Sage*, Halsbead, New York, 1976.

Brahme, Sulaba, "Economic plight of Hamal Women in Pune", ICSSR, 1978, unpublish mimeo.

Buch, A.N. and Bhatt Ela, R., *Fire-wood Pickers of Girnar*, SEWA, Ahmedabad, 1978.

Buchanan, Francis, *A Journey From Madras Through the Countries of Mysore*, *Canara and Malbar*, London, 1807.

Buhler, G., *The Laws of Manu : Sacred Books of the East*, Trans, Vol. 25, Motilal Banarsidass, New Delhi, 1964.

Census of India, *Technical, Personnel and Degree Holders*, Vol. 7, G. Series, 1971.

Chakravarti, Renu, *Communists is Indian Women's Movement*, People Publishing House, New Delhi, 1980.

Chakravarti, Uma, "The Rise of Buddhism as Experienced by Women", A Paper presented in the Seminar on Women's Life Cycle and Identity, Bhadkal, 1981.

Chakravarti, Uma, "The Sita Myth", Samya Shakti, Vol. 1, No. July, 1983, p. 70.

Chakravarti, Uma, "Towards a historical Sociology of Stratification in Ancient India", *Economic and Political Weekly*, Vol. XX, No. 9, 2 March, 1985.

Charvet, John, *Feminism*, Debt and sons Ltd., London, 1982.

Chaterjee, Mary, "Conjugal Roles and Social Networks in an Indian Urban Sweeper Locality", Journal of Marriage and Family, Vol. 1, No. 39, 1977.

Chaterjee, Meera, "Health For all : Whither the Child ?" *Social Action*, Vol. 35, July-Sept., 1985, p. 224-240.

Chatterjee, Ruchira, "Marginalization and the Induction of Women in Wage Labour, The Case of Indian Agriculture", *World Employment Programme*, ILO, Geneva, 1984.

Chattopadhya, Kamaladevi, "The Struggle for Freedom", (Ed.) Tara Ali Baig, *Women in India*, Govt. of India, 1958, p. 19.

Chattopadhya, Kamaladevi, *The Women's Movement Then and Now, in Indian Women*, (Ed.) Devaki Jain, Publication Division, Ministry of Information and Broadcasting, Government of India, 1975.

Cine Women, February, March 1982, Vol. 1, No. 1, 1982, p. 4.

Committee of Legal Literacy, *Rape and the Law*, 1983.

Cormack, Margaret, *The Hindu Women*, Asia Publishing House, Bombay, 1961.

Croft, A., *Review of Education in India*, 1886, p. 279.

Dandekar, Kumini, *Employment Guarantee Scheme : An Employment Opportunity for Women*, Gokhale Institute of Politics and Economics, Orient Longman Ltd., New Delhi, 1983.

Das, Veena, *Indian Women, Work, Power and Status* in *Indian Women*, (Ed.) B.R. Nanda, Vikas Publishing House, 1976, p. 135.

Das, Veena, "The Mythological Film and Its Frame Work of Meaning", *Indian International Centre, Quarterly*, Vol. 8, No. 1, 1981.

Deckard, Barbara, *The Women's Movement Political, Socio-Economic and Psychologically issues*, Harper Row, No. 1, 1983, p. 449.

Deptartment of Sociology, S. Gujarat University, "Report of a Seminar on Violence", *Economic and Political Weekly*, Vol. 20, No. 12, 23 March, 1985.

Desai, A.R., *Urban Family and Family Planning in India*, Popular Prakashan, 1980.

Desai, I.P., *Some Aspects of Family in Madhuva*, Asia Publishing House, Bombay, 1964.

Desai, Neera, *Women in Modern India*, Vora and Co., 1957, p. 20-24.

Desai, Neera, *Women in Modern India*, Vora and Co., Bombay, Chapt. IV and V, 1977.

Desai, Neera and Gopalan, Prema, "Changes in the Food Processing Industry from Traditional and Modern Forms and its Impact on Women's Role and Status", Project ICSSR, Indo-Dutch, 1983.

Desai, Neera, *Review of Studies on Middle Class Women in India*, MSS Research Centre on Women's Studies, Bombay, 1983.

Desai, Neera and Anantram Sharayu, *Review of Studies on Middle Class Women's Entry on Women's Studies*, 1984.

Desai, Neera, "Caste, Class and Gender", Paper presented at the Sociology Conference Surat, Dec., 1984, p. 15-16.

Desai, Neera and Patel Vibhuti, *Indian Women, Change and Challenge in the International Decade 1975-1985*, Popular Prakashan, Bombay, 1985.

Desai, Neera, "Review of Research on Middle Class Employed Women", Golden Jubilee Symposium Paper Women, Work and Society, ISI Calcutta, 1985.

Deshpande, Anjali, "Post Rape Ordeal of a Victim", *Mainstream*, Vol. 21, No. 33, April, 1983.

Dhagamwar, Vasudha, "Women who use The Marriage Act", *India International Centre Quarterly*, Vol. 12, No. 1, 1985.

Dimmit, C. Van Buitenen's (Translation), *Classical Hindu Mythology*, Rupa, Repro., New Delhi, 1983.

D'Mello, Flavia, *Domestic Violence : Difference between Working Class and Middle class*, Institute of Social Research and Education (ISRE), Bombay, 1980.

D'Mello, Flavia, "Our fight against wife Beating", Paper Conference, on Research and Teaching Related to Women held at Concodia University, Canada, 26 July—4 August, 1982.

D'Mello, Flavia, "Domestic Violence", *Women's Centre Publication Bombay, November, 1984.*

Dube, Leela, Sociology of Kinship : An Analytical Survey of Literature, Popular Prakashan, Bombay, 1974.

Dube, Leela, "The Seed and the Earth Paper presented at The Tenth International Congress of Anthropological and Ethnological Science", New Delhi, Mss., 1978, p. 8.

Dube, Leela, "Review of Studies on Women in South East Asia", UNESCO, Bangkok, 1980.

Eisenstein, Zillah, "Capitalist Patriarchy and the case for Socialist Feminism", *Monthly Review Press*, New York, 1979, p. 16.

Everett, Jana, *Women and Social Change in India*, Heritage Publishers, New Delhi, 1979.

Farouqui, Vimla, "Women—Social Victims of Police and Landlord Atrocities", National Federation of Indian Women, New Delhi, 1980.

Forum Against Oppression of Women, "Paper of National Conference on Perspective on Women's Liberation", Bombay, 1985.

Friedan Betty, *The Second Stage*, Summit Books, New York, 1981.

Gadgil, D.R., *The Industrial Evolution in Recent Times*, Oxford University Press, Bombay, 1954.

Gandotra, M.M. and Pandey, Divya, "Values Attached to Children in Indian Society and Family Size Norms : the Changes and Impact", *Journal of Family Welfare*, Vol. 26, No. 1, 1979.

Gandhi, M.K., "What is a Woman's Role ?" *Harijan*, 16 March, 1940.

Gandhi M.K., "To the Women of India", *Young India*, 10 April, 1938.

Giladia, Ishwarprasad, *Prostitution in Urban Centres' Studies: Perspectives and Positional Problems for Social Intervention*, Survey by the Indian Health Organisation, 20 June, 1982.

Githens, Mariamme, "Women and State Politics : An Assessment", Janet flammang Ed. In *Political Women*, Sage Publication, Beverley Hills, London, New Delhi, 1984.

Goode, William J., "World Revolution and Family Patterns", *Collier*, Macmillan Ltd., London, 1963.

Gopalan, C., "The Mother and Child in India", *Economic and Political Weekly*, Vol. XX, No. 4, 1985.

Gotaskar, Sujatha, *Politics of Rape*, Paper, First National Conference on Women's Studies, Bombay, 1981.

Gotaskar Sujatha, Banaji Rohini and Hanheve Vijay, "Health of Women in the `Health' industry", in *Socialist Health Review* (Special issue on `Women's Health'_, Vol. 1, No. 2, September, 1980.

Govternment of India, Ministry of Education, *Progress of Education in India*, Vol. II, 1897, 1902, New Delhi, p. 106, 110.

Government of India, Ministry of Education, *Progress of Education in India*, Vol. I, 1907-1912, New Delhi, p. 213.

Government of India Acts, *The Child Marriage Restraint Act*, 1929, 1978.

——, *The Hindu Marriage Act, 1955.*

——, (Grounds for divorce) *Special Marriage Act, 1954.*

——, *The Indian Divorce Act, 1969.*

——, *The Factories Act, 1948.*

——, *The Plantations Act, 1951.*

——, *The Mines Act, 1952.*

——, *The Bidi and Cigar Workers* (Conditions of Employment) *Act, 1966.*

Government of India, *Report of the University*, Education Commission, 1948-1949, Vol. I, Manager of Publication, Delhi, 1950, p. 393-395.

Government of India, *Report of the National Committee on Women's Education—1958*, New Delhi, 1959, p. 7-9.

Government of India, *Report of the Committee on the Differentiation of Curricula*, New Delhi, 1962.

Governemnt of India, *Census volume on Degree holders and Technical Personnel*, G—Series, Part VII, New Delhi, 1971.

Governemnt of India, *National Plan of Action : Sixth Five Year Plan 1978-1983*, (First Draft), 1975.

Government of India, Report of the Committee on the Status of Women in India, Ministry of Education and Social Welfare, New Delhi, 1975, p. 281-82.

Government of India, Women in India—A Statistical Profile, Ministry of Social Welfare, Government of India, New Delhi, 1978.

Government of India, Women's Activities in Rural India, A Study Based on NSS, 32 Round, Department of Statistics Govt. of India, June, 1981.

Government of India, Ministry of Health and Family Welfare, *Report of the Working Group on Health for All by A.D. 2000*, 1981.

Government of India, Ministry of Information and Broadcasting *Annual Report*, 1984, p. 10.

Government of India, Ministry of Education, *Challenge of Education*, New Delhi, 1985, p. 1, 34.

Government of India, *Women in India*, Ministry of Social and Women's Welfare, New Delhi, 1985, p. 47-48.

Griffiths, Dorothy, *Sex Differences and Cognitive Abilities : A Sterile Field of Enquiry*. Chapter in Sex Role Stereo typing, edited by Oonagh Hartnett, *et al.*, London, Tavistock Publication, 1979.

Guha, Ramjit, *Subaltern Studies, I, II, III*, 1982, Oxford University Press, New Delhi, 1984.

Gulati, Leela, "Inter-state Difference in Female Labour Force Participation", *Economic and Political Weekly*, Vol. 10, No. 1-2, Jan. 11, 1975.

——, Marked Preference for Sterilization in a Semi Rural Squatters Settlement, *Studies in Family Planning*, Vol. 10, No. 11/12, 1979, pp. 332-336.

——, *Profiles in Female Poverty*, Hindustan Publication, New Delhi, 1982.

——, *Fisher Women on the Kerala Coast*, ILO, Geneva, 1984.

Hall, Basil, *Travel in India, Ceylon,* and *Burma*, George Routledge and Sons, London, 1931.

Haskar, Nandita, "Dominance, Suppression and the Law", A Paper presented at the Second National Conference on Women's Studies, 9-12 April, 1984.

Hershman, P., "Virgin and Mother", in I. Lewis (Ed.), *Symbols and Sentiment*, Academic Press, London, 1977.

Hirway, Indira, "Women and Technology—A Study of K. VIC", Gujarat, Seminar Paper, MID., op. cit., Footnote 71, Oct., 1984.

Hole, Judith and Levine, Ellen, "Rebirth of Feminism", *The New York Times*, Book Company, U.S.A., 1971, p. 1.

Howe, Florence, *Seven Years later : Women's Studies Programmes in 1976*. National Advisory Council on Women's Educational Programme, 1976.

Howe, Florence, (Ed.), Every Women's Guide to Colleges and Universities, XIII-XIV, 1976.

Huntington Samuel, P., *Political Order in Changing Societies*, Yale University Press, New Haven, 1968, p. 444.

Lynne Iglitzin, B., "The Making of the Apolitical Women", Feminity and Sex Stereo Typing in Girls, in Jane Jaquette (Ed.), *Women in Politics*, John Wiley, New York, 1974.

Indian Express, 27 August, 1985.

Indian Social Studies Trust, *The Study of Utilization and Wasteage of Training Programme of National and Regional Vocational Training Institutes for Women*, Delhi, 1985.

Jacobson, J. and Wadley, Susan, *Women in India : Two Perspectives*, South Asia Books, Columbia, 1977.

Jain, A.K., *Determinants of Regional Variations in Infant and Child Mortality in Rural India*, Population Council, New York, 1984.

Jain Devaki, *Women's Quest For Power*, Vikas Publication New Delhi, 1980.

Jain, Devaki and Chand, Malini "Importance of Age and Sex Specific Data Collection in Household Survey", ESCAP, Bangkok, September, (mimeo), 1980.

Jain, Devaki and Chand, Malini, "Domestic Work : Implication for Remuneration of Workers", ISST, New Delhi, (mimeo), 1982.

Jain Devaki, *Displacement of Women Workers in Traditional Industries*, ISST, 1984.

Jain, Devaki and Bannerjee Nirmala, (Ed.), *Women in Poverty: The Tyranny of The Household*, Vikas, New Delhi, 1985.

Jain, L.C., "End of Handloom Industry", *Economic and Political Weekly*, Vol. 20, No. 27, 6 July, 1985.

Jain, Shobhita, "Women and Peoples Ecological Movement", *Economic and Political Weekly*, Vol. XIX, No. 41, 1984.

Jayaswal, Suvira, "Position of Women in Early India≤A Histographical reappraisal" Paper, Presented at the First Conference of Women's Studies, 1981, p. 2-3.

Jaising Indira, Evaluation of Changes in the Law relating to Women during the Decade 1975-1984". A Paper presented at the National Seminar on—A decade of Women's Movement in India—A Review of achievements and issues, Jan. 8-10, S.N.D.T., Women's University, 1985.

Jesudasan, Victor et al., *Non-Formal Education for Rural Women and Development of the Young Child*, Allied Publishers, New Delhi, 1981.

Jha, K.K., *Rethinking in Marriage Institution*, Chintamani Prakashan, Patna, 1979.

Johnson, M. Samuel and Erappa, S., "Women Workers in Silk Reeling Industry", Seminar Paper, Indian Historical Assocation, Madurai, 1983.

Joshi, M.N., *Urban Handicrafts of Bombay*, Deccan Gokhale Institute of Politics and Economics, Pune 1936.

Joshi, Rama, "Status of Women : Agricultural Workers", ICSSR, 1973, (unpub. mimeo), 1973.

Junjee, Monica and Vaid Sudesh, "Delhi Women Protest Dowry Deaths," *Alternate News and Features*, January, 1980.

Kakar, Sudhir, *The Inner World*, Oxford University Press, new Delhi, 1980.

Kale, C.V., "Female Participation in Farm Work in Central Kerala", Sociological Bulletin, Vol. 25, No. 2, September, 1976.

Kalpagam, U., "Women Workers in the Readymade Garment Industry," Mids, Madras, 1981 (mimeo).

Kane, P.V., *History of the Dharmashastra Literature*, Bhandarkar Oriental Research Institute, Pune, 1930.

Kane, P.V., *History of the Dharmashastra : Ancient and Medieval Religious* and *civil law in India*, vol. II, Pune, Bhandarkar Oriental Research Institute, 1947.

Kapadia, K.M., Rural Family Patterns, A Study in Urban Rural Relations, *Sociological Bulletin*, Vol. III, 126, 1947.

Kapadia, K.M., *Marriage and Family in India*, Oxford University Press, 3rd Ed., Delhi, 1980.

Kapur, Pramilla, *Life and World of Call Girls in India*, Vikas Publication, New Delhi, 1978.

Karkal, Malini, "How the Other Half dies," *Economic and Political Weekly*, Vol. 20, No. 34, 25 August, 1985.

Karkal, Malini, "Mother and Child Survival", in *Dynamics of Population and Family Welfare*, (Ed.) K. Srinivasan and S. Mukherjee, Himalaya Publication, Bombay, 1985.

Karlikar, Malavika, *Poverty and Women's Work*, Vikas Publishing House, 1982, p. 121-22.

Karve, Irawati, *Kinship Organisation in India*, Asia Publishing House, Bombay, 3rd Ed., 1968.

Kaul, R.N., Kalhat, H.S. and Shyam, M., "Potato Diggers Elevators—Performance Study, Punjab Agriculture University" quoted in Bina Agarwal, Footnote 50, op. cit.

Kelly Elizabeth, *Appropriate Technology for Women : Development Forum*, June, 1976.

King, U., "Women and Religion : The Status and Image of women in Major Religious Traditions," *In Women in Contemporary India*, Manohar, New Delhi, 1975.

Kishwar, Madhu, "Making life More Meaningful" —An Interview with Rinki Bhattacharya, *Manushi,* Vol. 4, No. 5, July, 1984.

Kishwar, Madhu, "Gandhi on Women", *Economic and Political Weekly*, Vol. 20, No. 4, 5 October and No. 41, 12 October, 1985.

Kolenda, M. Pauline, "Region, Caste and Family Structure : A Comparative Study of the Indian Joint Family," in Milton Singer and Bernard, S. Cohn (Eds), *Structure, and Change in Indian Society*, Wenner-Grin Foundation for Anthropological Research, 1968, p. 339-396.

Kolenda, Pauline, "Marked Regional Differences in Indian Family Structure," Paper presented at the Third Regional Conference on Women and the Household, Delhi, 1985.

Krishna Raj, Maithreyi, Mehta, Madhavi, *Unemployed Post-graduate Degree Holders in Science in Bombay*, Research Centre for Women's Studies and Council of Scientific and Industrial Research, 1982.

Krishna Raj, Maithreyi, *Newsletter of the Research Unit on Women's Studies*, SNDT, Women's University, Vol. 4, No. 3, August, 1983.

——, Socio-Economic Condition of Women Workers in Garment Industry in Greater Bombay : ICSSR, (mimeo), 1983.

——, "Why Study Women ? "*Sociology of Women*, Lesson 1, SNDT University Open University Programme, 1984.

——, "Where Do We Go From Here ? "*Women Work and Society Golden Jubilee Symposium*, Vol. ISI, Calcutta, 1985.

Kuhn, A. and Wolpe, Ann-Marie (Ed.), *Feminism and Materialism*, Routledge and Kegan Paul, London, 1978.

Suresh Kulkarni, N., "Demographic and Nutritional Background of the Status of women in India", Institute of Economic Growth, Delhi University (mimeo), 1978.

Kumar, Dharma, "Aminocentesis Again (Discussion)", *Economic and Political Weekly*, Vol. 18, No. 24, 11 June, 1983.

Kumar, Rajani, "Secondary Education for Girls : The What and the How", *Education Quarterly*, Oct., 1982.

Lakshmi, C.S. "Non-Textual Methods of Research in Women's Studies" (mimeo), Seminar Abstract, Research Unit on Women's Studies, SNDT, Women's University, Bombay, 1983.

Lewis, Oscar, *Village in North India*, Random House, New York, 1958.

Mala Usha, S., Female Wage Differentials in Urban Labour Market : A Case Study of Madras Metropolitan Area, Ph. D. Thesis, University of Madras, unpub., 1981.

Manushi, "Women Lecturers Mobilise Against Dowry Deaths", Vol. 2, No. 12, Nov.-Dec., 1982.

Mathew, Molly, "Women in the Unorganised Sector", Coir Industry (mimeo) (undated).

Mazumdar, Vina, *Role of Rural Women in Development*, Allied Publishers, New Delhi, 1978.

——, *Symbols of Power*, Allied Publishers Pvt. Ltd., Bombay, 1979, p. 74.

Mazumdar, Vina and Pandey, Balaji, "Perspective on Women's Education, 1971-1981", Unpublished Paper, 1985.

Mehta, Ajit and Jayant, K., "Perinatal Mortality Survey of India (1977-1979), Part-I : Identification of Health Intervention Needs", *Journal of Obstetrics and Gynaecology of India*, Vol. 31, No. 2, 1981.

Meis, Maria, *Indian Women and Patriarchy*, Concept Publishing Co., New Delhi, 1980.

Meis, Maria, "The Lace Makers of Naraspur", *In Indian Housewives Produce for the World Market*, ILO, Zed Press, London, 1982.

Milbrath, Lester, W., *Political Participation*, Rand McNally and Co., Chicago, 1965, p. 18.

Millett, Kate, *Sexual Politics*, Abascus, London, 1972, p. 23.

Minault, Gail, *The Extended Family : Women and Political Participation in India and Pakistan*, Chanakya Publication, Delhi, 1981, p. 13-14.

Minkin, Stephen, "Introduction : Contraceptive Use and Abuse Depa Provera : A Critical Analysis", Reprint from *Women and Health*, Vol. 2, Summary, 1980.

Mitra, Asok, *Implications of the declining Sex Ratio in India's Population*, Allied Publishers, Bombay, ICSSR, Programme of Women's Studies, 1979.

Mitra, Asok, *The Status of Women Literacy and Employment*, ICSSR, Allied Publishers, Delhi, 1971, 1979.

Mohan Lakshmi, "The Sex Determination Controversy Continues", *Eves Weekly*, 25 September and Ist October, 1982.

Mokasli, Sudha, "Maharashtra Rajyatil Sagari Masevari Vyavasache Swarup Va Jadan Dadhan", SNDT University, Ph. D. Thesis (unpub), (Marathi), 1982.

Morris, M.D., *"The Emergence of the Industrial Labour Force in India :A Study of the Cotton Mills*, Oxford University Press, Bombay, 1965.

Mukherji, "Impact of Modernization in Women's Occupation : A Case Study of the Rice Husking Industry of Bengal," *The Indian Economic and Social History Review*, Vol. 20, No. 1, 1983.

Mukherjee, Prabhati, *Hindu Women :Normative, Models*, Orient Longman Ltd., New Delhi, 1978, p. 7.

Mukherji, T.N., *Art Manufacturers of India*, Navrang, Delhi, 1974.

Mukhopadhya, Sudhir and Gosh, Bhanushika, "Sources of Variation in Female Labour Force Participation," A Decomposition, Technical Seminar on Women's Work and Employment, ISST, Delhi, 1982.

Murshid, Gulam, *Reluctant Debutant : Response of Bengali Women to Modernisation 1849-1905*, Rajashahi University, Rajashahi, 1983.

Nagbhraman and Sambrani Srikant, "Women's Drudgery in Firewood Collection", *Economic and Political Weekly*, Vol. 18, No. 1-2, Jan. 1-8, 1983.

Naik, J.P., *Equality, Quality and Quantity*, Allied Publishers, New Delhi, 1975.

Nair Arvindakshan, K., "Women Worker in Cashew Industry", ICSSR, mimeo, 1978.

National Institute of Education, *Monograph Series*, U.S.A., 1980.

National Sample Survey, *38th Round Report 315*, 1983, *Key Results*, Dept. of Statistics, New Delhi, July, 1985.

Nayar, Usha, "Education of Girls at the Secondary level in India", Unpublished paper, New delhi, 1983.

NCERT, *Report of the Education Commission—1964-1966*, New Delhi, 1971.

NCERT, *Status of Women through Curriculum,* Elementary Teacher's Handbook, New Delhi, 1982.

——, *Status of Women through Curriculum : Secondary and Senior Secondary Stages*, New Delhi, 1984.

——, *Status of Women through Teaching of Mathematics*, A teachers handbook, New Delhi, 1984.

Nehru, Jawaharlal, *Forward to Social Welfare in India*, The Planning Commission, New Delhi, 1955.

Nehru, Jawaharlal, *Towards Freedom*, Beacon Press, Boston, 1958, p. 161-162.

Newsletter, *The Asian Women's Research and Action Network* (AWRAN), vol. 1, No. 1, July, 1983.

Nishchol, Kamlesh, *The Invisible Women*, Amalatas, New Delhi, 1978.

Omvedt, Gail, "Rural Origins of Women's Liberation in India, *Social Scientist*, vol. 4, No. 415, Nov.-Dec., 1975, p. 45-46.

Omvedt, Gail, *We will Smash This Prison*, Orient Longman, Ltd., Bombay by arrangement with Zed Press, London, 1979.

Omvedt, Gail, *Land, Caste and Politics in Indian States : Teaching Politics*, University of Delhi, 1982, p. 11-12.

Padmanabha, P., "Mortality in India, A Note on Trends and Implications", Economic and Political Weekly, Vol. XVIII, No. 32, 1982.

Palmer, N.D., *Elections and Political Development : The South Asian Experience*, 1976, p. 72.

Patel, B.B., "Technology, Employment and Occupation of women Workers in Gujarat " MIDS", Seminar, on Women, Technology and Forms of Production, Madras, op. cit., 1984.

Patel, Vibhuti and Bakshi, Rajni, "The Women's Movement in India : A Historical Perspective", mimeo, 1982.

Patel, Vibhuti, "Aminocentesis and Female Foeticide Misuse of Medical Technology", *Socialist Health Review*, Vol. 1, No. 2, 1984.

Patel, Vibhuti, "Emergence and Proliferation of Autonomous Women's Groups in India (1974-1984)", mimeo, 1985.

Pathak and Amir, "Media and Sex Role", (mimeo), Ahmedabad Women's Group, AWAG.

Pathak, Ila, "The Handling of Rape News by News Papers", Ahmedabad Women's Action Group, Ahmedabad, (mimeo), (undated).

Parsons, Talcott, Robert, Bales F., *Family, Socialization and Interaction Process*, Free Press, New York, 1955.

Parsons, Talcott, *Social Structure and Personality*, Free Press, New York, 1970.

Parthasarathy, G., "Rural Poverty and Female Heads of Household Need for Qualitative Analysis", Paper, Technical Seminar on Women, Work and Employment, ISST, New Delhi, 1982.

Patriot, New Delhi, 25 May 1982.

Patwa, Subhadra, "Women's Studies Centres in India", Research Centre on Women's Studies, Bombay, (mimeo), 1985.

Pawar, Amarja, "The Pune Domestic Servant's Revolt", Institute of Social Research and Education, (mimeo), Bombay, 1982.

Prakash, Padma, "Editorial Perspective : Roots of Women's Ill Health", *Socialist Health Review*. Vol. 1, No. 2, 1984.

Ram, Kalpana, "Coastal Fisherwomen of Kanya Kumari", Tamil Nadu Paper, Second National Conference on Women's Studies, Trivandrum, 1984.

Rao, Rukmani, and Hussain, Shahiba, "Women Working in the Garment Industry", ICSSR, New delhi, (mimeo), 1983.

Raychaudri, "Historical Roots of Mass Poverty in India", *Economic and Political Weekly*, Vol. 20, No. 18, May, 1985.

Reddy, Atchi, "Female Agricultural Labourers of Nellore 1881-1981", *The Indian Economic and Social History Review*, Vol. 20, No. 1, 1983.

Reed, Evelyn, *Women's Evolution*, Path Finder Press, New York, 1976.

Report of the Committee of Experts on Unemployment, New Delhi, 1981.

Saheli, "Rape and Dowry Deaths", mimeo, New Delhi, 25 November, 1983.

Sakre, Seema, "Analytical Study of the Recent Rape Cases in Vidarbha Region of Maharashtra State in India", Paper, Second National Conference on Women's Studies, Trivandrum (mimeo), 1984.

Samya Shakti, Vol. 1, No. 1, July, 1983, p. 27-28.

——, *The Dowry Prohibition Act, 1961*, Vol. 1, No. 2, 1984.

Saradamani, K and Menchev, K., Muddy feet, Dirty Hands—Rice Production and Female Agricultural Labour : *Economic and Political Weekly*, Review of Agriculture, Vol. 17, No. 52, Dec., 1982.

Saradamani, K., "Changing Land Relations and Women : A Case Study of Palghat District in Kerala", in *Women and Rural Transformation*, Ed. Vina Mazumdar, Concept Pub., New Delhi, 1983.

Saraga, Esther, *Sex Role Stereotyping*, (ed.) Oonagh Hartnett *et al.*, Tavistock Publications, London, 1979.

Saraswathi, Baidyanath, "The Kashivasi Widows", *Man in India*, Vol. 65, No. 2, June, 1985.

Satyamala, C., "Is Medicine Inherently Sexist" ? *Socialist Health Review*, Vol. 1, No. 2, 1984.

Seal, K.C., "Women in the Labour Force—A Statistical Profile in Women in the Labour Force", Asian Regional Employment and Training Programme, *ILO*, Geneva, 1981.

Sen, Amartya and Sen Gupta, Sunil, "Malnutrition of Rural Children and the Sex Bias", *In Women and Poverty*, (Ed.) Devaki Jain and Nirmala Bannerjee, Vikas, New Delhi, 1985.

Sen, Anupam, *The State, Industrialisation and Class Formation in India*, Routledge and Kegan Paul, London, 1982.

Sen, Gita, "Inter Regional Aspects of the Incidence of Women Agricultural Labourers", in *Women in Poverty*, Devaki Jain and Nirmala Bannerjee, op. cit., 1982.

Sen, Gita and Grown, Caren, "Development Crisis and Alternative Visions : Third World Women's Perspective", DAWN, New Delhi, 1985.

Sen, Gita, "Women and Agriculture World Employment Programme", ILO, Geneva, 1985.

Sen, S.N. *History of Modern India, 1765-1950*, Wiley Eastern Ltd., New Delhi, 1979.

Sen Gupta, Padmini, *Women in India*, Ministry of Information, Govt. of India, New Delhi, 1964.

Sethi, Raj Mohini, "A Study of Agricultural Labour in Punjab", (unpub.), Dept. of Sociology, 1981.

Shah, A.M., *The Household Dimenstion of the Family in India*, Orient Longman's Ltd., New Delhi, 1973.

Sharma, Kumud, "Women in Struggle : A Case Study of Chipko Movement", *Samya Shakti*, Vol. 1, No. 2, 1984.

Sharma Meenakshi and Saksena, S., "A Chemical Study of Perinatal Mortality", *Journal of Obstetrics and Gynaecology of India*, Vol. 32, No. 3, 1982.

Sharma, R.N. and Sen Gupta, Chandan, "Women's Employment at Seepz Unit", Urban Studies, Tata Institute of Social Sciences (mimeo), 1984.

Sharma, R.S., *Indian Feudalism*, Macmillan & Co., Delhi, 1980, p. 112-113.

Sharma, Ursula, *Women, Work and Property in North-West India*, Tavistock Publications, London, 1980.

Shatrugna, Veena, *Women and Health*, Research Centre for Women's Studies, SNDT University, Bombay, 1984.

Sinha, J.N., "The Indian Working Force : Its Growth Change and Composition", *Census of India 1961*, Vol. I, Monograph, 11, Govt. of India, New Delhi, 1972.

Sinha, J.N., *Employment of Women in Mines and Plantation Labour Bureau*, Ministry of Labour, Govt. of India, Simla, 1978.

Sinha, J.N., "Economic Census Data—A Note 1981" *Economic and Political Weekly*, Vol. 17, No. 6, 6 February, 1985.

SNDT University, *Report of the First National Conference on Women's Studies*, Bombay, 1981, p. 41-45.

Srinivas, M.N., *Caste in Modern India and other Essays*, Media, Prompters and Publishers Pvt. Ltd., Bombay, 1978, p. 3.

Srinivas, M.N. *The Changing Position of India Women*, Oxford University Press, Bombay, 1978, p. 7.

Srinivas, M.N., *Some Reflections on Dowry : J.P. Naik Memorial Lecture*, Oxford University Press, New Delhi, 1983.

Shree Sangarsha, "Mass Rape in Santhal Parganas : Police

Repression Against Tribal Movement to Reclaim land : An on the spot study", *HOW*, Vol. 3, No. 5, May, 1980.

Susheela, Kaushik (Ed.), *Women's Oppression, Patterns and Perspectives*, Shakti Books, New Delhi, 1985.

Thaper, Romila, "Looking Back in History", in Devaki Jain, *Indian Women*, Publication Division, Ministry of Information and Broadcasting, Govt. of India, 1975.

Thaper, Romila, "Syndicated Moksha in the Hindus and their Isms", *Seminar 313*, Sept., 1985, p. 17.

Thorner, Alice, "The Secular Trends in the Indian Economy : 1881-1951,"*The Economic Weekly*, Special Number, Vol. 14, No. 28, 29, 30 July, 1962.

Trikla, K. Sushila, *Women Workers in Kandala Free Trade Zone* : Report for Indian Council for Research in International Economic Relations, New Delhi, 1985.

Twift, H.J.R., *A Monograph on the Arts and Practice of Carpet Making in the Bombay Presidency*, Govt. of Central Press, 1907.

UNESCO, *Women's Studies and Social Sciences in Asia*, Report of a meeting of Experts, Bangkok, 1983.

Upadhyaya, Bhagavat Saxsena, *Women in Rigveda*, S. Chand and Co., New Delhi, 1974.

Vaid, Sudesh, Rao, Amiya and Junje, Monica, *Rape, Society and State*, Peoples' Union of Civil Liberation, New Delhi, 1983.

Vana Mala, "Employment of Women in Andhra Pradesh, Public Enterprise", in K. Murli Manohar Ed. *Women's Status and Development in India*, Society for Women's Studies and Development, Warangal, 1984.

Vogel, Lise, *Marxism and the Oppression of Women : Towards a Unitary Theory*, Pluto Press, U.S.A., 1983.

Voices of the Working Women, Vol. 3, No. 4, July, 1983.

"Vimochana, Forum for Women's Rights, An Open Letter to Simi Grewal : Producer, *It's a Women's World*, A Doordarshan Programme, Bangalore, 1985.

Visaria, Leela, "Infant Mortality in India : Levels, Trends and Determinants", *Economic and Political Weekly*, vol. XX, No 32, Aug. 10, 1985.

Visaria, Pravin, "Indian Households with Female Heads, Their incidence, characteristics and levels of living", in *Women and Poverty*, op. cit., 1985.

Venkatachalam, "Maternal Nutritional Status and Its Effect on the New Born", *WHO* Bulletin, 26, 1962, p. 198.

Verba, Sidney, "Democratic Participation", *The Annals of the American Academy of Political and Social Science, CCCLXXIII, Sept., 1967, p. 55.*

Wadley, Susan, *Women and the Hindu Tradition,* Chapt. in *Women in India : Two Perspectives,* (Ed.) by Jacobson and Wadley, Manohar, 1977, p. 114.

Weiner, Myron, *Political Participation : Crisis and Sequence in Political Development*, Princeton University Press, Princeton, 1971, p. 164.

Women's Studies : International Forum, Special Issue on Strategies for Women's Studies in the 805, Pergamon Press, Vol. 7, No. 3, 1984.

Yadav, J.S. and Mohnet, Abilash, *Advertising and Social Responsibility*, Indian Institute of Mass Communication, Vol. 2, 1983, p. 70 ; Vol. 1, p. 73-75.

Yoon, Young Soon, "Women's Studies : Is it Relevant ?" *Samya Shakti*, Vol. I, No. 1, 1983, p. 5.

Zaidi, A.M. and Zaidi, Shaheeda, *The Encyclopaedia of the Indian National Congress,* Vol. 9, S. Chand and Co. Ltd., New Delhi, 1980, p. 29.

Zurbrigg, Shiela, *Rakku's Story : Structure of Ill Health and the Source of Change*, Published, George Joseph, Sidma Offset Press, Madras, 1984.

Index